METU NETER

Vol. 1

The Great Oracle of Tehuti

And the Egyptian System

of Spiritual Cultivation

The author and publishers acknowledge with thanks, first of all, the great devotion shown by Raar Mesh User (Jay Barker). We cannot thank him enough for the long hours, and love that he poured into the rendition of the art work for the deck of cards, the cover design, and the illustrations. A big thanks also goes out to Hrimgalah Amen and Greg Thomas for their editing assistance, to Merisa Amen for her typing assistance, to the priests and priestesses of the Ausar Auset Society who, in testing the Metu Neter oracle, trusted it with their lives.

METU NETER

Vol. 1

The Great Oracle of Tehuti

And the Egyptian System

of Spiritual Cultivation

RA UN NEFER AMEN I

Published by Khamit Corp. P.O. Box 281, Bronx NY 10462

ISBN 1-877662-03-8

NOTICE TO THE READER

THIS BOOK IS ACCOMPANIED BY A DECK OF CARDS THAT COMPRISES THE ORACLE. IF YOUR RETAIL OUTLET DOES NOT CARRY IT, WRITE TO THE PUBLISHER.

Contents

AUTHOR'S PREFACE 1
The Divine Plan 1
CHAPTER 1 5
Introduction 5
The Hemispheres of the Brain 9
A Brief Definition of Religion 13
Religion, Trance, and Ancestors 14
CHAPTER 2 20
The Black Founders of Civilization 20
The Three Fundamental Races of Mankind and the Principle of Geographic Contiguity 22
CHAPTER 3 38
The Source of the Light of the East 38
CHAPTER 4 46
Cosmology and Cosmogony 46
CHAPTER 5 49
The Two Great Realms of Being 49
The Subjective Realm 50
The Objective Realm 52
The Cosmogenesis of the Objective Realm 54
The Noumenal Plane 54
The Divisions of the Noumenal Plane 55
The Great Divine Trinity
The Phenomenal Plane 58
The Step by Step Manifestation of Subjective Being 59
The Paut Neteru (Tree of Life) 64
CHAPTER 6 69
Analysis of the Cosmogonical System 69
The Six Acts of Creation 70
The Creation of the Celestial Government 70
The Creation of the Celestial Workers 71
An Analysis Of The Process Of Creation 73
The Duality Principle In Cosmogony 77
The Complementary Dualities On The Tree Of Life 78
CHAPTER 7 82
The Cosmological View Of Man 82

The Spiritual Anatomy Of Man   82
    The Tree Of Life As A Guide To Man's Spirit Or "Mind"   84
    A Comparative Analysis Of Man's Complementary Faculties
        95
        The Five Principles Governing Man's Life   96
        Man's Self-identity   99
        The Will   101
        Man's Power   102
        Man's Knowledge Of Reality
                                                        103

CHAPTER 8   105
The Three Types Of Men   105
    Stage I of Man's Evolution   107
    Stage II of Man's Evolution   110
    Stage III of Man's Evolution   112
        Religion   118
        Economics   122
        Government   123
        Education   124
CHAPTER 9   125
The Spiritual Cultivation of Man   125
    The Ausarian Metaphorein   128
    The Metaphorein of Ausar in the Spiritual Evolution of
        Society   130
CHAPTER 10   133
The Tree Of Life Initiation System   133
    The Two Principles Underlying the Problems to be
        Overcome through Initiation   135
    The Four Principles Underlying Initiation   136
CHAPTER 11   138
The Ten Stages Of Initiation   138
    Preliminary Requirements to Initiation   138
    Sphere 10, Geb, The Khaibit   138
    The Care of the Life Force   138
    Level 1 - Stage 1 of Initiation   139
    Level 1 - Stage 2 of Initiation   142
    Sahu division of the Spirit, Sphere 8, Sebek   142
    Level 1 - Stage 3 of Initiation   145
    Sahu Division of the Spirit, Sphere 7, Het-Heru   145

Level 2 - Stage Four of Initiation

          152

Level 2 - Stage 5 of Initiation   156
Level 2 - Stage 6 of Initiation   157
Level 3 - Stage 7 of Initiation   158
Level 3 - Stage 8 of Initiation   159
Level 3 - Stage 9 of Initiation   160
Level 4 - Stage 10 of Initiation   160
CHAPTER 12   161
Meditation And Ritual   161
The Means of Realizing Spiritual Growth   161
The Principles of Meditation   161
The Fundamental Components of Man's Being   161
Stages in the Process of Meditation   162
The Process of Meditation   163
The Components of a Meditation   166
The Importance of Trance   168
CHAPTER 13   171
Level 1, First Three Stages of the Meditation Process   171
Care of the Life-force   171
The Four Principles Underlying the Process of Meditation   171
Level 1 of the Meditation Process, Stage 1, Sphere 9   174
Level 1 of the Meditation Process, Stage 2, Sphere 8   178
Level 1 of the Meditation Process, Stage 3, Sphere 7   180
CHAPTER 14   187
Level 2, Second Three Stages of the Meditation Process   187
Level 2 of the Meditation Process, Stage 4, Sphere 6   187
Men Ab em Aungk em Maat   189
Pert Em Heru   194
Level 2 of the Meditation Process, Stage 5, Sphere 5   195
Level 2 of the Meditation Process, Stage 6, Sphere 4   195
CHAPTER 15   199
Levels 3 and 4 of the Meditation Process   199
Level 3 of the Meditation Process, Stage 7, Sphere 3   199
Level 3 of the Meditation Process, Stage 8, Sphere 2   202
The Two Fundamental Actions of the Mind   202
Thinking vs. Thought Drift

          202

Level 3 of the Meditation Process, Stage 9, Sphere 1   204
Level 4 of the Meditation Process, Stage 10, "0"   205

Initiation and Society 205
CHAPTER 16 209
The Oracles 209
CHAPTER 17 212
The Deities Of The Metu Neter 212
   Amen 212
   Ausar 212
   Tehuti 214
      The Utchau Metut 216
         Spatial - Hierarchical Dimension 216
         Classification, and Evaluation (Utchau) of Life
            Problems 219
   Seker 221
   Maat 224
   Herukhuti 226
   Heru 227
   Het-heru 229
   Sebek 230
   Auset 233
   Seb, Or Geb, The God Of The Earth 235
   Sheps & Dark Deceased 236
   Ra 237
      Nekhebet And Uatchet 239
CHAPTER 18 244
The Metutu 244
      The Philosophical and Psychological Foundation of the Metu
         Neter Oracle System 244
      Shaping Factors of Success 248
      The Shaping Factors of Failure 255
   A Place and Time For All Things 261
CHAPTER 19 266
The Metutu 266
   Amen 266
   Ausar 267
   Tehuti 269
   Seker 271
   Maat 276
   Herukhuti 280
   Heru 283
   Het-Heru 287

Sebek	290
Auset	293
Geb	296
Sheps & Dark Deceased	297
Nekhebet	298
Uatchet	299
CHAPTER 20	300
The Meanings of the Combined Metutu	300
CHAPTER 21	356
Consulting The Oracle	356
The State of Mind, and Motives For Readings	357
Suggested Questions	358
How to Consult	359
CHAPTER 22	361
Interpreting The Oracle	361
The Suits	364
The Utchau Metut and Interpretation	367
Modes and Levels of Interpretation	367
Why Should Oracles be Used?	369
Significators	371
Rituals and the Readings	379
Rituals and the Significators	379
Initiation and the Readings	381
CHAPTER 23	382
Meditations and Rituals	382
State of Trance	383
Waking Trance States	383
Mediumistic Trance	384
Breathing The Key To Meditation	384
Tension Diaphragmatic Breathing	386
The Physiological Basis of Kumbhaka	387
Breathing And The Internalization Of Consciousness	387
The Harmonics Of Breathing	388
Breathing And Wakefulness	393
Rituals	394
CHAPTER 24	397

How To Meditate And Perform A Ritual   397
    Posture In Meditation   397
    The Procedure   398
        Functioning In The Meditation Stage   399
        Managing the Sphere of Awareness During Meditation
            400
        Meditating on your Readings   401
        Hekau Of The Deities   401
        Coordinating the Breathing with the Chanting   401
            The Rate of Breathing   401
APPENDIX A   404
Sesh Metut Neter   404
SELECT BIBLIOGRAPHY   411
INDEX   413

Author's Preface

The Divine Plan

We live in a world that was created, and is maintained by the *unified* working of a *multiplicity* of agencies.

We live in a world that is composed of a *multiplicity* of entities that are *unified* through a web of interdependence.

In the infancy of his spiritual evolutionary career, Man is unable to perceive the hidden forces and abstract principles that *unify*, the working of the shaping forces of the world, and the entities that make up the world. He creates, therefore, a way of life-systems of religion, science, economics, government, education, family, philosophy, etc. - that is incapable of establishing, and maintaining unity-law, order, peace, harmony-in the world. Thus the world has been plunged, and is sinking deeper, day by day, into the jaws of death.

It is true that he has amassed a great number of facts concerning the workings of nature, and a great collection of ideas concerning religion, and so on, but the possession of a mass of facts, however reliable the facts are, does not constitute the possession of a science, nor does the possession of a collection of ideas about religion, constitute the possession of a religion, for the knowledge contained in these facts regarding nature, and these ideas concerning religion, does not embody the principles that are necessary to unify the facts, and ideas. It is only when the facts concerning nature, or the ideas about religion are linked to each other, and to the whole, that a science, or a religion is formed.

Man's perception of the world, however, cannot change the reality that the world is shaped, and maintained by a unified multiplicity of agencies, and that the world is made up of an infinitude of interdependent entities. This reality has been known to Black and Oriental cultures, and ignored by Westerners as far back as history can take us. The Black nations of antiquity, through the cultivation of the science of inducing the state of waking trance, which enables Man to perceive the working of abstract principles, and the hidden shaping forces of the world, were able to create a way of life-systems of religion, science, philosophy, government,

1

economics, etc. - that was capable of establishing and maintaining unity, and thus led to the creation of civilization.

Unity, harmony, and order in society cannot be achieved through the making of laws by Man, and the policing of people's behavior. As Man's life on earth is a product of the Supreme Being's creative process, every aspect of Man's life, is therefore, controlled by the divine creative agencies. Unity, and thus, prosperity in society can only be achieve by Man's efforts to intuit the knowledge of how the divine agencies are shaping his life, i.e., to intuit the knowledge of the Divine Plan[1]. It follows, logically, that the Divine Plan would contain the knowledge of the unifying principles, of the multiplicity of shaping forces of the world, and of the entities making up the world. Through it, all things, and events in the world were unified. Religion with science with government with philosophy with medicine, and so on. Man with nature with God, etc. It achieved this monumental accomplishment by assigning to each event, force, entity, and idea a place in space (hierarchy, rank), and time. It is the purpose of this book to give the reader a working knowledge of this system. The Divine Plan is presented in this book, not as the museum pieces that are the delight and folly of historians, but as a system to be lived. The jab at historians was thrown, both in jest, and in seriousness. The fun side is dictated by the fact that they have, cumulatively, amassed a great deal of facts on our past, for which we must be grateful. The other side is dictated by the fact that, although most historians of religious subjects know of their lack of first hand experience of the religious phenomena they report on, it does not stop them from arrogating to themselves the aura of authoritativeness in reporting, "explaining," and passing judgments.

Although, the material in this book has the full support of historical documentation, I am writing foremost as a priest of over 20 years of practice. I am here presenting a practical syncretism of the best that the Kamitic (Ancient Egyptian), the Dravidian (Black India), and the Canaanite (true authors of Kabala) religions have to offer. They were among the six nations that laid the foundation of civilization. But it would be folly on our part to merely document this fact, and to compile and explain a list of who, when, why and what. Would it not be a sign of intelligence, to be more interested in

---

1. Maat.

2

the methods employed by them for the creation of civilization, that we may learn and apply them to its recreation? If the religious, and philosophical systems of ancient civilizations were so great, why aren't we practicing them?

Yes! In this volume, one of many as the topics are too broad to be fully explained in one book, I have given the world, the means through which everyone can discover the links between all aspects of life, the means of discovering the Plan-the structural continuum-that the Supreme Being has put in place to enable the events in the world, to unfold in an orderly, and harmonious way. Become the Plan, and let Peace, Prosperity, and Spiritual Realization reign in the world. Hetep!

Ra Un Nefer Amen I, Shekem Ur Shekem of the Ausar Auset Society. Ashem Ur Ashemu of the Shrines of Taui
New York, U.S.A., April 24, 1990

Chapter 1

INTRODUCTION

The world is on a collision course with disaster. Not only from, or because of the threat of nuclear war, but from the massive collapse of its institutions (political, social, economical, religious, spiritual, educational, etc.). It is the combined failure of these institutions, and traditions that is at the root of the widespread decay and stagnation that we are witnessing in just about every nation in the world.

"This state of affairs," a Kamitian (Ancient Egyptian) priest(ess) would say, "is due to 'Lack of Self Knowledge'." This injunction has been quoted often by scholars yet none have given much insight into its true meaning.

In explaining what is 'Knowledge of Self', I ought to begin, it seems most natural, at the beginning. But that would take us into such an abstruse discussion that it makes better sense to start, instead, at a very familiar midpoint.

Let's start with what you are doing this very moment. As your eyes race across these lines I want you to make the effort of becoming aware of the fact that you are involved in two sets of functions. On one hand, you are **making the effort** to keep your attention on the sequence of words as you read on. On the other hand, **without your conscious effort, and awareness,** the meaning of what you are reading is taking shape. These two sets of functions are more apparent in more complex activities. While you need to think of getting up and going somewhere, you need not think of the details of the muscular activities involved in getting up itself. They are taken care of for you. When you type, dance, play an instrument, perform in a sport, drive, write, etc., you can become aware of the fact that some part of your activities is performed without conscious effort.

Now, this dualization of your being into two fundamental sets of functions is the central theme of 'Self Knowledge'. One part of your being is concerned with activities that you have to direct, while the other deals with activities that occur without your attention to them. You may have noticed that I have gone to a little trouble to avoid the popular designations, "voluntary vs. involuntary, or conscious vs. subconscious" behavior. We will later see why. Let us for now label them "willed," and "automatic" respectively.

It might not surprise you, because you already know, that great performers make poor teachers. Yet, you might be surprised to know that you could not give an accurate description of how you walk, or articulate the words that you speak, etc. You fail for the same reasons that most great performers do as teachers. The performance of the tasks in question is carried out without your attention, and awareness of the intricate details involved. You direct your attention to the desired result and the other part of your being unattended takes care of the execution. In fact as you sit here, this other part is, without your attention, or consent, determining what understanding you are extracting from what you are reading, and at the same time, it is taking care of your breathing, exchanging oxygen for carbon dioxide in your blood, circulating the latter through every cell in your body, probably digesting some food, and getting ready to shut down the part of you that directs activities, that it (the automatic part of being) may have more freedom and energy to do some major repairs on your vehicle while you sleep . . . among many, many other, very complicated things[1].

It should be obvious by now that there exists a vast difference in the knowledge and capabilities between the two parts of our being. While the willed part of our being has to be instructed and is no better in its performance than the quality of the material taught it, the automatic part of being is directed by an omniscient factor, -let's realize that it directed the formation of the physical part of our being the very moment that our progenitor sperm and egg came together.

What if the willed part of our being, instead of learning from the nescient will of others, learned from the omniscient being that directs the automaton within us? I.e., instead of the "limited in knowledge" learning from the "limited in knowledge," learn from the omniscient.

The answers to these questions will provide full insight into the nature of our being, the cultures we have produced, the shaping forces of our history, and explain the causes of the problems besetting mankind, and will also show, definitively, the way to their solutions. It is sufficient to say for now that according to the African spiritual

---

1. This so-called subconscious mind is the Deity Ra of the Kamitic tradition.

tradition, the automaton within us is in touch with all functions in the world and is capable of manipulating them.

With the proper directions, we will come to see that there are three kinds of people in the world. One type inclines toward relying on the willed part of being for survival and flourishment, the second, on the omniscient intelligence and the automaton, and the third, on an equilibrium of both parts of being. In fact, all cultures fall into one of these categories.

These three categories do not represent distinct types, but stages in the spiritual development of individuals and nations. The first stage corresponds to the polarization in the willed (outer) part of being, the second, in the polarization in the inner, and the third to their equilibration. We can better comprehend this if we paraphrase it as the stages of 1) reliance on the part of being with limited knowledge and capability, 2) reliance on the part of being with infinite knowledge and capability, and 3) the equilibrium between the two. Another paraphrase will explain further. 1) Polarization in learning from outside of ourselves (from someone else), 2) in learning from within ourselves, and 3) an equilibrium of both approaches. Further still, 1) polarization in reliance on externals (tools, machinery, medicines, etc.), 2) polarization in reliance on internals (the power of the spirit), and 3) an equilibrium of both methods.

We can begin to see which cultures shape up to which categories. The 1st type, polarized in the cultivation of the external part of being corresponds fundamentally to Western Man and some Orientals, while the opposite, polarized in the cultivation of the internal, corresponds to the Black race, and some Orientals. Success in the cultivation of both parts has only been truly achieved by the Kamitians (Ancient Egyptians), who, for the record, belong to the Black race.

Now we can understand why, for example, all the fundamental skills and institutions of civilization began with Black nations (Kamit [Ancient Egypt], Sumer, Babylon, Elam, the Harappa Valley civilization, Kush [Ethiopia], Indus Kush [Black India], and Canaan). Because of their people's ability to learn from the internal part of being, with its storehouse of knowledge concerning every secret of the world, they were able to intuit, 6000+ years ago, the knowledge that forms the basis of our civilization (religion, mathematics, geometry, medicine, astronomy, writing, literature, agriculture, metallurgy, government, architecture, painting, sculpturing, algebra, science, etc.). Because Western man is polarized in the cultivation of the external part of his being, he had to learn these skills from others (Blacks and Orientals) who were able to learn these things intuitively.

This brings us to the critical part of our introductory discourse. Underlying all the functions of the automaton within us is a 'program of order'. The maintenance of our bodily processes in a state of order according to this program, is what we call health. We will come to see that this very same 'program of order'[2] is in charge of regulating the social behavior of people. Where it finds full expression in the social arena, there is morality, wealth, spirituality, and prosperity. True religion, we will come to see, deals with the techniques of communicating with the director of the automaton within us, in order to gain access to the power, storehouse of information, and the host of shaping factors of our lives.

The world is in the sorry mess that it now finds itself because the dominant culture in the world is that of the external part of being. It is not enough to say that the external part of our being does not know much about creating and maintaining order. For, even if it did, it lacks the ability to generate order in the life of people. Hearing sermons, and reading books (external means) on moral behavior will make you as moral as reading books on healing will heal your illnesses. The most that a book on health, for example, can do is to direct you to some means of directly influencing the automaton. Yet such information must have originated from some person's intuition. The same holds true for religious, moral, and spiritual behavior. All teachings on the subjects originated from the inner part of people's being. If you observe very carefully you will see that in the religions of the dominant cultures today, people are directed outside themselves (to scriptures, sermons from priests, etc.) for moral, and spiritual guidance. In contrast, African, and some Oriental cultures direct their members within themselves (trance) for intuitive guidance for the same ends. The differences are vast. We must recall the fact that the external part of being, however lucid on a subject, lacks the power to direct the processes that shape our behavior, and bodily functions. Now we can fully understand the lack of wisdom in denouncing Westerners as hypocrites for preaching doctrines of such high moral values, while their destructive acts in the world are unparalleled. The

---

2. This 'program of order' corresponds to Maat.

8

'inner culture' for accessing the 'program of order' that is the shaping force of a harmonious social life, an essential prerequisite for man's spiritual growth, and the flourishing of all social institutions, has been displaced by the 'outer culture', which is far from equal to the task although it is long on words on the subject of spirituality. A detailed account of the history of this phenomenon is necessary for the understanding and use of the teachings in this book. But first we must get a better grasp of the structure of the subject.

THE HEMISPHERES OF THE BRAIN

During the last forty years or so, the western scientific community has come to realize that the human brain is composed of two parts with diametrically opposed, yet complementary functions. They are known as the left, and the right hemispheres of the brain. To understand this subject, we must realize that underlying all mental activities are two sets of functions, one in charge of relating us, and the variety of things in our environment to each other, and to the whole, and the other function is in charge of separating us and the variety of things in our environment from each other. The latter function, which corresponds to the left hemisphere of the brain enables us, for example, to distinguish between the sounds made in speaking and verbal thinking, that we will be able to speak, and think verbally. The language function of the right hemisphere enables us to unify the words we perceive, into phrases, these into sentences, and so on into larger units, that we will be able to comprehend what has been spoken or thought. The acts of speaking and verbal thinking are processes that occur in a series of steps one at a time. The understanding of what is thought, and said is a process that occurs in one step. Since the acts of speaking, and verbal thinking are processes that occur at separate points in time they are therefore carried out by the left hemisphere, which is in charge of all processes of segregation, and differentiation. Conversely, the act of extracting the significance from a series of related units, which is carried out in one step, is under the jurisdiction of the right hemisphere, which is in charge of all functions of unification, and integration.

In summary, let's note that the left hemisphere of the brain is in charge of noting the differences between things, separating wholes into parts, and enabling us to deal with all sequential phenomena (wholes presented pieces at a time). This mode of thinking is popularly known as analytical, Cartesian, serial, linear, deductive, segregative, etc. The right side is in charge of noting the similarities between things, and their relation to each other and the whole thus unifying them. This mode of thinking is generally known as synthetical, holistic, congregative, etc. We must also note that the left side of the brain is extroverted and is therefore the means for the 'outer culture' noted above. The right side, is introverted and is the means for the 'inner culture'.

Although both functions are complementary, that is, their equal inputs are needed for every mental activity to be complete, most people have a predominance of one over the other. We all know too well of people who can generate a profusion of words, yet make little sense, or go off on tangents, etc. (too much left, and too little right). On the other hand, we know of people who are not very expressive verbally, - in fact are poor communicators- yet are profound. Critical to this book is the fact that these hemispheric differences are not randomly distributed through society. Men in general are more left-sided than women, and so are members of the White race, in comparison to non-Whites (a well known fact to Western psychologists). We will come to learn that hemispheric differences are one of the main shaping forces of cultural differences, and the historical events that such differences have engendered. In fact, without this concept there can be no science of history, or psychology, or anthropology, or understanding of religion.

The differences in thought patterns between the White and Black races are well known. To prove the point, I will quote from well established scholars. Writing about the Bantus of South Africa, Placid Temples, at the turn of the century states in his *Bantu Philosophy*, that:

This (European) concept of separate beings, of substance (to use the scholastic term again) which find themselves side by side, entirely independent one of another, is foreign to Bantu thought. Bantu hold that created beings preserve a bond one with another, an intimate ontological relationship, comparable with the causal tie which binds creature and Creator . . . Just as Bantu ontology is opposed to the European concept of individuated things, existing in

10

themselves, isolated from others, so Bantu psychology cannot conceive of man as an individual, as a force existing by itself and apart from its ontological relationships with other living beings and from its connection with animals, or intimate forces around it.

Writing about the same people, Janheinz Jahn, states in *Muntu*:

When we say that the traditional African view of the world is one of extraordinary harmony, then except for the word 'African' every single word in the sentence is both right and wrong. For in the first place the traditional world view is still alive today; secondly it is a question not of a world view in the European sense, since things that are contemplated, experienced and lived are not separable in it; thirdly it can be called extraordinary only in the European sense, while for the African it is entirely commonplace; and fourth, the expression 'harmony' is entirely inadequate, since it does not indicate what parts are being harmonized in what whole. And if we say 'everything' is harmonized, that tells us less than ever.

Jahn then quotes Adebayo Adesanya, a Yoruba writer:

This is not simply a coherence of fact and faith, nor of reason and traditional beliefs, nor of reason and contingent facts, but a coherence or compatibility among all disciplines. A medical theory, e.g., which contradicted a theological conclusion was rejected as absurd and vice versa. This demand of mutual compatibility among all disciplines considered as a system was the main weapon of Yoruba thinking. God might be banished from Greek thought without any harm being done to the logical architecture of it, but this cannot be done in the case of Yoruba. In medieval thought, science could be dismissed at pleasure, but this is impossible in the case of Yoruba thought, since faith and reason are mutually dependent. In modern times, God even has no place in scientific thinking. This was impossible to the Yoruba.

These observations extend to all contemporary Africans as well as ancient. A. A. Barb, writing in the *The Legacy of Egypt* states the following:

> Certainly scholars have since provided dictionaries and grammars of the ancient Egyptian language, but that is not enough to grasp the Egyptian way of thinking, so utterly different from our Western logical mind. There is first of all what has been called the multiplicity of approaches: statements (and answers to problems) which to us would seem absolutely contradictory appear side by side and did not in the least disturb the Egyptian, on the contrary, our own logical abstractions would probably have appeared to the Egyptian mind as an impoverishment and falsification of the fullness of significant truth . . . All this would lead--as a modern scholar has put it--to the impossibility of translating Egyptian thoughts into modern language, for the distinctions we cannot avoid making did not exist for the Egyptians.

In speaking of the Greeks and Romans, regarding their ability to comprehend Egyptian beliefs, Wallis Budge, in *The Gods of the Egyptians, vol. I*, states:

> The evidence on the subject now available indicates that he [the Greeks] was racially incapable of appreciating the importance of such beliefs to those who held them, and that although, as in the case of the Ptolomies, he was ready to tolerate, and even, for state purposes, to adopt them, it was impossible for him to absorb them into his life.

It is important to note that these observations on the differences in thinking between Whites and Blacks were all made before the appearance of literature concerning the cerebral hemispheres. I could have piled up enough evidence on the subject to fill this book, but the foregoing should prove the point.

The concensus on the differences between these two modes of thinking, is that they each represent, by and of themselves, legitimate approaches, -"schools of thought"- to knowing. On one hand, this belief must be rejected on the ground that as the two are complementary to each other, they are incomplete by themselves. On the other hand, we will see, as history records, that the evils arising from the unbalanced expressions of the left hemisphere far exceed in destructiveness those of the right hemisphere. While the former is responsible primarily for man's inhumanity to man, and all social disharmony, the latter is responsible for stagnation in physical technology.

The greatest problem arises from the fact that the greatest validators of our actions, i.e., religion, and science, which are intrinsic products of "right-sided" cultures are now used by predominantly "left-sided" cultures in the characteristic fashion of the left hemisphere. Although the left side is totally incapable of truly religious, and scientific thinking, the grafting of its processes onto these subjects has gone unnoticed due, on one hand to ignorance, and on the other, to the military supremacy acquired by Europeans in the last 2000 years. The results have been that "scientific" and "religious" validation has been given to false doctrines, practices, and institutions that now control the cultures of the nations dominating the world, and set the cultural trends for the others. It is important to see how this has come about.

A BRIEF DEFINITION OF RELIGION

An analysis of the word "religion" shows that it is to the right side of the brain what a glove is to the hand. The word is composed of the Latin prefix "re," meaning, "again, back" + "ligare," meaning "tie, bind, fasten," as well as the Indo-European root "leg," meaning "to collect," from whence the Greek "legein," and the Latin "legere," meaning "logic," and "legal." From this we can conclude that the coiners of the word religion applied it to those beliefs and practices aimed at tieing people back to something with which they had originally been one, and belong with by natural connectivity. The original oneness is implied by the prefix "re" (back, again), and the natural connectivity is explicit in the root meaning "law, and logic." Right at the outset we can see that in the meaning of the word itself, according to its components, religion was not thought to be opposed to reason and logics, which are the foundations of science, and philosophy. More on this later.

We have seen that the predominant function of the right side of the brain is a unifying, or collecting, or synthesizing one. Religion is therefore nothing more than one of its organized expressions. Its concern with realities existing beyond the visible is a further proof of its intrinsic relationship to the right hemisphere. We can thus conclude that all efforts by left-sided cultures that are aimed at creating religious doctrines and practices, must produce results off the expected mark. Western religions are good examples. We will see that the Hebraic, and Christian religions are hybrids resulting from the juxtaposition of a left hemispheric thought process upon religious doctrines created by right or balanced hemispheric cultures. The same can be said for Hinduism, and Islam, although they have maintained a greater faithfulness to the fundamental culture upon which they are based.

During the first 2000 years of history (4000 - 2000 B.C.), the only nations that attained to a high degree of civilization were Kamit (Ancient Egypt), Sumer, Babylon, Canaan, Harappa Valley, and Kush (Ethiopia). Although it is well known to all serious historians that all these nations were Black, to this day much effort is being made to hide the fact from the general population. With some it is due to racism. With others it is due to feelings of shame over the fact that throughout the first 4000 years of history (6000 - 1+ B.C.) it is well known that Western people had attained to very little cultural development, as well as the fact that they are indebted to the above Black nations for the foundation of their scientific, religious, and philosophical accomplishments. They repaid these nations by utterly destroying their civilizations, and enslaving their descendants. And with others, it is because they took the traditions of these Black nations, added a few touches here and there to make it more in keeping with some of their social values, and then claimed that the final product was a revelation from God to them.

RELIGION, TRANCE, AND ANCESTORS

As religion concerns itself with the inner realm of being, its main vehicle is the phenomenon of trance. Proficiency in this state, which we will later define, gives one full acquaintance with the metaphysical realm. On one hand, communication with the two classes of entities dwelling therein, - the dead (ancestors), and the spirits administering natural phenomena (angels, deities)- becomes possible. On the other hand, first hand knowledge of man's metaphysical (higher) vehicles, and the "insperience" of man's true

14

relation with God, and all other creatures are attained. The central theme of this discourse becomes clear when we take note of the fact that while Westerners believe in the survival of the spirit after death, they have no tradition of "ancestor worship," (i.e., communication with the deceased). Now the reason is clear. It is for lack of a culture of trance working, which is the only means to that end. The same holds true for angels. While Western religions claim belief in their existence, these metaphysical dwellers have been banished, of late, to the pages of the scriptures.

The ability, through trance, to communicate with deceased beings has led Blacks to the greatest understanding of the nature of Man. It has provided us with an inner empirical evidence of the immortality of Man. Immortality is not merely the survival of the spirit, but of one's identity across incarnations. On one hand, because of the pricelessness of the revelation that Man is immortal, and on the other hand, because of the unparalleled guidance that ancestors provide, rituals for communion with the ancestors (so called ancestor worship) play a prominent role in the religion of Black nations. It is instructive to note that the greatest architectural marvels of the ancient civilizations (Kamit, Mohenjo Daro, etc.) were burial shrines. Entire cities were filled with these structures (pyramids, etc.) that surpassed in opulence the dwellings of even the kings. In place of this insight Western scholars could only see what they believed to be the work of megalomaniacal builders.

Only from the ancestors, the "living proof of life after death," could have been learned the observances and practices that lead to immortality (the survival of an individual's identity across incarnations). Such practices and observances became the fundamental doctrines for the spiritual development of men and nations.

Participation in a series of African, and Oriental rituals will reveal to all that women in general can attain to the trance state with greater ease, and power than men. Societies that have a deep appreciation for synthetical thinking and introversion, due to their right-sidedness, or equilibration, cannot fail then to hold in great esteem their women. Just the opposite is found in left-sided societies. It is no wonder then to find that in all Black nations (not led astray by Whites) women, and Goddesses occupy positions, and play roles equalling those of the males. Women in Kamit, and other Black nations of antiquity occupied positions not yet achieved by Western women to date. As Queen Mothers they determined the transference of the kingship, and legitimized the king; inheritance was through them. That is they held the wealth of the nation. They were priestesses in their own right, and it is a matter of record that the Goddesses whose shrines they were responsible for, commanded greater importance than those of the Gods, in many cases. In contrast we find Western women just beginning to make headway in their struggle for equality, 6000 years behind their Black counterparts. Where is the female Rabbi, Iman, Bishop, etc.?

To summarize, I would like to point to the fact that what I have done is to simply carry to the logical conclusion well known facts regarding the division of the brain's functions. It was not until the early part of the 1950's that western scientists began to understand fully that the higher functions of the human brain were divided between hemispheres.

Teams of surgeons, psychologists, neurologists and biologists discovered that the two hemispheres process information regarding the same things in diametrically opposed, yet complementary ways. Unfortunately, western scientists went on to characterize the separate functions of each hemisphere by wild generalizations. "The left side governs language, scientific thinking, etc.," for example. Even wilder generalizations were given. The left, and the right hemispheres, respectively, were said to differ from each other in that the first is "intellectual, the other intuitive," "intellectual vs. sensuous," "secondary vs. primary" (Freud), "deductive vs. imaginative," "realistic vs. impulsive," "analytic vs. relational," "sequential vs. multiple," "rational vs. intuitive," "discursive vs. iedetic," etc. There is a bit of truth in some of these statements, but they cannot be accepted without due caution, and corrections. We will deal with them in later chapters. It has also been recognized that in some people the functions of the left hemisphere predominate, while in others, those of the right side do. Central to our discourse is the fact that the characteristics of western culture are predominantly the productions of the left hemisphere of the brain while the characteristics of Black and most other Nonwestern cultures are that of the right.

Let's return to the earlier quotation from Placid Temples' book. *"This European concept of separate beings, or substance which find themselves side by side, entirely independent one of another is foreign to Bantu(an African group) thought."* This observation, which is one of thousands, implicitly, but unequivocally states that something in the European makes them "see," and postulate differences, while something in the Bantu (as with all other Africans, which includes the Ancient Egyptians) makes them see and postulate unity, when viewing the same reality. Again, in the *Legacy of Egypt*, Barb states that although Westerners are now in possession of dictionaries, and grammars of the Egyptian language they are not in a position to understand it because *" . . . the Egyptian way of thinking, so utterly different from our Western 'logical' mind."* Again, one has to be obtuse not to see that what Barb refers to as the European 'logical mind' is the predominance of the left side of the brain. Of course the statement must be corrected to syllogistic logic, for the right side has a logical function of its own. Barb concludes by referring to the "impossibility of translating Egyptian thoughts into modern language, for the distinctions we cannot avoid making did not exist for the Egyptians." It begs several questions. Why can't European thinking avoid making distinctions that do not exist for the Egyptians? Or equally valid, why cannot the Egyptians avoid unifying, and synthesizing where Westerners cannot avoid segregating and analyzing? Before we answer these questions let's dispose of the racist statement "modern." It is a tool of the theory of evolutionism that holds that the Black races and their cultural expressions exemplify the primitive phase of mankind, while the White race, represent the more evolved (modern).

The observation made by many scholars concerning the difference in thinking between African people and Westerners can only be intelligently explained by reference to the hemispheres of the brain. If the cultural expressions of the individual nations of an entire race share the same trait,- analytical, for example, it can only be because their thinking is dominated by the left hemisphere. Fortunately we don't have to speculate on the issue for the simple fact that it is well known by professionals in the area. Western scientists have long arrived at the conclusion that western culture is predominantly left-sided, and is now attempting very strongly to introduce into the school system methods that would make more use of the right hemisphere. This has been especially encouraged by the discovery that such educational methods that appeal to the right side of the brain excel greatly over those of the left. "Super learning," "accelerated learning," etc. are the superlatives that are being thrown

17

around as they are finding that such methods shorten the learning period (2 to 20 times faster), and produce a greater yield in understanding, and retention (500% in the same time span) over the left side. Is this the reason why Black nations were the first to achieve a high level of civilization? We will see that it is. The techniques used in the current "Super learning" systems, are nothing more than a minor fraction of the techniques used in traditional Africa from time immemorial. By pretending that the whole thing is a recent western discovery, and invention, Westerners are dooming themselves to stagnation, again! They need to humbly ask the African people to show them the way.

A study of the literature on brain hemispheres will show that analytical, and segregative thinking are carried out by the left hemisphere, while synthetical thinking is done by the right side. Let's put it another way; the left side is responsible for the differences we make between things. It is the author, for example, of the western attitude of seeing themselves as being separate from nature, and therefore ruining the ecological balance (killing off whole species of animals, polluting the air, soil, etc.); of denying diet a significant role in healing - poisons play a higher role; of racial, and sexual discrimination, and so forth. On the other hand, the ecological mindfulness of most other Nonwestern people, for example, must be attributed to the dominance of the right hemisphere in their thinking; the respect and high regards for their women, is the result of the same function. A most important expression of the right side of the brain, concerns the Nonwestern belief in the indivisibility between all things in the world. Far from being a mere intellectual notion, it is the basis of their entire way of life. Affect one thing, and all others are. The Western Man's response to this is to call it primitive "animism" (fortunately it is just a word,- without objective reality!). But is this not the foundation of religion? To "tie (legion)" "back (re)" the things that have been separated? "Unity" states the Kabala is the foundation of good, while "disunity" is the foundation of evil. Egotism, a failure to experience the interdependence between humans, is a function of the left side, and a major problem that religion sees as a chief obstacle to the spiritual life. We will see that the cure for egotism is the activation of the right side of the brain. We also will see that the religions of Black nations were well acquainted with the dualization (the knowledge of good and evil) of the spirit, and made its unification the foundation of their spiritual tradition. What today the Western man

18

calls the functions of the hemispheres of the brain, the Kamitian referred to as the Two Truths (Maati), Ta-ui; the Taoist, as the doctrine of Yin and Yang; the Dogons, as the twin Nummo serpents that govern the various aspects of the world.

Finally, we must note that racial differences go beyond the color of the skin, type of hair, skeletal structure, and other physiognomical items. In future chapters we will accumulate all the evidence to show that *there is a cultural unity among all White nations, all Black nations, and all Oriental nations. And that the common factors in each are traceable to the hemisphere of the brain that dominates their thinking, their language, and cultural expressions.* And finally, that since the behavior of nations is a product of this part of their biological make-up they could hardly help the manner in which they created their cultural expressions, and reacted to others, determining thus the events that make up world history. This and only this, I dare say, can establish history, and anthropology as sciences, as well as to put the study of religion on a scientific basis.

CHAPTER 2

THE BLACK FOUNDERS OF CIVILIZATION

In the preceding chapter we saw that one of the main factors that is responsible for the differences in cultural expressions, is the division of the brain into two hemispheres, each with its own peculiar way of thinking. We were able to go beyond the mere listing of the cultural traits of nations, and to catalog them into two fundamental sets, based on the the traits of each of the hemispheres of the brain. I.e., if it is not shown why, it is of no use to say that the fundamental traits of Black cultures are the burial of the dead (especially accompanied by grave offerings), and communication with ancestors; high recognition of women (matrilocal marriages, matriarchal inheritance system, etc.), and "female divine powers"; high degree of social stratification; high degree of stratification of the "celestial hierarchy of powers controlling events on earth"; and the involvement of religion in every area of life. We saw how these are all the results of a people's mental output dominated by the side of the brain whose strong point is trance. White culture, which is extroverted (left hemispheric) produced and sustains a culture that (before contact with Blacks) cremated its dead, or exposed them to be eaten by animals, and has a negative attitude toward, and horror of spirits of the dead to this day; holds its women, and "female divine powers" in low esteem (the Christian divine pantheon is made of a Father, a Son, and a ghost, for example); low degree of social stratification and the love of freedom from authority that goes with it (laissez faire); separation of religion from all other social institutions (government, education, etc.), and the restriction of the divine to special places, and times (church, Sunday, holidays, etc.); the separation of the divine from healing, and so on. If you can't help thinking this way, it's because the left side of the brain is dominating your thinking.

Keeping these ideas firmly in awareness, let's attempt to establish the racial characteristics of certain nations of antiquity.

The importance of knowing the racial identity of the nations that were the founders of civilization lies in the fact that:

1) Religious doctrines, and systems cannot be understood in a vacuum. They cannot be separated from the social environment that produced them. The various components of the religious system of each nation are, for example, ritual vehicles to condition the population to support, or reject particulars of interest or

detriment to the nation. The ritual system of Ausar (Osiris) will always remain a mystery to people who have no understanding of the African Kingship, and the history of the peculiar difficulties that the Kamitians experienced with their kingship. In the same way, people who know little regarding the African Queen mothership, and high priestesship (e.g., the rituals performed with the skeletal remains of deceased kings) will understand little regarding the ritual system of Auset (Isis).

2) The White nations who became the heirs of these civilizations understood only the external aspects (what appealed to the left side of the brain), and distorted the spiritual (internal, right-brained). What passes for the world's major religions are attempts of the left side of the brain to practice what can only be done by the right side. Can you imagine where chemistry would be today if it were in the hands of poets (right-sided function)? Each element would no longer be a complex of exact weight, and electrical behavior, but, "grey clouds," or "wolves," according to the poet's mood. This is what the sons of Eurasia have done to the science of religion. The result is that, with the destruction of the ancient Black founders of civilization some 4000 - 2000 years ago, the world has been plunged into a spiritual dark age, and is sinking ever into that jaw whose fiery tongue flickers with death.

3) *The solution to our problem is the restitution of the science of life that actually gave birth to civilization.* The only way that this can be done is by correlating the spiritual doctrines, and religious practices of the founding civilizations with those of the Black civilizations of today. This is of extreme importance for the simple fact that most students of spiritual culture and esotericism have received their education from western organizations (Rosicrucians, Aryan Hindus, Semitic and European Kabalists, etc.) who have falsely claimed that they are the custodians of the wisdom of the ancients. After going through this book, the reader can decide if this is true. Last, but not least we will come to understand that religion cannot save mankind unless it is allowed to govern all social institutions. All such teachings regarding the lone sage, and individual salvation will be seen to be, on one hand, natural conceptions of the left side of the brain with its isolationist thinking, and on the other, to be impotent as far as being vehicles for the spiritual upliftment of the world. In our study we will see that when the White nations adopted the religious institutions of the Blacks

21

they allowed only those doctrines that did not interfere, for the most part, with their most cherished social beliefs, whether these were right or wrong. In fact many of the religious myths, and doctrines have their origin in the political competition that arose out of their contacts with Blacks. The extreme manner in which women were humiliated (made the source of all of mankind's suffering, the heavily lopsided adultery laws against them, etc.) in Semitic Asia 4000 years ago, for example, was chiefly due to the fact that the occupation of very high positions of the Black women of Canaan, Sumer, Phoenicia, etc., was a serious challenge to the patriarchal system of the Whites, as it filled the heads of their women with another view of social possibilities. In those days, the White people of Mesopotamia were under the cultural, if not political, domination of Blacks.

Establishing the racial identity of the founders of civilization is a simple matter. Yet, the issue needs to be heavily detailed so that there is no room for doubt. Western writers have tried so hard to hide the fact of the blackness of these civilizations, that their culture is so distorted, and misunderstood, and their descendants, modern day Blacks, have been totally culturally disenfranchised.

THE THREE FUNDAMENTAL RACES OF MANKIND AND THE PRINCIPLE OF GEOGRAPHIC CONTIGUITY

If we put the variations and admixtures aside, then we find that the races of mankind are the White, the Black, and the Yellow/Red (Oriental, which includes the American Indian). When we trace these people back to late prehistoric and early historic times we find that each of these people reside in separate geographic locations; the Oriental in the Northeasternmost part of Asia (and later, America), the Eurasian (White) in the Northwesternmost part of Asia and Northern Europe, and the Blacks, occupying from the Southern parts of Europe, Western and Central Asia, and all of Africa. Within each of these three great geographical divisions of the world we find, in late prehistoric and early historic times (before the great migrations of people), nations speaking related languages, with similar racial characteristics, and cultural patterns. We could say that the Supreme Being made men with certain differences and put them in different parts of the globe. Western historians have used these concepts to discover the kinship and origin of their people after thousand of years of separation.

When it comes to the great Black civilizations, it is a different story. Western historians are always postulating an unproven (and unprovable) geographic origin for them in areas where they have no kin. I.e., they seek the origins of the Sumerians in eastern Asia, when the people who most closely share their racial, and cultural characteristics reside in Africa. They do the same for the Ancient Egyptians. The exact locations of the origin of many of the great White nations of antiquity are unknown, yet no historian has proposed an origin for them in America, or Africa. It is such a natural reflex to search for their origins in the geographic location where all Whites have been known to inhabit since prehistoric times. We must take note of the fact that plants and animals of related characteristics have been thus distributed around the earth.

Trick number two has been to postulate that the "precocious" development of Kamitian (Ancient Egyptian) culture was either the product of an invading "master White 'Semitic' race (the Shemsu Heru)," or the result of the blending of the White and the Black races. First of all, it is important to realize that at work is the racist offshoot ideas of Darwinism. To wit: clearly, Blacks (a primitive race) could not solely, or primarily be responsible for such a culture. Period! Rather than pass in deserved silence the allegation that a White race was responsible for Kamitian civilization, wholly or in part, let's look at some facts. 1) No facts have ever been given to support the allegation, showing that the concept is born solely from the unwillingness to accept the fact that Blacks could have created such a civilization, 2) This alleged master "White race" has no other achievement. Previous or otherwise. They left no traces of civilization anywhere else. At the time when this alleged "dynastic race" is supposed to have come to Kamit (and placed themselves under the military leadership of the Kamitian leader Narmer?!!), Eurasia was still in the paleolithic stage (hunter, gatherer,- around 3500 B.C.), while all of North Africa was in the Neolithic, and early agricultural stage, and Kamit had passed into the historical stage. The proposal that they came from Arabia is even worse. At that time Arabia was mostly inhabited by Blacks who were less developed regarding civilization. Thus we are to believe that a people, who achieved nothing at home, came and established civilization in an entirely more advanced area . . . and then vanished, leaving no remains of themselves. No bones, cultural items, likeness of themselves in paintings, sculptures, etc. In reality, the Shemsu Heru, the people who historians have tried to equate

23

with their hypothetical race, are the very Blacks that are called Nubians.

What can you say of historians who ignore the fact that all the nations in the Northeastern section of Africa at that time were far ahead of Eurasia in the technologies that were chiefly responsible for the development of Kamit, and who prefer to invent a Eurasian cause for the development of Kamitian civilization?

An important part of this argument rests on the false theory that racial contact is a chief cause for the advancement of civilization. Let's look at the facts:

a)   The Hyksos occupation of Kamit for 150 years contributed nothing to the progress of Kamitian culture. In fact all historians are in agreement that it retarded it. So did the occupation of Kamit, by the Persians, Greeks, and Romans. In fact, the contact of Whites with the Kamitian culture ended in the destruction of the latter,- culturally, and physically. I cannot imagine one single historian who would not agree that the civilizations of Ancient Egypt, Sumer, Indus Valley, and Kush would far surpass anything in the present world had they not been destroyed by Whites. It is a very interesting subject to speculate upon.

b)   The same retardation, arrest of progress, and eventual destruction occurred with the mingling of White culture with that of Sumer, Canaan, Phoenicia, Indus Valley.

c)   The theory has only held true in the reverse direction, as Western man greatly benefitted from his contact with the ancient Black civilizations.

The point of this detailed look at the issue is not merely to prove historians wrong, but to emphasize the real source of civilization. Today's leading psychologists will tell you that when you have to come up with the solution of a problem for which there are no precedents, it's to the right side of the brain that you have to make your appeal. It is in charge of invention, and creativity. The progress of western science is more one of technological advancement and variation, than of invention without precedents. To this day, no one has explained how the Chinese were able to come so far in science since the end of World War II. They have done in less than 40 years, what normally takes over 150 years for Europeans. We will see that the Chinese is an eminently "right-sided" culture. The ability of the great Black nations to invent civilization, and make such rapid progress must be seen as the result of their advanced techniques for using the right side of the brain. In fact, Kamit out-distanced Sumer, Canaan, the Indus Valley, and Phoenicia because it adhered closely to a right side methodology of thinking, in which its hieroglyphic system played a pivotal role.

The third ruse used by historians is an insult to their intelligence. It concerns their play with the word Ham. In the Old Testament the races of mankind are classified as descendants of Ham, Shem, and Japheth (the sons of Noah). While it is accepted by all that Japheth corresponds to the European and Northern Asiatics, and Shem to the Semites, there is a great deal of, well, you would have to call it, idiotic talk regarding Ham. Since there are no Oriental people depicted in the paintings and sculptures of Kamit, Greece, and Mesopotamian nations, it is not far fetched to conclude that the compilers of the Old Testament were not familiar with this race. Especially given the fact that they were located so far away. This explains why the Orientals were not included among the races of mankind. Now we know, that the biblical compilers were very well acquainted with Black people,- after all their ancestors were heavily intermarried with them, to say the least. Now if the Semites correspond to Shem, the European to Japheth, then where do we assign the Blacks? Still don't know? Let's modify the question. If Ham does not correspond to the Semites, or the Europeans, or the Orientals, to whom does it correspond? The Old Testament compilers assigned Ham to Ancient Egypt, Canaan, Kush (Ethiopia), and Put (Punt, a nation that was located at the horn of Africa,- modern day Somaliland. The Ancient Egyptians claimed that it was the location of their origin, hence made regular pilgrimages to it. They called it Ta Neter,- Land of God. Incidentally, the people of this area dressed in the same fashion as that of the Egyptians, and their men styled their beard in the same manner as the false beard worn by the Kamitian "Pharaoh." These similarities clearly support the Kamitian claim that they descended not only from this area, but from these people. And through Kush (Ethiopia), Ham relates to the indigenous original inhabitants of Arabia, and Sumer, which last was referred to as Nimrod (ruler of Babel, Erech, and Akkad in the land of Shinear (Sumer)), according to the biblical Table of Nations.

Hebrew scholars claim that the etymology and meaning of the word "Ham" is uncertain (we will see that this is the case with many of the most important words in the Hebrew language, and why). Now the word is actually pronounced "Kam" as it is spelled with the guttural "H," Cheth (Keth). The popular pronunciation with the aspirated H is the product of sloppy scholasticism. It is a

25

loan word from the Ancient Egyptian language, where it means black. And the Ancient Egyptians called their country Kamit (land of the Blacks), and themselves Kamau (Black people). This can explain why of all races, the Black has been referred to since ancient times by the color of their skin,- "Negroes," from the Latin, "negro" meaning black. If it were natural to do so, we would find that other people would be referred to in a similar manner. Instead all other people of antiquity are referred to by the name of their nation. White people call Blacks black, because the Kamitian people started the whole thing by thus calling themselves. Their paintings and sculptures of themselves testify to the fact that they are of the Black (Negro) race, and so are the words of foreign eyewitnesses. Herodotus, the eminent Greek historian who visited Egypt around 450 B.C. describes the Kamitian people as having "black skins and woolly hair."

In *Eternal Egypt*, Pierre Montet describes the Kamitians (ancient Egyptians) as follow; *"They had clearly defined features, prominent eyes, usually large, almost flat, noses, thickish lips, and somewhat low foreheads. Such were without exception the kings of Egypt at the time of the Old Kingdom. Many individuals presented the same features--for instance Ranefer, who lived during the fifth Dynasty, of whom there are two statues in the Cairo Museum."* It is interesting to note that Montet fails to sum up these characteristics as Black,- especially when he has seen the statue of the priest Ranefer, which is indisputably that of a so called "negro."

So desperate have historians become, that in their attempts to identify Ham with another race (perhaps Martian will qualify) they have classified most Nilotic Blacks, like the Massai, and the Somali, as non-Negroes. Yet, they are Hamitic! Interestingly, the same historians label the same Blacks as Negroes, when they are referring to them during the Egyptian historical period. So how come today they are of the so-called non-black Hamitic, or Nilotic race (note: a race unknown by scientists)? The answer is to be seen in the fact that more and more evidence is pouring in showing that the Ancient Egyptians and the contemporary Negroes of the Sudan (the Galla, Bari, Dinka, Nuer, etc.), and northeastern Africa are linguistically related.

To show that Kamit is ethnically and culturally related to Africa, Frankfort wrote of several of the earlier African prehistoric cultures of the Sudan south of Egypt:

26

Together they represent the African substratum of Pharaonic civilization, the material counterpart of the affinities between ancient Egyptian and modern Hamitic languages; of the physical resemblances between the ancient Egyptians and the modern Hamites; and the remarkable similarities in mentality between these two groups which makes it possible to understand ancient Egyptian customs and beliefs by reference to modern Hamitic analogies. (*The First Great Civilizations*, p. 46, Jacketta Hawkes).

In the *Symposium on the Peopling of Ancient Egypt and the Deciphering of Meroitic Script*, 28 January, 1974, (Published in 1978 by the UNESCO), Theophile Obenga introduced the irrefutable evidence that the Ancient Egyptian language, and its descendant, the Coptic language used by the Coptic Church, are related to the African languages. He proved the point by giving a substantial list of words that are common in 'meaning as well as grammatical functions' to the Kamitian, Coptic, and modern Negro-African languages. I.e., he used the same principles that proved the unity of the languages that are classified as Indo-European-Iranian.

A very important aspect of the Kamitian language that I am sure Egyptologists must have noted but have kept silent is the widespread occurrence of words that are written in the same manner but differ totally in meaning. They have kept silent about this because it irrefutably ties Kamit to the rest of Africa. For example, the Kamitian word "a-au-au" has the following meanings: grave, tomb; to come; sleep, slumber; to punish, to do harm; to bespatter, to make a charge against; foreign interpreter. In every case, the word is written with the same letters. While the reader distinguishes the meaning from the added hieroglyphic symbolic determinant, the only way that speakers - listeners could do the same would be through variations of intonation and accents. For example, in the Twi language of the Akans of West Africa, "Me ba," means "my son," when the "ba" is accented, and "I (am) going," when the "me" is accented. In the Chinese language (which exhibits the same principle), the word "Shi" means "damp," "stone," "to cause," and "to be" when pronounced in an even pitch, rising pitch, dropping then rising pitch, and dropping pitch, respectively. The only way that Kamitian speakers could use the word "a-au-au" to mean so many things would be by such intonation differences. If we let " ^ " represent the accent, " < ," a drop in pitch, and " > ," a rise, we would get the following: a-au-au; a-au-au>; a^-au-au; a^-au-au>; a^-au-au<; a-au>-au>; a-au<- au<; a-au<-au>; a;au>-au<, and so on. It must be noted that this phenomenon is widespread in all African languages and is the main problem in the creation of alphabetical systems for recording these languages. This is one of the reasons why the Kamitians never abandoned their hieroglyphic system, - a fact that historians to this day cannot understand (Their chief explanation relies on the racist Darwinist theory of linguistic evolution, which explains hieroglyphic writing as the primitive expression of man's efforts to write.). Incidentally, this linguistic phenomenon is what gives the Oriental, and African dictions their characteristic sing-song pattern. Studies on the hemispheres of the brain have shown that this "melodic" superimposition on speech in relation to meaning is due to the right side of the brain. This ties in with my premise relating the Black and Oriental races to the right side of the brain. This pattern is virtually foreign to the diction of Western man, and poses a great barrier to their learning these languages.

Perhaps the real source of the Hamitic problem is to be sought in Canaan. Thus far it seems that historians are getting away with making it a White, and Semitic nation. The basic argument is that the Old Testament (OT) compilers believed that it was Hamitic because it had extensive economic and cultural dealings with Kamit. Jewish scholars know better. In their later religious texts commentating on the OT we find the following:

"Others say that Ham himself unmanned (castrated) Noah who, awakening from his drunken sleep and understanding what had been done to him, cried: 'Now I cannot beget the fourth son whose children I would have ordered to serve you and your brothers! Therefore it must be Canaan, your first born, who they enslave. And since you have disabled me from doing ugly things in the blackness of night, Canaan's children shall be born ugly and black! Moreover, because you twisted your head around to see my nakedness, your grandchildren's hair shall be twisted into kinks, and their eyes red; again, because your lips jested at my misfortune, theirs shall swell; and because you neglected my nakedness, they shall go naked, and their male members shall be shamefully elongated.' Men of this race are called Negroes; their forefather Canaan commanded them to love theft and fornication, to be banded together in hatred of their masters and never to tell the truth." This quotation was taken from *Hebrew Myths* by Graves and Patai. It cites the following Jewish religious texts as the original sources: B. Sanhedrin 72a-b, 108b; B. Pesahim 113b; Tanhuma Buber Gen. 49-50; Tanhuma Noah 13, 15; Gen. Rab. 341.

The above is one of many Rabbinical texts created for the purpose of "clearing up" difficult biblical passages. In order to "justify" taking the land of Palestine from its original inhabitants, the Canaanites, Genesis states that Canaan shall bear the curse of perpetual slavery to the Semites, and Europeans for the "sin" committed by his father, Ham. Accordingly, Ham committed an injustice against his father Noah by walking into the latter's tent unknowing of the fact that the latter was drunk (not sinful?), and naked. Later rabbis were uncomfortable with the passage, on one hand, because they could not justify the rationale for charging Ham with a crime, and the punishment, -sentencing his descendant to eternal enslavement, cannot stand up to a common sense of justice. On the other hand, they knew that the story was an adaptation of the well known Middle Eastern mythical theme of the father's castration by his son(s). It occurs with the Greeks in the story of Kronos' castration of his father Uranous in order to usurp his power. The Hebrew version is most likely derived from the Hittite myth (derived from the Hurrians) in which the Supreme God Anu curses his son and cup-bearer Kumarbi, because the latter bit off his genitals (who afterwards rejoiced and laughed as Ham was supposed to have done). I trace their version of the story to the Hittites because the Hebrew people originated ethnically from a mixture of Hittites, Amorites, and Blacks. Their language and religion is an adaptation of the Canaanite tradition,- which is Black. That the Jews got their language, and religion from the Canaanites, and Sumerians (through Babylon) is well documented by historians.

If the preceding is not convincing enough, let's quote from the *Babylonian Talmud* translated, or edited by Rabbi Dr. I. Epstein (*Sanhedrin*, Vol. II, pp. 608-609):

"For when the Africans came to plead against the Jews before Alexander of Macedonia, they said Canaan belongs to us, as it is written, the land of Canaan with the coast thereof; and Canaan was the ancestors of these people (ourselves)."

Here we find a Jewish Rabbi dealing with historical records of Babylonian historians who were eyewitnesses to the historical life of Canaan, calling its inhabitants "Africans," as the latter called themselves. The event described above occurred around 332 B.C. when Alexander took Palestine away from the Jews, who had initially taken it away from the Canaanites. Incidentally the taking of Palestine from the Canaanites by the Jews is the pivotal theme of the Old Testament,- the Hebrew's quest for a land of their own. Because of the Jewish involvement in the history of Canaan, I cite their references as the most authoritative regarding the racial identity of the people of Canaan. This fact must be extended to embrace Phoenicia which was merely one of the cities of Canaan.

It is very important to take note of the fact that racially speaking the Semitic people originate from the same stock as the European. They were the first of the Eurasians to migrate from the north (around 3000 B.C.) into Western Asia. There they became politically, and culturally subjected to the Blacks (Sumerians, Canaanites/Phoenicians, etc.) who were far ahead of them in civilization. Having adopted the culture, and language of the latter, they practically lost the knowledge of their original tongue, and most of their culture, as has happened to Blacks in America. The main stock of these people must be traced to the Amorites (Martu, Aamu, and Amurru), and Hittites. The Amorites as known from Kamitian paintings (as the Aamu), and other sources are tall, fair, blue-eyed, some are blondes, and others, brown haired. The Hittites appear in history as an essentially White people slightly mixed with Black, and Oriental. As they are depicted in their own sculptures, and Kamitian paintings they cannot be told apart from modern day Persians, and Armenians. The language of the Hittites was related to the Latin, and Celtic, which may account for the guttural element in Semitic speech. Once these people were assimilated culturally by the Blacks of Western Asia, they lost their language, but not their speech articulation pattern, as has happened to Blacks in the West Indies, and America. For certain, we know that the Hebrews were a mixture of Hittites, and Amorites, and Canaanites. In *Ezekiel* 16:3 we read of the Jews saying about themselves, "And say, thus saith the Lord God unto Jerusalem; Thy birth and thy nativity is of the land of Canaan; thy father was an Amorite, and thy mother a

30

Hittite." Why cannot we conclude that the guttural element of Hebraic speech came from the Indo-European language of the Hittites? Additionally, the terms "Hebrew" and "Arab" were derived from their common ancestor Eber, who was the grandson of Arphaxad ('arpksad), who was a direct descendant from Shem. But Arphaxad is a good Indo-Iranian name. I relate it to the Medeans.

My argument is finally strengthened by the fact that it should strike anyone as a great oddity, that studies of the "Semitic" languages which were written down long before that of the Indo-Europeans, and thus stabilized, have yielded no common parent "before they were separated" as has been done for Indo-European. Before commenting on this, let's take note of the fact that while the languages of the Indo-Europeans, Africans, and Orientals number over a hundred each, with hundreds of dialects, there are, with generous concessions, only three Semitic languages with no more than four dialects. They are 1) Akkadian and its dialects (Babylonian, and Assyrian), 2) Aramaic, and its dialect (Hebrew), and 3) Arabic. The reason for this is that the "Semitic" languages, are really variants of essentially Black languages (of Canaan/Phoenicia). Therefore, any attempt to find the original Semitic language must lead back to Canaan/Phoenicia. In fact this study has been done, but it is suppressed by mere silence on one hand, and on the other, by passing Canaan, and Phoenicia as Semites (Whites). We will see that in their mode of thinking, and therefore in their cultural expression they share everything in common with the rest of Africa.

The conclusion is inescapable. There is no such reality as a Semitic language! What we call Semitic languages, are really dialectical variants of African (Hamitic) languages. Let's quote a highly regarded Jewish author, and professor of Sociology at the University of Toronto. *Ancient Judaism* by Irving M. Zeitlin (Polity Press). On page 19, we read concerning Israel's debt to Canaan:

Canaanite influence on ancient Israel

What the Ras Shamra evidence shows beyond doubt is that the Canaanites did in fact have an influence upon the culture of Israel. The only question is not whether such an influence existed, but rather its nature, and how and when it occurred. Beginning with the biblical literature, it is evident that they are perfected and polished

31

writings, attesting to the existence of literary traditions going back many centuries. These traditions are neither Mesopotamian nor Egyptian, but Canaanite. Just as the Hebrew language developed from Canaanite, so Hebrew literature built on the Canaanite literary traditions which had crystallized long before the Israelites had become a people. Israel took over norms and techniques of literary expressions that were established in the most ancient Canaanite dialects. We find, first of all, many words common to both the Ugaritic and the biblical literatures. Rosh (head), Shamayim (heaven), Aretz (earth or land) are just a few examples.

And on page 23 we read:

Many contemporary biblical scholars continue to take for granted that the Israelites *borrowed* from the Canaanites *almost everything essential*. - language, elements of religion and knowledge of agriculture. This occurred, scholars believe, as a result of the well-known phenomenon of cultural assimilation. Denying the historicity of the Book of Joshua, where it related that a large number of Canaanite city-states were destroyed together with their inhabitants, these scholars argued that the Joshua narratives are largely fictional. The Israelites did not conquer Canaan in a series of wars, they rather settled gradually in the sparsely populated hill-country, far from the Canaanite centers of power. (Emphasis is mine).

The above material was quoted to show how Western historians have played down, and have sought to conceal the Canaanite origin of Jewish culture. The reason? It is obvious. The Canaanites were Black.

The book of *Joshua* is very important because it contains the fulfillment of Yahweh's promise to give to the descendants of Abraham the land of the Canaanites. Yet, excavations conducted at Tell-es-Sultan, 1951-1957 by the British School of Archeology totally disproves the historicity of a Jewish conquest of Canaan. The supposed destruction of the walled city of Jericho, leading to the downfall of Canaan was no more than a creation of priests writing during the exile (about 700 years after the alleged event). The only finding of the dig was a group of walled towns dating way before the Israelite period. Some even dated back to 6800 B.C.!

Let's examine one of the most desperate attempts to whiten the Hamites. The Coptic language is classified by White historians as Semitic. Now, what is the Coptic language? The word "Copt" is the Arabic corruption ("Quft") of the Greek word "Aigyptos," or "Aiguptos" from which is derived "Egypt." The Coptic language is the very same language of the Ancient Egyptians with dialectical modifications that survives today in the liturgies of the Coptic (Ethiopian, Kushite, Abyssinian) Christian Church. In fact, it was spoken in Ethiopia for over a thousand years after the fall of the Kamitian kingdom, until the Islamic invasion drove it out of popular use, and into the sanctuary of the Church. So, if Coptic is Semitic, then the ancient Egyptians are Semitic (no one would try this), and so are the Ethiopians. In fact, all biblical scholars make extensive use of the Coptic language to clarify the meaning of "obscure" and "archaic" so called Semitic words, as well as to understand the writings of the Ancient Egyptians. When we study the people of Canaan, and Phoenicia we find that in their fashion of dressing, and picturing their deities they followed the Kamitian pattern so closely that often times, you could not tell one from the other. If historians classify the Coptic language as Semitic in full knowledge that it is the survival of the Ancient Kamitian language, does this not show duplicity at work? But they had to do it on compulsion of the principle that makes a bad lie be followed with the most idiotic of lies. I.e., after having made the Canaanites and Phoenicians white, they had to make the Ancient Egyptian language in its Coptic form Semitic. In all of this we must not lose sight of the biblical table of nations that tells us that Canaan is descended from Kush (Nubia). There is much more evidence that can be given on this point, but that would take us beyond our theme.

According to the biblical table of nations, another descendant of Kush (Nubia) is Sumer (biblical Shinear). We must interpret this as meaning that these people originated in the Sudan from where they migrated to Mesopotamia. My theory is that these were the authors of the Qadan culture, which appeared between Northern Sudan and Southern Egypt from 13,000 and 9000 B.C.

The remains of these Paleolithic Africans include grinding stones, and sickle blades showing that they were already involved in agricultural operations (the earliest on record). This conclusion is supported by the findings of wheatlike and barley pollen in the area. I also contend that these same people, having moved out of Nubia, due to the desiccation of the southern Sahara were also the authors of the Merimden culture (3500 B.C.) in the Egyptian Delta. There they exhibit many of the technologies common to the Qadan, and early Sumerian cultures. It is of interest to see how historians treat the subject of the racial identity of the Sumerians, whom they agree are not of the White, nor Mongolian, nor of the Far Eastern races (What is left for them to be?). In *The First Great Civilizations*, p. 37, the eminent historian Jacquetta Hawkes describes the Sumerians as follows:

> Their sculpture suggests that they were round-headed, with large noses slightly convex in profile, and with well-shaped lips of medium breadth.

The description of a nose as "slightly convex" is interesting. Of course she means "not straight," but rounded,- i.e., broad, wide, Negroid! I will let the "well shaped-lips" speak for themselves.

Keeping with the fact that the Sumerians were ethnically and culturally similar to the Dravidians ("original" Black inhabitants of India), I will quote R. S. Tripathi, who in *History Of Ancient India*, p. 15, says about the Dravidians that *"Western Asia is, however, generally supposed to have been their original abode, and the similarity of the Dravidian and Sumerian ethnic types undoubtedly lends some colour to this view."* And on page 30, speaking of the destruction of the Black civilization of India by the invading Whites (Aryans) he states, *"the Aryans were engaged in struggles with the "Dasyus" or "Dasas." They were carried on with unceasing relentlessness for the two people had strong differences, both racial and cultural. The Aryans were tall and fair, and the Dasyus were dark-skinned and of short stature. Their features were uncouth, being flat-nosed . . . The characteristics indicate that the Dasyus probably belonged to the Dravidian stock."* It is a shame that we have to do so much detective work to get at the truth of such issues.

The motive for hiding the racial identity of the Sumerians must be found in the fact that they were the source of Semitic culture. They were the first to teach the Semites (Akkadians, later Babylonians, and Assyrians) how to write in their cuneiform script;

34

mathematics, science, religion, literature, agriculture, and all the other critical elements of civilization. Their religious and secular literature, proverbs, and "Myths" became the main source of Semitic, including Jewish religious scriptures (modified to suit their individual needs.) It seems that Western historians have problems admitting to the world that they received the fundamentals of civilization from Negroes. It is just now that a handful of historians are giving credit to Kamit, and Sumer, what has been dishonestly credited to the Greeks and Hebrews.

The importance of dealing with the subject of the racial identity of the great Black nations who founded civilization in this manner will become more and more evident later in this book. For now let's realize the following:

1. The contemporary major world cultures, religions, and esoteric teachings are adaptations of the cultures of the Black founders of civilization.

2. These adaptations have veiled the true original values and purpose of the original cultures.

3. As a result of the veiling of the true elements of civilization, the world, suffering from the cultural domination of the Western nations, has fallen into a state of decadence, and is verging on the brink of destruction, from nuclear war, and social decay (AIDS, drugs, etc.).

4. The majority of the material floating around as esoteric teachings suffers from the same perversion. We will see, for example, that the vast literature of Kabalistical science as known to date is such a distortion of the original traditions that students of the subject can only but fail to achieve the lofty goals promised by it. Similarly, a great part of the material passing as the spiritual wisdom of India, is in reality the work of the White conquerors of India speculating on the Black tradition which is the true foundation of Hindu culture. As the esoteric tradition in Europe (Rosicrucian, Cabalism, etc.) is based on the above mentioned traditions, it too is in a similar position.

Very few people are aware of the fact that the Kabalistical tradition is in reality a "polytheistic" (syntheistic[1])

1. I will explain this term in a future chapter.

system. The so-called archangels of each sphere of the Tree of Life are exact correlates to the deities in other traditions. In fact, most of them were taken directly from Canaanite sources. Long before the formation of Israel, "El" (Al) was the generic name for the deity in Canaan. We thus find the term combined with others to denote the various aspects of God; AngEl, ArchangEl, MichaEl, RaphaEl, HanaEl, Elohim, YsraEl, etc. In order to have a wisdom (esoteric, "mystical") tradition without seeming to be polytheistic, the Hebrews changed the Canaanite/Phoenician deities into so-called "angEls," virtues, heroes (Euhemerism), and "names of God." Shaddai, which was a Canaanite deity, appears as the name of God (incorrectly rendered "almighty") at the 9th sphere of the Tree of Life; RaphaEl (El heals, not the true meaning) appears, incorrectly, as the angel associated to the 6th sphere and so on.

A careful study of the literature of the Kabala, the Old, and New Testament will reveal that the angels depicted perform most of the functions of the "deities" of other so-called polytheistic cultures. Like Elegba of the Yorubas, for example, Raphael, the "airy" angel is a mediator between God and the prophets (mediums). John L. McKenzie, S.J[2]. states in his *Dictionary of the Bible* that, *"the conception of the angels in the Gospels does not advance beyond the OT conception, and in some ways is less imaginative. The angel is still primarily a messenger or a member of the heavenly retinue, and there is not always a sharp distinction between the angel as a personal being and as a personification of the divine word or the divine action."* I highlighted the latter because it forms the most important part of the statement. It is of great importance to find a professor of Judeo-Christian divinity referring to the angels as "personifications of the divine word." The "divine word" is of course a reference to the hekau, mantras, and words of power that are used in other traditions to invoke the angels (deities). This fact underscores one of the greatest shortcomings of Hebrew Kabala. While the Hebrew Kabala conceals, and downplays the fact that angels are to be invoked to possess the spirit of the meditator, in the African tradition, the angels (deities) are openly invoked. They possess the spirit and borrow the bodies of the meditators to heal, counsel, admonish, teach the community, and carry out many other functions. Hebrew Kabalists, obviously limited by the need to avoid the image of practicing "polytheism," which they are indeed practicing, have thus

---

2. McKenzie joined the faculty of the Divinity School at the University of Chicago in 1965, and is presently a professor at DePaul University, Chicago.

limited, and distorted their understanding of Kabala. In place of guiding the student of Kabala to the mystical experience of the deity (angel) itself in order to comprehend the spheres and the principles of the Tree of Life, they engage the student in a host of intellectual speculations regarding the realities of the metaphysical world.

5. In order to understand the true message of the Black founders of civilization, we have to identify the original tradition and separate it from the contemporary hybrid cultures. This can only be done by making correspondences to the cultures of the nations that are the present day survivors of Kamit, Canaan, Sumer, etc. These are the contemporary African, and Black Indian nations.

Chapter 3

THE SOURCE OF THE LIGHT OF THE EAST

While in the past decade, a great deal of progress has been made, at least amongst Black scholars, to document the fact that the Kamitians (the people of ancient Egypt),- authors of the great pharaonic civilization, were Blacks, a great deal remains to be done to show that the authors of the great civilizations of India, Sumer, and Canaan/Phoenicia were also Black. Although the facts have been clearly known by white scholars from time immemorial, there has been a conspiracy to hide it from the world. It is the mere product of the inability of Europeans to cope with the fact that the greatest contributions to the establishment of civilization (religion, science, geometry, algebra, astronomy, mathematics, writing, etc.) were made by the same race that they enslaved and dispersed throughout the Americas.

One of the greatest losses that mankind has suffered from this distortion of history, is the inability to truly understand the great spiritual wisdom of antiquity. Scholars have resorted to all sorts of intellectual speculation about spiritual matters that can only be known through direct experience, and practice. "How else, but through speculation can one discover the true meaning of teachings, and beliefs for which there are either no written records, or that has come down to us shrouded in the veil of allegories, and myths?" One may ask, with apparent justification. But, there is an alternative. Once it its realized that the "wisdom of antiquity" was that of the same Blacks who are today still dwelling in India, Sub-saharan Africa, etc., then the alternative will be made clear. Through one to one correspondences, for example, if I note similarities between the West African Yoruba deity Obatala (Oba Tala), and the Dravidian Goddess Tara, whose mantra is Aum, and the Kamitian Deity Ausar, whose name conceals the mantra Aum, I can test my hypothesis with the existing rituals of Obatala, the Goddess Tara, and the surviving material about Ausar. This work has been done extensively for the past sixteen years by the priests and priestesses of the Ausar Auset Society with the results that a syncretism between all Black civilizations, past and present has been achieved.

Very few people realize that the yoga teachings that are being disseminated throughout the world are fundamentally a creation of Africans. Hinduism as we know it today is a blend of prehistoric Western European religion, with many systems extracted from the original African cultural base.

The earliest evidences of yogic practices date back around 3000 B.C. Figurines of men seated in the Lotus pose, and symbols of Shiva and Shakti,- the main symbols of ancient Black Dravidian spiritual culture were found in the excavated ruins of the two oldest centers of civilization in the Indus Valley; Harappa, and Mohenjo Daro. These cities were neatly laid out with rectangular city blocks, streets crossing each other at right angles, brick houses, public baths with steam heating, underground sewer system, etc. --as early as 3000 B.C.! And they were senselessly destroyed by Whites (the Vedantic Aryans) who invaded them, and conquered the area between 1500 - 800 B.C.

In *The History of Ancient India* (Pub. Motilal Banarsidass, 1967), Rama Shankar Tripathi gives the following descriptions of the Dravidians who have been identified as the originators of the esoteric wisdom of India.

> The Dravidians, so called from the Sanskrit term Dravida, were one of the earliest cultured races of India . . . Western Asia is, however, generally supposed to have been their original abode, and the similarity of the Dravidian and Sumerian Ethnic types undoubtedly lends some colour to this view . . . . The Dravidians were conversant with the use of metals, and their pottery was of improved type. They knew agriculture, and were perhaps the earliest people to build dams across rivers for irrigation purposes. They constructed houses and fortifications . . . As observed by Dr. L. D. Barnett, Dravidian society was "to some extent matriarchal" . . . They worshiped the Mother Goddess[1] and a host of spirits . . . Presumably, the Dravidians were

---

1. The Mother Goddess is the synthesis of 10 major Goddesses of India-the Dasha Vidyas. Their words of power were later syncretized to the Yogic system. Aum, for example was the word of power of the Goddess Tara long before it was assimilated into the Yogic system as we know it today.

39

identical with the "Dasas" or "Dasyus" of the Rigveda.

Of great importance in the above quotation is the reference to the ethnic similarity between the Dravidians, the Sumerians, and the Dasas or Dasyus. Since it is well known from the written Vedantic records that the Dasyus were Black people, and that the Dravidians are black skinned (krishna-tvach)[2], as we know from the fact that they are still in existence, we must conclude that the Sumerians were black. Tripathi informs us that:

> the Dasyus were darked skinned and of short stature. Their features were uncouth, being flat nosed (anasah) . . . These characteristics indicate that the Dasyus probably belonged to the Dravidian stock, then occupying the parts over which the Aryans were seeking to establish their domination. . . . . Many of the Dasas became slaves of the conquerors, having been admitted into the society as sudras, but others retired into the jungles and mountain fastness, where we still find their descendants living in primitive conditions.

It is of great interest to learn that the creators of one of the greatest civilizations are today living "in primitive conditions" due to the barbaric act of conquest of others.

Regarding the origin of the system of Yoga, Vivian Worthington states the following in *A History of Yoga*:

> We shall see how yoga appeared in the Indus Valley at Harappa and Mohenjo Daro . . . It carried on as Sramanism through the Aryan, Brahminical and Vedic periods. Although fiercely contested and often persecuted by the Brahmins, its main writings, the Upanishads, were later adopted by the Brahminical establishment and tagged on at the end of the Vedas thus changing the whole complexion of Hinduism into its modern form known as Vedanta.

---

2. Krishna means black.

40

Regarding the nature of the religion practiced by the inhabitants of pre-Aryan India-the Dravidians-, Worthington states the following:

> Although tantra received its philosophical basis from the Vajrayana school of Mahayana Buddhism[3], its history is much older and takes us back to the early Sramanic stream of Indian thought. In its active aspect it can be looked on as a modern development of very ancient magical and fertility rites . . . In the excavations at Mohenjo Daro and Harappa can be found traces of the worship of the male principle in the form of the lingam (phallus) and of the female principle in the form of the yoni (vulva). From these early practices developed the Siva-Shakti cult which is so prominent a feature of tantrism. These early tantric practices were suppressed by the Aryans.

Of the whites who came later and destroyed the civilization of the Dravidians, Tripathi (see above) states:

> The Aryans were tall and fair . . . The general opinion is that the Indo-Aryans, as also the Avestan Iranians, were a branch of the ancient "Indo-Germanic" (Indo-European) peoples or the Wiros, and before their eastward migration . . . they occupied for long a common habitat, which has been variously located in Central Asia (Max Mueller); . . . This belief rests on grounds of the close similarity between the speech as presented in the Rigveda and the Avestan and the Indo-Germanic tongues.

The Whites imposed a rigid caste (apartheid) system in which the priests (Brahmins) held absolute power, followed by the secular leaders,- kings, military men, etc. (Kshatriyas), followed by the Vaisnas who made up the merchant class, and last the Blacks (the sudras), who could only engage in manual labor (cow-herding, agriculture, etc.). Needless to say that the whites were the only ones who could belong to the two higher caste, and Orientals and

---

3. It is not true that Tantra received its philosophy from Buddhism, as its philosophy appears in the Upanishads, which preceded Buddhism.

41

Mulattos belonged to the third. Intercaste marriage was prohibited. Nevertheless, they occured. M. M. Kunte, in his book *Vicissitudes of Aryan Civilization in India*, relates:

> Intermarriages-between the Aryas and the Shudras, Kolis, and other aborigenes-were frequent. The class of what the Americans contemptuously style Mulattoes, quadroons, and octoroons multiplied.

The new masters also outlawed the religion of the Blacks, as they made their religion the official one of the land. This caused the religion of the Blacks which involved Cosmology, meditation, Deity invocation (predominantly Goddesses), hatha yoga, pranayama, mantra yoga, kundalini yoga, yantras, spiritual initiations, talismanic magic, tantric rituals, etc. to break up into separate practices. Lacking the benefit of carrying on their training, and practice in the organized manner that freedom would have allowed, the priests led individual existences in the safety of the forests. They were the Rishis who had to hide and teach in the forests as they were bitterly persecuted by the Brahmins (Aryan priests). As time went on, several "traditions" emerged as these individual priests varying in degrees of knowledge, and ability, colored the material with their individual insight, temperament, opinions, ignorance, etc.

In *A History of Yoga*, Vivian Worthington informs us that:

> The Aryan religion was brutal and materialistic. The caste system was rigid and oppressive, and the Brahmins wielded great power.
> The Sramanas, as the yogis and other independent thinkers and teachers were known, were tolerated when the priests were not strong enough to eliminate them, but were hunted down and killed, and driven out of the area where the priests had full control.

It is interesting to note how Vivian Worthington sidesteps the reason for the Brahminical persecution of the Sramanas. Instead of stating that they were persecuted because they were Black, as any historian of ancient India must know, she makes it seems as if their persecution was due to their "independent thinking." She knows very well, as shown in her book, that the Sramanas were practitioners of Yoga, Tantra, so-called Mother Goddess worship, etc. I have given these quotations to show the depth of racism and deception that exists in the western reporting of history.

The Dravidians (Sramanas, rishis, yogis) succeeded, however, in one thing. By around 872 B.C., they wrote down their cosmological knowledge in the first of the Upanishads which dealt a death blow to the religion of the Whites,- the Vedas. It must be noted that the Vedic Aryan tradition has been totally abandoned in India since then, to this day.

These doctrines, which were interpretations of the prehistoric Dravidian religion gave rise to Samkhya philosophy, Gautama's Bhuddism, and Jainism.

Gautama's Buddhism, which was called the Hinayana (Little vehicle), was not able to transform people's being, because it was lacking in the techniques to achieve its lofty philosophy. So after his death, it was in danger of dissolution as it was kept alive in great measure by his charisma. To ensure its survival, his disciples, against his rules, blended his teachings with the tantric traditions of the Blacks. This aspect of Buddhism, which is called Mahayana (the great vehicle) was able to transform people's being as it is based on the causal psycho-physical principles that control Man's behavior and growth[4]. Gautama's Buddhism is based in part on intellectualism, and on the adherence to a code of conduct which is in reality the effect, and not the cause of spirituality. In other words, it failed because 1) Intellectual activity cannot transform behavior, and 2) It is a confusion of category, and ignorance of psychology and spiritual laws to try to make people good by telling them to behave good. You have to engage them in some activity which, without their conscious effort results in the desired behavior. This latter is the foundation of Tantrism (the Religion of the Blacks, and Mahayana Buddhism, which is based on the Tantras).

Incidentally, it must be noted that as the original Bhuddism (Gautama's Hinayana) was against the practices of Deity invocation (mantric chanting), and was also anti-woman, in conformity with its Aryan parentage, its followers, upon merging it with Goddess based Tantrism, took the mantras that corresponded to the Goddesses and syncretized it with their male Dhyani-Buddhas. For example, the mantra Aum which is the word of power used by Blacks from

---

4. These are the mantras,- words of power.

prehistory in their invocation of the Goddess Tara, the embodiment of Man's divine perfection on earth, became some 2500 years later, the mantra of the Dhyani-Buddha Vairocana. Similarly, the mantra Hum, of the wisdom Goddess Chinnamasta, became the mantra of the Dhyani-Buddha Aksobhya, and so on. In this manner, Buddhism was able to survive as these mantras gave to their adherents the power to achieve the spiritual virtues that these "Dhyani-Buddhas" represented. Before this, their followers would study the philosophy, aspire to realize the virtues, but fail in their aspirations for the lack of the power to achieve. It is not enough to understand. You must have the power of realization. In addition, this synchretism enabled them to convert many of the Blacks who could now worship their deities in the guise of the Dhyani-Buddhas. This is similar to what Blacks did thousands of years later in Brazil, Cuba, Haiti, etc. They syncretized the African deities with the Christian Saints (which were originally Black Deities. Things come back in strange guises!).

Buddhism, once synchretized with the Black religion as its power base was spread throughout India, and Sri Lanka by the Emperor Ashoka (264-227 B.C.). It then spread to China, 65 AD. In 552 AD the Hindu sage Boddhidharma founded the Chan (Zen) aspect of Buddhism in China; in 747 AD the Hindu Sage Padma Sambhava introduced tantric Buddhism to Tibet; in 1191 AD Eisai founded the Rinzai sect in Japan, and in 1300 AD Dogen founded the Soto Zen sect; around 1500 AD, the tantric Black religion was merged with Islam to give rise to Sufism. From China, India, Tibet, and Japan, this tradition spread to the rest of the Orient. Today those who do not know the history of the yogic tradition, nor understand its inner constitution speak of the "Light of the East" when in reality it is a modification of the Light taken by the Blacks from Nubia into the Tigris, and Indus Valley in prehistoric times. Anyone who takes the time to become acquainted with the pre-Aryan religion of India (e.g., See the *Agni Puranam*, published by the Chowkhamba Sanskrit Series, Varanasi, India) will see that it is the parent of all the fragmentary systems in vogue throughout the Orient. And that is the unfortunate truth. In place of the Dravidian integral system of living, and spiritual development, we are being offered its fragments colored by Aryan speculation into the nature of the spiritual dimension. This latter form of Hinduism-the latest reaction against the Tantric Yogic system of the Blacks of India-is known as Vedanta. It is the form that has been introduced into the West.

44

We must also note that another factor that has hidden the Black origins of the Tantric Yogic system, has been the fact that it has been presented to the world through translations into the Sanskrit language. And to make matters worse, due credit has never been given to the Black people who created the system. What else is new?

Chapter 4

COSMOLOGY AND COSMOGONY

Imagine the following scenario: You have come up on a man busily engaged in constructing something with wood, bricks, cement, etc. He is mixing cement in a kitchen blender, digging holes with a spoon, nailing boards with a rock,- he has already shattered 20, and so on. "Hum," might be your first reaction, "What are you doing?"

"Building a house. Isn't it obvious?" the familiar salt.

"Right" you nod, "what kind of house?"

"Don't know" as he picks up some cement with a fork and pours it into the blender.

"Shouldn't you be using the right kind of equipment?" you attempt to bring some sanity into the conversation.

"Whadya mean. Can't you see that these are working fine?"

"And how!" you quip. "Well let me see your blueprint"

"A what?! What is that?" he drops everything and transfixes you with an honest quizzical look.

As you are by now begging for this scenario to end, I will end it. But it is not really the end, as it is a good replica of how most people conduct their lives. Don't be too quick to exempt yourself. By chapter 10 you will be thinking very differently. Due to the lack of knowledge of Self, and the purpose of Life, most people in the world are going about the daily business of living with wrong ideas of what is life, what should be their true goals, how to correctly achieve their goals. There is not the slightest awareness that there ought to be, or that there actually exists a blue-print to guide our steps in life to the true fulfillment of our mission on Earth. Such a blueprint is called a Cosmogony.

Cosmology, the study of Cosmogony has two fundamental goals. First, it provides an ordered and unified (synthetical) view of who and what is God, Man, and the forces that administrate and sustain the world. No understanding of a subject can take place without an ordered and unified presentation of its whole and parts. Second, cosmology (like all blueprints and maps) provides a framework that guides thinking and action through the vast array of seemingly unrelated life situations to the successful identification and attainment of the goal of living. It achieves this by showing how all the events in a person's life are integrally related to his/her destiny.

Through it is revealed the spiritual value of each and every event in a person's life.

With a partial view of Man's identity, and worse no knowledge of his origin and destiny, people go on to create innumerable institutions, life goals and undertakings. What if someone offered proof to the world that all things making up the world are integral and inseparable, functional and structural components of one Being? The unity of all things in the world can be understood by the study of biological entities, as they are based on the same cosmogonical structure (blueprint).

The human body, for example, is made up of thousands of different types of cells numbering in the billions. Yet, they are all parts of one entity. They represent one life, and not billions of separate existences. Although each cell has its own individual need,- The nourishment that one cell receives doesn't take care of the others. Yet, we all know too well what happens when even one cell begins to go its own way,- Cancer! In spite of having individual needs, like all other creatures of this Earth, their activities interrelate to maintain the one being which they collectively compose.

But how do we know that all the cells in the body are integral parts of a whole? The answer is simple. Their interdependence, the harmony and order governing their interaction, and the fact that their individual activities can be shown to add up to the life of the whole they compose. Running through all the disciplines studying living things,- Biology, Physiology, Biochemistry, etc.,- as well as all other sciences are the factors of order, interdependence, relationship, and the integration of seemingly separate things into a whole. It is most interesting to note, that the Western world does not have a fully organized science of the shaping factors of order, harmony, etc. that permeates all sciences. Such a science, known in various degrees of sophistication to most Nonwestern nations is known as Cosmology. The term "cosmology" means the study (logy) of order (cosmos, from the Greek Kos, meaning order). It occurs in such words as Cosmetas, an epithet of the Greek god Zeus, meaning "the orderer;" we also find it in "cosmetics" and mathematics- from the Greek mathematikos. It is easy to see the relationship of the meaning of the term with the subject treated in mathematics. The term's antonym is "Chaos." *Webster's New World Dictionary*, Second College edition, defines it thus: the disorder of formless matter and infinite space, supposed to have existed before the ordered universe. --SYN. see confusion. (underlines mine). Although this fairly common definition clearly

47

establishes its relation to "cosmos," it has a major flaw. How can there be disorder and confusion in a formless medium? The text is clear that there are two states,- one in which matter is formless (incorrectly equated with disorder), and the other, of a later existence, in which there is order (implied is that here matter is formed, ordered). We must go further and note that the term chaos is of very clever coinage. It is composed of "A," the article of indefiniteness, sandwiched into the term K̲o̲s̲ (k̲A̲o̲s̲). To appreciate this fully, we must realize that indefiniteness denotes the absence of form. All forms are ordered, or defined states of substance,- hence "kaos" = formless (undefined) matter. In other words, the *indefinite* article "A" denies the existence of order (*definition*)in the term chaos.

Yet, in all truth, we will see that cosmology, the study of order, must start with the study of Kaos, for the ordered realm is a mirror reflection, according to its own laws, of the nonordered realm.

Keeping the above firmly in mind, it will be easy to see that present day Westerners have perverted the meaning of the words that are kin to "Kos." "Cosmos," is generally defined as the world, and universe; "Cosmogony" as the theory of the genesis and development of the world, and universe; "Macrocosm" as the great world, or universe; and "microcosm," anything that is regarded as a world in miniature; mankind, society, man, etc. What is at work here is the Western polarization in "thingish" thinking about a term that represents an abstract reality. Such thinking has kept Westerners from seeing that the so-called "creation" myths of Blacks are "Mythoscientific" expositions of how to bring order into an area where there is none. *The grand theme of the Cosmological mythoscientific literature of the Black spiritual tradition is the absence of order in the early part of the Man's life. Illnesses, social decay, and wars run rampant as a result. As long as this state exists, prayers, words of power, rituals, science . . . all measures are of no avail.* This is the state that all western nations find themselves in, to date. The bringing of order into the situation is the first prerequisite for the correction of the ills.

The value of these mythoscientific expositions resides in their appeal to the right side of the brain, which uses them as means of creating order in all other situations in our life. This is due to its synthetical ability.

Chapter 5

THE TWO GREAT REALMS OF BEING

All potters know that the clay they work with has two fundamental states; its original unformed or unordered state, and the other, which is formed, or ordered into things (pots, frogs, jars, and what have you). The same is true of Reality. All that is real falls into one of two fundamental divisions. By fundamental is meant that there is no possibility of further division. One division corresponds to a mode of reality that is lacking in form, objectivity, definition, etc. We will call this division of "kaos," the Subjective Realm. The other division corresponds to the mode of reality in which energy/matter has been ordered into forms, objects. This division is called the Objective Realm, due to the fact that it is in it that objects (thoughts, emotions, physical things) are found.

The Being that is the synthesis of Life in both realms, is called Neter in the Kamitic tradition. Its conceptualization goes beyond the concept of the Supreme God-head that is used by most spiritual traditions to represent the Supreme Being. All manifestations of itself, through which it creates, and maintains the world, including the God-head (Neb er Tcher,- Lord of the World), are called the Neteru. It is easy to see that this term is the origin of the Latin terms "natura," "neutral," "eternitas (eternity)," etc. Unfortunately, more space cannot be devoted to the subject, but discerning readers will see in the Kamitic notion about the Supreme Being, a deeper understanding than is to be found in other traditions, who limit It to the Subjective Realm.

For our purpose, a useful synonym for the world is "the Objective Realm." In this book the term "Objective" when referring to the World, manifested reality, etc. will always appear capitalized to distinguish our usage from one of its popular denotation,- "impartial, impersonal, unconditioned view, etc." The term, kin to "object," from the prefix "ob," refers to all that has form, and therefore denotes all that is perceptible (mentally, or physically). In the same manner we will qualify the term "Subjective." Excluded is the denotation of "partiality, conditioned view, personal, etc." The term, kin to such terms as "submerged, substrata, substance, etc.," from the prefix "sub," refers to all that is under, therefore, incapable of being perceived.

So, we have two fundamental divisions in the Realm of Being. One which is "submerged," i.e., imperceptible, and the other, perceptible. The imperceptibility of the Subjective Realm is based on the fact that in it, there are no objects. The derivation of the name Objective Realm from the fact that it is the place of objects is obvious. The importance of these concepts will be realized from the consideration of the fact that most people limit their acknowledgement of reality to what is perceptible. Yet, not only is reality not limited to the perceptible (Objective) region, it originates beyond it (in the Subjective Realm).

THE SUBJECTIVE REALM

If there are no things in the Subjective Realm, what then is there? It must be comprehended, first of all, that all the objects making up the world are modifications of an eternally "subsisting" energy/matter. As the term "exists" refers to objectified reality, the term "subsists" must be used to refer to Subjective elements in a homogeneous and unmodified state in the Subjective Realm. It must be understood that where there is absolutely no differentiation, there cannot be perception.

Contrary to the characteristics of Western "scientific" thinking, the modification of this universal underlying substance (Subjective energy/matter) into the set of related things we call the world, does not occur by chance. It is the result of conscious intelligent action. Although imperceptible, lacking form, the Consciousness and Will of Being (Neter) also reside in the Subjective Realm. With full consciousness of itself as Infinite Potential of expression, Neter wills its energy/matter to modify itself as the infinitude of forms manifesting in/as the world (the Objective Realm). Let's note, therefore, that the Creative elements of Being are imperceptible.

Soph and Aur are the Canaanite names given to the "unmanifested undifferentiated energy/matter" in the Subjective Realm. While Soph corresponds to the undifferentiated feminine polarity we designate as matter, Aur (root of aura = light), is the undifferentiated masculine polarity we designate as energy. They are the substance and energy underlying all forms and activities in the world. In the Kamitian tradition the matter side of the Subjective Realm is referred to as "Nu," and the energy polarity, Ra (pronounced Rau, hence aur, aura, radiation, etc.). In the Kamitic

Book of Knowing the Manifestations of Ra, written around 2500 B.C. (although the doctrine is much older), we have:

> The words of Nebertcher (Lord of the World) which he spoke after coming into being; I am he who came into being in the form of the "infinite power of manifestation (Khepera)." I became the creator of what came into being. After my coming into being, many were the things which came into being, coming forth from my mouth [words of power]. Not existed heaven (the noumenal division of the Objective Realm), not existed earth (the phenomenal division of the Objective Realm), not had been created the things of the earth, and creeping things in that place. I raised them out of Nu, from the state of inactivity (of energy). Not found I a place to stand wherein. I radiated words of power with my will, I laid a foundation in the law (Maau), and I made all attributes. *I was alone*, for not had I spit out the form of Shu (the thermal, yang principle of the world), not had I emitted Tefnut (the moisture, hydrogenoid, yin principle of the world), not existed another who worked with me. I made a foundation by means of my will, and there came into being the multitude of things . . . I became from God one, Gods three, that is from out of myself . . .

The text continues with the creation of men, and other things in the world through the interaction of Shu (yang) and Tefnut (yin). Besides corroborating what has been said thus far in this chapter, it introduces a very important point that cannot be passed up. **Here we have a written confirmation that monotheism existed in ancient Egypt much earlier than the birth of Abraham, and over 1000 years before Akhenaten, and Moses.**

In the Bantu (the South African nations) tradition, Subjective matter is "Ntu," in the Yoruba, it is Oladumare, in the Akan of West Africa, it is Nyame, etc.

Let's paraphrase the above by noting that all that was, is, and can ever be, are all modifications of the undifferentiated energy/matter, and unconditioned consciousness/will of Subjective Being. Therefore all that we have been, now are, and can ever be, are modifications of this original Subjective Being.

We can therefore make the following conclusions about our selves:

1. As the energy/matter, like unmolded clay is undifferentiated (i.e., not restricted to a particular form) it can assume any shape. It's power of attainment is omnipotent. If the energy/matter making up our being is rooted in this energy/matter, we also partake of its omnipotence,- of course, in kind, but not magnitude.

2. As the consciousness/will of Subjective Being is not conditioned by any limitations of energy/matter, as there are no forms there to do so, its potential to will is unlimited. It is therefore omniscient. As our consciousness/will is rooted in the consciousness/will of Subjective Being we also partake in its quality.

3. As there are no limitations of time and space in the Subjective Realm, Being is therefore eternal, and infinite. I.e., omnipresent. We also partake in this quality.

This may seem to fly in the face of experience. But objections are soon dealt with by noting the fact that there are many people with spiritual abilities that are out of the ordinary. And this is one of the chief roles of a cosmogony. It enables you to know what is ahead in the field of human growth. Like a map it guides you to where you haven't been. It keeps you from defining (delimiting, crystallizing) yourself around the present level of mankind's evolutionary attainment, or your growth to date. The defining of Man in terms of the common faculties that mankind has thus far evolved is the chief impediment to further growth.

THE OBJECTIVE REALM

It is not enough to know that the world (Objective reality) is a modification of Subjective Being (Unconditioned consciousness, and undifferentiated energy/matter). We cannot understand our Being, the purpose of Life, and how we should live, unless we have a clear understanding of how and why the Subjective Being creates the world (Objective reality).

Let's begin by recalling the notion that energy/matter in the Subjective Realm is not differentiated into forms (the world).

And that if there are no things to be perceived, then consciousness can only be conscious of being conscious. This state of consciousness can be achieved, and has been achieved by humans, and is called in the Kamitian meditation system, the "Deity" "Tem," or "Temu" (negative being), and in the Indus Valley system, Asamprajnata Sarvikalpa Nirvana (Pure consciousness without objects of consciousness). An indepth look at the subject will show that in the Subjective Realm there can only be one Being. *For there to be others, there must be differentiations of the energy/matter into bodies which serve as the means of separating each being from the other.* Infinite and eternal (unwalled by a body) this Being is all alone. It is one without a second. As a thought is a differentiation of the energy matter, it isn't even thinking. It has not even the thought "I am conscious." No-things. No needs, no identity. In the Kamitian tradition, Being, on this level, is called the Deity "Amen." Meditate on your being conscious and you will get a glimpse of the fact that what in you is conscious, is itself imperceptible, and "concealed." The Subjective Realm, therefore, is the hidden plane of reality where Being dwells. All manifestations are the differentiations of the energy/matter of this level,- the objectification of the substantive basis of all forms.

The reason, therefore, for the creation of the world,- the differentiation of the original energy/matter into things- is to give Being experience. The Subjective Realm is Life, the Objective is Living. Being vs. Doing. The slightest thought, the faintest feeling is already an objectification of energy/matter,- a world in itself.

All alone, without thoughts, without experience,- no me, and you and it . . . Subjective Being creates,- differentiates its energy/matter into-- the world that it may have experience. I like to use the following metaphor although it is crude, and somewhat inaccurate. Imagine yourself all alone suspended somewhere (nowhere?) in a dark bottomless, and surfaceless expanse of water. Bored to death aren't you? One day you realize that your body is composed of billions of cells. So you transfer your consciousness into several millions of your cells, and suddenly you are no longer alone, and the adventure begins. And suppose you forgot that you are not really the cells. And the drama begins, and goes on until you have been knocked around pretty good by some bacteria, and viruses. And the spiritualization begins.

Yes. All alone without thoughts, feelings, or a second with whom to interact, Subjective Being differentiates a portion of its infinite energy/matter into an enclosed circle. Within it, it differentiates its energy/matter (Nu/Ra, Soph/Aur) into billions of galaxies, with their trillions of stars, and how many Earths? In many of the latter it fills with people, and transfers it's consciousness into them and . . . the adventure begins. Temporarily, perhaps for a short period of billions of years, the embodied (incarnated) consciousness forgets that it is not really these things within which it dwells on these Earths. Then it tires of the knocks, and the journey back begins. Not until, of course, every single ray of incarnated consciousness has been liberated from its Earthly tomb. Men who have found the way back, and stopped at "the edge," in the Kamitian tradition are called Ausar, in the Indus Valley tradition Boddhisattvas, -they are the only ones who truly deserve the title, Sage.

The mapping of the way down and back is the function of a cosmogony.

The transition from absolute undifferentiation in the Subjective Realm to earthly existence does not proceed in one step. It is a graduated progression designed to maintain a connection- at each and every step- between the qualities of Subjective Being, and the purpose of creating the world. That is to say, that each step[1] toward the manifestation of earthly existence is qualified to maintain an equilibrium between Being, and Doing, Life and Living, the No-thingness of Subjective Being, and the infinite numbers of things of the earthly plane, the infiniteness and eternalness of the Subjective Realm, and the finiteness in time and space of the Objective Realm.

THE COSMOGENESIS OF THE OBJECTIVE REALM

The dual nature of the Subjective Realm (Consciousness/Will and Energy/matter) is the main organizing principle of the Objective Realm, which is divided into two main planes; the Noumenal, and the Phenomenal.

The Noumenal Plane

In this plane is found all metaphysical Objective reality. The spirits of things, thoughts, images, and those metaphysical beings called angels, spirits, etc.

---

1. Each of these steps is carried out by a Deity.

The Phenomenal Plane

This is the well known plane of physical energy/matter. From gluons to galaxies.

Each of these planes are in turn subdivided.

The Divisions of the Noumenal Plane

1. ATZILUTH: When the undifferentiated energy/matter of the Subjective Realm is acted upon by the divine will, its first manifestation is an objectification of a portion of its substance which maintains its undifferentiated quality. This state of Objective energy/matter is called Atziluth in the Canaanite Kabalistical tradition. In the Kamitic tradition, this plane is under the dominion of the Goddess Nut. Incidentally, Nut is not the "sky Goddess, or Heaven" as held by Egyptologists. "Sky and Heaven" are used as metaphors to convey the fact that what is referred to is not differentiated in space or time. Where does the sky begin? Where does it end? The sky is the emblem of the infinite, the boundless, the eternal. This holds true for all the so called "sky Gods." The fact is that the realities here described, Nu and Nut, can only be contacted by going into the "recesses of the mind." Close your eyes now. Didn't you find yourself looking into what resembles the night sky? Dark and endless. Think about going deeper into it! We will be talking a great deal more about this in the chapters on meditation.

As energy/matter on this plane (Atziluth) is undifferentiated, that is, there is only one "building element" it can give rise to only one entity. This entity is the one vehicle within which dwells all things in the world. It is the World Soul, the "Ba" of the Kamitians, the Yechidah of the Canaanites, the Honhom of the Akan, the first aspect of the Utiwetongo of the Bantu, and the Anandamaya Kosha of Hinduism.

The deity that resides in this division of the spirit is the first manifestation of the Supreme Being. Ausar of the Kamitians, Obatala of the Yorubas, Nyakonpon of the Akan, Tara, and Shiva of Indus Kush etc. The sphere of the Tree of Life is Kether. It is important to realize the connections between the functions of Unification represented by these deities, and the fact that their environment is composed of a single building "element" and that there is only one body, one Being at this level. We will later see that it is to this plane, and in this body that people's consciousness "ascends" to when experiencing those highest manifestations of trance called samadhi in Hinduism. Because there is only one Being on this plane, it is here that the unity between all things is inherently experienced,- I.e., one experiences that all things and events in the world are one, as one experiences that all of our bodily members are parts of our body.

2. BRIAH is the Canaanite name given to the second level of energy/matter densification. Here there are two "building elements" which allow for the creation of two bodies. The universal Spirit, Ba, in the level above, dualizes itself to give rise to two universal spirits within itself. One is the organ system through which it wills manifestations to be. This part of the spirit is called the Khu by the Kamitians, and Chiah by the Canaanites. Herein dwells Chokmah, the second sphere of the Tree, and the Wisdom Deities, Tehuti of the Kamitians, Ifa of the Yoruba, Odomankoma of the Akan, Chinnamasta of Indus Kush, etc.

The other spiritual vehicle is the organ system wherein resides the "seeds" of the individual forces that are responsible for the actualization of the types of things that are willed to be manifested by the second sphere. This part of the spirit is called the Shekem by the Kamitians, and Shekinah by the Canaanites. Herein resides Binah, the third sphere of the Tree of Life, and the Deities Seker(t) of the Kamitians, Kali of Indus Kush, Babalu Aye of the Yorubas, Kalunga of the Bantus, etc.

These two, the second and third divisions of the Spirit (in the World, as in Man), the Will, and the Power part of the spirit interact with each other in the manner of "creative organs" to bring into manifestation, and to affect all things, and events in/as the world. Together with the first division of the spirit, the Ba, they form the great Divine Trinity, which in the Kabalistical tradition of Canaan is called the Neshamah.

The Great Divine Trinity:

1   **The Ba (Yechidah):** The World Soul in which all things dwell as integral parts of the One Divine Being.
2   **The Khu (Chiah):** The Universal Divine Will which initiates the manifestation of each thing, and event. It appoints to each thing its place in time and space.

3   **The Shekhem (Shekinah):** The Universal Power which carries to physical manifestation the dictates of the Universal Divine Will through its 50 units of power,- the Beni Alohim, or the 50 Gates of Binah, as they are called in the Canaanite Kabalistical tradition; and the 50 Oarsmen of the boat of Ausar in the Sirius star, as they are called in the Kamitian system; or the 50 Garlands, or skulls of the necklace of Kali as they are called in Indus Kush; or the 50 matrikas (wombs, little mothers) of the body of the Great Mother Kundalini, or Kundala.

3. THE UPPER YETZIRAH is the third level in the graduated densification of energy/matter toward physical manifestation. Each of the two "building elements" of the preceding stratum, Briah, divide themselves to create four "building elements," which enable the manifestations of *four great spiritual bodies*. Although they are all referred by one common name, they are the *spirits of the four great kingdoms on earth*,- the Mineral, Vegetal, Animal, and Human. Each of these spiritual vehicles serves as the unifying body for all of its members. When a person is able to bring his/her consciousness to this level, the experience of oneness with all other humans is achieved, for the fact that we are all integral parts of the Whole represented by the spirit of the Human Kingdom in the plane of Yetzirah. The division of the spirit at this level is called the Ab by the Kamitians, Upper Ruach by the Canaanites, Okra or Nkra by the Akans, Utiwemuntu by the Bantu, etc. In addition, this part of the spirit links the "thinking principles" in Man with the "four-fold" organizing principles in the world, serving thus as an intuitive means of discovering the four-fold organizations in nature.

Herein reside the fourth, fifth, and sixth spheres of the Tree with their respective Deities. Because of their presence, this part of the spirit provides order in the manifestation of events in the world.

4. THE LOWER YETZIRAH is the Canaanite name for the fourth stratum of energy/matter differentiation of the Objective plane. Herein dwells the 7th sphere of the Tree, in relation to which the four building "elements" of the preceding plane are divided into eight building elements, and spiritual vehicles which serve as the "Families" classification set of species. These, in relation to the species creating sphere,- Hod, are further divided into 16, 32, 64,

57

and 256 sets of spiritual vehicles[2]. These latter "elements" contain the programs, or patterns, upon which are based the species of things or events in the world. Also found here is the ninth sphere in relation to which is generated the vehicle that defines each thing, or event as an individuated spiritual existence. This individuated spirit is called a "Ka" in the Kamitian tradition. The division of the spirit that contains all of these spheres (7th, 8th, and 9th) with their respective Deities is called the Sahu by the Kamitians, the Lower Ruach by the Canaanites, the Amandhla by the Bantu, and the Iye by the Yoruba.

The Phenomenal Plane

5. ASHIAH is the name given to the fifth and lower stratum of the organization of the Objective plane. At its densest point, it involves the physical molecules, and on the subtlest, it is made up of energies and substances that have to be classed as physical, yet are subtler than anything thus found by western scientists. This subtle aspect of Ashiah is called in the occult tradition of Europe the Astral Light. In the Astral division of Ashiah dwells the sixth division of the spirit which was called the Khaibit by the Kamitians, the Nephesh by the Canaanites, the Ojiji by the Yorubas, the Sumsum by the Akans, the Pranayama Kosha, or Linga Sarira by the Hindus, the Isitunsi by the Bantu, and the Astral body, or etheric double of European occultism. This part of the spirit is the "life vehicle" of the physical body. It is that which makes a person "live" on Earth. It is the seat of all physical forces, sensations, desires, emotions, and motivations of the person. I.e., all psychical and physical movement. It is that which breathes and lives on oxygen within the physical existences. Without this part of the spirit, physical bodies are nothing but lifeless shells. The Astral division of the spirit is under the jurisdiction of the Deities Ra, and Geb of the Kamitian tradition, and the Kundalini force of Indus Kush.

In the lower half of Ashiah, where we find the atomic, and molecular organization of physical matter. The part of the spirit dwelling on this plane is the well known physical body, which is called the Khab by the Kamitians, and Guph by the Canaanites. It must be noted that in traditional African metaphysics there is no distinction made between the physical, and Man's higher bodies.

---

2. These organizing factors are the basis of the units composing oracles.

I.e., the physical body is considered an integral part of the spirit,- its densest component.

The failure to realize that Man has seven, and not one body, and that all things have a spirit, is one of the major causes of people's stagnation, and errors - both in thought and action. An integral summary of the above will further elucidate the purpose of each division of the spirit, and their relation to each other and the whole.

1st division of the spirit: The *seat of Consciousness and Identity*. The true ego of Being.

2nd and 3rd divisions: The *creative organs of Being*. The Will, and the Spiritual realization power, respectively. Note that while the Will is the faculty of potential action, the Spiritual Power is the vehicle for the actualization of the actions.

4th division: The *administrative organs of Being*. Once the manifestations are set in motion by the three preceding faculties, the fourth division of the spirit programs them with the "laws" that will enable them to achieve their respective goals without violating each other's sphere of interest, as all manifestations occur for the sake of the One Being of which they are parts, and not for, and of themselves.

5th division: The *specializing organs of Being*. It is here that manifestations acquire the spiritual qualities that will distinguish them into families, and separate existences.

6th division: The *motive power of Being*. It is here that each manifested thing receives its breath of life (if "living"), or electromagnetic motive force (if "non-living") to enable it to act upon the physical plane.

7th division: It is here that each manifestation is finally segregated into an *individual existence*. This is achieved by receiving a physical body which separates each thing in time and space.

THE STEP BY STEP MANIFESTATION OF SUBJECTIVE BEING

The First Manifestation

The very first differentiation of energy/matter which in the Subjective Realm subsists as a homogeneous and undifferentiated vibration-'ng(K)'-is carried out by Neter's projection of the sound 'Au' into it.   It   creates the first manifestation, in which

59

consciousness looks back into the Subjective Realm and becomes aware of its original and true essential qualities; that it is eternal and infinite, i.e., temporally and spatially unlimited. In popular literature, this quality of Subjective Being is called "Omnipresence." It must be noted that the "Om" in the word is derived from the heka (mantra, word of power) "Aung" that was formed when Subjective Being projected the sound "Au" into the midst of the undifferentiated energy/matter vibrating as the homogeneous sound "ng(k)." This sound incidentally, is hieroglyphically represented by the so called Aunk cross. This sound, in the Indus Valley tradition is called "Nada," which is kin to the Spanish term "nada" which holds the same meaning,- "nothing." I write it "ng(k)" to signal that it could be rendered either as "ng," or "nk" because "k," and "g" are variant sounds of the same diction principle. Where "k" is used in one language, "g" takes it place in cognate terms. E.g., the English "know," the Greek "Gnosis," and the Sanskrit "Gnana" (variant of Jnana, Ajna).

The Second Manifestation

Neter projects the sound "Hu" into the undifferentiated "ng(K)" and gives rise to the second manifestation. It too looks back to the Subjective Realm, and becomes aware of another of its essential qualities. Here Subjective Being, dwelling in the Objective Realm becomes aware of the fact that as its energy/matter is essentially unconditioned, and undifferentiated it (Being) can will it to assume any conceivable form. This aspect of the knowledge of Self is the basis of Omniscience (infinite knowledge,- Omni, infinite, science, to know).

The Third Manifestation

Neter projects the sound "Kri" into the undifferentiated "ng(k)" and gives rise to the third manifestation. It too looks back into the Subjective Realm and becomes aware of another of its essential qualities. It becomes aware that as its energy/matter is essentially unconditioned and undifferentiated, it (the energy/matter) can realize anything that is willed for it to become. Thus Subjective Being realizes that it is unlimited power of creativity. I.e., it is Omnipotent .

60

Thus the first three objectifications of Subjective Being is the awareness of its true nature. These three objectifications of the essential attributes of Subjective Being forms the first three spheres of a cosmogonical diagram known as the Tree of Life.

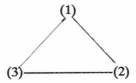

Subjective Being acts through the second and third manifestations,- the infinite Will, and the Unlimited creative power to give rise to the next set of three manifestations. We must note that up to this point, all that has been brought forth is the knowledge of Self, and the creative vehicles of Neter.

The fourth Manifestation

Neter projects the sound 'Shri' into the Nada ("ng(k") to give rise to the fourth manifestation. For the first time, Neter turns its attention to the things that are to be made. In respect to the making of things, its first act is to look, again into the Subjective Realm, the source of its Being, from which it realizes that all things will be modifications of the One Being, -the one consciousness, and the one energy/matter rooted in the Subjective Realm. This first thought about things, will therefore be the ruling principle of their existence. This fact is later elaborated into the principles of Law, Order, and Love (Maat),- the guarantors of Oneness in the lower world.

The Fifth Manifestation

Neter projects the sound 'Hlri' into the Nada to give rise to the fifth manifestation. Thoughts are once more about things. This time, for the first time, Neter looks outward to the world to come, and focuses on the requirements for experience. Where there is Oneness, there is aloneness, and no experience. No living. Thus, in order to live, the one Being must be "broken" into myriads of beings. The underlying substance of all forms, which sounded to the homogeneous "Ng," of "Nk," must scintillate in all colors of the sound spectrum. So, Neter becomes aware of the fact that the existence of the world depends on their being differences and opposition. It here guarantees them.

The Sixth Manifestation

Neter projects the sound 'Hri' into the Nada to give rise to the sixth manifestation. Neter looks, first back into the Subjective Realm, and next, outward, and becomes aware that a balance must exist between, the principle of oneness of the fourth manifestation, and that of opposition of the fifth. It realizes that to live safely and effectively it must be in the world, but not of it. Or, Be of the Subjective, but not in it. This is the foundation of the Law of Equilibrium.

What has now been brought forth are the Laws that will govern the earthly manifestations of Neter. Three more spheres have now been added to the Tree of Life.

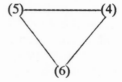

Acting through its creative vehicles, the second and third spheres, according to the laws carried out through the fourth to sixth manifestations, Neter creates the next set of three manifestations.

The Seventh Manifestation

Neter projects the sound 'Kli' into the infinite ocean of undifferentiated energy/matter to give rise to the seventh manifestation. Looking backward at the Subjective Realm, through the fourth, and previous manifestations it realizes that beyond the external differences between things there must be an emphasis of their interdependence, and relation,- i.e., a recognition of their oneness in the midst of their differences. This fact is later elaborated into the grouping of things by families. It gives rise to metaphor and harmony.

62

The Eighth Manifestation

Neter projects the sound 'Ai' into the infinite no-thingness to give rise to the eighth manifestation. Like the fifth, it looks forward into the world emphasizing the differences between things by focusing on their external differences. The groupings of the preceding sphere are broken into pieces. Here are created the species of things.

The Ninth Manifestation

Neter projects the sound 'Va' into the infinite (surfaceless, bottomless) Waters of Life,- "Ng(k)," Nada, undifferentiated energy/matter to give rise to the ninth manifestation. Acting on 'Ngk', "Va" creates a mirror-like watery manifestation that captures (reflects) all that is exposed to it. It thus integrates all of the preceding manifestations that they may each play their respective role in the generation of individual physical existences. The ninth manifestation is known as the "Mother of all Living things." It gathers the physical elements and forces, and coordinates the forces of the other eight manifestations to give rise to physical things. Although the physical plane is considered the tenth manifestation, the Kamitian Tree of Life, correctly, limits the spheres to nine, as the 10th sphere is an effect, while the preceding nine are parts of the causative mechanism. The Tree of Life, in the Kamitian tradition is considered under various headings. One of them is the Paut Neteru.

Thus does the Subjective Being proceed from No-thingness to physical thingness. Nine emanations integrate its sphere of Being, "0," with its sphere of Living, "10."

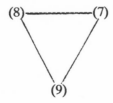

THE PAUT NETERU (TREE OF LIFE)

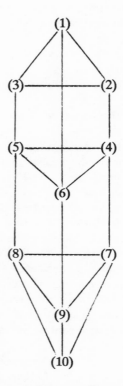

The greatest error that can be made at this point is to interpret the above diagram as an arbitrarily created conceptual, or theoretical explanation of the ordering system underlying physical reality. It represents the nine emanations that are the shaping factors of all physical structures, and events. They underlie, direct, and integrate all physical realities,- from the subtlest sub-electronic forces, to the complex of galaxies, to the organ systems making up the physical body of Man . . . from the most primitive instinct of a slime mold to the most divine manifestation in the spirit of Man. They are what the Kamitians called the Neteru; Yorubas call, the Orishas, and Westerners have translated as deities, Archangels, angels, etc.

It is very important to understand, that contrary to popular opinion, cosmology does not attempt to explain how physical things, on the atomic and molecular levels, come into being. It concentrates on the coming into being of the metaphysical factors that will function as the vehicles through which the physical things will come into existence, as well as the means of regulating their structural and functional components, hence external behavior. In other words, a cosmogony deals with the "generation" (from "gonus") of a "system." Properly understood, the terms "System" and "Cosmos" are synonymous; an assemblage, or combination of things, or parts working in unity, as a whole, cooperating to carry out the same function, to achieve the same goal, etc.

It was said that the emanations, one to nine, are the parts of a "system" through which Subjective Being,- represented by zero (the absence of things, but not of Being) creates, and administrates physical reality, "10." These nine "DEITIES" - The PAUT NETERU- compose the "organs systems" making up the spiritual bodies of all physical things. They link them with their source of being and subsistence, and direct their functions. African religion, better comprehended as a Way of Life, is based on the understanding of the functioning of these nine metaphysical vessels of creation, and administration. As they are shaping and governing functions, their activities carry the force of law. For example, you wouldn't attempt to feed on hay because the functions that govern your digestive mechanism can't digest it. It is in this manner that the attributes of the Deities (Neteru, Orishas, etc.) represent the laws governing our lives on Earth. Observance of these laws, allows them to fully bring forth their powers through our being. According to our chronological, age, state of health, and level of spiritual development, the manifestation of these "powers" will range from our basest urges, to the commonly evolved "mental abilities," to the psychical abilities held by a few, to the attainment of divine perfection, i.e., Man-Godhood on Earth.

Now we can fully take up the question of Monotheism versus Polytheism. for the longest time Westerners have held 1) that **Monotheism** -the belief that there is only one God- is superior to **Polytheism** -the belief in more than one God. 2) that Monotheism first appeared in the world with the Hebrews, and that 3) Monotheism represents a higher evolutionary understanding of divine reality than Polytheism. The latter was explicitly, or implicitly cited as evidence for the supposed low level of evolutionary attainment of Blacks. If you read between the lines, you will see that all that in historical, anthropological, and other literature is referred to as "modern, progressive, evolved, etc.," correspond to Western cultural expressions. And what is referred to as "primitive, unevolved, etc.," correspond to Nonwestern cultural expressions.

First of all, the above shows clearly that the religion of Blacks cannot be classified as polytheistic, nor as monotheistic, as these terms are commonly understood. From the earliest appearance of Western man on the historical scene (2500 B.C.), until the end of the nineteenth century A.D., his thinking and perception of reality for the most part can be described as "linear." That is to say that all manifestations are the result of "single things acting upon single things." As western science took a turn for the better toward the end of the nineteenth century A.D., it began to become more and more apparent that all manifestations in the world were the expression of multiple things coordinating their functions. This "new" insight received the names of Gestalt theory, Field theory, Systems theory, and dethroned the belief, and expectation of finding any thing that was not composed of a multiplicity of co-acting components. It ushered in the host of "fantastic" scientific technologies that make up today's world,- computers, rockets, bioengineering, etc. A study of all of these "new" Systems theories will show that they are all pale versions of the "Systems theories" (Cosmogonies) developed by Nonwesterners in antiquity, and contemporary Africa.

The question is begging. Why did it take Westerners so long -at least 6000 years behind Blacks- to arrive at this realization? In previous chapters we detailed the facts concerning Western man's polarization in the left hemisphere of the brain. Now this part of the brain is only capable of linking sequentially following units. I.e., it is incapable of "Systems thinking." That is a task that belongs to the right side of the brain with its unlimited integrative capability. Western people would look, for example, at seven integrated sets of one to one relationships and see seven separate sets of one to one relationships. On the other hand, Blacks, and Orientals will see one set of seven integrated subsets of one to one relationships. Polarized in the segregative part of the brain, Westerners could not integrate the host of deities of the Black pantheon. They just couldn't see how the many were integral parts of the One. This stuff about co-acting multiple factors shaping and determining each and every physical entity was way beyond them.

So they described our religious practice as "polytheistic." We must reject it for obvious reasons. And since the term Monotheism fails to convey the reality that the One God functions (lives) through a plurality of integral parts, it too must be rejected. In this book, I will use my coinages, "Systheism," and "Syntheism." Both "syn," and "sys" are variants of the same prefix carrying the basic meaning of a "whole compounded of several parts." Sys is the root of System, and syn, that of Synthesis,- both analogous terms.

It was said that the nine emanations direct the behavior of physical things. In the case of humans, this depends on our living in harmony with the laws governing the functioning of the deities. This is due to man's freedom of will to determine the quality of his destiny. Other creatures, not possessing this faculty of free will are obligated to follow. In future chapters we will see how Nonwesterners, in following the laws of these emanations operating within their being, achieve personal and social harmony by living a unitary, or systematic life, while Westerners, in spite of the claim that they believe in one God, live polytheistically, that is, a way of life in which the various personal and social interests are not integrated. *Universal in lip-service, pluriversal in living.*

It must be understood that the greatest evil in life, as understood by Blacks, was the lack of integration in thinking; lack of integration between beliefs, feelings, and actions; between the various social interests, etc. Integration in these areas was achieved through their cosmogony and its application to daily living, and spiritual practices. Our religion had to be integrable with science, government, economics, medicine, education, and every human institution. It had to integrate all areas of our lives. This idea of Unitarianism, extremely important and highly elevated in our culture, was reinterpreted by Westerners (Europeans, and Semites) when they adopted our culture, according to their "thingish" way of thinking. By thingish thinking is meant the reduction of abstract realities to sense perceptions. While "one" denotes "singularity" (one apple, one book, etc.), "Unity" denotes the *abstract tie* between a plurality of things. Thus the belief in, and living as the "Unitarian" God was reduced to the belief in the one God, and the disintegrative way of living. Once more we must see that this "thingish," or materialistic way of thinking belongs to the left side of the brain. Relational thinking, which is needed to understand the Black understanding of God and religion, is the property of the right side of the brain.

Once the true nature, purpose, and functions of a cosmogony is fully understood it will be realized that it is to religion and all life "sciences," what mathematics is to science, and the periodical table of elements is to chemistry,- and more. The great strides in progress made by Western scientists with the appearance of their "Systems theories," which made their prior progress look seemingly slow by comparison, must be equated with the great strides in progress made by Blacks when they were founding civilization, while Westerners at the time were still in the paleolithic situation.

Chapter 6

AN ANALYSIS OF THE COSMOGONICAL SYSTEM

THE FIRST ACT OF MANIFESTATION

THE SUPREME BEING BRINGS ITSELF OUT OF THE SUBJECTIVE STATE

Before creation can begin, the Supreme Being must first make objective its qualities of Being ("Sphere" 0). Note that in the Subjective state there cannot even be so much as a single thought. The very first manifestation of a thought is already a process of objectification. The only consciousness that there is, is that of "consciousness being aware that it is conscious." Creation, then is preceded by a process whereby the Supreme Being brings itself into manifestation.

The first act of manifestation, which corresponds to the first sphere of the Tree of Life, Kether, is the Supreme Being's identification with the unlimited potential, and unlimited presence in space (infiniteness), and time (eternalness) of the Subjective Realm. I.e., The Supreme Being brings forth the awareness that its identity is the capability of being whatever it chooses to be, and that it is immortal, and eternal.

THE SECOND ACT OF MANIFESTATION

THE SUPREME BEING BRINGS FORTH ITS CREATIVE FACULTIES

The second act of manifestation is the Supreme Being's bringing forth of its creative faculties. These are the Will, and its Spiritual Power.

The Divine Will, the second sphere of the Tree of Life, is the faculty that indicates what will take place, and is thus the initiator of creative events. At this level, there is the awareness that as the energy/matter from which all things are made is an eternal and

69

infinite continuum, no part of it can have a separate existence in time or space. Therefore, all things are parts of the whole and are related to, and interdependent upon each other. From another perspective, this states that no thing has a quality in itself. That qualities are the result of a thing's relationship to the whole, and to other things. As we shall see later in this book, that the intuitive and automatic operation of this principle in Man's thinking is the foundation of wisdom. The creative faculty of the Supreme Being at the second sphere is therefore the Divine Wisdom. It is omniscient. It is also realized that the will is infinite in its potential to initiate activities, as the energy/matter which will carry them out is essentially unlimited.

The Spiritual Power, the third Sphere, like the second sphere, looks back to the Subjective Realm, and the essential state of Being and realizes that as the energy/matter that is the basis of all creations is essentially unlimited, there are no limitations to its ability to carry out what is willed by the second sphere. It is the Divine Omnipotence. Note that the Will is the potential, while the spiritual power is the actualizer or producer of the effect in the world.

THE SIX ACTS OF CREATION

Now that the Supreme Being has brought itself and its creative faculties out of the Subjective Realm, the process of creation can begin. But before the physical creatures can be created, there is a need for the creation of a metaphysical system of government or directors, and metaphysical entities that will carry out the work of administering the physical world.

THE CREATION OF THE CELESTIAL GOVERNMENT

THE FIRST ACT OF CREATION

The first act of creation, which corresponds to the 4th sphere of the Tree of Life, is the framing of the laws reflecting the workings of the forces of the third sphere. These forces are deployed through a structure that allocates to all things its place in time, and space for the purpose of maintaining order in the world. The Tree of Life, the canons of Divine Laws, the Cosmogonies,

Mandalas etc. are all representations of this grand structure. It corresponds to the fourth sphere of the Tree.

It is important to realize that "order" is not merely "a fixed plan," or "a regular series," or "a law of arrangement," etc. Where there is no more than one entity there can be no order. And where a number of things are not related or interdependent, there is, implicitly no order, or the possibility thereof. *"Order" is essentially dependent on the existence of the interdependence (oneness) between things.* It is the means of safeguarding their mutual dependence. The full import of this will be realized when full consideration is given to the fact that the goal of creation is the division of a whole (the one energy/matter) into an infinitude of parts (things).

THE SECOND ACT OF CREATION

Next is created the means of enforcing Order (the 5th sphere). No thing can encroach upon another. Yet, although things are protected, the chief interest is the preservation of the whole.

THE THIRD ACT OF CREATION

Next is created the faculty through which the metaphysical workers will be coordinated in their activities to bring forth and administrate the physical creatures. This is the work of the 6th sphere. The work of coordination is based upon the Canon of the 4th sphere. Its application to specific situations is communicated to the 6th sphere by the second sphere.

THE CREATION OF THE CELESTIAL WORKERS

Now that the means of establishing and maintaining order are in place the Supreme Being proceeds to create the faculties/Deities that are directly in charge of the work of creating the physical entities.

THE FOURTH ACT OF CREATION

Next is created the faculty through which the designs of the various species of beings will take place. What is actually achieved at this point, the 7th sphere, is an image of the type of thing that is to be created. E.g., the species tiger. The emphasis of our

71

understanding must be placed on the "ordering" function of images. When we imagine something, although we may not realize it, we are organizing the shaping forces of things, or events to a defined objective. The imaginative faculty takes the set of forces governing a particular set of events or things and organizes it into a concrete objective (image). It is the great "celestial designer", inventor, artist, Goddess of beauty, harmony, etc.

THE FIFTH ACT OF CREATION

In the preceding stage, we arrived at the design of the species of things. But as we know, species are broken down into individual existences. This faculty, the 8th sphere, has the task of making the distinctions that will distinguish each member of a species from another, by creating variations amongst the parts of things, and events.

THE SIXTH ACT OF CREATION

The next faculty created, the 9th sphere, uses all of the preceding shaping factors to make a vehicle that will serve to coordinate physical energy matter into the physical thing or event. This vehicle is the soul of the individual thing or event. In the Kamitic tradition it is called the "Ka," and in the Hindu tradition, the "Jivan Atma." Because this faculty is directly in charge of the organization of physical energy/matter into the creature, it is referred to as "the Mother Goddess creator of all the living, and of the Earth" (Auset, Yemaya, Nana Esse etc.).

The preceding exposition of the creative process is one of the best examples of the claim by kabalists that the mythologies and religious scriptures of nations cannot be fully understood without the knowledge of Kabala. The above six acts, or stages of creation correspond to the original and true understanding that was misrepresented by the biblical version, as the *"six days of creation."* We must also note that in mythological symbolism, the will (2nd sphere) is personified as a male, and the spiritual power (3rd sphere), as a female. This is to be understood by the fact that we are free to express our will to do something at anytime in the same manner that a male is always ready to impregnate a female. Our spiritual power, however, is only receptive to being impregnated at fixed recurring points in a cycle. E.g., women can only be impregnated at the midpoint between menstruations. Thus we can paraphrase the second act of manifestation-the Supreme Being's bringing forth of its creative faculties- as the Supreme Being's bringing forth of its 'generative organs'. And because Man is made in the creative likeness of God, (Genesis I:26), i.e., with the same creative faculties, Genesis I:27 informs us that "God created man in his own image, in the image of God he created him; *male and female* he created them" (emphasis mine). There are many factors that prove that the "male and female" correspond to the Divine Will (2nd sphere), and the Divine spiritual power (sphere 3).

In the original Hebraic version of the bible, the word translated as God is "ALHM" ("Elohim"). This word is composed of "El," the Canaanite name for God, and "Him," a suffix indicating plurality. This is why the God speaking at Genesis I:26 says "let *us* make Man in *our* image, in *our* likeness." The author of this text has simply personified the two creative faculties of God.

AN ANALYSIS OF THE PROCESS OF CREATION

The Creative Activity of the fourth sphere

According to the Tree of Life cosmogonical system, the act of creation is carried out by the first sphere, using its two creative faculties (spheres 2 and 3). The first act of creation, which occurs at the fourth sphere, is the framing of the law embodying the activities of the set of metaphysical forces of the third sphere, which act as the structural framework upon which is built the physical world and each thing in the world. It would be appropriate, according to the demands of the order for presenting the details of cosmology, to embark at this point upon an explanation of the blueprint of the entire physical realm. Such a task requires certain supportive information that cannot be given at this time in the discourse. I will therefore explain the blueprint of creation through one of its minor applications. Let's consider the creation of the animal kingdom.

Animals, like all other members of the world-spirits, deities, humans, vegetables, and minerals- are modifications of the universal energy/matter and pure consciousness of the Subjective Realm. This oneness of origin, we said earlier, is the basis of order. According to the cosmogonical forces operating in the third sphere, and framed into law at the fourth sphere, all animals are parts of a circle of manifestation that encompasses all modes of forces making up living beings. When the universal Subjective energy/matter

73

differentiates itself to bring forth living things, it dualizes itself into two modes of energy. For the sake of simplicity I will for now simplify the explanation by skipping certain steps and details, and state that one of the forces is the source of the thermal (heat) factor (Shu) that determines the level of biochemical activities. The other force is the source of the hydration (water) factor (Tefnut) which represents the universal medium in which all living things dwell[1]. The upper and lower boundaries of the thermal factor for specific living forms are relatively denoted as "hot," and "cold." The upper and lower boundaries of the hydration of bodies are denoted as "moist," and "dry." Meditation on the subject will show that all biological activities can be reduced and explained by these two modalities[2]. The interaction of these two factors produces the four modalities underlying all manifestations in the world. They have been symbolized as the four elements of Alchemy.

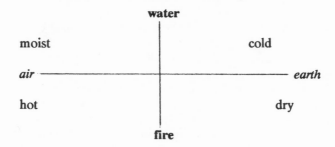

1. Water is cold and moist; Water accumulates in bodies as they cool down.
2. As bodies begin to heat up, and have not yet lost their humidity, they are metaphorized as "air" (hot & moist).
3. When the temperature rises to the upper range, and bodies lose their humidity, they are metaphorized as "fire" (hot & dry).
4. When they begin to cool down, but have not yet regained their moisture, they are metaphorized as "earth" (cold & dry).

All bodies go through these changes daily with the rise and fall of temperature that follows the sun. The same happens during the course of the year. Besides being applicable to the cyclical changes that life forms go through, these four "elements" are also used as classification sets for the four fundamental types of all

1. The life dwelling in each cell making up all living things actually lives in water.
2. This is the basis of Chinese medical theory.

manifestations. Thus there are four fundamental types or "temperaments (temperature types)" of animals, vegetables, minerals, and humans. Applied to the types of animals we get the following:

Ferocious

Predators: Fiery (hot/dry); tigers, lions, etc. Carnivores.
Non-predators: Airy (hot/moist); rhinoceros, elephants, etc. Vegetarians.

Non-ferocious

Passive: Watery (cold/moist); sheep, doves, etc. vegetarians.
Non-passive: Earthy (cold/dry); hyenas, jackals, buzzards. Scavengers, Omnivores.

To summarize, in the creation of animals, what is achieved at the fourth sphere is the creation of the four "temperaments" of the animal kingdom. As each of these symbols of temperaments (the elements) ties a vast number of types of beings together, across lines of genre and kingdoms, the activity of the 4th sphere is of a *synthetical* and *analogical* nature.

The Creative Activities of the Fifth Sphere

The next step in the creative process, which occurs in the fifth sphere, is the separation of the beings of each temperamental set. As they are held together through the *"analogs"* of the 4th sphere, their separation (lysis) is called *"analysis."* We will later have a full discussion on the incorrect views that are popularly held about this mental process, as well as its opposite- synthesis. Here at the 5th sphere, fiery animals are analyzed into the various genre of predators (feline - the general class for all types of cats; canine, etc.). The same is done for the other temperaments.

The Creative Activity of the Seventh Sphere

We must pay particular attention to the fact that the creative acts of the 4th and 5th spheres are on the abstract plane. Images cannot be formed of "fiery" or "earthy" animals, or plants, etc. Neither can they be formed of "felines" or "bovines." It is at the 7th sphere that we arrive at the images of the members of the general sets of creatures. In place of felines, for example, now we have tigers, angoras, leopards, etc.

The Creative Activity of the Eighth Sphere

In the 8th sphere, dogs, horses, tigers, etc. are distinguished into specific dogs, etc. Here we get the distinctions that set Lassie apart from the collie matrix created in the 7th sphere.

We can summarize the process of creation in a most far reaching manner which will greatly reward the reader's efforts to memorize and understand:

Sphere   Cosmogonical Correspondence

0	According to my unlimited potential of Being (unlimited resources)
1	*I, God*, (or Man, the likeness of God!)
2	*Will*
3	*Make* (with my spiritual power)
4	According to the divine blueprint (Laws)
5	which will be enforced
6	assisted by a centrally located coordinator
7	assisted by a designer (imagery)
8	assisted by a technician
9	*through my divine womb*
10	*a world, worldly events, etc.*

And

0	The infinite
1	Manifests its Self, and
2,3	its creative faculties, and
4,5,6	Makes a celestial government, to administrate
7,8,9	the celestial workers which will shape
10	the world.

And

0	No things, which implies
1	Unity
2,3	makes

76

10	an infinitude of things which are in unity
4	through a set of reciprocal, and interdependent factors.
5	Which relations are enforced
6	and maintained through coordination of
7,8,9	the celestial workers.

THE DUALITY PRINCIPLE IN COSMOGONY

Let's recall the fact that the entire expanse of reality can be divided into two all-comprehensive divisions: the Subjective and the Objective Realms. The Subjective Realm corresponds to the Supreme Being's essential or unmodified nature, while the Objective corresponds to its conditioned or modified nature. I.e., the infinite, eternal source of all things, versus the infinite, time conditioned plane wherein things dwell. Whatever was, is, and shall be must fall into one of these two, all-comprehensive categories. Thus, at the most fundamental level of classification, we find an indivisible duality of Being. By indivisible duality (usually contracted to "individuality"), it is obviously meant that the two modes of being are complementary halves.

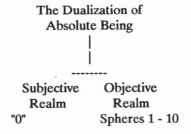

This duality manifests itself in all areas, and on all levels of being as a major organizing force. In order to understand God, ourselves, the world, and life, we must be able to identify, understand, and live in harmony with the dualizing shaping forces of Life.

In the Subjective Realm the duality manifests itself, on one hand, as Consciousness/Will (two polarities of the same reality), and on the other, as energy/matter. The former is referred to in the Kabalistical tradition as Ain, and Amen in the Kamitian. The latter is Soph, and Nu/Nut in the Kabalistical, and the Kamitian traditions respectively.

The Dualization of
Subjective Being

Consciousness	Matter
Will	Energy
Ain	Soph
Amen	Nu/Nut

The Dualization of Objective Being

In the Objective Realm we also have two fundamental divisions. The noumenal or metaphysical planes wherein dwell the Deities (spheres 1 - 9), on one hand, and on the other, the phenomenal or physical realm (sphere 10).

In order to make this information useful in our daily lives we must first note that both the Subjective and Objective Realms are *indivisible halves* of Absolute Being. We saw that without the Objective Realm, with all of its limitations, the Supreme Being cannot have experience. This enables us to reject such pseudo spiritual teachings that deny the validity of objective existence, with its phenomenal manifestations. They are there to give the Supreme Being experience.

What is important, missed by the pseudo sages, is the maintenance of the equilibrium between the dualities on their respective levels. The *Doctrine of Equilibrium*, we will see, is the major theme of cosmology, The Tree of Life, and of Living. These two fundamental divisions of our Being, the Subjective and Objective factors reside in our being as primordial driving forces. The failure to satisfy either of them, as the Subjective is denied in the West, and the Objective, by Hinduism (Aryanized yogic philosophy), leads to serious problems in life.

THE COMPLEMENTARY DUALITIES ON THE TREE OF LIFE

In order to use the Tree of Life as a means of ordering our thinking and our living, it is necessary to understand the complementary relations between certain sets of spheres.

The 0 - 10 Complementary Relation

0 and sphere 10 obviously represent the two extreme polarities of the expanse of reality. They stand in relation to each other as

SOURCE	GOAL
infinite potential	infinite beings
explicit oneness	implicit oneness
freedom	limitation
NU	Geb

The 1- 9 Complementary Relation

While sphere 1 looks back to the Subjective Realm and identifies with the infinite potential of being of the unstructured energy/matter, sphere 9, as the soul of the individual physical creations identifies with each physical being. We shall later see that this duality is the basis of individuation of human consciousness into Self and Person, or Higher and lower Selves, or Alter Ego and Ego, Selflessness and selfishness that has not escaped the attention of many spiritualists, and psychologists. In the Kamitic tradition, it is the well known complement of Ausar and Auset (Osiris and Isis).

The 2 - 8 Complementary Relation

While sphere 2 (the wisdom faculty) is concerned with the interdependence and relationships (unity) between things, and their place in time and space, sphere 8 (the linear logical faculty) is concerned with creating differentiations (disunity) between members of the same species, by varying their parts. The former is integrative while the latter is segregative. In addition, the thought processes of sphere 2 are purely abstract, while that of sphere 8 is concrete.

The 3 - 7 Complementary Relation

The subtle particles (atoms, electrons, etc.) making up all things are in a state of constant vibration, western science informs us. And all vibrations generate sound waves in one medium or another. We can paraphrase the foregoing by stating that sound waves underlie the structure of all things and events. This has been known by African spiritual scientists since prehistoric times, who have taught that the third sphere is the vehicle from where is generated the sound waves that underlie (create, maintain, and destroy) the structure of all things and events in the world. These sounds are the words of power (mantras, hekau, etc.) of spiritual cultures. Words of power have a special relationship with the faculty of imagination (the 7th sphere). As anyone who has successfully worked on mantras knows, chanting them results in the filling of the sphere of awareness with a certain set of images that are specific to each mantra. In other words, before these special sound waves can effect their desired objectives, they must be translated into the images that literally serve as matrices for the physical manifestations. This relationship between the 3rd and 7th spheres, has led dabblers into the esoteric to mistakenly believe that the imagination, unaided by words of power, can effect changes in the physical plane. "Nurture a clear image of what you want with faith, and in time you will have it," many books have told us. The half truth in this belief is the reason it works only some of the time. The truth regarding magic, success, and failure is a very simple one. *All events, talents, etc. in a person's life are created by the sound waves (mantras, hekau, words of power) that are in an active state.* Where these sound wave forms are in a latent state, then there will be the absence of the talents that they govern. The nurturing of an image without awakening its associated sound wave, is like trying to incubate an unfertilized egg. The subject is a rich one, and we will return to it many times in the course of this book.

The 4 - 6 Complementary Relation

We have seen that the fourth sphere corresponds to the blueprint upon which the world and all physical events are built. The sixth sphere corresponds to the faculty that governs the metaphysical beings (spheres 7, 8, and 9) that are in charge of creating physical reality, and maintaining order within it, according to the blueprint of the fourth sphere.

The 5th Sphere

The Tree of Life shows that the creative process of the world is based on a plan in which all the things in the world are modifications of one and the same material substance and Being. Although they are different in their needs, mode of existence, and appearance, they are all parts of *One Whole*. The equilibrium between this oneness at the top and difference on the bottom, must be maintained. This is the function of the fifth sphere. In order to carry out this mediating role, the 5th sphere must be unrelated to all others. It is thus posited at the exact center of the entire span of reality (0,1,2,3,4) 5 (6,7,8,9,10).

Chapter 7

THE COSMOLOGICAL VIEW OF MAN

OR

THE SPIRITUAL ANATOMY OF MAN

Everything stated thus far regarding cosmology is of no value, unless it can be translated into a means of giving Man an understanding of Self and serve as a guide to correct living. "Self Knowledge," it will be seen, is the beginning and end of all knowledge.

Who and what is man can only be understood by reference to the purpose of the creation of the world. Earlier we learned that the essential state of the Supreme Being is one in which Its energy/matter is not differentiated into things. Hence, God lacks experience in Its essential state. God modifies Its essence into the World as the means through which to have experience. *Although there is an infinitude of creatures making up the world, only one of them was created for the express purpose of serving as the vehicle through which God can transfer Its consciousness into, and realize the fullness of its Being. This creature is Man.* The knowledge of this spiritual fact has been expressed in many of the scriptures of the world. In the Kamitian (Ancient Egyptian) scripture, *The Book of Knowing the Manifestations of Ra* (about 2800 B.C.), we come across the following statements regarding Ausar, who is the symbol of the man, or woman who has completed his/her spiritual growth, enabling God to manifest Itself in the world through him, or her:

I produced myself from primeval matter. My name is Ausars, (from) the primeval matter of primeval matter. I have succeeded in all that I have willed on earth . . . I was alone, not born were they. Not had I spit, in the form of Shu, not had I emitted Tefnut. I brought through my mouth, my own name, that is to say a word of power, and I, even I, came into being in the forms of the infinite power of being (Khepera) . . .

The same awareness is expressed in *Genesis* I:26, which states that God makes Man in *their* own likeness. Or, as was earlier stated in this book;

The Supreme Being (and Man). 0
through Its creative organs. 1 - 9 (Paut Neteru, Deities)
creates physical realities. 10th sphere.

While the above makes a great deal of sense from a spiritual philosophical standpoint, it flies in the face of Man's common experience. If Man is made in the likeness of God, then why is this fact not evident in our daily experience? The answer is a simple one. Mankind as a whole has not completed its evolution (growth). In the same way that a three year old has the faculties of an adult in a latent state, so do the majority of people today, have their divine faculties in a dormant state. The various stages, and goal of our evolution (growth process) are shown by the Tree of Life.

We are born with spheres 10 (our physical body with its animating spirit) and 9 (the personality division of our spirit, and learning faculty) in an awakened state, and we develop from the bottom up. All of the other faculties, represented by spheres 8 to 1 are in a dormant state. In the same way that the development of our physical faculties is cued to our chronological age, so is the development of our spiritual faculties. The first 28 years of our life is spent awakening and developing the 8th and 7th spheres. These are our syllogistic logical and inventive/artistic faculties respectively. The 8th and 7th spheres, which as we saw in previous chapters, correspond to the "celestial workers," and are, therefore, the faculties that we utilize primarily in making a living (Sphere 8 = technologies, commerce, etc. Sphere 7 = scientific, and artistic invention). If the social order is enlightened, the following 21 years are devoted to the awakening of our moral and mental abstractive faculties. It will seem strange to most people to hear that the moral faculties in Man are not developed until after the 28th year of life. Yet, this is supported by conventional wisdom. What do you think will happen if the police and the armed forces in America or most nations were to be disbanded? The answer can be inferred from previous riot situations in which many otherwise "law abiding" persons have been seen, always to their dismay, in the act of stealing and vandalism. Unfortunately, most societies lack the knowledge of how to spiritually cultivate their citizens, so that the majority fails to develop the moral part of their spirit (spheres 6, 5, and 4). We will later see that there are a great number of behavioral expressions of an immoral nature that the majority of people in the world is incapable of recognizing as such. Take for instance, the act of smoking tobacco in public which forces others to inhale gases that are well known poisons. Before the discovery of DDT, tobacco was one of the major insecticides. While you would not be permitted to even slap strangers, you are permitted to poison them in socially acceptable ways. This is one of innumerable examples of the inability of the majority of people to think on an abstract level (spheres 4, 5, & 6). They only recognize as immoral those specific examples of immorality that have been pointed out to them. On their, own they cannot see that forcing others, children even, to inhale tobacco smoke is even more immoral than, let's say, slapping a stranger. If an individual is able to develop these moral faculties (spheres 4, 5, and 6), he becomes a candidate to develop the divine faculties. When an individual develops the faculty of the 3rd sphere he/she has the ability to influence events in the environment through the use of words of power. I.e., the person shares in the omnipotence of the Supreme Being, although not in the same magnitude. The second sphere faculty enables the person to intuitively understand all of life's situations. This is wisdom or omniscience. The development of the first sphere enables Man to experience the fact that his person, and that of all others, are parts of one Being. For example: Although a person's physical body is made up of billions of cells (individual creatures), it is experienced as one creature. This experience of oneness is beyond the intellectual understanding of oneness that most people hold in common. Before we can embark on a full explanation of the differences between the various stages of Man's development, we must have a full understanding of the faculties making up his spirit.

THE TREE OF LIFE AS A GUIDE TO MAN'S SPIRIT OR "MIND"

We have seen that mankind (certainly 99% of the people) has not completed its evolution. We cannot therefore understand Man by merely studying the behavior of Man through the ages. It is like arriving at conclusions about adults through the study of children. In the same way that we know that there are potentials residing in children waiting to be awakened, at the time appointed by the biological growth process, by studying adults, we know that there are potentials in mankind, and what they are by the study of people who have evolved beyond the present level of human evolution (Sages). We also know of others, although not more evolved, who have revealed faculties not yet awakened in the majority of people (mediums, psychics, etc.). To understand Man, we must therefore begin by analyzing the faculties and behavior of those people -Sages-who have completed their evolution. We will see that all of Man's faculties can be catalogued in one of the spheres of the Tree of Life.

SPHERE   FACULTY OF MAN'S SPIRIT

0   It has already been said that Man's true essential and original Being is composed of an energy/matter that is devoid of limitations. Hence, the cipher "0" symbolizes the absence of conditionings, and limitations characterizing the essential state of energy/matter, which can neither be created nor destroyed, as we know well from western science.

1   The first sphere corresponds to Man's *Self-identity*. As we are speaking of the perfected (fully evolved) Man, Her identity is with "0" (with the fact that the root, and essence of Her Being is unconditioned, and unlimited in its creative capacity). In other words, there is no identification with any personality complex that is characterized by specific human preferences (likes, dislikes, inclinations), abilities or inabilities, etc. At this level the Self-identity rises beyond sexual class, race, occupation, nationality, etc. There are no conditioned reflex patterns in the spirit that can force the individual to respond in a determined manner. In everyday life this means that the person will not be controlled by conditioned responses. He will be totally free of the control by likes, dislikes, loves, hatreds, fear, anger, and the whole host of emotions, and desires. As each personality type is a pattern of conditioned ways of thinking and emotional responses to given situations, the individual who has attained to the realization of her essential nature (0, and sphere 1) is able to change personalities as changing situations demand. Here, the Self identifies with the unstructured state of Subjective energy/matter composing the spirit at the 1st sphere level--the Ba. In the Kamitic tradition, an individual who has attained to this level of development is called an Ausar.

The ability to manifest any personality is of utmost importance. An individual succeeds when the demands and challenges of life are to be met by his *natal personality* traits. A fiery person will carry the moment if a situation demands courage, zeal, rashness, etc. But life's challenges will not always come to the fiery person through a fiery window. What would such a person do when challenges demand patience, calmness, following, etc? If the person identifies not with his natal fiery personality, but with the evolved higher *Ausarian nature*, then he will be able to assume the personality type that can best meet the situation of the moment. In other words, the individual will go through life without any limitations imposed on his Self image. This is the state of *The Great Liberation* sought by all sojourners on the spiritual path. It is obvious that what most people in the world identify as their self is not the first sphere of the Tree of Life.

2   The second sphere of the Tree of Life corresponds to the Will of God and of the evolved Man. In Chapter 6 we learned that all of creation is the differentiation of one and the same eternal and infinite energy/matter. Even Man's Being is an individualization of the Being of God. It follows then, that as all things are integral parts of one Being encompassing the world, *everything that a person wills to achieve must be in harmony with the Will of the whole (God). The ability to intuit the Will of God is, according to spiritual tradition, Wisdom.* We will have a great deal more to say about this. What is important here is to understand that with the fully evolved individual, what is willed is not based on personal needs or wants. The person will intuit from God the what, when, how, and why of events that are to take place in people's lives. It is the only way in which all human actions can be in harmony with each other, leading thus to peace, and prosperity. The other implication of the unlimited potential of the energy/matter that is the source of all things, is the fact that as there is no limit to what it can bring forth, there is no limit to what Man can will. One of the greatest causes of human failure is the imposition of limitations on what we can achieve in the world.

3.   The third sphere of the Tree of Life corresponds to the spiritual power of God, and of the evolved Man. This is the vehicle that carries out all that is willed at the second

sphere. We must recall the fact that *the will* is nothing more than what the word denotes in everyday speech. When a person says "I will do so and so," she is expressing a possibility. Its realization depends on the means, or the power to carry the potential into actuality. We will later see how the common error of taking the will for a faculty of power is a major cause of people's failures in life. The actualizer of what is possible is the third sphere of the Tree. Residing in this sphere are 50 creative forces that are in charge of all manifestations in the world. Each one of these forces has its own specific vibratory wave and rate, and can be evoked (literally "called out") into creative activity by chanting in a state of trance. They are the "matrikas" (matrices) or "little mothers" of the Kundalini Tantric Yoga tradition of Indus Kush; the 50 oarsmen who propel the boat of Ausar; the 50 gates of life and death of Binah, -the third sphere of the Tree; the 50 Beni Aelohim (Sons of God(s) which reside in the third sphere; the 50 skulls making up the necklace of the Great Black Mother, or Kundala of the Indus Kush; and most revealing, it corresponds to the 50 single sound units making up the Kundalini (Life-Force, Ra) body in God and Man. They are the basis of all mantras or hekau (words of power). We shall see later that they are the divine forces that western historians and theologians have translated as "the Gods" of the various religions of Black people. Arthur Avalon in the *Serpent Power* states:

Each man is Shiva (a deity,-Ausar), and can attain his power to the degree of his ability to consciously realize himself as such. For various purposes the Devata (deities) are invoked. Mantra (a word of power) and Devata are one and the same . . . By practice (japa) with the mantra the presence of the Devata is invoked. Japa or repetition of the mantra is compared to the action of a man shaking a sleeper to wake him up.

The biblical claim that "Man is made in the likeness of God," is substantiated by the fact that these 50 powers, which are the sources of all events and things in the world, are shared by both God and Man. The latter, of course,

87

expresses these powers to a much lesser degree. As I said earlier, God and Man, like the Ocean and a drop of water, have the same creative qualities (forces), but differ quantitatively in the expression of these qualities. It must be kept in mind, however, that for the majority of people in the world this faculty with its vast powers is dormant. Its awakening is the subject of Kundalini Yoga, the 12 Hours of the Night initiation ritual of the Ra theology of Kamit, etc.

4.   The fourth sphere of the Tree of Life corresponds to the seat of Man's intuitive sense of law and order. To fully understand Man's behavior *we must abandon the belief that law and order in the human world is dependent on the framing, and enforcement of rules by men*. It takes little to see that there are natural forces regulating all natural events in the world, as well as in Man's biological makeup. These forces have their seat in the fourth sphere (in the 4th division of the spirit of God and Man--the Ab) of the Tree of Life. When an individual evolves to this level, its ordering influence is extended to the mental operations of the individual. The result is instinctive emotional order (moral behavior) and intuitive cosmologically ordered thinking. Cosmo-logical thinking, which is beyond and superior to syllogistic logic, is based on the ability to intuitively perceive the abstract general class (whole) to which the specific issues of life belong. Let's illustrate this principle. As the majority of people in the world have not yet evolved this faculty, they are unable to intuit (learn from within) all of the specific manifestations of the general class "morality." All of their moral notions are extuited (learned from the outside- i.e., from others). Such a person, for example, may believe himself to be moral because he would not steal, beat up on others, or even pour a non-lethal dose of arsenic into someone's drink. Yet, he fails to see the immorality of poisoning the body of those he smokes around, making others pay for his medical bills (medicaid, and medicare) for illnesses induced by such purposeless and irresponsible acts as smoking, or self poisoning by eating artificially colored, preserved, and flavored foods, etc. Able to think only on a concrete level, such people can only identify specific instances of immorality that have been pointed out to them by their instructors and society. It is easy to see how the majority of the problems in the world

arise. A government claims that the citizens don't have the right over their bodies, when it comes to taking unproven medicines for deadly illnesses (laetrile for cancer, etc.), yet it gives the citizens the right to poison themselves with tobacco, devastate themselves and each other through alcohol, and so forth. There is a very far reaching and subtle principle at work here. The ability to perceive abstractions enables an individual to connect and unify events and things that may differ widely in form and external appearance. It enables the person, as shown above, to see that the introduction of non-fatal amounts of tobacco into another's body is no different from lacing someone's food with non-fatal doses of arsenic. In both cases the deadly cumulative effect is the same. As this faculty enables us to see through the differences between people, it is the intuitive intellectual basis of Love. This faculty in Man's spirit is symbolized in the Kamitic tradition by the Goddess of Law and Order, Maat. As the foundation of Love, which is the source of wealth, it is the Goddess Lakshmi, or Shri Deva of Indus Kush. Wealth, according to spiritual tradition results from the pooling of human resources in a harmonious, peaceful and cooperative manner. That this faculty is not developed in the majority of people in the world should be clear from the above examples. If anyone takes exception to the statement that the majority of the people cannot yet intuit moral principles, let him ponder on what would happen if the police in any major western nation were to be abolished. Would anyone be surprised to find that many people hitherto thought of as moral would be engaged in criminal activities? Have we not seen this exact type of event take place every time there was a riot, natural disaster, etc.? The mental application that ties *externally unrelated species* through an abstraction is called *"synthesis."* It must be noted that the popular use of the term synthesis is incorrect. There is a common misunderstanding of the mental application that the term denotes.

5.   The fifth sphere of the Tree of Life is the seat of Man's analytical faculty. As with "synthesis" the popular conception of the meaning of the term "analysis" is mistaken. In an earlier chapter it was observed that the term was literally composed of "analog" + "lysis." I.e., to separate (lysis) through analogs, which are abstractions. It

is the opposite of synthesis. Analysis separates, through abstractions, 1) things which on a concrete level may be members of the same species, or 2) establishes abstract differences between even more abstract categories. We must recall the example given in which the 5th sphere separates the abstract category "ferocious predators" into the lower abstract categories "feline," "canine," etc. We shall have occasion to see how the definitions of synthesis, and analysis that are given in this book are the only means of distinguishing such sciences as Chinese or African medicine from western medicine.

One of the most important principles that the Tree of Life has provided to Sages is the fact that the ability of an individual to be just depends on the faculties of analysis and synthesis as they have been explained in this book. On one hand, individuals cannot truly be held morally accountable for their deeds, until they have evolved the 4th (synthetical) sphere within their spirit, as this is the seat for intuiting moral behavior. Now the 5th sphere is the faculty through which Man is able to intuitively understand and apply the correct application of the principles of *Justice*. *It is essentially based on the individual's capacity to separate his Self from his person, thus making it possible to invoke upon his person the punishments, constraints, and regulations that he would place on others*. It does not take much to see that all over the world these are applied unequally. This inequality is the major cause of wars and conflicts in society. In a future chapter when we deal with the astrological symbolisms of the Tree, we will see and understand why the 5th sphere corresponds to the planet of violence and war - Mars. The fact that the greatest threat to the flourishment and survival of mankind is war, is proof of the fact that this faculty is not awakened in the majority of people, including those in leading positions.

6.   The sixth sphere of the Tree of Life is the most important of all the spheres. It is the faculty where the *equilibrium* of Man's being is established. All references to the *Golden Mean, to being centered, of being in the world but not of it*, refer to this sphere. When we consider the fact that the Supreme Being in Its essential state, has no other beings with which to interact, then we can understand why It must create the world, which is a diversification of Its Being. Life

on Earth, then, is a process in which *unity* governs the internal and higher levels of *organization*, and *diversity* governs the external and lower levels of *expression*. When our consciousness is established in the 6th sphere, we are able to maintain the equilibrium between the forces that unite us internally to the world and each other, and the forces that separate us externally. It also enables us to maintain the equilibrium between our higher true Self and our lower personality that unevolved people mistake as their self (identity). There are many factors in the world that demand this ability.

Most people are caught in the quandary of knowing, on one hand, that all men are integral parts of one whole, yet on the other hand, do not know how to acknowledge that oneness in action, because of their need to defend themselves against others whose attitudes to life are in violation of the oneness of life. The 6th sphere intuits (teaches from within) Man how to accomplish this task in all of its manifestations. *As most men have not yet completed their evolution, there cannot be total expression of unity amongst them.* It is important to realize that people are not going to manifest behavior without the necessary intuitive guidance from their spirit. The shaping forces of unity in Man's spirit (spheres 4 and up) are still dormant. Their awakening and functioning are in mankind's evolutionary future.

In the same manner, the way people live must reflect an equilibrium between their current level of growth, and the spiritual goal they are seeking (and are being pulled toward! More on this later). It's a question of genuinely acknowledging our limitations as a temporary point in our growth, as opposed to a finite and essential quality of our spirit. Accepting our temporary limitations within the process of growing toward our divine essential nature, will keep us from such pitiful acts like those made by many who felt that their innate divine nature would protect them while picking up rattle snakes, etc. On the other hand, it will keep us from defining ourselves around our failures in life.

The failure to understand this principle of equilibrium is the reason for the erroneous beliefs held by many Aryanized Yogis (Vedantins) to the effect that life on Earth is without merit. Like the Western crass materialists, who reject all that is not of the physical plane, many Yogis have erred, but in the opposite direction. Since many problems in the world can be traced to the absence of this faculty, it is safe to conclude that most people in the world have not yet evolved it.

7.   The 7th sphere of the Tree of Life corresponds to the faculty of imagination. At last we are on familiar ground. Although it is not fully evolved, as we shall see, most people in the world have developed it to a high degree. The role played by the imagination in artistic creativity is well known, as well as its role in the coordination of details into a whole. While this latter function might seem to overlap with the synthetical function of the 4th sphere, we must take note of the fact that while synthesis deals with abstractions, the 7th sphere deals with concrete thoughts. It is *"congregative"* rather than synthetical. Art, as well as scientific invention, over which it has dominion involves the coordination, and special arrangement of forms based on their external components. Whereas synthesis uses a symbol, "fire" for example, to bring together all specifics that share in its expansive, violent, centrifugal, and rising nature, the congregative thinking of the artistic faculty seeks to bring together fiery things with watery, with earthy, etc. into an aesthetic and harmonious arrangement. Put more familiarly, its function is to coordinate different forms,- different tones, and harmonies into musical compositions; different shapes and colors into paintings, etc. In other words, while synthesis *groups* together species that are different outwardly, but similar inwardly, congregative thinking *assembles a whole* by *coordinating* species that are outwardly, and perhaps inwardly different. While synthesis classifies, thus giving order to thinking, Congregative thinking builds wholes out of parts.

The highest function of the imaginative faculty is to be seen in its, not so well known, control over our physiological and psychological processes. Western science has extensively documented the use of the imagination in the cure of diseases, the cultivation of behavior, and performance. Many athletes and artists have perfected their performances through imagery. Its power can be extended beyond our own persons to influence other people, and to help shape events as well. But we must recall what was said in an

92

earlier chapter. Such uses of the imagination are limited to coordinating the activities that have already been initiated in the third sphere of the Tree of Life. Failing to understand that the imagination is a coordinator of subtle physical forces, and not a "creative faculty," despite its popular reputation as such, many so-called experts in esoteric matters have erroneously recommended its use for the solution of all problems in life. We shall later see the great role it plays in life as part of the team of spheres that are in charge of the creative process.

8   The 8th sphere of the Tree of Life is the exact opposite of the 7th. While the latter coordinates parts to build wholes, the 8th sphere separates wholes into their parts. To illustrate: The 7th sphere takes the different components of language (nouns, verbs, adjectives, etc,) and assembles them into meaningful units (sentences, paragraphs, stories, etc.). Oppositely, the 8th sphere will focus on each component, the nouns, the verbs, etc. in isolation from each other, and the whole, in order to study some aspect of them (definition, part of speech, etc.). While the 7th sphere deals with how each component works with the others to create a workable and meaningful whole, the 8th sphere deals with *the specific identifying characteristic of each member of a species.*

These two faculties make very important contributions to the nature of society. The 7th sphere is not only responsible for people's ability to work harmoniously, it recognizes the fact that the creation of complex wholes cannot be achieved without the element of differences between the parts. You can't have a painting with one type of shape and one color, or a musical composition with one type of tone and one type of rhythm. In the same way, the world requires the vast diversity of ethnic, and cultural elements in order to achieve prosperity. On the other hand, the 8th sphere focuses on the external and superficial differences between people (racial, ethnic, sex, age, etc.) and things, and segregates them accordingly. Although there is a legitimate function for the segregative thinking of the 8th sphere, we will see that due to the lack of input into peoples' thinking from the higher faculties (spheres 6 to 0), the 8th sphere is the chief architect of Man's social ills.

9.   The ninth sphere is the faculty that governs Man's learning during the early part of life. As this sphere is part of the lower divisions of Man's spirit, it corresponds to His spiritual infancy. A person's learning, therefore, comes from the outside, i.e., from other people and creatures. All acts of learning involve imitation and following. And given the immaturity of this level of being, such imitation is indiscriminate. This applies to all educational experiences, from the cradle to post-graduate; from the streets to the academic halls; secular or spiritual. It is *indiscriminate imitation* that makes professional scientists swear by the "scientific facts" of their days that are later on proven to be no more than false theories. Peoples' adherence to traditions and customs, whether these are secular, "scientific," religious, cultural, etc. comes about in the same way. The danger inherent in this mode of learning is clear, yet it cannot be avoided.

This sphere is also the seat of memory, which is essential to learning. There are two very important facts concerning memory that must be understood. One is the fact that nothing that has been experienced is ever forgotten, no matter how out of view, or difficult to recall it may be. The other is that, many of our stored memories, especially, those that are difficult to recall, because of psychological suppression, exert powerful influences in shaping our beliefs and behavior. Given the fact that these types of memories (patterns for imitation) are stored in the infancy of our spirituality, they are illogical, and irrational in their makeup. Contributing to this irrationality is the characteristic mode of functioning of this faculty. Not only does it store experiences, it associates them on the basis of external qualities. Unfortunately, external qualities which serve well for identity tagging purposes (naming, definitions, etc.) do not contribute much to meaning. However, when we are trying to understand, memory (the 9th sphere) throws up associated items linked through their external qualities. As a result, most people misunderstand more than they understand. We will later see the full implications of this concept when we deal with the fact that the majority of people who, due to the fact that the faculty of Self-identity - the first sphere- is unevolved (dormant), assemble their self-identity out of the memories of experiences that are stored in the 9th sphere. It amounts to "I am these failures, and successes as my memory informs me."

10   The tenth sphere corresponds to two sets of principles in Man. Her sensory and physical bodies.

10a   The sensory body is the seat of our faculties of perception, sensual cravings and expression (sexual desire, appetite, seeing, hearing, emotions, etc.). A study of human behavior based on the principles of spiritual science will reveal that there is *a qualitative connection* between the types of desires, types of emotions, and modes of perception dominating an individual's personality. These patterns of sensory mechanisms are integrated in the conception of "temperamental classes." The various sets reflect the order established in the 4th sphere of the Tree of Life. Thus, humans are classified as "fiery," "watery," "earthy," and "airy." These are metaphors for the various types of human classes according to their metabolic differences. "Fiery" people are "hot and dry" -that is to say- of a high catabolic activity, which places their body heat in the higher ranges. This increases the rate of their physical and psychological activities. They are lively, impatient, easy to anger, zealous, prone to acute illnesses, etc. "Watery" people are just the opposite. They are "cold and moist." We will detail this principle of temperamental ("temperature") classifications later on.

10b   The lower part of the 10th sphere corresponds to the physical body, which is the vehicle that allows Man, who as we have seen, is a metaphysical being, to communicate with, and act in the physical world. It is also the means through which the attainment of the illusion of being separate existences takes place. All things are differentiations and structuralizations of one infinite continuum of energy/matter. While their essential unity is maintained in the higher metaphysical regions, their sense of separateness is effected through the physical state of energy/matter.

A COMPARATIVE ANALYSIS OF MAN'S COMPLEMENTARY FACULTIES

In order to use the Tree of Life as a means of ordering our thinking and our living, it is necessary to understand the complementary relationships between certain sets of spheres. We will recall that in chapter 6, the spheres of the Tree were arranged in sets of complementary spheres; 0-10, 1-9; 2-8; 3-7; 4-6; and 5 by itself. A function of this *a priori* duality principle is that it holds the key to how people substitute the higher principles for the lower ones during the early part of their evolution. In place of 0 and 1, they identify with 10 and 9, etc. The best way to understand these principles is to view them within the perspective of *the five principles governing Man's life*. Correlating to the Tree we get the following:

The Five Principles Governing Man's Life

	Prin-ciples	Spheres	Meaning
1.	Peace	0,10	The ultimate *Why* behind all actions. The emotional/pleasure factor in life.
2.	Self	1,9	*What* Man thinks He is.
3.	Will	2,8	*What* Man thinks He can achieve.
4.	Power	3,7	*How* Man achieves Her goals.
5.	Laws	4,6,5	Man's relationship to God, other men and the world.

The Why Behind Man's Actions
"0," Our Essential Nature vs. the 10th Sphere

In whatever way they have defined it, whether they have articulated their view of it or not, underlying all human endeavors is the quest for *happiness*. But what is it? While philosophers and psychologists have vexed themselves for ages seeking an answer, the Tree of Life, with its marvelous thought ordering functions guides us swiftly and easily to the answer. All things and events originate from the primordial energy/matter (the Subjective Realm, "0") which we know by now, is a substance devoid of forms, structures, etc. This is due to the fact that its energy is in a state of perfect stability or serenity. *Movement comes into being at the demand of Time.* Time is the ordered (rhythmic) apportioning of things, their place for manifesting and expressing themselves, given the fact that no two things can occupy the same space at the same time. As matter in the Subjective Realm has not been structured into things, there is no need or justification for time. This state of serenity or peace is the master and primordial energetic configuration of our spirit. In the Kamitic tradition it was called *Hetep*. What we want and need most is peace. To achieve it we must return the focus of our consciouses to "0"--the Subjective Realm. This condition is the highest goal of meditation. It is the state of Hetep of the Kamitic tradition; Samadhi Sarvikalpa Nirvana, in the Hindu; Satori, in the Zen Bhudhist, and so forth. It is not a serenity that depends on outward conditions, such as the amount of money, weapons, the state of our love life, etc. Neither is it the "fleeing" from the cares and troubles of the world. Granted that returning consciousness to the Subjective Realm, its original level, enables Man to go through life with an unassailable and independent calmness. But along with this achievement there is the knowledge that one has also contacted the root of all divine power. Implicit in people's quest for happiness is not only the urge for emotional gratification, there is also an urge for security. And *there is nothing that can give one more security than the acquisition of divine power*.

But as shown earlier, the return of consciousness to "0" is the last step in our evolution. We are born with only the 9th and 10th spheres active. That the 10th sphere is complementary to "0" means that they are the ultimate motivators of our actions. As 0 is dormant in the infancy of our spiritual evolution, there is no intuitive or instinctive influence urging the person to attain peace by the withdrawal of consciousness into the higher part of being. All urges in people's lives at this point in evolution originate from the 10th sphere, which we learned is the seat of desires, passions, emotions, etc. As this sphere is also our vehicle for communicating with the physical world, all emotions, and desires are stimulated by information streaming in from the external world. Gratifying desires, and emotional drives depend then on externals which are under very limited control of the individual at this point in his evolution. Happiness to people at this stage of growth, then, is the gratification of emotions, and desires which are dependent on achieving, or manipulating externals. Getting a job, having someone's love or acceptance, having wealth, fulfilling the necessities of life, indulging the cravings for food, sex, etc. All emotions and desires are in reality states of tension and disequilibrium of the energies of the spirit. All responses to our emotions and desires are attempts to resolve the tensions that they represent. Unevolved Man strives to return these energies to their original state of balance and serenity by gratifying the external stimuli that activated them. One day we will all, like Sages have done, realize that the spirit's energies can only attain their equilibrium and serenity by being elevated to their original primordial level of being in the Subjective Realm. While the gratification of emotions and desires can bring only temporary joy, elevating our consciousness to the highest part of our being gives eternal peace. This is true happiness. The value of this reality can be appreciated when we recall to mind the individuals who, in spite of having acquired great wealth and fame, ended by destroying their lives, either through an overt suicidal act, or indirectly through living a very self destructive life. The reason for this is that the 10th sphere is the animal division of Man's spirit. It is called the Khaibit in the Kamitic spiritual tradition; Nephesh and Nachash in the Canaanite Kabalistical; Umzimba, in the Zulu; Ojiji, in the Yoruba; and Pranayama Kosha and Linga Sarira, in the Hindu. It is the blind principle that tempted the woman Aisha, who in turn tempted the man Aish[1] and caused, according to the Hebraic tradition, the "Fall of Man." It is unfortunate that so many bible scholars have debated for centuries whether serpents at one time or another were able to speak to people. The fact is that in the Kamitic spiritual system, which is the source of most of the Hebraic tradition, the hieroglyphic symbol for this part of the spirit is a serpent (Apep, Nak, from whence Nachash,- the "serpent" that spoke to the woman in the Garden of Eden). This part of the spirit is composed of subtle electromagnetic energies that have the function of animating Man's life, especially the physical body. Hence, the name "animal spirit," or "anima and animus," as it was called in the Latin spiritual tradition. Our modern use of the term "animal" to denote the creatures that are thus identified is an example of muddled thinking. All things in this world are infused with this animating spirit. This agrees with the law of physics which states that all things are in a state of motion. The creatures that we call animals are simply those that allow the greatest expression to this universal principle. But it is of utmost importance to know that all things, minerals, vegetals, and humans are ensouled by this animal, or animating spirit. To follow one's feelings, and desires . . . to do it because you like it, and so on, is to identify with the animal part of being. And as anyone would expect, to allow oneself to be led by an animal can lead only to disastrous

_____

1. Few readers of the bible know that according to the original Hebraic version of the bible, the characters that took part in the Fall of Man scene were not Eve, and Adam, but Aisha, and Aish. A study of Kabala reveals that the so-called woman, and man were in reality symbols of parts (the intellectual) of Man's spirit.

results. One's emotions, cravings, and desires can never be guides to living, and to what is correct. This explains the violence and irrationality that so controls the life of the majority of people in the world. *The goal of spiritual culture is to lead Man to the realization that the happiness -resolution of spiritual tensions- that He seeks through worldly achievements, or direct sensual indulgence can only be satisfied by returning consciousness to the level of being that is the only and legitimate place of equipoise of the energies of His being.* Life on earth is by necessity an unending ebb and flow of tension and relaxation. It is an expression of movement, rhythm, and music. But we cannot let the blind tensions be our guides. We can never abolish them, but we need not allow our consciousness, the essence of our Self, to dwell in their place of manifestation. It is to eat very low off the Tree.

Man's Self-Identity

The First Sphere vs the Ninth Sphere

Our Self vs Our Person

We have already seen that Man's identity belongs at the first sphere. When an individual says "I am so and so," this "so and so" must equate with *"the likeness of God,"* which according to the Old Testament, Man has been made. As this sphere identifies with the unstructured primordial energy/matter which can thus become anything, so is Man's potential of becoming unlimited.

Yet we must remember that the purpose of manifested Life is to bring about a reality of *unity in the midst of diversity.* One essence appearing to be an infinitude of separate beings. Thus Man, like God, and all of creation is an *individual.* The term is made up of "indivisible + dual," therefore denoting a reality which contains elements that are separate yet cannot be separated. Thus, properly understood, the term "individual" cannot be confined to denoting Man, but must be applied to God, and all things in/as the world. These dual elements making up Man's being are the results of the unifying action of 0 and the 1st sphere, and the separating action of the 10th and 9th spheres. In this book we will establish the convention of equating the higher part of our being, our true identity with the term "Self," and the lower part of our being, where we establish a temporary identity reference point, with the term "person."

99

We are born with only the 9th and 10th spheres in an awakened state. It will be a long time before we evolve to the point where the faculty of our 1st sphere will inform us intuitively of our true Self. Thus we begin life equating the information acquired through our 9th sphere with our self. The 9th sphere, which is the seat of learning of the lower part of the spirit, learns from the 10th sphere only of our separateness from other beings. This is in direct opposition to what the 1st sphere intuits us. It also identifies with the specific pattern of emotional (energy) inclinations (fiery or earthy temperament, etc.) that the animal spirit of each person accentuates. Thus the person believes that he or she is a shy or brave person, and so on. It also stores the memories of our experiences, and through its associative (but arational) function, assembles a "belief system" of our capabilities and limitations. These *three* fundamental factors- our sense of separateness, identification with a limited expression of our emotional capability (i.e., with our temperament), and with the history of our accomplishments and failures- are the major building elements of what most people falsely call their Self. As this lower part of being is a legitimate point in our evolutionary process, it must have an appropriate label. This is the term "person." It is derived from two Latin words. "Per" which means "through," and "sona," which means "sound." It literally denotes something *"through* which a *sound* is made." The understanding of this point is to be found in the science of mantras. Anyone who has worked extensively with mantras may have verified the fact that what we call personalities are effects of sound complexes. For example, the sound (mantra) "Kling," taken into trance often and long enough will generate an artistic, peaceful, and amative personality in an individual of a different personality. The sound "Hring" will transform a shy, yielding, follower into a courageous and fearless leader. In future chapters we will also see that these words of power are also the forces of nature that Westerners have translated as "deities." Correlating this with the previous observation leads to the understanding of why in many African traditions, many people claim to be the incarnation of a Deity. We will later see that each of the spheres of the Tree of Life represents one of nine personalities ("Deities") that Man must learn to invoke at any given moment to meet the changing demands of life. In addition, they are each the "steps" of our evolutionary ladder.

It is important to realize that Man's placement of His identity in the 9th sphere, thus equating Himself with a lower part of his being, is the second master cause of all of mankind's problems

100

(the first master cause is his being controlled by his animal spirit). The unity that must exist between people in order for there to be peace and prosperity for all, can only come about by the leadership of the world resting in the hands of people who have evolved the first sphere, which is the natural faculty of unity.

The Will

The Second Sphere vs the Eighth Sphere

The will is the faculty through which we express our future undertakings and actions. What we will to achieve is ultimately determined by our self-identity. We saw that our true self-identity belongs at the 1st sphere, and shares the same qualities of the Supreme Being. In reality, Man's true self is one with God, qualitatively. Similarly, Man's will belongs to God. It shares thus in the omniscience of the will of God. The principal underlying determinant of success is not "having a firm will" or "thinking positively," as "mind experts" will have us believe. It comes from Man's ability to intuit God's will. The ability to do so resides in the 2nd sphere of the Tree of Life. An individual who has evolved to this level of being is able to unite her personal will with that of God. In other words, the person seeks to be guided by God's will in all undertakings in life. Since all of the person's actions is guided by God, success is always the outcome[2]. In addition, all actions are always in harmony with all other events in the world, given the fact that God's will is a reflection of its Self-identity, which is the sphere of unity (sphere one). This is the opposite to the common experience in which people's actions and attempts to solve problems, result in new and even worse problems (the Hydra serpent of Greek mythology that sprouted two heads for each one that was severed[3]). But the faculty of the second sphere belongs to the higher division of Man's spirit and, therefore, to the evolutionary future of the majority of people in the world. It has only been manifested by a few Sages.

When most people express their will to achieve a particular goal, lacking the input from the 2nd sphere, they take their cue from

2. From the spiritual standpoint, success is not in reality the accomplishment of one's goal, but the spiritual upliftment,- increase in knowledge, and power- derived from the undertaking.

3. This is a symbol of Sebek, the 8th sphere.

the 9th and the 8th spheres. The 9th sphere, the seat of their personality, informs them, basically, that they are limited in their potential of being and separate from all other beings. The superficial and segregative thinking of the 8th sphere hides the connection between the things that people think about. This results in a limited view of what can be achieved, and causes most undertakings to end in conflict with other events in the world. Meditation on the subject will reveal that most of what people achieve in the world is at the expense of something else in their life or that of others. This is the master source of all the personal and group conflicts in the world. In the same manner that the lower principle that unevolved Man identifies with as his self (the 9th sphere) is not his true self, neither is the 8th sphere Man's true will. What most people call their will are really their desires, hopes, and wishes masquerading as such.

Man's Power

The Third Sphere vs. the Seventh Sphere

We learned earlier that when an individual develops the faculty of the 3rd sphere, she has the ability to influence events in the environment through the use of words of power. I.e., the person shares in the omnipotence of the Supreme Being, although not in the same magnitude. The difference between this faculty and the seventh sphere, which is the faculty of the imagination, is that while the 3rd sphere is able to create effects in the environment even when the materials and circumstances to enable them do not yet exist, are in opposition to it, the 7th sphere can only coordinate the shaping forces that already exist, and are not in opposition to it. Unfortunately, the "gurus" of the "achieve your goals through creative 'imaging'" school do not know this fact. "All that you have to do is to imagine your goals. See yourself the way you want to be. Doing the things you want to achieve, etc., and you will achieve your goal." This process works only by reorganizing and coordinating the wayward shaping forces of a particular event.

Man's Knowledge Of Reality

The 4th Sphere vs. the 8th Sphere

The next major determinant of the quality of Man's life depends on *what He believes is real*. Whether they have articulated it or not, everyone operates from certain ideas regarding what is real and what isn't. The exposition of Cosmology in this book has shown us that reality encompasses a range of states of energy/matter from the unformed, hence imperceptible, to the finite and restrictive physical matter that we are well acquainted with. And all things are none other than divisions within this infinite and eternal substance, hence, essentially one in being. And that *all "beings" are in reality the percolation of one original consciousness through each separate form in the world.* Imagine sunlight flowing through glasses of different colors. The same colorless light will come out yellow, through one, red through the other, and so on. In each case it will have different qualities and limitations, yet they are all separate expressions of the same entity. In addition, it is important to realize that there is no separation, cannot be any separation between the whole (holy!) light entering the glass and the light fragment (of a particular color, wave length, etc.) leaving the glass on the other side. This is the message, stripped of poetry, of the Tree of Life. The message originates in the second sphere, and is codified in the fourth. People who have evolved to the 4th sphere are able to intuit the cosmological principles that give order to existence. They are thus able to create systems to integrate the lives of people with each other, the environment and God (i.e., religion, morality, etc.); systems or ways of life that integrate the various affectors of health, etc. This integrative (synthetical) ability, we must remember, depends on the 4th sphere faculty's capacity to think abstractly. Unfortunately, this faculty is also in the evolutionary future of most people.

Unevolved people are therefore forced to process their information about life through the surface thinking, and external form-limited faculty of the 8th sphere. They cannot, therefore, avoid segregating things that belong together. This faculty is the author of biases and segregation by race, religion, sex, age, etc. It separates medicine from nutritional science, religion from science, government from religion, etc.

In addition, whereas the 4th sphere is informed from within and above (i.e., the divine omniscience), the 8th sphere is informed from the physical plane. It is limited then to 1/10th of the Objective

Realm and is totally excluded from the Subjective. Thus limited, the unevolved Man, regardless of how well educated, whether in science, morality, health, religion, etc. is not truly able to apply the higher teachings efficiently in life. He can only see the external and lower side of religion. To Him, it is a system of worship and adoration of God. Morality is limited to the specific acts that have been pointed out to be immoral or those acts that are not condemned by enough people in a society. So limited is his thinking to surface and external appearances that he cannot see that there is no biological or physiological or spiritual support for homosexual sex, for example. We can go on.

Fundamentally related to the functions of the 4th sphere are those of the 6th, which is the seat of our ability to live according to the principles of cosmogony (innate order) residing in our spirit. This faculty which is also in the evolutionary future of most people enables people to intuitively and instinctively live according to divine laws, as opposed to the tyrannical influence that the 10th sphere (seat of emotions, etc.) exerts upon the 9th sphere (Man's person). The same is true of the 5th sphere. It is the source of a Judicial system based on the divine laws codified in the 4th sphere. Its acts of punishment are for the reestablishment of equilibrium in the world, as opposed to the disorder spreading acts of revenge that the 10th sphere motivates.

Chapter 8

A COSMOLOGICAL GUIDE
TO THE THREE TYPES OF MEN

INTRODUCTION

That there are in this world, people of widely differing mental, moral, and spiritual abilities we must all agree. We will see that the similarities and differences between people, when sorted, arrange themselves into three fundamental types of Men. In the Taoist tradition of China, for example, we find that people are classified as the masses, superior men, and Sages.

The division of people into three types, is based on the various stages in human evolution. In an earlier chapter it was said that Man's spirit is not a single body. It consists of seven divisions or levels, which include the physical body as its lowest and densest portion.

A brief look at the subject, from this perspective, will reveal the following outline of the various types of people.

1. People who are controlled by their emotional and sensuous being (10th sphere). And who only "know" what they are taught by others (spheres 7 - 9), and whose mental perception is limited to the external and concrete side of things. Because of this their lives are full of contradictions. I.e., they are devoid of "understanding." As this type of Man has not risen above the 5th division of the spirit (the Sahu),- counting from the bottom-we shall refer to him as "Sahu Man." Recall that the Sahu is the 5th division of the spirit. The "masses" or "inferior men" of Chinese Taoism correspond to this level.

2. People who are able to rise above the influence of their emotional and sensuous being. And although their "knowledge" is only limited to what they are taught, they are able to understand-think abstractly about-the subjects that are taught to them. This is due to the fact that their mental faculties (spheres 4 - 6) are able to perceive the abstractions that underlie physical events. This enables them to avoid the contradictions (falsities) that beset the previous type of man. As the soul qualities of this type of Man originates in the Ab part of the spirit, we shall refer to him as the "Ab

Man." They correspond to the "superior men" of Chinese Taoism.

3. People who are able to intuit the knowledge needed to avoid and solve all the problems that can face Man. They also possess the ability to achieve such goals (influence physical events) by manipulating their spiritual power through the use of hekau and visualization. As this type of Man has completed his/her evolution we shall refer to him as "an Ausar."

Each of these three types of people represents a stage in Man's evolution. Let's take a more detailed look at the subject.

The most important factor that determines a person's behavior is his level of consciousness. It will determine her level of perception, which in turn will determine what she knows or believes, and her attitude toward her emotions and sensual appetites.

When our consciousness is focused in the Sahu part of the spirit and below (the animal spirit--Khaibit) our mental perception is limited to the external side of things. We are able to recognize concrete specifics but not the abstract principles from which they are generated. For example, the abstract perceptive ability of an Ausar Man (fully evolved person) reveals that there is no such thing as "a medicine" or "a poison." All substances can be used medicinally or toxically according to their dosage. There is a level above which arsenic will poison, and below which, it will heal. Although we all know this from our experiences with vaccines, very few people are able to arrive at the above conclusion regarding "medicines" and "poisons." The point to be emphasized here is that there are no concrete realities called "medicines" or "poisons." There exist "medicinal relations" and "toxic relations." But, Sahu people are not able to properly understand such abstract entities, so they lower them to their level of perception. They cannot help but think in terms of "this medicine" and "that poison," etc. The result is that they fail to avail themselves of the healing potential of the things in their environment that are intoxicating them[1]! I.e., the very pesticide that added to the crops gives us cancer, is the best remedy against the very cancer it causes. Hundreds of examples of this belief in the existence of non-existing realities can be given. It is one of the major causes of problems in the world.

---

1. Every environmental poison can be antidoted by homoepathically preparing them into a medicine.

A very important question is raised by the foregoing. If Sahu Man believes that there are such things as medicines and poisons, when they don't in fact exist, it cannot be said that he has *knowledge*. What he does have is the *belief* that the information that he has received is factual. When we fully examine this issue and see that this is the rule with Sahu Man, we will arrive at the conclusion that he is incapable of "knowing." There is a general confusion of "knowing" with "believing," and acquiring "knowledge" vs. acquiring "information." Beliefs are what the Sahu Man has. Because the faculties of inner (abstract) perception is dormant in the Sahu man, he is unable to intuit (learn from within his spirit) the nature of things, and must therefore learn from outside of his being. All of his beliefs are shaped by what he has been taught by others or what his senses report to him. He has no way of knowing whether what he has been informed about is true or false, as truth or falsehood can only be determined by the knowledge of the relation between parts with each other and the whole. As a result, he falls into a host of contradictions.

When our consciousness is raised to the Ab level of the spirit, we are able to understand and significantly function with such relations as explained above. All of the contradictions and our vulnerability to falsehoods are thus avoided. At this level, however, we are still not able to intuit for ourselves these abstract relations, although we are able to fully understand them and live accordingly.

The ability to intuit the abstract relations between things, and the whole to which they belong, is a function of the second division of the spirit -the Khu. This mental function is the true constituent of wisdom and knowledge.

These three levels of Man's being are stages in his evolutionary growth. We must therefore look at it from this perspective.

Stage I of Man's Evolution

Sahu Man

Although the Sahu is the 5th division of the spirit, we are here coining the label "Sahu Man" to refer to people who's behavior is dominated by the 6th division of the spirit (the Khaibit, sphere 10) and the 5th division (Sahu--spheres 7, 8, & 9).

When we are born, our consciousness is focused in the 6th division of the spirit, and the 9th sphere of the 5th division of the spirit. The 6th division (10th sphere of the Tree) is the animal part of the spirit, which is the source of the sensuous behavior that dominates the early part of Man's life (first 28 years) and its entirety unless it is brought under control through spiritual practices (rites of passage, Bar Mitzvah, etc.). The ninth sphere is the faculty that makes it possible for us to learn. As we know well, the early part of Man's learning career is characterized by indiscriminate imitation. This influence comes from the 9th sphere. Rather than "knowing," Man at this level "believes" what is perceived through the senses and the ideas communicated from others. His thinking is limited to the concrete and external side of reality, as the faculties for perceiving the abstractions underlying physical realities are dormant at this stage. Examples of indiscriminate imitation are numerous. Anyone who exercises discrimination in adopting other people's practices would not wear high heel shoes, eat the host of refined foods (white sugar, white flour products, white rice, etc.), or abuse alcohol, smoke tobacco, do drugs, etc.

From the 7th year of life on, the faculties of the 7th and 8th spheres achieve their full state of awakening, although it will take another 21 years to develop them fully. If the person functions more out of the left hemisphere of the brain, the 8th sphere will dominate the mental character of the person. An inclination to the right hemisphere of the brain will result in the predominance of the 7th sphere.

The 8th sphere corresponds to Man's ability to give "concrete verbal" form to his feelings, beliefs and knowledge[2]. It is our faculty for separating things from each other, and parts from the whole to which they belong, through the act of defining, describing and naming. We saw earlier how this faculty, due to its inability to perceive the abstract relations between things and parts and their whole, creates such false "concrete" categories as "medicines" and "poisons." If studies were to be conducted on this premise, they will show that western education is predominantly a process of providing definitions, descriptions and names. The problem is aggravated by the fact that, besides the creation of false distinctions, it thus deludes the person into believing in the existence of things that don't exist. E.g., once we understand the above we will understand that poisons and medicines do not exist. We are forced to think relationally.

---

2. Therefore, the enlightment achieved at the second sphere-eight stage of meditiation-may be distorted by the person's 8th sphere deficiencies (impoverished conceptual bank, poor vocabulary, inadequate belief system, etc.).

This is the reason, for example, why western societies, which function predominantly through the 8th sphere--the lower portion of the left side of the brain--cannot conceive of a female Pope, a female Rabbi, and are obsessed with segregation in all things. Not only are differences made between the sexes, races and nationalities but in the sciences as well. Until the 1950's psychiatrists knew virtually nothing about the physiology and biochemistry of the brain; physicians to this day know virtually nothing about nutrition and so on. They cannot help confusing the exclusiveness of the definitions of "healing" and "nurturing" with the actual healing and nurturing processes themselves which are never nor cannot ever be separated from each other.

The 7th sphere corresponds to Man's ability to coordinate things based on their external forms. Colors, shapes, rhythms, people, etc. are arranged into aesthetic or functional wholes. This is our faculty for artistic and scientific invention. Although this faculty brings things together based on their differences and makes them work harmoniously together, like the 8th sphere, it is still limited to the perception of externals. As a result, the criterion for the value of its creations is based on their impact on the animal spirit (gratification of the senses). There is no real concern with the healing and consciousness altering functions of music and art[3], for example.

As the animal spirit--the Khaibit--is the first and oldest part of the spirit to be awakened, it dominates the Sahu. In learning (9th sphere function), the immature person inclines toward imitating those behaviors that cater to his sensuous and emotional being. The prowess of the 8th or 7th spheres is mostly used to rationalize or gratify the influences from the animal spirit, respectively.

The behavior of Man during the 1st stage of his development can be summed up as one in which he is dominated by 1) the urge to gratify the sensuous (emotions, appetites, desires) part of being, 2) the urge to use the mental faculties to rationalize the gratification of the sensuous expressions, 3) the inability to know. He can only be "informed." And can only "believe" what he is taught or what he can perceive through the senses. 4) His mental perceptions are limited to the concrete and external side of things. As the highest division of the spirit that this person attains to is the Sahu, we refer to him in this book as the "Sahu Man."

---

3. In the branch of science called Kinesiology is clearly shown how images, musical forms, etc. affect peoples health.

Stage II of Man's Evolution

The Ab Man

If the society in which the person lives knows how to spiritually develop its citizens, they will begin to develop the 4th division of their spirit (the Ab) by around the 28th year of life. Unfortunately, this is not the case with the majority of nations in the world. When our consciousness is raised to the Ab part of the spirit, a reversal in the relationship between our intellect and emotions takes place. In opposition to Sahu Man, in whom the intellect is subordinated to serve the sensuous part of being, with the Ab Man the Self uses the intellect to subjugate the sensuous division of the spirit. The faculties of this part of the spirit- spheres 4, 5 and 6- we will remember, correspond to the "Celestial government." The 4th and 5th spheres possess the ability to perceive the abstract principles underlying and uniting things and events in the world. They thus enable the person to transcend the divisive emotions and mental functions of the lower parts of the spirit (spheres 7 - 10). The sixth sphere corresponds to Man's personal will. Although a great deal has been written about the will, we will see that there are a lot of misunderstandings concerning it. The common beliefs held by Sahu men that the will is "the power of choosing the course of one's destiny," that it is the expression of one's wishes or desires, etc. are full of flaws. Since most people's "choices" and wishes are primarily underlaid by their emotions and sensuous feelings, it cannot be argued that their will is at work in such instances. Essential to the definition of the will, therefore, is a choice of action that is on one hand, free of emotional and sensuous motivations, and on the other, based on knowledge or beliefs. The faculty that enables us such an expression resides in the 6th sphere of the Tree. Although it does have the freedom to decide on a destiny course, this is not the major function of the personal will[4]. It is the freedom to choose to live for the gratification of the lower divisions of the spirit, especially the 6th division or according to the divine laws governing the higher/true part of one's being. When the person realizes that he or she does not have to obey the emotional nature, and lives according to truth,

---

4. If Man is made in the likeness of God, He must therefore possess the same attribute of free will as God. In fact this faculty is what separates Man from all other creatures on earth. It is his ability to step outside of the instinctive automatic reflexes that guides his lower nature.

then the will is being exercised. The true function of the will, then, is to deny the animal division of the spirit (source of our sensual and emotional expressions) its control over the life of the individual.

Another important fact concerning the will is its dependence, not on power, but on abstract intellectual insight. In a previous chapter we saw that the sixth sphere corresponds to the Kamitic Deity Heru, whose actions are judged by the 4th sphere, Maat. This translates into the western verbal mode of thinking, by saying that the will (Heru) depends primarily on mental synthesis (Maat). It is very interesting to note that the word Maat is kin to Maa (to see, hence, insight), and it (the 4th sphere) is diagonally opposite the 8th sphere which expresses thoughts in verbal form. In other words, at the 8th sphere, the Self is informed by verbal thoughts, while at the 4th sphere it is informed by thoughts that are seen[5]. To know a definition--8th sphere function--is not to know the thing or event defined. It is "hearsay," when on one hand a dictionary gives us the definition "poison, n 1. a liquid, solid or gaseous substance which has an inherent property that tends to destroy life or impair health," and on the other hand our experience shows us that such substances as arsenic, the venoms of snakes, bees, spiders can be used either to destroy life or to cure illnesses in relationship to their dosage. In the future chapters on meditation we will focus at length on this delusive effect of verbal thoughts. While we can easily be deluded by definitions and names as their contents are heard and not seen, it is the opposite with visual thoughts.

Unable to function through the 4th sphere, Western scholars have always believed that the visual thought--hieroglyphic--system of Kamit communicated mainly, and only, concrete thoughts. In an earlier chapter I showed how the ancients used the image of "fire" as a synthetical symbol to serve as a common category for diverse things and events that share its centrifugal, rising, expansive and exciting qualities. It becomes the common set for classifying and abstractly uniting courageous men, ferocious predators, the summer season, acute febrile diseases, hot and pungent plants (cayenne pepper, mustard, etc.)[6], etc.. Knowledge of the characteristics of fire or anyone of the analogies will provide insight

---

5. Images of the Sesh Metut Neter.

6. Unfortunately for the west, Plato and other Greek philosophers could not get beyond the elemental concrete fire that cooks our food. This use of fire as an abstract symbol illustrates the foundation of the Chinese, African, and Homeopathic medical systems.

into the others. This is the essential means through which the Cosmo-logical or Kabalistical system of correspondences yields to the Cosmo-logician's insight into all things. All things are subsumed under one of 4 essential universal categories through the 4th sphere's ability to see analogies. Readers desiring to acquire a magnificent working knowledge of this sphere should study the Taoist and Five Elements principles of Chinese medicine. The synthetical or abstract unifying functions of Kamitic hieroglyphs is thoroughly shown in part 3 of this book in the section dealing with the Metu Neter oracle.

Stage III of Man's Evolution

The Ba Man

Once the faculties of the Ab division of the spirit are perfected, the person is able to move on to raising her consciousness to the divisions of the spirit wherein dwell Man's God-like faculties. The third division of the spirit -the Shekem- enables the person to influence the course of physical events through the use of words of power (mantras, hekau). These powers cannot be used as long as the person is under the control of emotions and appetites, as the words of power work through the latter. When consciousness rises to the Khu division of the spirit, the person acquires wisdom and the power to learn from within his spirit. Again we arrive at a block upon which most men have stumbled. Their definition of wisdom as erudition, sagacity, discernment, insight and so on is either false or tells us nothing about it. The well read student of spiritual science would most likely be acquainted with the common description of meditation as a process of "emptying the mind of thoughts." The reason for this is rooted in what was said of the faculties of the Sahu and the animal division of the spirit. As long as there are thoughts embodying the definitions (hearsay) that we have been taught, supposedly telling us what things are and are not--"Man is a rational animal." "He ascended from the apes." "Foods have nothing to do with healing," etc.--we can never truly arrive at the knowledge of reality. All that we can ever know are the symbols--the verbal or visual thoughts--that interpose themselves between us and the reality we are trying to know. There is a point of adeptship in meditation where we are able to elevate the *focus of our consciousness* above the sphere of thought manifestations. In the absence of thoughts, consciousness is able then to directly perceive the reality it is trying to know.

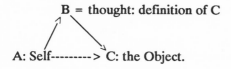

B = thought: definition of C

A: Self--------- > C: the Object.

In the above diagram, AB corresponds to the perception of the thought-the symbol representing C, i.e., its definition or description. If we do not suppress the "AB" manifestation, everytime we want to know "C," the reality itself, what we get is "B"-a stand in for C. We will always be trapped, as "B" could be false, or if correct, it can never fully embody the reality of C. At best, definitions and descriptions provide no more insight than that received by the three blind men who felt, each, a part of an elephant and concluded-the first, that it was a tree trunk (he felt a leg), the second, that it was a wall (he felt the stomach), and the third, that it was a snake (he felt the trunk). The "AC" line corresponds to the direct perception of the object that enables one to see the reality itself, without symbols (thoughts) interposing themselves and distorting the perception of reality.

Knowledge, then, is achieved by the direct perception of reality. It is an act of understanding without the use of thoughts. The reader should take time out from time to time to engage in the practice of suppressing the process of thought formation. It will be discovered that thinking is a process of giving verbal form to a reality that is already known but lacks verbal form. Of course you are well aware of the countless times in which you knew a fact--a person's name, an answer to a question, a telephone number--but couldn't reclothe it in verbal form. You know it but are not in-formed at the time! These are extremely far-reaching points to be pursued in the chapters on meditation. The ability to suspend thinking, enables the omniscience that Man shares with God--in truth, God's knowledge-- to manifest itself through the 2nd sphere. When this knowledge embodies a directive for Man's actions, then it becomes the true will that must be followed.

The focusing of consciousness in the Ba, the highest division of the spirit, enables the person to realize that his Self is one and the same as that dwelling in all things, as well as being one with God. One becomes, then, an Ausar.

113

We shall now turn our attention to how the three types of men, according to the faculties shaping their behavior express themselves in the areas of self knowledge, religion, government, economics, and education.

Knowledge of Self vs. Beliefs regarding Self

One of the most important teachings to come out of Kamit is that Man must place the utmost importance in the quest of knowing his Self. The unsuspecting might believe that the acquiring of knowledge of Self is a simple act of studying the appropriate literature. But we have already seen in the earlier part of this chapter that the Sahu Man is incapable of acquiring knowledge, which depends on the second division of the spirit, which is awakened and developed in the Ausar Man. Unless we experience our "true self," we can only believe what we are taught. We have already pointed out that although the spiritual traditions of most nations are in agreement that Man is made in the likeness of God-- i.e., that God and Man share the same essential qualities of being-- there is nothing in the experience of the person who has not evolved above the 4th sphere to give evidence to this "fact." The evolved Man directly experiences--knows--his divinity in the same manner that we all experience our arms, legs, etc. Intellection is neither required or useful. It is obvious then that we cannot teach Self knowledge in this, or any other book. We can only provide information regarding it, and the steps toward its realization. A classical technique for the direct experience of Self has been preserved by the tantric Buddhists of Tibet[7] in the Great Tar Lam Yoga (Path Without Form), or the Mahamudra Yoga (The Yoga of the Simultaneously-born Great Symbol) as it is known in India[8]. The yogi assumes a cultivated posture that guarantees full relaxation, and the unimpeded flow of energy. He then engages in a special form of deep diaphragmatic breathing--pot shaped breathing--which withdraws the focal point of consciousness from the senses, and induces a state of trance characterized by a state in which the mental wakefulness is as much as 50 times the norm, yet the person is asleep to the physical world or fully detached from it. In this state the

---

7. It must always be kept in mind that the wisdom tradition of Tibet was taught to them by the Blacks of India--the Dravidians.

8. Tibetan Yoga And Secret Doctrines, Edited by W. Y. Evans-Wentz, Oxford University Press, 1958

meditator assumes an attitude of complete indifference to the thoughts that enter and leave the sphere of awareness. There is no attempt to engage in thinking--organizing thoughts to a meaningful end--or following up thoughts, and ideas that present themselves. This meditation process leads to several experiences.

1. There is the clear experience that:

    a. There is an entity that is conscious of the thoughts. Although this entity can perceive, it cannot be perceived.

    b. The thoughts come and go independent of the entity that is perceiving them. This fact, which we have all experienced is magnified by our inability to suppress thoughts by merely willing it, or by those situations when we are trying to recall well known things to memory and can't.

    c. The realization that the rate at which thoughts manifest, the manner in which they are organized (analytically, synthetically, etc.), and the dependence of their contents (concrete, or abstract thoughts) on the breathing (the spirit!)[9], leads to the knowledge that thought activity is processed by the spirit ("mind"), and not by the will.

Now, this entity that sees, hears, smells, tastes and feels, yet, cannot itself be perceived, is the Self. And the goal of the Yoga of the Simultaneously-born Great Symbol--the Mahamudra--is to clearly separate the "Seer" from the objects of perception, and the formative basis of objects of perception (the spirit, "mind"). The great problem in life, the great impediment to Self knowledge is the general misperception that one is one's body, feelings, mind, etc. Once it is clear that thoughts rise into one's sphere of awareness independent of oneself, it is then impossible to identify with the host of thoughts that profess to describe, or define our being; "I am shy," "strong," "sick," etc. And once it is clear that thoughts arise from our bodies (various divisions of our spirit), it becomes impossible to identify our spirit as our Self. We realize that that which is conscious cannot be perceived itself because it is immaterial--our Self. These experiences have many implications for our day to day existence.

---

9. In reality the thoughts themselves do not change. The manipulation of the breath (spirit) causes the focal point of consciousness to be transferred from one division of the spirit to another.

When there is Self-knowledge there is the direct experience that the essence of one's being is unconditioned, therefore, one's true Self lacks predetermined automatic behavioral response patterns. There are no automatic thought and emotional reflexes to impel or compel us to act in predetermined ways, because our consciousness is focused, then, in the Subjective Realm where the energy/matter that is the basis of all creation is undifferentiated, infinite and eternal. This is the foundation of the meaning of the statement that Man is the likeness of God.

When there is knowledge of Self, there is also the direct experience that for one to incarnate to experience earthly life for its own sake, or to enjoy and suffer for the sake of one's person, in the end makes no sense- especially if life is limited to one life-span. The evolved Man ostensively experiences that his spirit and physical body are not personal properties. Not only is Man made in the likeness of God, but his life belongs to God. Man has been given the same qualities--same kind of powers--because it is God's intention, and sole purpose in making Man, to use his spirit and body in order to enter and live in his creation. This is the true meaning of the "Glory being done on Earth, as it is done in Heaven." These divine powers are not for the purpose of occult, psychic display, or for the magical accomplishment of our earthly desires, but for the furthering of God's divine plan.

If our true self is the likeness of God, then what must we call that part or those parts of our being that in the early part of our evolution we identify with, but are not the likeness of God? The term "person," coined for this purpose, which literally means "through" (per), and "sound" (son, sona), implies that a part of our being serves to convey (per) a sound (sona). This insight, which is totally alien to Westerners, would make full sense to a present day Dravidian[10], or to an ancient Kamitian, as it is a common practice in their religion to teach people how to manifest any personality type through the use of words of power (metaphysical sound technology). Why would a word that is compounded of *sound* + *through* be used to indicate people's "self-image"? Skeptics must ponder this question; see if they can come up with an alternative answer. St John's words are even more provocative. He states in the New Testament of the Christian Bible, that "In the beginning was the Word, and the word was God, and that the word became flesh and came to dwell among Men." Putting aside the argument that this

10. The Dravidians are the Blacks who authored the Yogic, and tantric tradition.

116

"word" is Jesus, we must ask why is he being equated with "a word that is God, and enters flesh?." As for the word being Jesus, there is nothing that he has done that had not been done and taught by Sages before and after him. In fact others have done more, and have given the world a better spiritual system. That is another story that we must leave alone, for there is no space, nor interest here to go into the questions surrounding the veracity of his existence; the fact that many of the teachings--the Sermon on the Mount, for example-- credited to him are thousands of years older than he, and so forth. What is of greatest importance is the fact that in the midst of the attempts to render Jesus a unique individual--the one and only Son of God--the authors slip and make Jesus state that all Men will do greater things, in reference to the miracles which were supposed to be the evidence of his divinity, thus revealing the divinity in all men; the third sphere of the Tree of Life in this case.

John was not the only one, or the first to equate "the word" with "God," a fact that has gone without comment from biblical scholars. Faithful to the tantric tradition of the Blacks of India, in the translation of their sacred scriptures, Arthur Avalon in the *Serpent Power* states:

> Each man is Shiva (a deity,-Ausar), and can attain his power to the degree of his ability to consciously realize himself as such. For various purposes the Devata (deities) are invoked. Mantra (a word of power) and Devata are one and the same . . . By practice (japa) with the mantra the presence of the Devata is invoked. Japa or repetition of the mantra is compared to the action of a man shaking a sleeper to wake him up.

When a word of power (deity) is awakened and becomes functional in our "psyche," we manifest the personality expression that belongs to that particular deity/mantra. Along with its personality traits, we gain possession of its talents and occult powers. We shall see in future chapters that each of the so-called human mental functions and talents are in reality the expression of the deities. Once this is understood, then it will be clear that the ancients and Africans do not "anthropomorphize their Gods." It is the other way around. That the Gods resemble Man is because Man is made in the likeness of God and the host of metaphysical intelligences (Gods) that It has created through which to make and administer the world.

117

That we can take on any of the personality types through the manipulation of mantras (words of power) is the logical conclusion of the fact that we are made in the likeness of God. Our true Self is no-things, hence capable of assuming any personality type, of knowing, and accomplishing all things,--through time. It is of interest to note that while the common western belief that each Man has a personality, the Kamitic tradition states that each Man has, in addition to his Self, seven personalities- Kau (the plural of Ka, the Kamitic word for the person and personality), and must learn to give full expression to all of them; just not the *natal personality* that dominates the early part of our incarnation.

Religion

An analysis of the word "religion" shows that it is composed of the Latin prefix "re," meaning, "again, back" + "ligare," meaning "tie, bind, fasten." From the preceding we have seen that the Sahu man, because he has not evolved above the 7th sphere, is incapable of intuiting the "ties" between things. Thus, he is the Man that is in need of religious instruction to tie, bind, or fasten him back to something with which he had originally been one, and belonged to by natural connectivity. The original oneness is implied by the prefix "re" (back, again). It is important to note that the word "Yoga" also bears a similar meaning--"to yoke," "to unite"-- although it lacks the meaning component of the prefix for "again." The things he has lost his oneness with are the Supreme Being, other men, other creatures, and all other things in/as the world. It also signifies the inability to unite the will with the spirit at will. As he identifies with his physical body (E.g., when it dies he thinks he has died, when it is sick he thinks he is sick, etc.) he believes that he is a separate existence, and thus looks out for himself at the expense of the whole. Just the opposite is true for the Ausar Man. As he has developed the 1st sphere of the Tree of Life he does not need religious instruction, as it is the natural function of this faculty to intuit and establish unity amongst all things in/as the world. He is already "tied, bound, fastened" as a natural essence of his being. What is already tied cannot be, nor need be "re-tied."

The term "religion" is also related to the Indo-European root "leg," meaning "to collect," from whence the Greek "legein," and the Latin "legere," meaning "logic," and "legal (law)." The men who coined the word therefore had in mind that it is a system to "collect, or unite things that belong together by logic, and natural law (hence, it is scientific)." Once more, it is clear that it is the Sahu Man who is in need of instructions regarding the legitimate and logical ties between things. As the fourth sphere of the Tree is the faculty wherein is understood the laws that govern and connect things and events, Ab men, who have developed this faculty are truly able to practice religion.

Unfortunately, the issue is not confined to the education of Sahu Man in religious matters. As religion is a natural product and function of the higher faculties 0 - 6, it can only be truly practiced by people who have brought forth these faculties. When it is taught to Sahu Men, they cannot help but bring it down to their level of perception. If the first and 4th spheres within one are dormant, the most that one can achieve is the *belief* in the teachings regarding the oneness underlying all events, as opposed to the actual knowledge of it. The experience, and thus the capacity to live according to the shaping forces of unity is lacking. This is the reason for the fact that there are so many bigots, haters, and segregationists in high religious places. They comprehend the doctrine of oneness, but find it impossible to live it, earning thus the smear of hypocrisy. In reality they are not. There is nothing inside of them that can respond to the religious values on their true level. The light shines in the darkness, which fails to comprehend it.

When we consider the fact that the Sahu Man is dominated by mental faculties that cannot perceive the unity between things, then it is easy to see how his attempt to practice religion is full of fatal contradictions. Despite religion's central theme of unity, we find him invoking God to aid him in vanquishing his "enemies;" claiming that God has given him the right to enslave the generations of Ham (Black people); claiming that women cannot hold the highest religious offices, etc.

The fact that Sahu Man is unable to truly understand abstract categories shows up in his misunderstanding of the term "God." To him, the term "God" represents a concrete entity, hence his use of the term as a proper noun. In the African tradition, the term is an abstract relational category. Like the terms "governor," "president," etc., it denotes all that "presides" or has dominion over a sphere of activity. The African scholar, therefore, has no problem in understanding that a Supreme God (presider) can create and administer the world through a number of agencies to whom have been delegated dominion or presidency or governorship or godship over specific spheres of activities. This is no different from the hierarchical administration of the physiological functions of our bodies, or of the government of a nation, business, etc. Once we understand the categorical relational abstractness of the term "God," then we are in a position to understand how Man and God are of the same category of being, and that *so-called polytheism is in reality a Systheism; that is, a whole (Supreme God) compounded of several integral parts (gods) acting in concert with each other to fulfill the will of the Whole.* But the Sahu faculties (spheres 7 - 9) cannot perceive the connection between things, and fails, thus, to see the unity between "the gods" with each other, and with the Supreme God. As they close their minds at the outset to all teachings that expound the deities, they fail to avail themselves of the assistance that such knowledge can bring to them. Imagine a person who believes that all of his problems must be solved by the Supreme leader--the president--of the country. When Sahu Man sees Ausar men healing and affecting nature through the power of their spirit (3rd sphere) he then talks ignorantly, but fluently of course, about "miracles," "the supernatural," "spiritual gifts," "only Son of God," etc.

If the etymological and semantical structure of the word "religion" shows that the term denotes a system for tying back, reuniting elements that lawfully belong together, then what can we say for Sahu Man's definition of the term. There is nothing in the semantical structure of the word that directly supports its being defined as "an expression of the belief in and reverence for an eternal being that creates and controls the destiny of the world." It cannot be argued that this is a description of an important aspect of religious expression, but it is not the definition of the word itself. History has shown quite well that men have found it extremely easy to profess their faith in the existence and power of God, to feel a great reverence, and devotion to God, while actively nurturing their sense of disunity from other men and other departments of nature. What would the course of history be, had the world religions placed into the foreground the unifying--yogic, yoking, at-onement-- principle that is essential to the definition of religion?   Let's remember that this unity cannot be achieved by the intellectual assimilation of the appropriate literature, but by the spiritual practices that result in the raising of one's consciousness to the higher divisions of our spirit. Consequently, we must also change our outlook regarding the process of worshiping. While Sahu Man's worship is an act of veneration, love and admiration for the Deity, the Ab and Ba Men add to this, the cultivation of the moral virtues, and spiritual practices that culminate in the elevation of consciousness to the higher parts of the spirit wherein dwell the faculties that Man shares in common with God. No one can be saved by living a sinful life, breaking the laws of nature, then begging God for forgiveness. Nothing short of living a God-like life will do.

Regarding the scriptures, we are told that they were acquired through the divine inspiration of particular men. Once we have acquired true knowledge of Self, we will know that all Men are capable of intuiting divine wisdom through the agency of the second division of their spirit (the Khu and 2nd sphere), once they have awakened and developed this faculty. But Sahu man lives with the impression that the reception of scriptural information is a phenomenon that is limited to a very few men of the past. Can anything be more absurd? Spiritual guidance is to be found outside of his self, he believes. So he does not strive to contact the source of wisdom within himself. Imagine what the world would be like, if most men, during the past 6000 years, were striving to perfect themselves in order to manifest the wisdom, and spiritual power that lies within them. It is interesting to note that the religion of African people, from ancient Egypt to the present sub-Saharan cultures, is characterized by the practice by priests and priestesses of going into trance to contact the source of wisdom to guide people, and the source of spiritual power in order to assure success in the events of life. We shall have a great deal more to say about this later.

A major theme that we find in some religions revolve around the issue of Man's salvation from "a power of evil." As such religions are essentially aimed at, and are the products of Sahu Man, both, the power of evil that Man must be saved from, and God upon whom the salvation depends, are conceived as being separate from Man. In the African traditions, especially those of Kamit, Indus Kush, and Canaan we find the teaching that Man's failure to control the lower part of his being is the source of all of his problems. His salvation does not depend on claiming belief in a divinity, nor membership in a religious system, nor from the intervention of some entity outside of himself. It depends on his elevation and establishment of his consciousness in the higher part of his spirit which is the likeness of the Supreme Being. Instead of a religion of an essentially sinful, ignorant, and impotent being who cannot transcend these character traits, and must thus remain so and seek the assistance of a divine being, the African tradition encourages the individual to strive daily toward manifesting his higher nature. In the Sahu type religion, the Man must succumb to sinful behavior with the hope that he will be somehow forgiven. His sins are excused as

121

the work of something separate from and outside of his being--Satan. But research into the subject will reveal that the Satan of the Christian religion is a perversion of the Kamitic symbol "Set" that depicts the expression of the combined behavior of Man's rational and artistic faculties in the service of his sensuous nature. The segregative way of thinking, the perception limited to externals, and the domination by the sensuous nature which characterize the behavior of Sahu Man, are the irreligious factors, verily, that Man must be saved from. All moral decrees are aimed at them. And all fire and brimstone dooms day, waiting in ambush of the wayward soul, as taught by some religions, find their rationale, if not justification, in the fact that Sahu Man only understands the language of the animal part of the spirit. Emotions (affection, kindness, fear, pain, etc.) are, ultimately, the coercers and persuaders of his behavior.

Once we understand the true nature of Man's spirit--that it is made up of seven divisions--it will be plain to see that a true religion can only be a system that aims at raising Man's focus of consciousness to the higher divisions of his spirit to allow him to function in a God-like manner. Not only are the religions aimed at Sahu Man lacking in this perspective, they even lack words for the various parts of the spirit, let alone know that it is a composite entity that contains both the saving and damning parts of Man's being. But things have gotten even worse. With each passing day, we find more and more Sahu people assuming the role of leadership in religious matters and in the world.

Economics

Economics deals with how people can best share the natural resources of the earth, the human resources (labor, skills) for mobilizing the earthly resources, and the rewards of their labor. It is important to note that the Sahu Men, who are today in control of the economy of the world, classify it as a science, as opposed to a system of ethics. When Ab and Ba Men are in control of the economy of a society, the sense of oneness (unity, 'ligion) between men, and between man and nature are the dominant principles. All efforts are made to make sure that the wealth is distributed in proportion to peoples' efforts, skills, and social (spiritual) responsibility. It is not surprising that the western world, which is built around Sahu principles, would invent an economic device that would enable wealth to be concentrated in the hands of certain individuals in total contravention to the ethics of fairness. This device is the prime use to which money has been put. Basically, it is created out of nothing (simply printed), made available to an elite circle--many of whom control its very creation--who in turn use it to acquire ownership over the lion's share of the natural resources, the means of production and the vehicles of violence, in order to impose their will on others. That it is an extremely efficient and successful means of mobilizing human resources cannot be denied. But the absence of moral restraints, which gives the highest priorities to turning a profit, results in the fouling of the earth, the waste of precious natural resources, the waste of the world's genius and lives, in the extravagant pursuit of trivia. 75% plus of manufactured goods is not only unnecessary, it is waste of natural resources that will be sorely missed in decades to come. All those trivial plastic products, for example, divert materials from which drugs can be manufactured. All the human efforts expended in the mastery of manufacturing, marketing, etc. of these trivial things are at the expense of the time and energy needed for the moral and spiritual development of the citizens of the world. The result is that police states are becoming more and more necessary for the maintenance of order, due to the moral vacuum that has been created.

Government

When consciousness rises to the Ab or higher levels of the spirit, it understands that the purpose of government is to coordinate the various self interests amongst the individuals making up a nation, to promote the equilibrium between the needs of the individual and of the group. The only means of achieving these ends is religion (as the semantics of the term shows, its purpose is to re-unite). It is the working of the segregative mental functions of the faculties of the Sahu and Khaibit (animal spirit) that are responsible for the selfishness (segregativeness) that characterizes the governmental systems of Sahu Men. Their governmental systems are primarily means of securing and protecting the economic advantages, and privileges of the "elite." As this cannot be done in the presence of a true religion, then the latter must be banished from government. Law and order must come, then, from the use of force. Incidentally, this, like all fallacies[11], is a lost cause. There will never be enough

11. All evils have their built in self destructive mechanisms!

money, for the hiring of enough law enforcement people, many of whom are crooked themselves, and for the achievement of a significant level of social order. It cannot be policed, nor forced into being. The shaping forces of law and order must emanate from within people's spirit. To separate government from religion is to betray not only the incapacity to govern, but the total ignorance of the meaning of the word and the subject. In the social correspondences of the Tree of Life system, the king is represented by the sixth sphere. It is located in the very center of the Tree in order to carry out its coordinating function. In the Kamitic tradition, it is Heru (Shango, in the Yoruba) who must defeat Set--the creator of a governmental system in which the lower intellect's (spheres 7-9) main function is to rationalize the sensual and emotional gratification of the animal spirit (sphere 10).

Education

The men who coined the term "education" to denote the process of training, had in mind a procedure in which something is being "lead, or drawn out," as the etymology of the word shows; from "educere" <e- out + ducere, to lead, draw, bring>. It is obvious that there is nothing in Sahu Men's common understanding of the term education that relates to the process it symbolizes. Western education does not "draw out," but seeks to put something into the minds of people. In contrast, the Kamitic system of education focused on drawing out of the spirit its dormant talents and spiritual powers. Unlike Western education which seeks to teach people to make better things, the African traditional educational system aims at making better people. This will explain the low interest, hence low output of technological wizardry of Africans. That they are fully capable of rising to the challenge is more than proven by the great contributions that they have made to civilization, especially in laying down its foundations.

Chapter 9

The Spiritual Cultivation of Man

At the very beginning, I must call the reader's attention to the fact that I am using the concept of "spiritual cultivation" as an alternative to the concepts of "religion" and "religious systems." This is made necessary by the common misconceptions that surround the two latter terms. Of these, one of the most important misconceptions is the belief that all groups of people have a religious consciousness, and the other, is the belief that under the surface of the differences between religious systems that they are all essentially the same, or at least aspire to the same goal, or ultimately worship the same God. The falsehood of these beliefs will be proven as the material of this chapter and subsequent ones unfold. The key is provided when we consider the fact that we can evaluate all religions, or people's claim of having it, by their degree of spiritual growth.

What is spiritual culture, its chief methods, and goal are defined by the essential nature of Man, which we saw is the "likeness of God." When Man is born, his consciousness is confined to the three lower divisions of his spirit--the physical, animal, and concrete intellectual (Sahu) divisions of the spirit. As these irrational and divisive faculties are the only guides to his consciousness and will, his behavior is subject to error. This is the cause of all that is wrong in the world. Spiritual culture, then, is a system that methodically leads Man's consciousness to the higher parts of his being, wherein dwell those faculties that contain the essence of God's attributes. In short, its goal is to raise his consciousness and spiritual power. The acquirement of wisdom--the intuitive knowledge that frees Man from errors-- and the spiritual power to achieve his will--making criminal acts unnecessary--is the result of achieving the goal of spiritual cultivation. We can already begin to see that not all religions share this understanding and this goal. For some, Man is essentially a sinner--i.e., confined to his animal spirit and concrete intellect--and can therefore only be saved by the intervention of a saviour outside of himself, or can only be kept from doing wrong by threats of a doomsday, or eternal damnation that awaits the sinner. In the traditions of Kamit, Canaan (its Kabalistical teachings), and Black (Dravidian) India, Man's salvation can only be achieved by the elevation of his consciousness to the higher part of his being, and the

125

increase of his spiritual power that he may be free of the limitations of the physical world. Ignorance and impotence are the father and mother, respectively, of all evils in the world.

The exact manner in which the spiritual cultivation of Man is to be undertaken--the schedule and the method--is shown, once more, by the Tree of Life and the metaphorein (incorrectly called myth) of Ausar, which, incidentally, is the oldest recorded initiation doctrine known to Mankind. I have adapted the Greek term "metapherein" to "metaphorein" to coin a new term to be used in place of the term "myth." The distinction cannot be encapsulated by a mere definition. As you read through the following chapters you will realize that these stories don't fit neatly into the category of allegories, neither do they bear much similarity to the myths of Rome, Greece, the Middle East, etc. When they are related to the Tree of Life, and to its related initiation and meditation systems, they will be seen to be poetically rendered, spiritual, scientific principles. According to the story, in the most ancient of times a Kamitic king named Ausar discovered the method of raising his consciousness to the highest division of his spirit, and increasing his spiritual power to its highest potential (spheres 0, 1, 2, and 3). As a result he was able to bring civilization--a spiritually controlled way of life--to the people, with its accompanying social harmony, peace, and prosperity. The reader must recall what was said in previous chapters regarding the Ba, or Ausar Man. Order in the land was maintained by a system that effectively developed the moral faculties in people, and by allowing only such men and women who had developed their moral faculties (spheres 4, 5, and 6) to hold positions of government.

It wasn't long before his youngest brother, Set--symbol of the dedication of our intellectual faculties (logical and artistic) to the service of the sensuous, and emotional nature--became jealous of all the adulation and homage paid to Ausar. Driven by his lust for power, and the rebelliousness of the animal spirit against the order and laws imposed by Ausar, Set, with the assistance of a confederacy of no-gooders (the Sebau, from Sebek, Deity of the 8th sphere), killed Ausar. They then hacked his body into fourteen pieces, and scattered them all over the land. It is said that a shrine to a Deity emerged at each place where a part of his body fell. Those with understanding will grasp what is implied regarding "polytheism." With Ausar out of the way, Set usurped the Kingship, and proceeded to terrorize the world. He created the first empire--rule of a foreign power over others--and replaced the system of maintaining social

126

order through moral cultivation with a policing system; as symbolized by the fragmenting of the body of Ausar into pieces, he separated religion from the state, education, separated God from nature, from Man, separated spirit from physical matter, the divine from the mundane--in short, he instituted an insidious system of dividing and segregating all things and people from each other and the whole. In short, he alienated Man from God, the world, and himself. Set's rule, of course, is that of all Sahu men, on the social level, and the rule of the faculties of the animal spirit and Sahu (spheres 7, 8, and 9) parts of the spirit in all men.

Everyone, Deities included, feared him. He was invincible in war and violence, which were his chief means of settling differences, as well as the objects of his worship. No one opposed him. Many even basked in the material pleasures with which he bought them off--all except Ausar's two youngest sisters--Auset and Nebt-Het (9th and 7th spheres, respectively). They searched for, and found the dismembered parts of Ausar's body, reunited them, wrapped the body in white linen (as a mummy), and buried his body at the bottom of the river. They set for his protection, the great serpent Kematef (Kundalini).

Some say that with the words of power given to her by Tehuti, others say that with Ausar's choicest part, she immaculately conceived a son--Heru--to Ausar, who as a legitimate heir to the throne could challenge Set, who had usurped it. And as in the Christian myth, which was copied from the Ausarian metaphorein thousands of years later, Set, hearing about the birth of a king who would challenge his reign and save the kingdom, sent his agents out to find and kill the child. But Auset was able to elude them and raise Heru to manhood.

Grown into full manhood, he engaged Set in a series of battles that lasted for hundreds of years. Victory slipped in and out of the hands of each combatant. But this stalemate was a victory to Set, for as long as morality and spirituality did not rule the world, he was achieving his goal.

Eventually Heru learned of the existence of a Deity that Set could not bother, who remained aloof of the events going on in the world. This Deity, Tehuti, it was written, was the only one that could guide Heru to a sure victory over Set. Heru sought his guidance, and was thus able to defeat Set. It was not accomplished militarily, but in the court of law, where Set was tricked into accepting the very laws that he had deviced to enslave others--"maintaining law and order," he called it. As one of Set's strong points was communication (Sebek--the 8th sphere was his main component), his penalty was to serve as the wind that propels the boat of Ausar-- i.e., to disseminate the wisdom of Ausar throughout the worlds.

The kingdom of Neter (God) was now reestablished with Heru as the king, but guided by Ausar, whom he "reawakened," or "resuscitated," from time to time. This can only be understood by taking note of the fact that it describes the foundation of the African system of divine kingship. At prescribed times, rituals are performed by the African kings (Heru) and their royal priesthood to communicate with the spirits of the deceased kings (the Ausars) in order to receive their advice. This type of ritual is incorrectly called by Western scholars "ancestor worship." It must be called *Ancestor communication rituals*.

The meaning of the Ausarian metaphorein has different levels of application.

The Ausarian Metaphorein
In the Spiritual Evolution of the Individual

1. Ausar established order, harmony, and prosperity: It is the Ausar--sphere one--within us that unites and harmonizes all of the separate functions in our body, enabling them to work as one. It is this metaphysical nucleus--God manifested within us--that coordinates the development of the human being from the very moment following conception. At the center of all acts of creation, whether they are of a galaxy or of an atom, is the Supreme Being-- who/what else? All questions regarding abortion must consider this fact, and can only be resolved by a master of cosmogonical law.

2. Ausar is killed by Set who usurps the Kingdom: Although our divine Self (Ausar) is present at all times of our life, it cannot make its presence felt because we are born with our consciousness focused in the lower part of our being (Spheres 7 - 10). The domination of our lives by our emotions (sphere 10--Khaibit, the animal part of the spirit), and the Sebek faculty (8th sphere) is symbolized by "Set's" usurpation of the Kingdom of Ausar. We dedicate our lives to the gratification of our emotions and desires. What we do, want, how we do it, etc. is dictated by our likes and dislikes. And since our passions and sensual desires are not guides to what is correct, or beneficial, we create a great deal of trouble for ourselves, and others.

3. Ausar's body is cut into fourteen pieces, and spread over the land giving rise to shrines: This corresponds to the loss of the sense of unity (religion) that accompanies the suppression of our Ausar faculty by the lower parts of the spirit. In past chapters we saw how the domination of our consciousness by the 8th sphere (Sebek) results in our segregation of the whole into unrelated pieces. Doctors separate healing from nutrition, scientists separate God from nature, psychologists separate the spirit from the body, and so on. Later in this chapter we will take a look at the integral system for the spiritual cultivation of Man which has been separated by many cultures (some Africans included) into stand-alone spiritual systems (shrines). The Sebek faculty also creates concepts that lack objective reality; X is "a medicine," Y is "a poison," there is "a devil" fighting for the soul of people, etc.

4. Auset and Nebt-Het collect the pieces of his body and bury it at the bottom of a river, and protect it with the serpent Kematef: This section deals with the beginning of the process of reintegrating Man's consciousness through the functions of mediumistic trance (Auset), and creative visualization (Nebt-Het, Het-Heru) one-pointedly (devotion) directed at reestablishing Ausar as the dominant faculty in our lives. That Ausar is buried at the bottom of a river symbolizes that he is accessible only through trance. His being guarded by the great serpent Kematef (Kundalini) means that the type of trance that will awaken him has to be of the ecstatic modality.

5. Through the use of words of power, Auset immaculately conceives and gives birth to Heru who is heir to the usurped throne of Ausar: Heru, we learned, is the will of Man. It is awakened by taking into ecstatic trance our devotion to reestablishing our divine Self, through the aid of the appropriate words of power (Hri, Hru, Hrau, etc.). It is an immaculate conception because it is a manifestation of our spirit that does not result in ourselves creating or reinforcing conditionings within our spirit. Normally, every goal in our life depends on our creation or reinforcement of a habit (conditioned state of the spirit). This is important from the standpoint that our ultimate goal is to liberate our spirit from the compulsion of all conditionings superimposed upon it.

6. Set sends his agents to look for and kill the boy-king: This symbolizes the antagonistic reaction of our animal spirit, and lower intellect toward our efforts to alter our behavior pattern to reflect the values of our higher divine nature. Most people are comfortable with "spiritual culture" as long as it does not entail giving up their likes and dislikes, following a teacher, living in harmony with cycles, interacting with things in a purposeful manner, etc. This stage

129

cannot be understood unless we adhere to the definition previously given regarding the true purpose of Man's will. Freedom of choice-- the exercise of the will--is not the freedom to chart the course of our destiny, but our ability to embrace truth, or the lower part of our being (opinions, emotions)--to undertake actions that are in or out of harmony with the whole. So at this stage, when the will of Man begins to make its presence felt, either as a result of spiritual instruction or the trance work of the previous stage, he often rebels against the higher values. There is a dichotomy between what he believes or understands, and what he feels.

7. Grown into full manhood Heru engages Set into battle but cannot achieve anymore than a stalemate, which ultimately is failure: This corresponds to the use of the will to fight the lower part of being. Its inability to defeat it--it wins some battles and loses others--is caused by the fact that the will is being guided by the very faculties it is trying to bring under its control. For example, you resist an emotion or desire because you are afraid of getting caught. There is a failure to understand that as long as you are motivated by an emotion (fear of getting caught, of being embarrassed, of dying, of going to jail, etc.), you cannot successfully oppose "undesirable" emotions and desires, because in each case you are being controlled by the emotional part of the spirit.

8. Heru is able to defeat Set with Tehuti's assistance: At this stage, the will is guided by the wisdom of Tehuti--through meditation, counsel from Sages, and oracles--which, as we learned, is the Will of God.

9. Set's penalty: As the core of Set's being is the 8th sphere--Sebek-- which is our faculty of communication, Set's penalty is to disseminate the wisdom of Ausar throughout the world.

10. The reestablished kingdom of God: Here the individual realizes his divinity and becomes a Sage. His words and teachings serve to guide others to the life of peace, love and prosperity.

The Metaphorein of Ausar in the Spiritual Evolution of Society

1. Ausar established order, harmony, and prosperity: This is symbolical of the fact that the nations that established civilization were governed by religion and a higher moral code than exist in contemporary--so-called modern--societies. It is interesting to note that imperialism--the subjection of a foreign nation by another--did not occur until the coming of the Semites to Mesopotamia. It started with Sargon I of Akkad. Until then, the great powers Kamit,

Sumer, Kush, Harappa, Mohenjo Daro, and Elam lived in relative peace with one another. Skirmishes and quarrels over routes, etc. existed for sure. But never did they set out to plunder, destroy, or subjugate each other. Neither did they go up to the north to enslave or exploit the militarily weak Caucasian.

2. Ausar is killed by Set who usurps the Kingdom: This corresponds to the period since the coming of the Eurasian to Western Asia (Mesopotamia), India, Africa, the Mediterranean, and later to the rest of the southern and western hemispheres. The conquerors reinterpret the religious teachings and cultural elements of the ancient civilizations in light of their level of understanding, biases, interests, etc. Motivation of human behavior is no longer through moral cultivation, but through fear and violence. Spiritual values are replaced by crass materialism, etc. We know the story well.

3. Ausar's body is cut into fourteen pieces, and is spread over the land giving rise to shrines: This speaks of the dispossession of the people from their land by the conquerors and their dispersion throughout the world. In a more significant manner, it refers to the breaking up of the integral spiritual initiation system into its components, and their being spread over the world as separate "religious systems." We will see later that the great initiation systems of Kamit, and Canaan were composed of 10 major stages and 23 minor (the so-called 33 degrees of Masonry) ones. Once these nations came under attack, signalling the beginning of the end, as their prophets had foretold, they began to send priests with their shrines into different parts of the world in order to preserve the teachings.

4. Auset and Nebt-Het collect the pieces of his body and bury it at the bottom of a river, and protect it with the serpent Kematef: This corresponds to the masses' (Auset) adherence to their religious faith, however unsophisticated, and their undying hope for a world of peace, happiness, and plenty.

5. Auset immaculately conceives and gives birth to Heru who is heir to the usurped throne of Ausar: The preceding stage eventually leads to the birth of revolutionaries.

6. Set sends his agents to look for and kill the boy-king: This symbolizes the typical reaction of conquerors and oppressors to those who revolt against their immoral rule.

7. Grown into full manhood Heru engages Set into battle but cannot achieve anymore than a stalemate, which ultimately is failure: This is the stage of revolutions in the world. But it does not lead to success, as one dies by the sword if one lives by it. Might,

131

however justified or unavoidable, does not make for right. We are presently at this stage in our social development.

8. Heru is able to defeat Set with Tehuti's assistance: At this stage, moral and legal values are wedded to serve as a basis for adjudicating the international and social conflicts in the world. The blatancy of the hypocrisy of the conquerors will be a major factor in the resolution of these conflicts as they will be shown to be in constant violation of the very laws that they propose for others. For this to take place there must be a philosophical and moral restructuring of the United Nations. The oracles (Ifa, Metu Neter, I Ching, and Dilogun) will play a major background role in the restructuring of the philosophical principles that will dominate in scholarly, religious, and governmental circles.

9. Set's penalty: The entire network of communications media will be used to establish and maintain a world order based on the principles embodied in the Tree of Life.

10. The reestablished Kingdom of God: This is a way of life where all things are in unity with each other. Peace, harmony, and prosperity will prevail. But . . . since we could prophesy into our future, it's because we are reading the past. So, the summit of Ausar will not last forever. Nothing on earth does. All is transitory and ephemeral here. Before long, Set will be back. Do not be oppressed. Keep your spirit like the Sun at midday, forever. *"En Aungk Heh, em Hetep."*

Chapter 10

THE TREE OF LIFE INITIATION SYSTEM

AN OUTLINE

While metaphoric stories like the Ausarian system explained in the preceding chapter enables us to get an integral understanding of a complex process, they do not lend themselves to giving the details and precision that are necessary for carrying out the process. For this we must go to the Tree of Life.

Sphere 10, Geb, the Khaibit (animal part of the spirit): This part of the spirit sets the foundation of the problem to be overcome. We are born with this part of our spirit already programmed for the preservation of our survival. Its basic program can be reduced to an attraction (likes, cravings, desire) for what gives us pleasure and a repulsion (displeasure, dislike) for what causes aversion or pain. It is a very rudimentary mechanism that can assist us somewhat efficiently against physical dangers, but if not transcended, it becomes the greatest impediment to our spiritual development. Since we can become in love with things that are not good for us, and hate that which is most beneficial, then this part of the spirit cannot be the guide for what is right or wrong. All that threatens to interfere with our pleasures, or cause pain leads to a response of anger or fear--responses that are not capable of solving problems or conflicts. For this understanding is essential.

Sphere 9, Auset, the foundation of the Sahu part of the spirit: Due to its extreme receptivity, this part of the spirit is greatly affected by the Khaibit (animal spirit). We are more inclined to imitate (learn) those ideas that cater to the domination of the emotions, and imitate the behaviors that portray receptivity and impotence in the face of our emotions and sensuous nature. Crying because of pain, displeasure, anger, etc. Manifesting anger because of contradiction, differences, etc. If the adults in the society into which we are born have transcended the expression of this part of the spirit, then we would have just the opposite as examples to imitate!

Sphere 8, Sebek: It is through this faculty that we become informed. We receive names for things and events, definitions, descriptions, and explanations. An unwise society will fail to teach its citizens the difference between "knowing" (experience of a reality), and "believing acquired information." If people, for example, "knew"

133

what is love, when they said to another "I love you," they could not, for example, manifest anger to another person, for love--an expression of the 4th sphere--is a perpetual expression of joy and optimism that is totally independent of external circumstances. It is giving, not seeking in return. At the 8th sphere, we "know the words," but lack the experience behind the words, so our actions contradict our claims and beliefs. In addition, because the 8th sphere is also receptive to the 10th, and is rooted in the 9th (we imitate the definitions given to us, etc.), we are inclined to accept and incorporate into our belief bag of tricks those ideas that allow us to rationalize ("justify") the dominance of our animal spirit. We go as far as creating a set of complex myths to give power to the animal in us. It is at this point that evil comes into play. All Nonwestern traditions are in agreement that cleverness, deception, and cunning are the fundamental expressions of evil. By evil (deception, etc.) we mean, the invention of names, slogans, concepts, etc. that allow us to gratify and cater to the animal spirit, regardless of the price to our well being, and that of others, and worse, when they, the slogans, etc. are used to exploit and oppress others by manipulating them through the lower part of their being. It is very easy to do in a society that is ignorant of the difference between knowing and believing; that is ignorant of the fact that the possession of information (names, definitions, explanations, and description) is not the possession of knowledge of the reality symbolized by the information. For example, at this level, people receive information (are taught a scripture) regarding God (definition, description, etc.). Because they now confuse the knowledge (experience) of the scripture defining and describing God with the actual knowledge of God they have no qualms about murdering others whom they accuse of paganism, heathenism, etc., because the latter professes a different belief (or experience!) of God. In this book the reader will see all of the challenges that a person must meet before he can qualify himself to have actual knowledge of God, then he can judge for himself. He can take a hint from the fact that this realization takes place at "0" above the Tree of Life!

In short, the disintegrating effect of this part of the human spirit is what enables the person to separate his beliefs from his actions; he worries about his health, yet smokes, and eats junk food (his animal spirit controls him); claims that he is concerned about the health of the public, and its economic well being, yet he spends billions of dollars subsidizing tobacco growers, hospitalization for the cardiac and cancer victims of tobacco, and cancer research, etc.

Deceptions like these, which number in the thousands on all levels are caused by the failure of the individual and the society to transcend this expression of the 8th sphere. This is the one and true Devil. We must remember that the bible defines him as "a deceiver." It is not an arch-enemy of God that is lusting after our souls. It is the immature intellect in man in the service of the emotional and sensuous--the animal--part of the spirit. Earlier we saw that it is called Set in the Kamitic tradition. This is the origin of the Christian Sat-an, even to its color--red.

Sphere 7, Het-Heru: Without knowing it, we integrate the "building blocks" of all that we accomplish through the use of our imagination. This is why we spend a great deal of time visualizing the things we aspire to in life. Unfortunately, what the spiritually uncultivated wants in life, is once more again, dictated by what causes pleasure. Sebek (the 8th sphere) by now has found artful ways--clever words-- of smoothing the way; He substitutes "pleasure" for "happiness," "pleasurable" for "spiritually uplifting," "rebellion against spiritual law, and spiritual teachers" for "the pursuit of liberty," etc. But the glitter of Het-Heru's metal which is copper must not be confused with gold.

These four influences, spheres 10 - 7, seal the way to the spiritual development of the individual. They insure that his consciousness remains imprisoned in the lower part of being (the Sahu and Khaibit divisions of the spirit). But now that we have a technical understanding of the problem, we can proceed to solve it. Underlying the problems to be overcome are two principles, which with the four principles underlying the initiation process itself, yield six principles that must be kept in mind in order to properly understand initiation.

The Two Principles Underlying the Problems to be Overcome through Initiation

1. The identification of the individual with the person or the four lower faculties (spheres 7-10), instead of the Self (0-sphere 3). This can be summarized by the following statement, "I am the person." This is the source of all of Man's problems. The use of summarizing statements such as this one, and others to follow will be fully appreciated when applied to meditation.

2. A struggle to overcome the lower part of being that ends in failure. As the individual is identifying with the person, then the

person is fighting with the person[1]. This corresponds to the ineffectual struggle of Heru against Set. It can be summarized as, "I deny my person to assert my person."

The Four Principles Underlying Initiation

1. Level 1 of initiation, which is carried out in three stages (spheres 9 to 7), corresponds to the return of the individual's identity, away from the person, to the Self (Ausar, spheres 1 & 0) and its faculties (spheres 3 & 2). In the Ausar story it corresponds to Auset's devotion to finding, and reuniting (re-membering) the parts of Ausar's body. It can be summarized as, "I am Ausar."
2. Level 2 of initiation, which is carried out in three stages (spheres 6-4) corresponds to the successful struggle of the individual in opposing the lower part of being--the person. In the course of the meditation work given in this book, it will be shown that the efficacy of the will is not based on power, although the latter plays an auxiliary role, but on the spiritual liberation of the individual, which is ultimately dependent on his identification with the Self (sphere 1, Ausar). This level can be summarized as, "I deny my person to assert my Self." It corresponds to the success of Heru over Set through following Ausar communicating through Tehuti.
3. Level 3 of initiation, which is carried out in three stages (spheres 3-1), corresponds to the actualization of the ability to live as the Self in the world, once the individual has gained total freedom from the lower part of being,- the person. It can be summarized as, "I live as Ausar." This corresponds to Heru's assimilation of the qualities of Ausar after defeating Set.
4. Level 4 of initiation, which is carried out in one stage (0, the Subjective realm), corresponds to the direct insperience of the essential formlessness of one's Being. Until then, all that we had to go on was the intellectual argument to the effect that "in order for us to transcend a particular habit or conditioning, our spirits must be essentially unformed." Here we come face to face with the reality.

The importance of the above outline cannot be overemphasized. I so often come across individuals claiming to be

---

1. This is the true explanation for the so-called inner conflicts that lay people, and psychologists speak so much about. They are prevented, and resolved by the identification of the individual, when trying to transcend the (lower) person, with the (higher) Self.

undergoing initiation, yet they are totally unaware of the fact that the source of their problems is their identification with their persons (the habitual complex of ideation and emotional responses to everyday life situations). This is so deeply ingrained that they vehemently resist all attempts to pry them away from this lower complex. The four levels of initiation, then is a process of (1) preparing the individual for the struggle against the lower part of being (Level 1) (2) the struggle itself (level 2) (3) the coming forth of the Self, and its faculties (level 3) and (4) the Realization of the essential nature of the Self as the unconditioned, unformed, eternal, and infinite capacity of actualization (level 4). Let us now proceed to detailing the 10 stages composing the 4 levels of initiation.

Chapter 11

THE TEN STAGES OF INITIATION

Preliminary Requirements to Initiation
Sphere 10, Geb, The Khaibit

Essentially, spiritual development is a process of raising consciousness from the lower divisions of the spirit (the Khaibit-- sphere 10--and Sahu--spheres 7, 8, 9) through the higher ones (spheres 6-1) to its original place, "0" in the Subjective Realm. Once the individual has insperienced the essential unconditionedness of his being, then he can live in the world in total freedom from all objective conditioned reality (not just simply the lower part of being). In addition, the spiritual power that is required to effect the raising of consciousness can also be directed by the will of the individual to affect his physical body, the life of others, and the external environment.

How the ascent of consciousness is achieved can be made clear by a common analogy. Imagine a room with a furnace and a thermometer. By increasing the heat output of the furnace, the mercury is made to rise in the thermometer. Let us now equate 1) the mercury with consciousness, 2) the heat with a specific expression of our life-force (Ra, spiritual power), and the measurements on the thermometer with the spheres of the Tree of Life, and divisions of the spirit. Besides affecting the mercury, the heat will affect other things in the room. The kindling of the heat corresponds to the metaphysical effects of sex, and its increase, to the effects of the austerities imposed on the initiate from the fourth to the 9th stage of initiation.

The Care of the Life Force

The heart of the work to be done at the tenth sphere concerns itself with the replenishment, conservation, free flow, and equilibrium of the modalities of the life-force. This life force is known as Chi in the Chinese tradition, Ki, in the Japanese, Kundalini, in Dravidian India, Ra, in the Kamitic, etc.

Its replenishment is optimized by observing proper dietary principles; by following a very nutritious and wholesome diet.

It is conserved by exercising moderation in eating, drinking, sexual activity, work, emoting, sensual gratification of all kinds, etc.

Its free flow throughout the body is secured by judicious and periodic fasting, the practice of cleansing breathing techniques (Nadhi Shuddi Pranayama, etc.), and a lifestyle that is free of emotional suppression.

This life force has four modes of expressions that can be described through the metaphors of the four elements that we discussed in earlier chapters. It is subject to a cyclical alternation of phases in which it heats and dries the body at one extreme, and cools and moisturizes the body on the other. In between these are phases of cold and dry (following the hot and dry), and hot and moist (following the cold and moist). These four phases are, metaphorically, fire, water, earth, and air, respectively. Over or under generation of any of these modalities result, not only in illness, but in problems in the generation of the special expression of our spiritual power that is needed to raise our consciousness, and to manifest our psychic powers.

The equilibrium of these four modalities of our life-force is achieved by a well balanced diet, not according to the western concept of food components, but according to their effect on, or analogy to the four modalities of the life force. I.e., foods are also classified as "fiery" (hot peppers, garlic, etc.), "watery" (watermelons, lettuce, wheat, etc.). The Dravidians of India have left extensive treatises on this aspect of food classification and utilization in their work entitled the Ayurvedas, which the Aryan (Vedantic) Hindus are now claiming to be their work. As everything that we do depends on, and affects one of these modalities of the life-force, we must also observe moderation in our activities, as well as the time for which certain activities are in harmony with the cyclical manifestation of these forces. We will take a look at these later on.

These are considered outer teachings, and their imparting are not considered part of the initiation itself. In fact, the teacher takes advantage of this stage to determine the level of receptivity, and discipline of the student, for most people, unfortunately, do not make good candidates for initiation.

Level 1 - Stage 1 of Initiation
Sahu division of the Spirit, Sphere 9, Auset

It is here that the most important step in our spiritual development is taken. Can you imagine setting out on a journey without a destination in mind? Writing a novel without a theme to give unity to the multiplicity of scenarios and actions? An educational system without a curriculum? Yet, this is the manner in which all men live without a true system of initiation. It is the effect of taking the person as one's identity. This step is the identification with Ausar, sphere 1, as our Self. We will see how this identification becomes the basis of the work that is to be done in each stage (sphere) of initiation. This identification of our Selves with Ausar, which has been equated with the "projection" of the Supreme Being as the core of our being, does not take place as an act of faith. Let's begin with the fact that the immense complexity, yet, order and unity of the functions of Man's body and spirit can only be attributed to a guiding intelligence. While most Western scientists are mute on the point, others, of a more progressive mentality, allege that this intelligence is the so-called sub-conscious mind. A study of the history of psychology will reveal that no one has ever proven the existence of such a "mind." It was merely a concept invented by Western scientists in their atheistic attempt to speak of spiritual processes without seeming to do so. When the true nature of the spirit is understood, from the study of spiritual literature, and verifications through rituals and meditation it will be seen that *the spirit is not the integrator or director of its own functions*. This is evidenced by the fact that the functions of the spirit (hence, the body) can be altered at will through meditation. In its capacity of directing and integrating the operations of the spirit (mental, emotional and psychical functions) and the body, this intelligence dwelling within our being shows that it has, qualitatively, the same capabilities as the Supreme Being. Although smaller in magnitude, the making and running of Man's spiritual body encompass the same degree of intelligence. In fact, this intelligence is an unseparated share or apportionment of the Supreme Being dwelling within Man as Her Self. That is why it knows how to direct the spirit in its functions of transforming a fertilized egg into the billions of cells of many different types that we call the human being. That is why it knows how to direct the body in its functions of digesting and assimilating food, in its functions of healing the body, etc. It stretches intelligence to the breaking point to believe Westerners' claim to scholarship or science regarding their belief that these infinitely complex physiological functions are guided and kept in harmony by the blind mechanical functions of atoms, "bio-feedback mechanisms," etc. This indwelling intelligence is none other than our Self--Ausar, the first sphere of the Tree of Life, the apportionment of the Supreme Being within our being. It is the concrete validation of Man having been made in the likeness of God. It is the "word" that came to dwell in flesh. It is the concrete validation for the claim that the Kingdom of God is within.

It is with this indwelling divine intelligence that we must identify as our Self. Unlike with Christianity, this is not an act of faith. It is a concrete reality that is amenable to being experienced. And not only must it be experienced, we shall see that in the same way that it plays an active role in directing and unifying our mental and bodily functions, it will play a similar role in our initiation, and all aspects of our lives. Imagine having this indwelling intelligence that knows how to run the machinery of your body, running your career, your education, your marriage, your nation, and so on. At this moment it is limited to running the "involuntary" and subconscious functions of your being. Through initiation, ritual, and meditation you will learn to expand its functions to the external part of your being, as well as to gain voluntary control over the "involuntary" processes. The fact that it dwells within you and can be experienced through "mediumistic" (slumbering) trance is symbolized in the Ausar story by its being buried within an acacia tree (physical body), or at the bottom of a river (innermost recesses of the spirit). Going into mediumistic trance, which is symbolized as being submerged under water[1], is the first spiritual skill that the initiate must acquire. Besides enabling the initiate to experience that his Self is this indwelling intelligence, this form of trance serves a number of other functions at this stage of initiation. It is the key to memory, and unification of experiences. People who have the so-called photographic memory are able to go spontaneously into a mild trance while reading, etc. This is the key to the "mindfulness" that plays a major role in the initiate's quest. Anyone who has made resolutions to change some aspect of his life, has discovered that the main reason for failure is primarily due to forgetting. It is at the fifteenth ounce of that pound of chocolate cake that you remember your dietary resolution. Since the identification with Ausar must underlie the initiate's thoughts and actions throughout his life--i.e., serve as the theme of the initiation and life--it must be firmly impressed through mediumistic trance upon the spirit. The perseverance in maintaining one's identification with Ausar is symbolized in the Ausarian story as Auset's devotion to him. We

1. Many religions have mistaken the symbol for the actuality and subject their new converts to various sorts of dunking. We of course know this as "baptism."

141

also learn in the metaphoreisis of Ausar that she (along with Nebt-Het) re-collects all the parts of his body which Set had broken into fourteen pieces, and reconstructed (re-membered) it. The breaking up of Ausar's body is symbolical of the segregative nature of the 8th sphere (Sebek) dominated mentality of people before initiation (Sahu Man). This process of re-member-ing symbolizes the dynamizing effect that trance has upon our thinking. It helps to link up and bring to our awareness the host of associated ideas that have stood separated in our memory bank. This process exposes contradictions within our being, and creates new revelations. Incidentally, this slumbering (mediumistic, hypnotic) trance is a major significance of the lunar correspondence to this sphere, and to Auset, as it is most pronounced at the full moon, and analogous times (winter, midnight, etc.).

As we saw in an earlier chapter, the word of power that corresponds to Ausar is "Aung(k)," and to Auset, "Dhung and Vang." It is by working with these mantras that the initiate is able to accelerate and guarantee success in the work of this stage. There is another very important event that is initiated as a result of the work that is undertaken in this stage of initiation, but we will discuss it in stage four.

<h3 style="text-align:center">Level 1 - Stage 2 of Initiation
Sahu division of the Spirit, Sphere 8, Sebek</h3>

At this stage the teacher provides the initiate with a new set of definitions, descriptions, and explanations for what is life, what are emotions, etc. In short, the teacher redefines the basic ideas operating in the life of the student. Before this, all of the individual's beliefs are based on the identification with the person. We have already seen that up to this point the individual has been victimized by the host of illusions, segregative thinking and rationalizations of emotions due to the operation of the lower faculties making up the person. Now his beliefs must be redefined using the Ausarian Self-identity as their basis.

The reshaping of one's belief system in light of the identification with the indwelling intelligence that is at the center of all our mental and bodily processes, is called the *Opening of the Way*. It is important to understand that in reality we don't learn how to grow spiritually. We learn how to remove the impediments to the coming to the foreground of our submerged divine Self. I.e., wrong ideas close the door to the full operation of the Self in the life of the individual. One cannot overstate the fact that the indwelling intelligence was not intended to be limited to operating your background mental process, and involuntary bodily functions. And as it is omniscient, it cannot be taught. The reformed Sebekian faculty reflecting rationalizations based on one's true self (Ausar) is called Ap-Uat (the Opener of the Way). The "way" is a symbol for our beliefs and ideas as conduits of the course of our lives. As we believe, so we act. As we act, so goes our destiny. According to our unreformed Sebekian faculty--Set--we are in the habit of rationalizing our actions according to our identification with our person. We would, for example, firmly believe that we could not help doing so, and so because of the way we felt (emotional influence), or didn't feel, etc. Can you imagine the indwelling Self running the body according to whims and feelings? Surely, its functions must be based on divine law and order (Maat, the 4th Sphere).

This process of redefining the belief system of the student is made very difficult by the use of our everyday language. Most African societies of initiates[2] possess "secret" languages for such purposes. One of the reasons for this is that such languages create order in the thinking of the person through their semantical structures. We get glimpses of this in some of the South African languages in which the categorical word for God-"Muntu"-is the same for Man. As a result of using such languages for our thinking, we are able, without conscious effort (a very important principle), to keep in our awareness the facts of our true nature. If your language constantly reminds you that your self shares the same qualities as God, by using the same term for both, if it reminds you of the difference between being informed and knowing, by using clearly distinct terms for each, it facilitates the process of spiritual development. If we use our everyday language we have to rely on personal definitions of the terms that we use. I have found it necessary in this book to establish such special usages of terms like "person" for the lower part of being (spheres 7 - 10) and Self for the higher part of being (spheres 0 - 3), and so on. Another benefit of

2. For example, the Bundu, Ampora, and Poro of Sierra Leone; the Ogboni, Egbo, Eluku, and Orisha of Nigeria; the Homowo, and Oyeni of the Gold Coast, and several hundred other "masonic" initiation societies that can be found throughout Africa.

such languages is to be found in their close relationship to the "language" of words of power. These languages use many devices, some of which are known as gematria, notaricon, temura, etc. in order to hide the words of power in the body of other words, and to serve as a pnemonic device to the initiate. Take for example the name of the deity of wisdom, Tehuti. It conceals the mantra "Hu." The Kamitic cosmology states that the God of the senses is Hu. Now it is well known that the highest goals of meditation cannot be achieved unless thinking is stilled. So this hekau (word of power) is used to quiet the senses as their operation stimulates thought activity. This fact will constantly remind the initiate that wisdom is achieved by stilling the thinking process to enable our omniscience to come to the foreground. Similarly, the Kamitic phrase for "I am" is "anuk," which is a transposition of the hekau "aunk" (aung). Each and every time that the Kamitic initiate says "I am" he is reminded that this I am is the same, qualitatively, as the Supreme Being. Although the classical Latin and Greek that are used for saying mass lack the same degree of cogency, and have no relation to words of power, it is on the basis of these principles that the Catholic church has reserved them for their masses and litanies.

In the same manner that mediumistic or hypnotic trance was used in the preceding stage to reestablish the proper Self identity, so must it be used to establish these new definitions as operatives in the spirit (mind) of the individual. Comprehending them is not enough. This is why people find themselves doing things that they are convinced they should not do. It is why the mere reading of scriptures, and hearing of sermons is not enough to do much to alter people's behavior. The inculcation of this new set of values into the spirit serves additional functions. Ideas and beliefs only have power to influence our lives when they have been charged with emotional force. Expertise in meditation will reveal that emotions are primarily states of mediumistic trance. In this state, independent thinking and the will are to a large degree paralyzed, and consciousness is withdrawn from the external plane. The idea or image in the sphere of awareness becomes the reality of the moment. That is why people who, in reality, know better cannot at the moment of a powerful emotion rescue themselves. Why do some people loose control at the sight of a picture of a serpent, spider, etc? Why do most people loose their common sense during emotional moments? How about the profusion of wise thoughts that visit you only when you are dealing with other people's problems? The mediumistic trance, of which emotions represent a variety, is

144

akin to the state of dreaming and death. And the guide of our behavior at such times is the idea or belief associated with the emotional complex. For example, what we call "anger" is a negative mediumistic trance in which the guiding factor is the image of our person carrying out some anti-social act, perhaps the idea that we are angry, etc. These negative thought/energy complexes are symbolized as Set, and Aupep in the Kamitian tradition. The positive thoughts (rationalizations of our actions based on our identity with Ausar) are symbolized by the deity Anpu (Anubis), the *Guide of the Dead*. I.e., it corresponds to the positive thoughts that must guide us when we are in the grips of an emotion. Since the will, and independent thinking will be by degrees paralyzed, according to the strength of the emotion, our only guide at such moments are the thoughts reprogrammed into our behavioral patterns. Once the work of this stage of initiation is completed (which takes place at the 8th stage, sphere 2, Tehuti), the initiate will be impervious to the visitation of any emotion, craving or temptation. This is why it is said that Anpu (Anubis) is the embalmer of Ausar. I.e., he renders him incorruptible. During the 4th stage of initiation we will see how this process truly unfolds.

Level 1 - Stage 3 of Initiation
Sahu Division of the Spirit, Sphere 7, Het-Heru

Once the initiate's belief system has been brought into harmony with truth, he is then ready for the intensification of the life-force or spiritual power in order to raise the consciousness to the higher parts of the spirit. This power which is called Kundalini by the Blacks of India, Ra, by the Kamitians, Shekinah by the Canaanites, Eros, by the Greeks (though misunderstood), libido, by the psychoanalysts (though misunderstood) is none other than our life-force. The arousal of Ra--our life-force--to the point of manifesting psychic phenomena (prophecy, clairvoyance, psychic healing, etc.), and raising consciousness to the higher parts of the spirit can take place when we are experiencing intense pleasure; extreme joy, heightened sexual excitement, orgasm, ecstatic trance, etc. It is of great importance to note that of all the intense pleasures that Man can experience, only two--orgasm and ecstatic trance--can be deliberately induced. This explains the fundamental nature of Black religious practices (as well as shamanism) which are centered around ecstatic trance. It also explains the sex-based ritual systems (tantra[3], etc.) that are widely disseminated throughout the so-called pagan religions of the world[4]. It also explains the heavy use of music and festivities--all Het-Heru (venusian) correspondences--in religious ceremonies and meditation. The reader must recall that this stage of initiation belongs to Het-Heru, the venusian[5] deity--Goddess of art, festivities, joy, etc.--of Kamit. While in the first stage of initiation the initiate's trance is dedicated to establishing devotion to realizing Ausar as the embodiment of his Self, and in the second stage his trance is dedicated to impregnating into the spirit a belief system that is in harmony with truth, *in this stage, the trance is dedicated to manifesting an intense joy for those earthly goals that are in harmony with the new belief system implanted during the second stage*.

A clue to the function of emotions is provided by its etymological structure (e = out, external + motion, the power to move, etc.). It is the energy, or moving principle, or work-capable factor that has the power to overcome the resistance of physical (external) matter. A law of nature is that all activities require energy. There is no achievement of the will without energy, and no extraordinary achievement of the will without an intensification of

---

3. Most books on tantra deal with it starting from the time that it gained social acceptance in Hindu society (circa 400 A.D.), in order to make Vedantism, the religion of the Aryans much older. The fact is that the tantric practices date back to the earliest time of India as a chief element of the religions of the Blacks of India (Dravidians, Austric, etc.). This is, of course, pre-historic to the Nordic Aryans who had not yet appeared on the historical scene. We must also note, that tantrism as known to the world, is already a mixture of elements of the Black religions that originated it, and the Aryan which modified it to harmonize it with their Brahmic principles. We thus find it reflecting a male chauvinistic and patriarchal bias by its primary concern with the initiation of males, while women are used primarily as their support.

4. What can be more pagan than the host of Western irreligious sexual practices; homosexuality, oral sex, prostitution, pornography, etc?

5. It is a very curious fact that the Jews prohibit all kind of work, and pleasurable "nonreligious" acts on the Sabbath. Yet, sex is not only allowed, but encouraged. When we note that the sexual engagement is to take place on friday night, ruled by venus, which is the beginning of the Sabbath, it all falls into place. Of course, Jews will never admit this openly. But as they have adopted many of the esoteric beliefs and practices of the Blacks of Canaan, we find them reiterating that the Shekinah,--the spiritual power--hovers over the nuptial chamber on the Sabbath.

the power of the nervous system[6], or without intense emotional pleasure. There is a very important story in one of the chief scriptures--the *Rudrayamala*--based on the religion of the Blacks of India. It tells of how the great yogi Vashista, who was very skilled in the orthodox teachings of Yoga, who after 6000 - 10,000 years (about 70 - 125 incarnations) of yogic exercises, fasting, and asceticism had been unable to bring forth his spiritual power--kundalini--into full manifestation. He was about to give up and curse the Goddess declaring that it was all a hoax, when Tara (the Goddess of the mantra Aum) appeared to him and told him that he could not manifest the Mother in her full glory because he was practicing in the wrong manner. He should go to Mahacina and learn the correct method. When he got there he found the God Vishnu intoxicated, and in ecstatic embrace with a beautiful maiden. Forgetting that it was the Deity itself that he was speaking to, Vashista criticized Vishnu for engaging in practices that went against the "sacred teachings." Vishnu challenged Vashista to prove how, and why sex was not sacred. After Vashista was not able to prove his point, Vishnu explained to him that during the sexual act, he and his yogini were involved in intense visualization aimed at preserving the world from extinction, while the "sexual energy" provided the motive force to achieve the goal of the visualization. He then initiated Vashista into the great Kula Yoga Ritual of the Blacks of India, thus enabling him to achieve his goal in bringing forth the Goddess, fully effulgent as 10,000 suns. This is the basis of the Tantric Yoga System of the Blacks who gave India, and the world the yogic teachings.

In his book *Reflections On the Tantras*, Sudhakar Chattopadhyaya, p. 13, states *"Then the sadakha (initiate) should worship the Goddess in her (the female partner) private parts according to the prescribed manner. The worshipper should then resort to pranayama (breathing practices) and remain ever calm in mind thinking that the Mother Goddess is there."* Although all teachers of yoga in the west have remained silent on the subject, all such procedures as pressing the heels against the pubic area and the perineum during pranayama (breathing practices), and the Bandhas are, primarily, measures to help suppress ejaculation. All pranayamas that have as their objective the raising of the kundalini must be practiced during the sexual ritual. Most of what appears as separate practices of yoga (mudras, bhandas, pranayamas, asanas)

---

6. For this purpose, such hypnagogic/aphrodisiac herbs as Yohimbe, Damiana, Ginseng, etc. are expertly used.

are in reality segregated parts of an integral system. The Aryan ignorance and contempt for certain aspects of Yoga--a Black creation--was the cause of their acts of selection and rejection of parts from the system that were in harmony with their thinking. Imagine having functional parts of a television set, but the parts are not hooked up together. This is the state of the world practice of yoga.

While engaging in sexual intercourse, the couple concentrates on visualizing a goal, success in the career of the husband, or the wife, or both, for example. Before and during the ceremony, judicious use will be made of certain foods and drinks with aphrodisiac properties in order to realize the greatest ecstasy possible. The association of the image of the objective with the sexual ecstasy serves to keep the image constantly in one's awareness, and endow it with great power to attract to the individual in an occult manner, the resources to achieve the goal. Do not pleasurable experiences keep reflecting themselves in our awareness, motivating us to renew the experience? This is the great secret for maintaining oneself motivated, which is a major key to success in any undertaking. It is this principle that advertising experts are using when they advertise a car with a beautiful half clad woman, or pictures of political candidates with the word "sex" embedded in such a manner that it is not visible to normal vision (subliminal seduction), etc. We "pagans" would rather meditate on transcending our lower nature and manifest our divinity during sex, than dwell on the physical sensation of the act, let alone use it to sell candidates, crackers and cars. Is not the latter truly prostitution . . . of the spirit? An experience that is so alien to Westerners is the breaking out of a person having sex (most often the woman) into trance possession by a deity or an ancestor. Instead of the usual "I love you," "how sweet you are," etc. the person, now possessed with the deity engages in psychic healing, prophecy, moral admonitions, counselling, warnings, giving guidance relating to the meditation goal, or some heavy theological abstractions. If they only knew who, in reality, is the pagan.

Once this part of the spirit has been developed through repetitions of this Kula Yoga Ritual, the initiate finds himself spontaneously, and readily manifesting ecstasy regarding revelations that occur to him throughout the normal course of living. This development accentuates the importance of the two preceding initiation stages. Had his belief system not changed in the preceding stage, he would find himself becoming ecstatic about wrong ideas.

And if he had not placed himself humbly under his teacher's guidance in the first stage of initiation he would not have been receptive to the reformulation of his belief system in stage two. The result would be, that once he learned how to empower his imagination through ritual sex and other means of arousing the life-force, he would find himself giving power to all kinds of false beliefs. The outcome is predictable.

Our spiritual power is defined in the Kamitic and Black Indian traditions as an expression of the solar force (Ra and Kundalini, respectively). And like the solar force it nurtures all that is within us. It does not discriminate between harmful and beneficial beliefs. This is the chief danger that Kundalini Yogis warn students in relationship to the arousal of Kundalini. One is going nowhere spiritually without arousing Ra, and one is courting all kinds of problems--persistent obsession with false ideas (insanity)--if one attempts to arouse it without a teacher.

We must take note of the fact that the ritualistic use of sex is not the only means of arousing one's spiritual power (manifesting ecstatic trance). It can be done with the mere repetition of words of power, through the use of drugs (Anamita, Peyote, Marijuana--called Bhang in India where it is used extensively for this purpose--etc.), and through the employment of hatha yogic sexual self stimulation; this is asvini mudra in which the perineum is contracted and relaxed throughout the visualization, coordinated with breathing. This is the muscle that we contract when we want to stop our urine in mid-stream. It also undergoes automatic contractions during sexual excitement and orgasm. Achievement of the goal by meditating with words of power by themselves requires so much time, and so many meditations that it is not practical for the majority of people. Yet, when such methods are combined with Kula Yoga, success is attained in a short time. As for the use of drugs to aid in the achievement of ecstatic trance, the price of damage to one's health and social status makes this a poor option. Not only does the sexual ritual approach leads to a speedier success, it also helps to emancipate the practitioners from the physical side of sex, as their attention never dwells on the sexual act itself. For example, the *Kamakhhyatantra* instructs that the practitioner must not allow himself to lose his semen. Throughout the ritual which usually lasts for 72 hours, in which the participants must remain in sexual embrace, they must concentrate on chanting the words of power and perform the dhyana (visualization of the meditation objective)[7]. Furthermore, the woman must be seen as the embodiment of the female aspect of God and the man as the masculine.

Students of Hinduism--the Aryan biased mixture of Indo-European religion with that of the Blacks of India--might protest, claiming that the extinction of desires and emotions (asceticism) is the true means of achieving spiritual liberation. But this is pure spiritual philosophical and scientific ignorance. Our emotions are none other than the expression of the activity of our spiritual energy. Not only is it impossible to extinguish it, but its suppression results in a diminution of our libido and overall ability to meet the demands of the world. Physicians are very well aware of the detrimental effects that suppression of pleasure has upon the endocrine organs, especially the gonads. In fact, the gonads are the organs represented by Het-Heru. Her name literally means, House (Het) of Heru (the libido, erotic force, sexual vitality that supports the will). The proper care of the gonads (prostate in the man, ovaries in the woman) and the judicious cultivation of pleasure builds up our libido (the power behind our will, ambition, psychic power, etc.). Unlike the Aryan religions, which in typical Sebekian fashion, segregate pleasure from the divine, Black religions have always understood that spiritual liberation depends on assigning the proper place to each thing in the world. The quest for pleasure must not lead us. Pleasurable acts are to be allowed only after they have been investigated and found to be in conformity with truth, and always in due measure. Can you imagine the effect on a people's consciousness and spirituality if every time they engaged in sex, their attention was directed to the achievement of a spiritual goal? What if they thought of themselves as engaging, not in a mere carnal act, but as divine beings using the energies of the lower part of their spirit to bring forth the higher? Do you know now why there are so many neuroses and sexual perversions in western societies? We are not dealing here with "schools of thought." Our "sexual energy" which is the driving force for all of our accomplishments--spiritual and mundane--is an expression of the universal creative power of nature/God. Misunderstand it, misuse it, suppress it if you want. But you will have no say when it avenges itself on you.

Another important skill that is developed in this stage is the creative use of the imagination. We have already described its

---

7. Reflections On the Tantras, Sudhakar Chattopadhyaya, p. 15. Published by Motilal Bansarsidass, Delhi.

function as the coordinator of the shaping forces of the events in our lives. When we take a belief into a state of trance and elaborate upon it in our imagination, unknown to us, we are manipulating and coordinating the forces that are responsible for shaping the event. This takes place regardless of whether the goal is harmful, undesirable or beneficial to us. The imagination will organize the powers of the spirit to make the goal a reality. This is one of the reasons for the work during the preceding stage. If the initiate increases the creative power of his imaginative faculty without first realigning his belief system with truth (based on the Self as Ausar), his wayward beliefs will direct his imagination to all sorts of harmful ends. Take for instance, the persons who believe that the "falling in love" process is beyond their control (this is one of those myths created by Set). These people, who are the ones who are vulnerable to infidelity while married, are not aware that it is their self-image identified with the person that is the cause of their "falling in love." If a thing like this (and there are so many other manifestations) can happen with the "normal" amount of spiritual power, imagine what would happen to individuals with a great deal of spiritual power, but wrong beliefs.

Success in this initiation stage gives the initiate the ability to achieve all minor undertakings, many of which are not so minor, primarily through the use of his ecstatic trance empowered imagination. This is why venus, the planetary correspondence to Het-Heru is called the "fortuna minore." The worst thing that the initiate can do is to stop at this point in his work. He will eventually discover that as he arouses his Ra force to greater activity, that it will begin to reawaken the erroneous beliefs and harmful desires that were set aside in the Sebek initiation. Unless he moves on to the next level he will discover that Het-Heru's external beauty conceals a most foul internal corruption.

The third stage of initiation marks the completion of the preparation of the initiate for higher initiation. We must note that thus far the initiate has not been directed to confront his lower nature. In fact, the method around it was one of "persuasion." The initiate entered into mediumistic trance, which has the significant property of silencing thoughts and energies of resistance to change, and was then presented with a new belief system, calculated to replace the false dichotomies and wayward beliefs in his spirit. But this replacement is only temporary, for no spiritual growth has yet taken place. The key to understanding why the lower nature has not

151

been challenged resides in the fact that the three faculties involved (spheres 9, 8 and 7) are feminine--i.e., receptive to the animal spirit. Their planetary symbols are the moon (Cold/moist), mercury (Cold/dry) and venus (Cold/moist). The cold--yin--quality that they share symbolizes that the heat (sexual passion) of the life-force is not yet strong enough. The next triad of planets that correspond to the spheres wherein the next set of initiations will take place are all hot; Heru, 6th sphere, the sun (Hot/dry); Herukhuti, 5th sphere, mars (Hot/dry); Maat, 4th sphere, jupiter (Hot/moist). This heat makes them masculine--unreceptive to the animal spirit. For consciousness to function through them, the libido must be raised.

The key to understanding why spiritual growth has not taken place, even if there has been a successful replacement of negative behavior, is due to the fact that the initiate has not yet become "awakened." We must again take note of the "coldness" of the three faculties involved. It is no mere metaphor, for as we know, the body (animal spirit) cools down to allow us to sleep, and heats up to allow us to awaken. Changes in our behavior can only be credited toward spiritual growth if we do the work ourselves. So far it was done for us by the initiator, while we were in a state of mediumistic (receptive, hypnotic) trance.

Level 2 - Stage Four of Initiation
Ab division of the Spirit, Sphere 6, Heru

The initiation at this stage aims at teaching the initiate to establish his will as the master of his behavior. It is amazing that so much ink has flowed in regards to the will, yet so little is known about it. "Willing" is "an action" of the Self[8], and not of the person. When we will, we are involved in the action of setting into motion functions of the spirit or the body, from the level of the Self. Actions that are set into motion from the level of the person are acts of desiring, wishing, hoping, etc. The fundamental difference is that the will originates from the Self which is unswayed by emotions and sensuousness, while desiring is influenced and dictated by them. This is cleverly embedded in the Ausarian story. Auset mates with the deceased Ausar, and conceives Heru. Het-Heru carries him in

---

8. As the Self is submerged within, we must go into trance to establish our will. Thus we can make the needed changes in our behavior patterns. I.e., hypnotherapy, etc.

her womb, and gives birth to him[9]. It is a grand metaphor for the union through trance of one's identity with the indwelling Self (Auset mates with Ausar), and the empowerment of this identity through the spiritual power intensification rituals in stage 3 (Het-Heru), which gives birth to the personal will (Heru). It is important to keep in mind that a goal of initiation is to attain to the point where one is able to set the so-called subconscious (the spirit) or involuntary functions into motion at will. Not only does the indwelling intelligence control the "involuntary" functions of the body, it also controls all phases of our behavior, and is the major shaping force of everything that happens in our lives. I.e., it influences the course of our career, marriage, safety, and so on to our destiny. As the chief director of the spirit (subconscious), Ausar, is free of emotional influences, so must be the will, which it gives rise to. This is to say, that the will is the child of the Self, as desire is born of the person.

The initiate also learns that the freedom of his personal will is not for the purpose of choosing and determining the various undertakings in his life; careers, marriage, etc. Such a concept must be alarming to Westerners (Whites and Blacks!). But Africans have a long standing tradition of consulting oracles in such matters to discover if the want is in harmony with the divine will, and if it is, which part of the spirit (as symbolized by a "deity") is in control of the undertaking. This subject raises the question regarding predestination in people's lives. As this is a false concept we need not entertain it. The practice of consulting an oracle to see if the proposed undertaking is in harmony with the divine will is based on the fact that, like all intelligent undertakings, all lives are planned. Do you plan before you undertake something important? Do you believe that your life is a haphazard, hence, accidental sequence of events? Where there is no planning, there is no intelligence. The plan of each person's life is revealed by the second division of their spirit. This plan and parts of it can be made known through such oracles as Ifa, Afa, Dilogun, I Ching, the Metu Neter (the oracle revealed in this book), by initiates who have awakened their 2nd sphere/Tehuti faculty, and in some cases, by mediums. What then is the function of the personal will?

---

9. It is interesting to note that this is the story upon which Egyptologists base their allegation that Kamitic people advocated marriages between brothers, and sisters. It is supposedly proven because Auset and Ausar are sister, and brother.

The function of Man's will is to allow him the freedom to choose between good and evil. What is good, and what is evil? We go to the Tree of Life for our answer. The first and highest manifestation of divinity (sphere 1) is the unity of all opposites, which is the good. The lowest manifestation, the 10th sphere is the source of our emotional behavior, which makes our life irrational if we allowed it control over our lives. This is the evil. Heru's job--the will--is to keep the lower part of being--emotions and the Sahu--from directing our lives, in deference to the higher.

Beyond the importance of insuring that all of our undertakings are in harmony with each other, the use of oracles involves a set of one of the most important rituals in our lives. In many cases we will find that the direction of the oracle is at odds with our desires and conditionings. Complying with the oracular pronouncement in most such cases involves the individual in a pitched battle against the lower part of being. This is the manner in which the Deities--metaphysical intelligences--reveal to us which conditionings are to be overcome in relation to a specific undertaking. I.e., we are informed of the spiritual significance of a specific worldly undertaking. A person might be told by the oracle that in order to succeed in the marriage, rituals must be done to Sebek. It means that this person's marriage is a vehicle for the development of this spiritual faculty. A set of key oracular readings serves to map out a fully personalized spiritual curriculum for the individual, while the success in carrying out the directions provides an objective way of measuring the degree of spiritual development. Anyone who has tried to measure objectively and accurately his/her spiritual progress will be able to appreciate this fully.

The ecstatic trance rituals performed in the preceding stage, and certain breathing practices introduced in this stage, result in the "awakening" of the initiate. A chief distinction between the states of sleep, and wakefulness, is that in sleep our will does not function, while it does when we are awake. And since most people are for the most part unable to successfully use their will, we are justified in concluding that they are not fully awake during their "waking state." A "waking trance" induction method is therefore introduced at this stage. It is based on a special way of breathing that is characterized by the decrease of the rate of breathing and the increase of the volume of air breathed in. This method of breathing, which is called Dhumo or Gtummo (Fire breathing) leads to a state of wakefulness that is many times more intense than "normal." The waking trance (opposite to mediumistic/hypnotic) is the subject of one of the greatest books ever to come out of Kamit. Known as the "*Egyptian Book of the Dead*, a name given it by Arab grave robbers because they found copies of the book buried with the corpses, it is really the, *Pert em Heru* (book of *Becoming Awake*; "Pert em" means "Becoming," and "Heru," which means "day," "sun," and by extension, "the day consciousness (wakefulness)." In this state of trance, the senses are fully asleep. There is little, to no awareness of the external world or the body, while the person is in a state of full mental wakefulness.

The wakefulness enables the meditator to see the falsehoods and contradictions in the beliefs that were cultivated in the early part of life.

Related to the initiation at this stage is the beginning of a spiritual responsibility that serves as the determinant of the effectuation of spiritual growth. In other words, when do we know that the living of truth has led to spiritual growth? Can you say that growth takes place when the observance of a virtue does not involve a challenge? While exercising at a heart rate of 140 beats per minute signals improvement for someone whose peak exercising rate was lower, it does not for someone already there or beyond. Similarly, spiritual growth only takes place when we are challenged to embrace a truth or directive of the oracle (the wisdom part of our spirit) and it runs into opposition from our conditioning. Your mind is set on doing something, and the oracle or spiritual law reveals to you that you will achieve your goal at the expense of someone else. Doing the right thing will--from the narrow view--cause you losses. These types of scenarios which are called "crossroad" situations, have given rise to the belief that the best place to make offerings and do rituals are at crossroads.

Success in the living of truth at such crucial moments is made possible by the Heru/sexual power that is generated in the gonads (house/Het of sex/Heru) and a great meditation system entitled Men Ab em Aungkh em Maat. We will detail it in future chapters.

In conclusion it must be noted that the opposition to the living of truth by our conditionings demands that we summon extra spiritual power. Spiritual power, kundalini, Ra can only be aroused to its greatest heights by the genuine challenges in life. Thus, it takes power to get power. It is hoped that the reader will begin to understand that discipline cannot be achieved by meditating on the abstraction "discipline." All sermons to such effects or hypnotic autosuggestions like "I am disciplined," etc. must fail.

Level 2 - Stage 5 of Initiation
The Ab division of the Spirit, the 5th Sphere, Herukhuti

Herukhuti is the dispenser of divine justice. It is the faculty that protects us from our enemies. It is the spiritual mechanism behind our physical and spiritual immunity[10], and our ability to overcome the resistances of the physical environment.

In the same manner that our physical immunity cannot protect us if we violate the laws of our body (eat incorrectly, indulge in excesses, etc.), this part of our spirit cannot protect us from the injustices of others and from psychic invasion if we violate its law.

In conformity with the law that you reap what you sow, the initiate at this stage meditates on being just with others, and makes a commitment to confess to his peers and kin (not enemies) any injustice that has been done to another. The spiritual strength that must be raised to carry this out awakens this faculty to its role of providing psychical protection. If only the major political and religious leaders of nations were to know the reality behind the word "justice." Can you see how much the knowledge of the definition, but not the reality itself is costing us? Can you imagine what would happen to an oppressor if all the individuals in a nation of oppressed people got together and made a commitment to give justice to everyone, as well as a commitment to confess all transgressions against each other? Did the thought heat you up? If it did, congratulations. You have just verified for yourself the basis of the Ra ritual system of Kamit and the Kundalini Yoga of the Dravidians[11].

But where would one find the strength to live up to the demands of this sphere? We must once more draw upon the fact that our Self-the indwelling intelligence at the center of our being-is not swayed by emotions. The ability to carry out the demands of this sphere is merely a natural outgrowth of identifying with Ausar. What about the fear (the Pachad that Jewish kabalism attaches to this sphere) that one must surely suffer in this situation? Once more again we must realize that identification with Ausar (Kether)

---

10. As the faculty of spiritual immunity, Herukhuti protects us against psychic attack (witchcraft, dark deceased beings, etc.)

11. Psychic heat thus raised is called Tapas in the yogic system.

involves the realization that the spirit is essentially unconditioned. That is to say that we are free to revert to the original state of our spirit in which there are no predetermined inclinations or response patterns.

Level 2 - Stage 6 of Initiation
The Ab division of the Spirit, Sphere 4, Maat

In an earlier chapter we saw that as the functional needs of the world are varied--hence, the cycles of food, water, oxygen, etc.-- the existence of different types of beings is required. If any one of them were to "evolve" from their station and function, the world would cease to function. What would make food if plants were to evolve into animals? How would plants make protein if the nitrogen fixing bacteria were to evolve into some higher form of life? It is time to rid the world of the "inter-species evolutionary theory," whose main function is to serve racist policies. In the same manner that the various cells in our body have been made with different degrees of structural and functional complexity in order to carry out the functions specific to them, so are the various creatures in the world. As much as some people may want to trace their ancestry to cockroaches or apes, the fact is that creatures do not evolve (progress) above their appointed function in the cycles that sustain earthly life--unlike obsequious civil servants--to become other types of creatures. When we speak of spiritual evolution, we are referring to the graduated coming into being of the hierarchy of faculties of the individual or the species.

Similarly, the human kingdom is made up of different racial temperaments. Each one is to make its contribution to the unfoldment of the divine drama. The lesson that the initiate has to learn here is that while his personality or that of his group might be "watery," he must share with, and let the "fiery" type live. This is not to say that one must acquiesce in evil or sleep in bed with the "enemy." Fire cannot mix with water, but they must both recognize that the whole, and therefore theirselves cannot exist without each other.

For many people, the oppressed especially, this is more difficult to carry out than the initiation demands of the preceding stage. Some people would sooner kill themselves than, recognize a place in the scheme of things for their enemies and oppressors. Once more again, we see how the genuine living situation demands

157

that the initiate summon a great deal of power in order to carry out the laws of the initiation. In each of the three last initiations we can see that there is a progressive moving away from an identification with our natal personality and earlier conditioned behavior pattern. We must also appreciate the fact, that unlike all other spiritual traditions and scriptures, this Tree of Life based initiation system lays down a careful, graduated set of challenges. It is at the fourth sphere (stage 6 of initiation) that the initiate is asked to "turn the other cheek." Christianity and many spiritual traditions do violence to people by making spiritual demands that have not been properly prepared for. Once you analyze the matter you will see that the various virtues require different levels of intellectual abilities and spiritual power.

The planetary correspondence of the fourth sphere, Maat, is Jupiter, which astrologers tell us is the major fortune (major success). It comes not simply from the act of sharing (giving, therefore receiving), but from the spiritual power generated by the ability to forgive and to work with one's "enemies." The sign that this power is fully developed is given evidence by the initiate's ability to maintain a sense of joy and optimism in the face of opposition-- even when facing death. Woe unto him who fails to realize that this is the greatest "occult secret" for generating the spiritual power to achieve earthly objectives.

Level 3 - Stage 7 of Initiation
The Shekem Division of the Spirit, Sphere 3, Seker

This is the first of three initiation stages that involve a total break with worldly interests. We must never lose sight of the fact that such an attitude to life, with proper understanding, and life-force generation rituals serve to increase the spiritual power to its highest levels of manifestation. This individual has already gone through initiations that have revealed the fact that psychic power increases in direct relationship to the individual's living of truth in genuine life situations (at the crossroads), and not from the mere performance of spiritual exercises (meditation, rituals, etc.). As this sphere is the center of the 50 sound units of power that are the basis of all physical manifestations, we must realize that they cannot be utilized for purposes that are predominantly personal. During the 4th stage of initiation (sphere 6) it was said that the objectives in Man's life are indicated by the oracular (2nd sphere) faculty. One of the results of the practice of consulting oracles is the unification our undertakings with the Divine historical plan. When we get a reading indicating, for example, that the success of our marriage depends on the development of our spiritual faculty represented by the Deity Sebek[12], success in the undertaking goes beyond the marriage itself. In the same way that the "normal" Sebek talents (communications skills, etc.) are now available for other areas of life, so are the psychic powers of the deity developed in the course of the ritual. The difference is that we must use these powers for the benefit of the world.

The ecstasy that must be cultivated at this sphere is not for the mundane objective, but for manifesting the personalities of the Deities and their powers in our life for the benefit of the world. For this to be, we must "die" to the personal mundane goals. The world must cease to hold wonders and pleasures for us. Our pleasure is in manifesting the likeness of God in whose image we have been made. When it is said that Seker is the God of the dead, a double sense is intended. The "dead" are both the deceased and the initiates who have died to the interests and pleasures of the world[13]. This is easy to understand when we keep in mind that *the initiate is here trading off earthly pleasures for divine power*.

Level 3 - Stage 8 of Initiation, The Khu Division of the Spirit, Sphere 2, Tehuti

Earlier it was said that Man's will must be directed by God. Up to this point this was achieved through the use of oracles, which are means of communicating with the spiritual faculty of the second sphere--Tehuti. In this stage of the initiation, the person learns how to still the thinking mechanism in order to allow this faculty to manifest its omniscience. One of the most important accomplishments resulting from this initiation is the ability to intuit what divine intelligences--Deities--are responsible for the various events in the world. This is the kernel of the true meaning of wisdom. In other words, the initiate becomes a Sage, i.e., a living

---

12. This might be phrased in another tradition as "success will come from making sacrifices to Deity X."

13. We must distinguish "the dead" when referring to Seker, as opposed to when referring to Anpu (a form of Sebek)—so called Anubis—as "guide to the dead." In this sense, "the dead" refers to trance mediums. We will explain this in the chapters on meditation.

oracle. These are the individuals that authored the great oracles that are now in the world.

Level 3 - Stage 9 of Initiation, The Ba Division of the Spirit, Sphere 1, Ausar

Here the initiate experiences that her Self is the One and only Self dwelling in all things in/as the world. Thus all oppositions are transcended and unity with all creatures is achieved. The initiate becomes an Ausar. The greatest challenge for the initiate here is to refrain from taking sides in the seeming conflicts of life. All adversities exist for the sake of making demands upon the individual to reach into the depths of his spirit to awaken the spiritual power to overcome them. One cannot push--exert force--if there is no opposition. There can be no manifestation of spiritual power without adversity. All is peace--Hetep.

Level 4 - Stage 10 of Initiation, Body and Spirit Transcended, 0, Amen, Nu

Here it is finally realized that all that has been transcended was made possible by the fact that the energy/matter that makes up our spirit is essentially unconditioned and unformed, otherwise the transcendence could not have taken place. This is the realization of "Sunyatta (the Void)" of Buddhism. It is Amen--the immanent aspect of God--in the Kamitic tradition. Ritualistically, the initiate becomes established in the ability to still all thought activity, and raise consciousness beyond the spirit even (remember that the Ba-- the spiritual vehicle of the 1st sphere--is the highest manifestation of Man's spirit). Now that Man's consciousness is in the Subjective Realm, and there are no things to occupy consciousness, the Self can only be conscious of being conscious. It becomes aware that it is an immaterial reality. In the Kamitic tradition this is symbolized as "the God Amen." The Jewish kabala calls it Ain, the "negative existence."

160

Chapter 12

MEDITATION AND RITUAL

The Means of Realizing Spiritual Growth

The Principles of Meditation

In chapters 9 and 10, we learned that the goal of initiation is the liberation of the Self by raising consciousness from below the faculty of the 6th sphere (Ab division of the spirit) to the highest part of being, the development and right use of the "personal will," and the raising of the spiritual force to the level of being able to affect physical phenomena. Meditation is a catch word for the set of practices to the realization of these ends.

The Fundamental Components of Man's Being

In the past two chapters, we saw that spiritual development aims at allowing the indwelling intelligence that directs our involuntary mental and physiological functions to extend its sphere of operation to the social events in our lives (career, marriage, education, performances, etc.). The benefits to our lives can be appreciated when we consider the omniscience that the indwelling intelligence shows that it possesses in its handling of the infinite complexity of our physiological processes. What then can we expect from its handling of the affairs of our lives, which are simpler?

The comprehension of the processes of meditation and ritual as means of extending the operation of the indwelling intelligence to the external part of our lives depends on a clear understanding of the fundamental components of Man's being.

1. We are all aware of the fact that the major part of our physiological and mental processes occur independently of our will. This automaton or spirit or life-force, which has been mislabelled "the subconscious mind"[1] provides the matrices or molds or "programs" that guide the physical functions of our bodies and events in the world. It is important to realize that this principle is not conscious, nor

---

1. If the mind is the conscious faculty (an incorrect definition, by the way), how can there be a consciousness below consciousness?

does it initiate or program its activities. Its direction and programming are the property of the indwelling intelligence. Health, success and happiness are the results of the direction of the life-force by the true Self, which bases its functions on divine (cosmogonical) law. Unfortunately, the spirit is also receptive to man's will, which is, as we know, nowhere as wise or capable as the indwelling intelligence. It is also receptive to the ideas we assimilate and to the impressions streaming in from our blood stream and the external environment (colors, odors, shapes, electromagnetic currents, etc.). As the influence that these agents exert upon the spirit are not ordered by laws, as it is with the indwelling intelligence, their influences, if unchecked, create illness, unhappiness and failure.

2. The second major component of our being is the inner intelligence and source of consciousness. It is Ausar, the first sphere, our Self, which from here on, will at times be referred to as our "true self"- although redundant.

3. The third major component of our being is the outer intelligence and *focal point of externalized consciousness*. It is Heru, the sixth sphere, our will, that is in charge of our voluntary mental and physical actions. It is the external point where consciousness grasps (perceives) and manipulates objective reality.

4. The fourth major component of our being is the faculty that houses the spiritual matrices that govern the conception of the events of the physical body and environment. This is Auset, the ninth sphere. This is one of the reasons why she is called the Mother of all living things.

Stages in the Process of Meditation

We have seen that if the Self-the indwelling intelligence-is unobstructed it will maintain the physical organism in good health and extend its functions to running the social aspects of our lives as well. The first source of interference to it comes from the failure to regulate the emotional and sensual activities of the animal part of the spirit. The second source of interference originates from our will when it is directed by our earthly education as opposed to our inner intelligence. These interferences, which cause physical and social disharmony are symbolized in the Ausarian metaphorein as

162

the usurpation of the kingdom by Set, and the stalemate (failure) of Heru's battle with Set, respectively. The essence of meditation and ritual then, lies in the harmonization of the will with the inner intelligence. This is symbolized as Ausar and Auset giving birth to Heru, and the latter directed to victory by Tehuti, the mouthpiece of Ausar. The function of the will, therefore, is to check the influences of the lower parts of the spirit, to enable the Self to direct the spirit according to the cosmogonical (divine) law and order (Tehuti/Maat).

The Process of Meditation

Thus far we have been speaking of an indwelling intelligence that is in charge of directing all of the involuntary mental and physiological functions. We have been saying that it is our true self. And you may have been wondering, quite correctly, why then you have not been able to "sense," to "feel" or to be conscious in some form of the existence of this intelligence. The answer is a simple one. Consciousness resembles a stream of light, in that it has a source of origin (inner), a path of propagation and a point where it makes contact (outer) with, and grasps the objects of perception. In our habitual mode of consciousness, whether we are dreaming or are awake, our consciousness is mostly "focused" at the point of contact with the objects of perception. You will recall, however, that there are times when as a result of being so absorbed in your thoughts, you find that your awareness of yourself, your surroundings and your thoughts are just returning to you from a moment in which you are at a lost for what you were thinking about. Some people call this being "spaced out," "absent minded," etc. What has really taken place? At such moments the focal point of consciousness has been withdrawn from the external point where it grasps objects (thoughts, feelings, the external environment), and it has been returned to its source within our being. Because of the immateriality of the Self and the manner in which the consciousness was withdrawn to it during such spontaneous occurrences, it is not possible to insperience the indwelling intelligence. The result is that we are only conscious of forms that consciousness perceives (our thoughts, feelings which we sum up as our persons, the environment, etc.), and not of the source of consciousness-that which is consciousness itself. The ultimate and highest aim of meditation is, therefore, the withdrawal of the *focus of consciousness* from the objects of perception-the goal of consciousness-and its return to its source.

163

When this is realized, we have no consciousness of objects (our thoughts, feelings, body and the environment). *Freed from objects of consciousness, we are conscious only of being conscious.* It is then that we are able to "sense," "feel" or insperience our inner true self. We will have much to say about this. We must first examine all of the possible manners in which consciousness can be altered.

The **"normal" waking state** is characterized by the tendency of the will to impose itself over the mental functions and its command over the voluntary physical functions. In this state the will is primarily engaged in determining what ideas should be associated according to the sense of logic and reference to the person's belief system, and what actions are to be allowed in the person's life.

The **"normal" dreaming state** is characterized by the dormancy of the will, which gives the spirit full control over the body and thought associations. The spirit's activities are of course determined by its programs, the condition of the blood, environmental influences, etc.

In both states, the "normal" waking and dreaming, the focus of consciousness is located in the external, lower part of being. A very important characteristic that they both share is their distractibility or the shortness of the concentration span. The inability to keep the attention on one object or train of thought for very long, during "normal" waking and dreaming is very well known.

Mediumistic or hypnotic (dream) trance, a state of meditation, is very much like the "normal" dream state with the fundamental difference that consciousness is fully undistracted. It becomes totally focused on an object or stream of thoughts. This hyperconcentrated state of the focus of consciousness is the key to impressing upon the spirit the programs that will determine its activities. For example, a thought to heal ourselves, expressed in the "normal" waking or dream states will fail simply because it was not held long enough in the sphere of awareness. In the mediumistic trance it can be held long enough to be strongly impressed upon the spirit. There are, of course, other variables to this procedure which will be considered in the later chapters on meditation. As the will is dormant, the contents of the awareness and the behavior of the person are directed by the spirit's program or by whatever else is influencing its activities (environmental forces, the will of the initiator, the hypnotist, contents of the blood, etc.). The full concentration of the focus of consciousness on a personality archetype (a deity) or a fragment of a personality (a "spirit," "demon," etc.) is known as "possession," as the behavior of the

164

person takes on the full characteristics of the elements of the personality in question. Because the spirit, and not the will, is directing the person's voluntary physical vehicle during this state, possessed individuals experience either a diminution or enhancement of their physical capabilities. Its full concentration on an idea, e.g., a virtue, which in turn directs its activities, is called an "obsession." This form of at-onement of our focus of consciousness with objects of perception is called in the Yogic system *Samprajnata Samadhi* (Samadhi = full concentration; Samprajnata = object of consciousness). Although it is very powerful and useful, it does not confer wisdom and Self knowledge, and when not directed by a wise teacher, it can lead to deep spiritual bondage. In fact, it is the mechanism that binds us (as the One Self) to one of the seven personality types. Although we are all the same one Self, we are each born in Samprajnata Samadhi (possessed) by one of the seven personality types modified by individuated physical circumstances.

The waking trance is a state of inner hyperwakefulness, and it exhibits two modalities. The first of these is similar to the "normal" waking state, with the differences that its degree of wakefulness is greater, it is confined to the mental sphere (the meditator's physical body is partially or fully asleep), and the focus of consciousness is fully concentrated on its objective. In the second of these modalities, the focus of consciousness is withdrawn from the objects of consciousness and returned to the source of consciousness-the indwelling intelligence. Here, the Self, which is immaterial, beholds itself; consciousness grasps consciousness. The yogic tradition calls it *Asamprajnata Samadhi*; At-onement of the focus of consciousness (Samadhi) without objects in the sphere of awareness. In his *Yoga Sutras*, Patanjali defines yoga as follows: *"Yoga (union) is attained from the inhibition of the mental energy/matter (citta). Then the Seer is clothed in his essential nature."* The things that are united (yoked, yoga), a question that has plagued yogis for the longest, are the *focus of consciousness* and the *source of consciousness*. The inhibition of the mental energy/matter (citta vrtti-nirodhah) is attained by the deactivation of the will (ignoring of thoughts, letting them come and go without expressing interest in them or directing them). When this happens during the hyperwakeful state of waking trance, there comes a point where the sphere of awareness becomes free of thoughts, allowing the consciousness to "sense" "That" which is conscious. When this happens during the "normal" waking or dream states, it leads to the non-REM (non-rapid eye movement) state. This is why we do not achieve consciousness of Self when we "space out" or enter into non-REM during sleep. It must be clear to the reader that our dreamming, and non-REM experience are not confined to sleeping. In fact, the thought drift activity that we experience during the waking state is in reality a different degree of the dream activity during sleep. The key, therefore, to attaining to the point of insperiencing, "feeling" our Self as the indwelling intelligence, as "that which is conscious" depends on the full awakening of ourselves, and the inhibition of the will's function of grasping and directing thoughts. This is the theme, incidentally, of the oldest religious text in the world. The *Pert Em Heru* (Coming Forth By Day (Awakened)), which is known, incorrectly, as the *Egyptian Book of the Dead*. This latter name originated from the Arab grave robbers who first discovered copies of it buried with the deceased.

The Components of a Meditation

Since the essential objectives of meditation--the raising of consciousness and the supporting of the will--depend on the raising of spiritual power there are certain health principles that must be observed before undertaking a course of meditation. These aim at the life-force (Ra, Kundalini): purifying its channels, equilibrating its modalities, nourishing it and optimizing the body's ability to relax. Tension impedes meditation by blocking the flow of the Ra (Life) force. These involve special dietary observances, yogic exercises, breathing practices, living in harmony with the cycles of the body, etc. The principle involved is no different from the preparation for an athletic contest.

The first set of meditations (9th sphere) involves going into a mediumistic trance with the objective of identifying with Ausar, for it is only through this action that we can *lay the foundation* for transcending our conditionings. We have already seen the importance of this procedure.

The second set of meditations (8th sphere) involves going into mediumistic trance with the beliefs that are to replace those incorrect beliefs that may block the way to achieving our goal. It is here that we "Open the Way" to allow the indwelling intelligence to extend its functions beyond the internal mental and physiological functions to the social aspects of our lives.

The third set of meditations (7th sphere) involves going into mediumistic trance with the image of our person as the deity governing the situation achieving and enjoying the goal that we are seeking.

The fourth set of meditations (6th sphere) aims at going into waking trance in order to oppose the conditionings that are opposed to the goal that we are seeking to achieve. We may find it necessary to repeat the first set of meditations once more again. The reason for this will be given later.

The fifth set of meditations (5th sphere) aims at going into waking trance to protect one's goal from outside obstructions. This is achieved by making a commitment to achieving one's goal without transgressions against others, or by being willing to face the consequences amongst our peers if this has been done.

The sixth set of meditations (4th sphere) aims at going into waking trance with the commitments to share the fruits of our accomplishments with others, regardless of our differences from them, and to maintain optimism in the face of "setbacks" and difficulties. It is here that the mundane goal is achieved. As it is said, "It was done in 6 days, and on the 7th, He rested."

But in reality, it is not time to rest. During the first set of meditations, we invoked the spiritual powers for the sake of our mundane objectives. It is now time to realize that the demands of earthly life exist for the sake of forcing Man to develop his spiritual powers.

The seventh set of meditations (sphere 3) aims at developing our spiritual power to the highest level that we are capable.

The eighth set of meditations (2nd sphere) aims at intuiting the true significance of the mundane objective that we achieved at the 6th stage.

The ninth set of meditations (1st sphere) aims at fusing the realizations of the past meditations into the realization of our Self as Ausar.

The tenth set of meditations (0 above the Tree) aims at realizing that the success of the meditations--fundamentally involving manipulations of our spirit--is due to the fact that our spirit is essentially unconditioned ("no things").

These ten components of a meditation are the substance of the traditional Kabalistical statement to the effect that all ten spheres or Deities must contribute to all of our undertakings in order for them to be of spiritual significance to us.

167

The Importance of Trance

We have seen that trance is an essential component of spiritual transcendence. The possession of the ability to go into trance at will, and to function in the state is a skill that all people must possess. Many people are now experimenting with so-called techniques of accelerated learning, which when understood are all based on the induction of a mild state of trance. They have discovered that by studying in a mild state of trance, learning can be sped up 2 to 50 times. The political, economic and military significance of this has not been lost to many nations that are secretly funding the development of these educational techniques. Imagine turning out a 20 year old Ph.D. in the most advanced concepts of nuclear physics, who at 30 would have the education and experience of a 60 year old. Incidentally, it was through the use of such "super" or "accelerated" learning techniques, and more, that enabled the ancient Black nations to forge in civilization, way ahead of the Western, and Eastern nations[2].

The studious reader would have noticed that the segregative functions of the left side of the brain correspond to spheres 2, 5 and 8, while the integrative functions of the right side of the brain correspond to spheres 3, 4 and 7. Sphere 9 unifies 7 and 8; 6 unifies 4 and 5, and 1 unifies 2 and 3[3]. The 6th sphere also unifies all spheres of the Tree. Of greatest importance to us at this point is the fact that while the left hemisphere of the brain is more concerned with the extroversion of consciousness, the right hemisphere is the introverter. Meditation, which is a process of introversion, relies heavily, then, on things that stimulate the right hemisphere to greater activity and deactivate the left hemisphere. This is achieved by concentrating on images and sensations, which are processed by the right side of the brain, while engaging the left side with the chanting of words of power. Since the left side of the brain deals with verbal thinking, it can be deactivated by engaging it with words of power, because the latter lack meaning (they are power holders, and not message holders). Repeating the word, prevents the process of verbal thinking which depends on the

2. Contemporary Black nations have fallen behind because they have been subjected to unrelenting warfare from the North for the past 4000 years, as well as the Western invention of that most Sebekian of tools,--money.

3. In reality, spheres one to three work out of a unified brain state.

stringing together of different words. In addition to this, the word of power contributes to the realization of the meditation objective.

The failure to understand this principle has been the cause for one of the greatest stigmas placed upon Black people for thousands of years. The use of images in thinking and meditating, in order to exalt the functions of the right side of the brain and thus introvert consciousness to bring about trance, is the basis of the religious use of "idols" and hieroglyphs. It is the reason Kamit (ancient Egypt) never abandoned the use of hieroglyphs for its religious and literary writings, while all of its civil records (inventories, bills, contracts, etc.) were written in phonetic script (hieratic and demotic). The well known concept that a picture is worth a thousand words is an allusion to the synthetical power of pictorial symbols. It is because of this that the kamitic initiates called the hieroglyphic script the "*Sesh Metut Neter*" (Sacred Writing). Its sacredness is due to its use in meditation and ritual. If for example, I want to heal myself through meditation, instead of going into trance with a thought such as "I am Ausar, the power to heal myself," I can chant the heka of Ausar "Aung," while visualizing my person holding a Uas staff (see Appendix A), which symbolizes well being and happiness. The string of meaningful words in the first example stimulates the left side of the brain, which by its very nature fights the internalization of consciousness. In the latter example, the right side of the brain is stimulated, therefore taking consciousness into the deeper recesses of consciousness, wherein reside the shaping forces of our behavior and physiological functions. This special use of the hieroglyphs has escaped all Egyptologists who have treated hieroglyphs in the only way that their limited understanding has allowed them. Westerners, who cannot help interpreting the Kamitic hieroglyphic script on the basis of their use of language, can do no better than to make the racist claim that it represents a primitive form of writing[4]. The hieroglyphic script is made up of 1) a set of alphabetical symbols representing vowels and consonants. 2) a set of non-alphabetical symbols that have been all lumped indiscriminately into a class Egyptologists call "determinatives" (some indicate that the word represents a deity, others, a person, etc.). While some of these symbols clearly function in this capacity, many of them are parts of what can be called the *Kamitic right side*

---

4. This is not a strong charge since Western scholars know very well that the Kamitians invented the script in use by the West. Do they call themselves primitive for not having even invented a script of their own?

of the brain symbol set. With the use of these symbols, which I have compiled and explained in Appendix A, all ideas that can be put into words for meditation purposes can instead be expressed pictorially, i.e., acted out in the spirit. Not only does this facilitate meditation, it eventually helps to unify the thinking of the initiate by providing him with a wealth of synthetical symbols for the use of his fourth sphere faculty. This esoteric or symbolic function of hieroglyphs is under the dominion of the Goddess of wisdom Seshat (also Seshait), also known as Sefkhit Aubut(related to the seven "liberal arts"), a female aspect of Tehuti. Tyros in Kamitic esotericism will be able to see the connection to "magic."

Chapter 13

Level 1, First Three Stages of the Meditation Process

Care of the Life-force

As the raising of our consciousness to the higher parts of the spirit and the achievement of our will cannot take place without a strong life-force, care of the life-force is the most important preliminary requirement to success in life and meditation. It is this force that is the energetic and substantive basis from which our physical bodies and higher parts of our spirit are made. It is also the basis of our metaphysical faculties that we call "deities." These are the spiritual complexes that are in charge of the operation of the host of physiological and mental functions. Het-Heru, for example, is in charge of the gonadal, gestational, artistic, imaginative functions, and so on; Sebek is in charge of the cerebro-spinal, verbalizing, sequential logical functions, and so on. It is for this reason that the life-force was called by the Kamitians Ra, the "father of the Gods and of all living things." It is not "the sun god," it is the solar force, which is the substantive and energetic basis of all things on earth[1]. While the Kamitians knew this fact over 6000 years ago, Western scientists have just recognized it in the past 100 years.

The observances that must be upheld to keep our life-force strong involve proper diet, conservation, moderation in our activities (mental and physical work, sex, eating, etc.), and living in harmony with the cycles and modalities of this life-force.

The Four Principles Underlying the Process of Meditation

The Fundamental Principles of Meditation

1. Level 1 of meditation, which is carried out in three stages (spheres 9 - 7), aims at a) <u>positioning</u> the Self (the inner guiding intelligence of our being) as the performer of the meditation and the undertaking, in place of our person. It is important to realize that our person is a limited, conditioned and defined entity-i.e., it is

---

1. Ultimately, food is transformed sunlight. Plants absorb it through their chlorophyll, and transform it into all of the substantive, and energetic material of the animal kingdom.

composed of a portfolio of capabilities, incapabilities, sensual and emotional orientations. As such, it is not capable of functioning outside of its portfolio. A martial personality cannot achieve a goal that requires mercurial, or venusian talents, but our Self-the indwelling intelligence guiding all of our spiritual (subconscious) and physiological activities can.

It must be realized that we are not merely positioning our Self as the executor of the meditation. Ultimately all meditations have as their purpose the realization of our true Self-Ausar, the inner guiding intelligence-as our identity. It is this that is meant by the archaic phrases, "achieving spiritual liberation," "attaining to nirvana," "Yoga is the union of the self (they mean person) with God," and so on. These nominal definitions, however, do not work for the student. What are needed are procedural definitions. To wit: Meditation has as its purpose, the uniting (yoga) of the will of the individual (Heru) with the indwelling intelligence (Ausar/Self), which is responsible for directing and unifying all physiological and spiritual functions. This union enables the individual's conscious needs-what is willed (for health, wealth, security, marital success, wisdom, etc.)- to be accepted and carried out by the indwelling intelligence[2]. This inner intelligence is always ready to do so, but the union between it and the personal will is interfered with, in most cases, by the set of disunited, conflicting, and contradictory ideas (the person/Set) that make up the belief systems guiding the actions of people.

2. Level 2 of Meditation, which is carried out in three stages (spheres 6-4), corresponds to the exertion of our will to establish the domination of the law of God-Cosmology, Maat Tehuti-over our thinking, feelings and actions. It is the living of this law that gives substance to our identification with Ausar as our Self. What are the "laws," or shaping forces, that govern your personality? Are they not a set of "I can do so and so," "I can't do so and so," "I like or don't like so and so, hence I do it or don't," and so on? What would happen if the indwelling intelligence running your body functioned in such a manner? "Well today I don't feel like directing the manufacturing of blood sugar, and I will not detoxify the body. I don't like doing that kind of work. It is so repugnant, etc." Shall we not thank God that it functions according to divine law? Yet, what it

2. In the metaphorein of Ausar, this corresponds to the making of Heru king of the world of the living, and Ausar, king of the underworld, as well as the resuscitation of the latter by the former.

does for your body and "subconscious mental activities" it can do for your marriage, career, etc.   But it is not a simple process of imagining what you want with a strong desire.   You must identify yourself as the indwelling intelligence, which is to think, feel and live according to divine law (Maat and Tehuti).

3. Level 3 of meditation, which is carried out in three stages (spheres 3 - 1), corresponds to the ability to utilize the divine powers, and omniscience of the spirit as a result of having established the law of God as the guide for living.   It is important to distinguish these powers from those obtained through the "occult" (subtle physics) use of herbs, gems, blood, and so on.   While the latter functions through the lower part of the spirit, requiring no spiritual transformation in the practitioner, the powers of the higher parts of the spirit (spheres 1-3) work primarily through divine law and words of power.

4. Level 4 of meditation corresponds to the realization that as our Self is inseparable from God, and shares in the same qualities of God, it is God that is ultimately responsible for all of the good things in our lives.

The 10 Stages of the Meditation Process

We will illustrate the meditation process with two scenarios. In the first, we have a woman who is having difficulties with her reproductive organs, and as a result, cannot become pregnant. All medications (allopathic, homeopathic, acupuncture, etc.) have failed. She consulted the oracle in the latter part of this book and was told that Het-Heru, the venusian deity will help her. The reason for this reading is that she has been too "hot" in her daily activities. The "fire" generated by the intensity with which she carries out her job (she is a boss lady), and the sharpness with which she deals with her subordinates are taking a toll on a reproductive system that was already congenitally weak, and harmed by earlier abortions. In the second scenario, we have a man who was told by the oracles that his career will be advanced by Maat. He came to the diviner because he could not understand how and why his acquaintances with significantly less talent, were steadily making progress, while he was stagnating, in spite of well planned and calculated career moves. Maat's prosperity generating force was choked off in his life because he failed to share with others. He was always too busy trying to make a buck, and would not make time to give some of his skills to his community. Although he was a devout church goer, his constant worrying over his financial situation betrayed that he had no understanding of, or faith in the laws of God. Let's call our woman Nefert-ra, and our man Sehu. They will achieve their goals through the series of meditations. Although the methods (chanting of hekau, breathing, etc.) that they will employ are efficacious, their success will depend on their ability to carry out the instructions.

Level 1 of the Meditation Process, Stage 1, Sphere 9

The first meditation aims at positioning Ausar as the executor of the meditation. Nefert-ra and Sehu will go into mediumistic trance chanting the heka "Aung Ausar Hung" (see Chapter 24), while visualizing themselves wearing the White Crown of Ausar (see Appendix A). Before performing this meditation they would have thoroughly studied the metaphorein of Ausar, and the meaning of Ausar as the indwelling intelligence that is guiding all of their spiritual (subconscious), and physiological functions. All of this information is to be equated with the White Crown of Ausar. As a result, the act of visualizing ourselves wearing this crown symbolizes our identification of ourselves as the embodiment of the ideas associated with Ausar. But more importantly, it enables us to express this act of identification without verbal thinking (left side of the brain activity, which resists the internalization of consciousness). That is to say, it enables us to think with the right hemisphere of the brain, which is in charge of the internalization of consciousness. This is the meaning of the Kamitic teaching to the effect that *"what the house of Neter (the Supreme Being) dislikes is much talking. Pray thou with a loving heart, the utterances of which are all in secret."* The "talking" during prayer (meditation) is the verbalization of our thoughts. The praying, which is uttered "in secret," is conducted through the graphic representation of our thoughts. This can be proven by comparing the attempts to meditate with verbalized thoughts, in comparison to using imagery. The fact that mental chattering is inimical to meditation, and that visualization aids it, is well known to seasoned practitioners of meditation.

Another important reason for bypassing the left side of the brain resides in the fact that it is the seat of our segregative, or disintegrative thinking and behavior. It is dominated by Set, the evil principle within us. It is the origin of the thoughts that delude us.

It is important to realize that the scope of this meditation is limited to initiating the process of identification of the individual with the Self. The realization of this identity, and the struggles to establish it, make up the theme of level 2 of the meditation process.

174

It is also important not to equate the process of this stage of meditation with western hypnosis. The individual is not being hypnotized into accepting the idea that his true self is Ausar. We must always keep in mind that Ausar is not an idea, but an actual entity[3]. It is the inner intelligence within our being, to which we are returning our identity. The closest that this meditation comes to hypnosis will be seen in those cases in which a person's ability to perform a particular task at a certain level is restored through hypnotherapy. The person is led to identify with his original capabilities, in place of the faulty performance that has replaced the former. It is not uncommon for athletes and artists to restore their confidence, or bring out their full potential through hypnotherapy. The major differences between the method employed here versus hypnotherapy reside in the fact that here the individual is identifying with the indwelling intelligence as his Self, whereas, in western hypnotherapy he maintains the person (the lower part of being) as his identity. While our method avails itself of the omniscience, omnipotence, and omnipresence of the inner intelligence of our being, western hypnotherapy confines the individual to the limitations of the personality. We must remember that our persons are defined entities. Some are martial, others lunar, others mercurial and so on. Each represents a set of capabilities and limitations.

The second meditation that must be done in this stage involves chanting the heka "Aung Ausar Hung," while visualizing your person wearing the White Crown of Ausar, as you plant a grain of cereal (corn, or barley, etc.). See it grow into a tree full of ears of grain. This is a right side of the brain way of expressing 1) your understanding that your Self-indwelling intelligence- is the source of all prosperity and sustenance in your life. 2) It also states that "from One comes many." This is to remind you that Ausar, your Self, is the one and only Self dwelling in all things. It is also symbolical of the fact that all of people's problems stem from their failure to identify with their true self. They thus invent millions of false causes for man's problems, and, of course, millions of like solutions. While Sehu has been blaming his lack of advancement on the inabilities of others to appreciate his true worth, Nefert-ra has been oppressing herself with the belief that life is just not fair. "Why me?" She asks herself over and over again. The truth is that all problems stem from the lack of knowledge of Self, or that the true self is the

---

3. This is why I coined the term "metaphorein," in place of myth, and allegory.

indwelling intelligence. Once this is known and taken as a base from which to build our thinking, feeling and action patterns, then we will avoid and solve all problems. That is, from one measure comes the solution to all problems. This unitary outlook on life is the true basis of monotheism.

The next set of meditations of the first stage aims at breaking the indiscriminate imitation flaw of the 9th sphere.

The third meditation at this stage involves chanting the heka "Aung Vang Duhung" (see Chapter 24). Once you are in trance, seek to recall one of the earliest times in which you manifested a particular emotional or sensual behavior. You will always discover that their earliest manifestations occurred when you were a child. Make the attempt to relive-just not remember-the situation, and you will notice that you expressed such behavior because you had no other option. You lacked the experience and the intellectual maturity to react rationally and philosophically to the situation, so you had no choice but to follow the emotions that reflected themselves in your awareness. You must therefore proceed to 1) meditate on the fact that now that you are an adult, you now have ideas, in place of emotions, through which to express yourself, 2) if you are going to continue this child-like behavior you must make a commitment to go and seek counsel for your life's problems from a child. You must also take note of the fact that the emotional expressions of anger, sensual craving, fear, shyness, greed, jealousy, etc. are not only common to both man and animals, but are the primary mode of expression of the latter, while man has a superior intelligence through which to alter his behavior. We must ask ourselves then (during the trance state), "How can we claim to be superior to animals, if we allow our emotions and sensualism to direct our thoughts and actions?" We must also identify each of these emotions, which originate in our animal spirit (the Khaibit, sphere 10), with one of the symbols of the Sesh Metut Neter (see Appendix A). Western biologists have just recently discovered that the human brain is in reality a number of brains, some of which are the centers for the traits that we share with animals. This fact was known to Kamitic priests thousands of years ago. They communicated this information through their hieroglyphic constructions of human-headed animals, and animal-headed humans. E.g., Anpu (Anubis), the jackal headed man symbolizing the cunning and cleverness that man shares with the canine species (also with the baboons[4], and other apes); the hawk, a trainable bird of prey, was used to symbolize the higher combative and destructive aspects of Man's spirit. These are the Deities Heru, Herukhuti, Seker, etc. An uncontrolled sensualism, for example, was equated with the pig-a correspondence of the "deity" Set-which symbolizes the self-destructive nature of an unbridled strong sensual drive. It is founded on the fact that the pig is known for its greed, which does not stop at even eating its own piglets. One must meditate with the following aims: 1) to realize that, to follow our emotions, is to imitate the animal part of the spirit[5], and 2) to detach our identity from our emotions. A major source of delusion and spiritual bondage comes from the belief that our emotions are expressions of our Self. People are in the habit of saying, "This is the way I feel . . . this is what I desire . . . I like so and so, etc." The Tree of Life offers us a means of seeing the difference between our Self, which resides at sphere one, with its roots in "0," and our emotions and sensual passions, which reside at sphere 10. We can begin to break these false identifications, by seeing our emotions and cravings for what they are; expressions of the animal part of our spirit (the Khaibit-sphere 10). The ultimate goal of our meditations, is the return of our focus of consciousness to the unprogrammed and unconditioned part of our spirit. Again, I must remind the reader that these meditations are not to be conducted through verbal thinking. The information associated which each symbol of the Sesh Metut Neter (Appendix A) must be thoroughly studied, understood and accurately amplified. While you are in trance, you must see your person with the head or body of the animal symbolizing your emotion or desire, indulging in an emotional situation. Jealous or hateful people might see themselves as serpents, filled with venom (ill will), waiting to ambush others. All negative emotions can be symbolized as worms eating away at one's vital force (Ra). Sehu, whose emotional problem is one of selfishness (8th sphere), will see himself as a canine (a jackal, or a dog). Have you noticed how dogs

---

4. Hence the baboon that is "sacred" to Tehuti. It is in reality a symbol of the 8th sphere that has close association to the 2nd. Yoruba initiates will understand this by analogies to the relationships of Elegba, the trickster, cunning Orisha to Ifa, the God of wisdom.

5. Emotions, and sensual pleasures, it must be understood, are to be allowed expression, only when they are in harmony with the truth. The "truth," though, is to be arrived at either through oracular inquiries, meditations taken sometimes to the 6th stage (sphere 4/Maat), and at other times to the 8th stage (sphere 2/Tehuti).

for the most part do not like to share their food? Nefert-ra will see herself on her job as the Goddess Sekmet--the lion-headed, destructive aspect of the sun's desert and barrenness making power. Please note that the third meditation is subdivided into four components.

The fourth meditation at this stage involves chanting the heka "Aung Vang Duhung." Once you are in trance, seek to recall one of the earliest instances in which you imitated your present emotional expression from someone else. You will notice that in most cases this took place when you were a child. Meditate with the aim of realizing that the emotion that you are presently harboring has its roots in the indiscriminate imitation of others. This is a form of "age regression meditation"

Level 1 of the Meditation Process, Stage 2, Sphere 8

The first set of meditations aims at positioning Ausar as the foundation of the reasons that we give ourselves for our beliefs, ways of feeling, and acting.   People are in the habit of basing the rationalizations for their actions on their identification with their persons.   In contrast to our indwelling intelligence, which is unconditioned, each person is the embodiment of a set of conditioned behavioral patterns. Fear, anger, sensitivities, shyness, failures, likes, dislikes and other shaping factors of personalities serve to limit an individual's ability to achieve his goals, not just simply from the fact that emotions can make him act irrationally, or paralyze his capacity for action, but more importantly, from the fact that they can interfere with the activity of the indwelling intelligence. This is symbolized as the killing of Ausar by Set. We must therefore realize that it is not a simple matter of "thinking positively," which must in the long run fail as long as the individual continues to identify himself with his person, which is in essence, limited in its capabilities. *A positive thought cannot succeed if it is contradicted by an innate limitation of the personality. We must therefore identify with the free part of ourselves-the indwelling intelligence-in order for our positive thoughts to be successful.*

The chief meditation of this stage is suggested by the function of one of the Deities of this sphere, Anpu (Anubis). He is the embalmer of Ausar, and assists in his mummification. In the Sesh Metut Neter, embalming and mummification symbolize the incorruptibility of the higher parts of the spirit. The initiate who has elevated his consciousness to this level is beyond the decadent influences of earthly things, which are symbolized by worms (see Appendix A). These earthly things-worms-that corrupt us are the earthborn ideas (the Sebau) that we hold about ourselves and life. As we saw, they originate in the left side of the brain (sphere 8) of Sahu Man. They are the emotion based rationalizations that we give ourselves, to "justify" indulging and following our emotions and sensualism. "I am only human so, naturally, I had to . . . or couldn't, etc." "I didn't live truth, but I am doing my spiritual work." To overcome this way of thinking we must thoroughly study and understand the fact that our true self-Ausar-is beyond the influence of emotions. No matter how often, and how strongly they reflect themselves in our awareness, we can resist and ignore them. What would happen if you didn't respond as an emotion suggested? Make an honest, and determined effort to ignore them the next ten times that they visit you, and you will see that they really don't have power over you. It is for this reason that emotions (Sebau) are called "the children of impotent revolt" in the *Pert Em Heru* (*Egyptian Book of the Dead*). Most people are controlled by their emotions mainly because they believe that they must follow them. Or, because they believe that emotions are the validators and justifiers of their actions. As if emotions were signifiers of truth, most people believe that they cannot do what they don't feel, and must do what they feel. All of the ideas of the Self's-indwelling intelligence's-imperviousness to emotions and sensualism must be equated to the depiction of Ausar as a mummy. Chant the heka "Aung Aing" (see Chapter 24) until you are deep in trance. Once in trance, recall a rationalization that you give yourself for indulging an emotion, while seeing yourself unmoved by it. Visualize yourself as the mummy Ausar[6]. The objective is for you to get in the habit of reasoning that if you identify with your true self, as opposed to your person, you can never use your emotions as justification of your actions. When we get to stage 4 of the meditation process we will see how the rationalizing faculty (8th sphere, Sebek) helps us to become impervious to temptations--i.e., how it embalms us (prevents moral decay). Nefert-ra must reject the belief that she cannot help getting upset by other people's lack of capability. As this fieriness is an intrinsic

---

6. It is important to appreciate the fact that here the problem is verbalized (stated by the left side of the brain), and the solution is pictured (expressed by the right side of the brain!).

quality of her personality (martial), she cannot become a calm person by simply nourishing positive thoughts to the effect. She must identify with her Self, Ausar, which is able to manifest any behavior, and personality that is required. We will have more to say on this in the third stage. Sehu's belief that his goal of achieving financial security can only be reached by devoting all of his time to his personal pursuits, will be transcended by his realization that as his true self is the same Self in others, what he does for others, he does for himself. His true self is not bound by time and energy limitations in the accomplishment of its goals. The indwelling intelligence directs thousands of physiological functions at the same time. By identifying with it as our true self we are able to transcend the limitations of our persons. This identification is the "Opening of the Way." Our rationalizations of what we can and can't do, which are the intrinsic limitations of our personalities, close the way to the working of our indwelling intelligence in the totality of our being. It limits the Self to the task of directing the "subconscious" mental and bodily processes. To sum up, the objective of the meditation at this stage is the realization that as our true self is infinite in its potential to know and do, we must never accept any limiting thought regarding the things that we need to accomplish in life. We must always be ready to say "I can . . .," with the understanding that this "I" is not the complex of capabilities, limitations, and inclinations that we call our personality, but the unconditioned, hence, infinitely capable indwelling intelligence of our being--Ausar.

Level 1 of the Meditation Process, Stage 3, Sphere 7

Now that we have positioned the infinite potential part of our being-the indwelling intelligence-as executor of the meditation (stage 1), and have brought our rationalizations of what we want, in harmony with the Self (stage 2), we are now ready to meditate on achieving the goal. A fundamental principle at work in this stage is based on the fact that our life-force does not make distinctions between the actions that we visualize during trance, and the same actions when they are carried out physically. Western scientists have objectively verified that the visualization of ourselves doing exercises, while in a mild state of trance, effects the same physiological responses as actual exercising. Many athletes and artists are currently improving their performances in this manner with the help of hypnotherapists. The spirit ("sub-conscious") does not distinguish between a successful performance (singing, playing tennis, typing, lecturing, having sex, etc.) that is carried out in one's imagination during trance, from one that is carried out physically. To wait for success in the physical performance of an act, before you can feel confident of your ability to succeed, is backward and dangerous. In the mediumistic or sleep (hypnotic) mode of trance, the animal spirit with all of its conditioned resistances to change is lulled to sleep[7]. This enables us to carry out perfect performances in our imagination while in trance. On the other hand we might hit or miss our objectives when we physically carry out our actions without such preparations. If an individual were to conduct 100 perfect lectures, or golf swings in the entranced imagination, as far as the spirit is concerned, the individual has, "in actuality," perfectly performed these acts, even though they have never been done physically. When the time comes for these actions to be done physically, the spirit will guide the body to the flawless execution of the acts. This is due to the fact that the spirit (the "sub-conscious") is the executor of all actions.

We are just not simply speaking of some esoteric way of rehearsing. All behaviors, and physical functions are controlled by matrices composed of sub-atomic energy/matter. This energy/matter is the substantial basis of our thoughts. We must realize that the sounds, and images that are perceived as thoughts, must be formed from some type of energy/matter. It is this energy/matter that we manipulate into images to direct and control, not only our physiological and emotional behavior, but events in the social dimension of our lives, as well as the environment, as you will verify from your success in meditation.

Assistance From the Deities

"Seek assistance from deity A," "Deity B will protect you," etc. are expressions that can only be placed in proper perspective through the Tree of Life. While our Self is located at Sphere 1, and is unconditioned and unqualified, personalities are located at sphere 9, and are conditioned by the set of qualities of the 10th sphere. Where the 10th sphere (animal spirit, Khaibit) emphasizes the fiery mode (Aries, Scorpio, Leo, etc.) of the Life-force, the individual's Ka (personality), barring illness, etc., excels at fiery tasks and

---

7. This is the main reason for employing this type of trance during the first three stages of the meditation process.

challenges. The person is zealous, enterprising, quick in deciding and acting, short tempered, a leader through force of character, etc. But this heat, which makes this type of person successful when challenged to respond in a fiery (hot/dry) manner, will be the cause of failure when challenged to meet a situation that requires the calm reflection, and flexibility of the watery (cold/moist) type of personality, or the persuasive and clever rhetorical skill of the earthy (cold/dry) personality, or when challenged to a long protracted fight that requires the blend of law and power of the airy[8] (hot/moist) personality type. Thus we can understand the "indivisible duality" between the two components of our being (hence man is called "an individual"); the Self, which is the constitutional component, and the person which is the functional. This is to say that the constitution, or law of our being, which is the Self's infinite capacity of expression, is united at our birth to a finite functional complex--the personality. A fiery person, for example, will not find in his personality portfolio the means of genuinely, convincingly, consistently, and most importantly, satisfying to his nature, being calm and yielding in confrontations. Similarly, the watery person will be afflicted when called upon to be zealous, enterprising, and domineering. In the archaic mode of speaking, each person must seek assistance from the "personality complex"-the deity-that governs the set of behavioral attributes that are outside of our natal personality. Since we are each born in intimate association with only one of these seven personality types, the practice of invoking, or evoking (calling out[9]) the non-natal personalities, seems to the spiritually immature as if beings external to ourselves, were being called upon. We must clarify this point. Although all personalities are latent in our Self, the other six that a person is not born with are outside of her person. Unfortunately, this subtle arrangement--*inside the Self, but outside the person*--has given rise to the widespread belief that the deities are outside of our being.

---

8. It is important to separate the Kamitic "airy" metaphor which is the hot and moist principle, from the Chinese (Taoist) "air" which corresponds to the Kamitic "earth." Similarly, the latter is not the same as the Chinese "earth" which corresponds to the Kamitic "ether," also known as "akasha," to use the Hindu term.

9. Note that the terms associated with bringing forth the deities, "evocation and invocation" are based on the root, "voc," to call. It hints at the method of bringing out the inner powers. They are called, or chanted out through the use of hekau (words of power, mantras).

To invoke a deity, then, is to call a personality complex out of its latent state within the Self, and actualize it as a temporary substitute to our *natal personality*. The fact that the *non-natal personality complex* that is needed to solve the problem must be called out of its latent state within the Self, underscores the premise of the first stage of meditation. We cannot benefit from the infinite potential of the indwelling intelligence if we do not identify with it as our true self, which transcends all personality qualities. We cannot call out behavior from our personalities that are not intrinsic to them. Calmness cannot come out of fire, zealousness cannot come out of earth, or water, etc. Thus, to the degree that we can identify with Ausar, we can manifest personality qualities that are not natal to us. We find many *"Chapters of transformations (Kheperu)"* in the *Pert em Hru* (*Egyptian Book of the Dead*), in which the initiate ("deceased") who has realized himself as Ausar is thus able to transform himself into a hawk of gold (Heru), Ptah, a phoenix, a lotus, Temu, Sobek, etc. We read in plate XXVII, *"Said Ausar, the scribe Ani, justified in peace. I came into being from the unformed matter, I came into existence as Khepere (the principle of transformation). I unfolded into plants, I am hidden in the tortoise. I am the te (atoms, essence) of every deity. I am yesterday as the four, and the uraeus of the seven which came into existence in the East."* Note that the initiate, the scribe Ani[10] is addressed as Ausar showing that he has achieved this level of being. Unlike western "scholars" who claim that Man evolved from apes, the Kamitic sages taught that Man came from the "unformed matter" (the paut). Note that his Self, Ausar, is the "te," the essence, or "atom" of all the deities. The "four of yesterday," correspond to the four fundamental transformations of the life-force (the four elements) underlying the seven personalities, of which the initiate says that he is their "uraeus."

Another important concept to be comprehended, deals with the manner in which changes in our behavior, and life is achieved. An effect of anti-polytheism has been the substitution of abstract ideals for the deities, which we have seen are personality complexes. As a result, people will pray or meditate on getting "courage," or "patience," etc., which are abstractions, instead of meditating on manifesting the entire personality complexes that govern these

---

10. Although the papyrus was prepared for the deceased scribe Ani, the very nature of the material, and the spiritual tradition of Egypt, leave us to conclude that the lofty spiritual teachings in the "Pert em Heru" reflected the teachings of the initiates into the mysteries.

attributes. This takes us back to the Sesh Metut Neter. *The spirit can only react to wholes, concrete thoughts, images, and sensations.* While it cannot react to the abstract word "evil," it can react to the image of something considered so, unless the former gives rise to the latter in the person's mind. In the same way, it cannot react to the *fractional abstraction* "courage," but it can react to the description (a concrete indication) of a personality (a whole) having courage as one of its qualities. Good creative writers know this well. To move their readers (affect their spirits) they know that they must "show," more than they "tell." This is why the Christian tradition promotes the concrete image of the life and suffering of Jesus, above the concepts regarding the Father in heaven. The truth is to be found in the fact that the Father in heaven is just too abstract to serve as a model for affecting the spirit of its followers. The process is better known in Africa, where it is well known, that there are seven distinct personality types (archetypes) which cannot be united into one synthetic archetype, as the Christians have tried to do with the Christ[11]. Each deity is the archetype, or perfect exemplar for a specific personality type. Heru in Kamit, and Shango (Jakuta) with the Yorubas is the archetype of mature manhood, fatherhood, male leadership and kingship. Auset in Kamit, Yemaya with the Yorubas is the archetype of mature womanhood, motherhood, female leadership, and queen-mothership. Herukhuti in Kamit, Ogun with the Yorubas is the archetype of the enterprising, pioneering, defensive, and aggressive personality type, and so on. So rather than meditate on the fractional abstraction "courage," for example, we bring out of latency the full personality complex (a whole) of either Heru, or Herukhuti. The process is exactly as that encountered in the practice of Homeopathic, or Chinese medicine. We don't prescribe medicines for fractions such as "suppressed menses," or "fever." We consider the entire complex of symptoms, and if needed, all of the personality traits of the patient, and search for a remedy which addresses the entire complex. For example, what will truly cure (just not palliate) the suppressed menses of a fiery woman, will not only fail to help a similar disorder in mild woman, but may even aggravate the condition.

Nefert-ra will therefore meditate on manifesting Het-Heru, as opposed to the fractional abstraction of "becoming a calm

---

11. I say the Christ, and not Jesus, because the Nazarene from Galilee has been turning in his grave for the past two thousand years over what Paul has done with his Jewish Messianic movement.

person," or on visualizations of her womb healing, etc. She will chant a heka of Het-Heru, "Aung Tang sutcha-a Het-Hert" (See Chapter 24). Once she is in trance, she will see herself wearing the crown of Het-Heru[12], dressed in yellow and green to enhance the required mood. Visualizing herself thus, she will recall those recurring situations in which she tends to function in a fiery manner, but seeing herself functioning in a sweet, yielding, and mild manner. She will support this meditation by indulging in lively music, keeping herself entertained, surrounding herself with beautiful things, and other correspondences to the deity Het-Heru. As she works more and more with the heka (word of power, mantra), and its energies flow into energize the imagery of the meditation, Nefert-ra will find a growing motivation to function as ritualized. Once she begins to manifest the desired behavior, which will be established at the end of the 4th stage of the meditation process, the avoidance of fiery behavior, and the expression of sweetness in the face of confrontation will result in a lowered metabolic rate which is conducive to the healing of the ovaries, increase in body fat, etc.

Since Sehu was told that Maat will help him achieve his goal, he will enter into trance with the Heka of Maat, "Aung Shring." Crowned with Maat's feather he will see himself giving some of his time and skills to his community. The bringing of balance into his life will be symbolized by the visualization of himself holding a scale with his heart in one pan, and Maat's feather in the other (See the Maat card). It symbolizes the balance between all complementary elements; in this case, the needs of the person, and those of the group.

In the chapter on initiation it was said that this stage also corresponds to the intensification of the life-force. Let's recall the observation that our emotions are the psychical driving force of the spirit. Nothing that is willed can be realized if there is no e-motive force behind it. A mistake that most people make is to think of joy as an effect, or reward for success, when it is the psychic motive force that is needed to succeed. This motive force can be cultivated by a practice known in the yogic tradition as asvini mudra. It consists in the rhythmic contraction and relaxation of the perineal muscle. This is the small annular muscle that is contracted in order to stop the urine in mid stream. It is also the muscle that goes into spasms at the moment of sexual arousal and orgasm. The practice of asvini mudra (as well as mula bandha) throughout the meditation

---

12. Symbolizing that she has succeeded in acquiring the qualities of the deity.

at this stage generates a feeling of sexual arousal, which the spirit, unlike the rational part of our being, does not distinguish as "sexual excitement." To the spirit, this pleasure is associated with the contents of the mind during trance. As far as the spirit is concerned Sehu is experiencing pleasure from sharing, and Nefert-ra is enjoying being sweet in the face of confrontation. And as we have shown earlier, the sharing, and the sweet behavior carried out in the entranced imagination are as real to the spirit, as the physical undertaking of the actions.

It is important to realize that the method given here for conducting this stage of the meditation process is a mere adaptation of the actual practice which consists of a full blown ritual involving trance induction through chanting, drumming, dancing and the use of many other techniques.

Summary
Nomenclature

It is important to pay particular attention to the special manner in which the words "person," "individual," and "self" are being used in this book. While they are generally used synonymously, their etymology shows that they are fundamentally different in meaning.

Person: is compounded of "per" = through + "son" = sound. We have seen that the various personalities are expressions of the deities (words of power, sounds) working through the lower part of the spirit. At times, for the sake of communication, I will sometimes use "lower self" for person. It corresponds to our being at the 9th and 10th sphere levels.

Self: is a term allied to the concept of identity. It is thus reserved in this book for the higher part of being. This will be understood by the capitalization of the term, as Self, or by the construction "true, or higher self." It corresponds to our being at the 1st sphere level, and 0.

Individual: is compounded of "indivisible + dual." It is obvious that this word, like "person," is not the kind of word that accidentally comes into being at the fish market, or the barber shop. It is created by men working on a subject with the precision and discipline that is demanded by chemistry, and mathematics. "Individual," thus denotes the indivisible duality between the higher and lower parts of our being. The Self and the person. It corresponds to being at the 6th sphere; the point of supreme equilibrium on the tree.

186

Chapter 14

Level 2, Second Three Stages
of the Meditation Process

The procedure of separating the meditation process into stages, is a strategy that is dictated by the behavior of our life-force (Ra, kundalini). While, on one hand, its arousal is essential to the realization of the meditation objective, on the other hand, its arousal also vitalizes the conditionings, and beliefs that are opposed to the meditation goal. For example, when a person meditates to give up smoking, the arousal of the life-force to realize this objective will also vitalize the habit of smoking. It is clear, then, that something must be done as a safeguard before arousing the life-force. This is the objective of the first two stages of the meditation process. A nonarousal of the life-force mode of meditation (mediumistic trance) is used during the first two stages to impress upon the spirit the goal of the meditation. Once this has been established, a life-force intensifying mode of meditation is used in the third stage to vitalize the objective. If an antagonistic conditioning to the objective, or the virtues that must be cultivated to achieve it exists in the spirit, it will also be vitalized. This will result in a crisis, or several of them, in which we must choose between the new objective, or the new virtues, on one hand, and on the other, the old habits. These crises are called, in the spiritual tradition, "crossroad" situations. This is the theme governing the second level of the meditation process.

Level 2 of the Meditation Process, Stage 4, Sphere 6

This stage corresponds to a set of meditations revolving around man's will. It was said earlier that for an indication of an expected accomplishment to be considered an act of the will, it must be free of emotional or sensuous influence. Otherwise, it is a desire. Since all personalities are indissolubly tied in with emotions, only those expectations arising from an identification with the indwelling intelligence can be considered willed events. There can be no such as a free will where the individual's choices are dictated by emotional or sensuous compulsion. It is important to note that the failure to distinguish between willing and desiring is a major cause of the failure to grow spiritually, for we fail to transcend our emotionality when we avoid an emotional act, because of another emotion. This is the reason for Heru's initial failure to defeat Set.

We must also recall that the true purpose of our will is not for choosing the path of our destiny, which is determined in the spiritual realm before incarnation. This is why competent astrologers can read a person's destiny from their charts. In most traditional African societies, it is a common practice for the character, and destiny of an individual to be revealed by diviners shortly after birth. The Goddess of destiny, for example, accompanies Tehuti when he makes his appearance at the individual's birth. This can be viewed from another perspective. Every person's destiny is under the control, and direction of the indwelling intelligence. The true purpose of the will is to ensure that the thoughts, feelings and actions that we undertake are in harmony with the plan of our indwelling intelligence. All truly successful people, who have not been guided by diviners, manage to intuitively, or instinctively discover their career, or destiny objective as determined by their true self. Unfortunately, they are in the minority. Most people must discover their earthly mission from their indwelling intelligence through the use of oracles, or in-depth meditation.

In most cases, the effort to live according to the dictates of the Self, which are based on divine law, brings us into opposition with the emotionally dominated personality. These crises, which are intensified by life-force arousal procedures, are symbolized in the Ausarian metaphorein by the battle between Heru and Set, and in other traditions, they are the "crossroads," which are the chief places for conducting rituals, and making offerings to God. These spiritual crises are the most important events in our spiritual development. They are the only events that mark our spiritual growth. It is of utmost importance to understand that spiritual growth does not take place from the studying of scriptures, spiritual literarure, doing rituals, meditating, deity or ancestor possession, etc. These are merely means of preparing you to live truth at the crossroad. Unfortunately, about 97% of students of spirituality do not know this truth. They pick and choose when and where they will observe a spiritual teaching, oblivious to the the fact that spirituality is the living of truth, each and every time that one finds oneself in a situation of having to choose between the laws of the higher parts of being, against our feelings, and opinions regarding the situation.

"Crossroad" situations have very marked characteristics. On the side of the lower part of being, we experience strong emotions, and rationalizations to the effect that we will suffer irreparable harm if we give in to the truth, or ignore the emotions. A person who is endeavoring to transcend selfishness will find himself in a critical situation, not of his choosing, in which he is called upon by the circumstances to share with his worse enemy, or to be nice with a most obnoxious person who has humiliated him, and so on. It is then that Sebek, his faculty of rationalization, will provide him with very clever, yet transparent, excuses for not living truth. A careful and objective examination of these rationalizations will reveal that they are made up of all sorts of half-truths, and out and out double talk (forked tongue). Good examples can be found in the arguments given by the American government for subsidizing tobacco growers, while banning tobacco ads from the air waves.

It is only when we transcend the dominance that our emotional and sensual vehicle exerts upon us, that spiritual growth takes place. This is easier said than done, as we all very well know from the trouble that most people encounter in dealing with their bad habits and emotions. Yet, with the proper meditation technique, and spiritual education, it is much easier than is generally believed.

Men Ab em Aungk em Maat

The meditation technique for transcending the emotions was called Men Ab em Aungk Em Maat (Keeping the Heart stable to live Truth) in the Kamitian tradition, and Satipatthana (Right or stable mindfulness) in esoteric Buddhism. Contrary to popular opinion, the way to successfully deal with emotions, is not by "controlling" them, but by ignoring them. This is the essence, not only for establishing the dominion of the will, but as we will later see, for the experiencing of our Self as the indwelling intelligence.

What would happen if you did not obey an emotion, or sensual craving? Nothing! This thought seems not to have occurred to most people, who believe that they must follow their feelings, and that their feelings are the validators of their will, and their actions. I.e., that unless they have a feeling for doing something, they cannot do it, or that the action is not genuine, and so forth. Most people succumb to this delusion, even though they have already overcome a habit (smoking, alcohol, meat eating, etc.) that should have taught them once and for all the truth. The day you made up your mind to

189

give up a habit, the craving did not stop. You succeeded by ignoring the craving, and following your knowledge of the facts, even though the latter lacked power to generate feelings of pleasure. In fact, the pleasure was with the habit you were seeking to transcend.

Essentially, the Men Ab meditation process is a practice of ignoring the thoughts, sensations and emotions that motivate you to think, give attention to feelings, and act in opposition to what the truth of the situation demands. A person, for example, experiences emotions that pressure him to withdraw, and to dwell on feelings and thoughts of insecurity and inferiority, whenever his wife declines to become intimate, whether she is justified or not. The Men Ab meditation will consist of 1) ignoring such thoughts, and making every effort to act in a contrary manner, and 2) as you will most likely be visited by a) thoughts of guilt and recrimination for harboring the negative thoughts, and feelings, you must also ignore this set of thoughts and emotions as well. You may also experience a sense of anguish manifesting as an intolerance of the sensations of oppression associated with the emotion of guilt. Rather than alowing yourself to get caught up in hoping to be free of these sensations, and doing things to expedite the deliverance from them, you must learn to accept their presence. In time, the emotions will cease to visit you, as long as you persevere in the above meditation procedure. Incidentally, it must be noted that this meditation technique is practiced, not sitting in a quiet place, but in the thick of our everyday life experiences. It aims at giving us expertise in the management of our thoughts, emotions, and states of consciousness. The governing principle of Men Ab is that *there is never a 'reason' for an emotional reaction.* In other words, the tie between an emotion and what prompts it is not a rational one. It is based on the law of association, which was well explained by the Russian psychologist Pavlov. He would ring a bell each time he fed his dogs. Eventually, the ringing of the bell would by itself elicit the salivation, and flow of digestive juices, as if the food had also been presented to the dogs. *The spirit could not tell the difference between the bell and the food*[1]! All of our emotional and sensual responses are based on this non rational associative mechanism. As Man's spirit is originally, and essentially free of emotional conditioned reflexes, all emotions are superimpositions on Her true nature. Must you become angry in

---

1. This is the master key of ritual. Once you are experiencing your objective during trance, associate it to a perfume, a heka, etc. The latter will serve as a trigger of the former, and a quick way of empowering the hekau.

order to defend yourself? Have not thousands of years of oriental martial arts practice proven that the calmer the warrior, the better is his performance? Are animal faces, screaming, tensing of the body and shouting obscenities necessary for expressing one's dissatisfaction? Don't they reduce the clarity of our communication of displeasure? "What about suppression?" some people may ask. They may argue that the Men Ab technique involves suppression of the emotions and sensual "needs," and may therefore be harmful. "It is best to let it out," some will argue, ignoring the catastrophic results in many cases; murders, broken marriages, high blood pressure, etc. We must return once more to the truth concerning the original and essential nature of Man's spirit. It is free of all emotional and sensuous conditioning. This is what enables us to remove the pain conditioned reflex, through suggestions given in trance, to allow surgical procedures to be done without anesthetics. The pain mechanism is a protective condition (hence, a conditioned reflex) imposed upon the organism, due to the slowness and corruptibility of the voluntary thought mechanism. If the removal of a part of our physical organism from a harmful source depended on our thinking, we would be in a great deal of trouble (most people freeze up in threatening situations, etc.), thus, the indwelling intelligence has programmed (conditioned) the spirit to react automatically to threatening situations. When, however, we know that we must subject the organism to pain, as with surgery, parturition (labor), etc., we can remove the superimposed pain reflexes. This "fight or flight" mechanism is very primitive. It has its centers in the portion of our brain, which is dominant in the life of animals[2], and influences us to animalistic behavior. Failing to distinguish between real, imagined and interpreted threats, it automatically prepares us to fight, or flee whenever we believe that we are threatened. If we keep our minds on the fact that the successes experienced by people in overcoming their habits (smoking, alcoholism, etc.) was due to the fact that the cravings and emotional drives to indulge, eventually disappeared, as a result of their being consistently ignored, then there was no suppression at work. In fact, the avoidance of the possibility of suppression is the aim of the second practice of the Men Ab meditation system.

Let's return to our gentleman above, who is visited by emotions pressuring him to withdraw and indulge thoughts of insecurity whenever his wife says to him, "no honey, not tonight. I

---

2. The R-complex (brain stem), and the mid-brain.

don't feel like it." He has read up to the last paragraph, and tells the author, "Ok. I am with you. I realize that my spirit is originally, and essentially unconditioned, therefore, these emotions are not who I am. I have been ignoring the pressure to withdraw and to dwell on thoughts of self-worthlessness, etc. But the fact is that, even though I make the effort to interact in a normal way with my wife at such moments, I nevertheless feel terrible. The feelings and the thoughts are still there in the background. I really want them to go away." We can all identify with our gentleman friend. Again, the answer is the same. Ignore this second set of thoughts and emotions, for the simple fact that our spirit is essentially and originally free of emotional conditionings, and the aim of spiritual development is the removal of the emotional superimpositions on the spirit. In other words, armed with the knowledge that our true nature is lacking in intrinsic emotional programs we make the effort to ignore the conditioned reflexes pressuring us to accept the thought that we cannot stand the sensations accompanying our emotions. Ignoring these thoughts is not merely our inattention to them. We must not seek ways to rid ourselves of the feeling, nor indulge thoughts to the effect of wishing that the feeling would soon go away ("I will be glad when I stop feeling this way, etc."), nor indulge the thoughts that we are unvirtuous, immature or unspiritual for having such emotions. We must remember that all emotions and sensual cravings are expressions of the lower part of our being-the person-and not our Self-the indwelling intelligence. Identification with our Self-Ausar-involves non-identification with our emotions.

It is interesting to note, that while Western man identifies his emotions as the expressions of his Self, in the Kamitic tradition they are identified with the animal part of our being. The latter is kept uppermost in the understanding of the people through the widespread symbolization of human[3] nature as animal-headed people or human-headed animals (E.g., the Deities Heru, Set, Anpu, etc.). This allows us to keep our emotions in their proper place, instead of elevating them, and thus giving them power over our lives, as Westerners have done.

What are emotions anyhow? In all the behaviors so labelled, we will discover that they involve a response in which we become _tense_, especially in our breathing which gets restrained and focused in the upper chest region at the point beneath the sternum.

---

3. We must not confuse the "human," with the "man." The term human reflects the understanding that there is an earthly side to man. Human = humus (earth) + man.

Because of this our breathing is shallow (less than 500 ml) and irregular. Stuck in this tense, shallow and irregular breathing state, we are thrown into a negative trance with the belief that 1) some external situation or agent is the cause of our sensation (we give it a meaningless label: anger or shyness or fear, etc.), and that 2) we must follow the behavior suggested by the thought component of our emotion. As emotions occur at the junction of the 9th and 10th spheres, the trance that is experienced is of the mediumistic modality, which means that the will becomes inactive. A characteristic of the mediumistic trance, is that the contents of the sphere of awareness are accepted as reality. This is how emotions exert their power over people's lives. This insight into *emotions*, that they *are mediumistic trances, accompanied with tense abnormal breathing* (painful as well as pleasurable!), gives us the clue for disarming their power to compel us. 1) Do not dwell on the thoughts that accompany them 2) focus your attention on each spot where you feel tense, and will your body to relax itself 3) regulate and harmonize your breathing, by naking it deep, slow and rhythmic, and 4) if applicable, do just the opposite of what the thought accompanying the feeling was suggesting. Make a strong effort to carry out the last instruction. When a powerful emotion threatens to overwhelm us, at step number 3, we can zap it by forcibly pulling the lower abdomen in and up. Lift the upper chest, and hold it as you breathe out. Make sure that the lower abdomen is the only place in the body where tension is felt. This cannot be overstated. Follow this outbreath by expanding the lower abdomen as you breathe in. At the end of the inbreath tense the lower abdomen and hold the breath. Repeat the cycle starting with the forcible contraction as shown above. Do this for as long as is needed to defuse the emotion[4]. It should not require many repetitions. Its effectiveness is due to the fact that the forcible contraction of the lower abdomen applies pressure on the pneumogastric nerve, which stabilizes the activity of the heart, and sends a reflex stimulus to the waking center of the brain (the R complex) and the cerebral cortex. This manipulation of the nervous system serves to awaken the person from the mediumistic trance of emotion, as it is the basis for inducing waking trance.

---

4. This is the great Mahabhanda that male hatha yogins use to forestall an orgasm, in order to arouse the kundalini during tantric rituals. Authors of Hatha Yoga manuals have removed it from its proper context, and teach it as a mere "pranayama" technique.

Another important goal of the Men Ab meditation system is the sharpening of mindfulness. How many times haven't you said to yourself that you will not indulge a particular habit, only to find yourself knee deep in the act before you remembered your pledge. A simple, yet very effective technique, consists in taking away something that you like very much from yourself for each infraction. Another extremely useful exercise that is a must, consists in going for several days without laughing or smiling. Because these emotions are so powerful, the ability to ignore them gives the individual a great deal of skill in handling the negative ones.

Beyond the issue of emotional transcendence, the practice of ignoring our emotions strengthens our awareness of the duality of our nature. Through the Men Ab meditation, we have repeated experiences of the fact that on one hand there is a part of our being saying, "I will not allow my body to follow the impulses to laugh, cry . . ," while there is another part that is generating these impulses independent of our will and consciousness. This is the objective reality behind the term "individual" (indivisible duality).

Pert Em Heru

It was noted at the beginning of this chapter that the first three stages of meditation employ the mediumistic trance technique. It is based on putting the will and the left hemisphere of the brain-our syllogistic and analytical information processor-to sleep[5]. Although this enables the implantation into the spirit of suggestions for changes in behavior, because there can be no opposition from the slumbering segregative and analytical thinking dominated will, the absence of these faculties makes it impossible for us to consolidate our knowledge. We have seen that the latter cannot be attained in the "normal" waking state, as full wakefulness, and concentration is not achieved in this state.

To attain full wakefulness, upon which insight and the efficient use of the will depends, we must triple our oxygen intake, and reduce the flow of the life-force to the voluntary organs (senses, legs, arms, etc.) of the body. The increased supply of oxygen gives us a degree of internal wakefulness far exceeding that of the "normal" waking state. This is why the waking trance was called "Pert em

---

5. It is this that allows for the spirit to be directed by another's will (hypnotist, initiator, ancestor), or for its own faculties, stimulated by meditation or ritual, to "act on its own"-as in spirit, or deity possession.

Heru" (Becoming Awake, or Coming by day) by the Kamitians. Besides giving us the insight and clarity of perception to transcend the host of false beliefs clouding our understanding, this mode of trance also provides the force and vitality needed for the successful carrying out of our need. This is especially needed at the "crossroad" situations spoken of earlier. It is then that our eighth and tenth spheres overwhelm us with the fear of losses and harms that we will incur if we live according to divine truth. The successful practice of the Men Ab meditation process, and the waking trance are the foundations of the following meditation stages.

The meditation at this stage involves going into trance with the heka "Aung Hring," as we go into trance visualizing ourselves as Heru (see the Heru card) resisting or destroying the animals that symbolize our emotions (see Appendix A).

Level 2 of the Meditation Process, Stage 5, Sphere 5

In this stage we use all of the techniques developed in the preceding stage (Men Ab meditation and waking trance) to establish our sense of justice. The ability to give justice depends on our skill in ignoring fear and anger. I.e., it depends on a skillful and vitalized will. An analysis of all acts of injustice will reveal an underlying fear or anger at work. Thus, we see once more how important is the return of our identity to our true self, which is essentially free of emotional and sensual conditionings.

It must also be noted that to the degree that we can give justice to others, to that degree will we receive spiritual protection from the injustices of others.

The meditation at this stage involves going into waking trance with the heka "Aung Hlring" while visualizing ourselves as the Deity Herukhuti in the act of destroying the animals symbolizing our fear or anger. The objective is to rise above the temptations to achieve our goals through transgressions against others, or having observed this law, to succeed against the injustices of others.

Level 2 of the Meditation Process, Stage 6, Sphere 4

While the preceding stage corresponds to our ability to detach ourselves from our person by sacrificing our personal interest for the sake of being just to others, this stage demands an even greater act of detachment. We are here called upon to rise above

195

our egotism by sharing with others. It is not uncommon at this stage to find ourselves, as a result of rituals and meditations at a crossroad in which the circumstances make a clear and inarguable argument for us to share with our enemies. In fact, this is the highest test of our ability to truly love. I.e., to give not seeking anything in return, but to fulfill a genuine need.

To be able to share, especially in such challenging situations, is not only a revelation of our transcendence of our persons and the understanding of our oneness, it also liberates a great deal of energy which is in turn used by the spirit toward the realization of the meditation objective.

It is important to realize that beginning with the 4th stage (6th sphere) of the meditation process, the detachment of the identification from the person begins to be established. The person, with its characteristic set of emotional and sensual patterns of behavior, is denied in order to assert the unconditioned Self. At stage 5 (sphere 5), the wedge is driven even further by our commitment to be fair with others, even if it means incurring great material losses. At this stage, the call to share with strangers and enemies, alike, drives our identity so far out of our person that we can almost begin to "feel" our true "inner" self. This budding experiencing of the indwelling intelligence takes on the form of a sense of joy and optimism that is independent of externals and success. In fact, as stated earlier, joy is the force that heals and brings success. Unfortunately, the majority of people reverses this relationship, and make joy the result of being healthy and successful.

The meditation at this stage, therefore, consists in going into trance with the heka "Aung Shring[6]" while visualizing yourself holding a scale in which your heart is in one pan, equally balanced by a feather in the other. See the Maat card in the section of the oracle. The scale symbolizes the balance that must exist between all dualities in our lives. For example, between our personal, and our Self interests; between our empirical information, and our spiritual intuitions (a priori knowledge); between our left-brained sequential verbal thinking, and our graphic, spatial and wholistic thinking, and so on. A light heart, i.e., a heart that weighs no more than a feather is a sophisticated symbol of the evidence of living truth (Maat = truth). But what is Truth? It is something to be attained through reading the scriptures, or through dialectical argumentation

---

6. The heka "Shring" is concealed in the name of the deity Seshat, which is an aspect of Maat.

196

according to Westerners. According to the African tradition, it can only be known through living. Man discovers Truth by living according to the laws of his true nature. It is of interest to note that according to the bible, Man and God share the same qualities of being. This is a theme that is dropped as soon as it is stated. We read in Genesis 1:26, "And God said, let us make man in our own likeness." It does not take much to realize that the likeness of God in which Man is made cannot refer to man's physical image, or to the set of personality qualities (habitual fears, likes, dislikes, etc.). Man, "the likeness of God," must then be a formless, incorporeal immaterial, spiritually unconditioned being. That is why it is said, "Make not graven images of God, thy Lord." The absence of emotional pressure from the immaterial, incorporeal, and unconditioned Self, is symbolized by the weight of the heart (the will) equalling that of a feather. I.e., if there is force motivating our actions, then we are not exerting our will, but our desire. We can illustrate this readily. Your doctor has placed you on a diet. On one hand you have a strong emotional and sensual pressure to indulge in a prohibited article of diet, and on the other, the cold, non-emotional truth embodied in your prescription. If you follow your desire and eat the prohibited food, it can be metaphorized that your heart (will) has been overpowered by a forceful (heavy) cause. If, instead, you follow the truth, which does not elicit any pleasure, which in fact is strongly opposed by your weakness for the banned item, it can be metaphorized that your heart (will) has been influenced by a forceless cause, symbolized by the feather of Maat. The importance of this concept cannot be overstated, as the majority of people believes that unless an idea has emotional or sensual force behind it, it should not, or cannot be carried out. But the crux of living truth is just the opposite. It matters not how unemotional or unpleased you are about the truth. If it is true, you can and must live it. The absence of emotional and sensual support for an idea simply means that our spirit has not yet been conditioned (programmed) to generate such energies for it. Living an idea, with an appreciation for the good it can do, will in time lead to the generation of enjoyment for it.

Last, but not least, the symbolism contained in the heart's weight equalling that of a feather, refers to the will being under the influence of the immaterial, hence weightless and unconditioned Self, as opposed to the very material, hence heavy and conditioned person. It symbolizes, then, that the individual has succeeded in establishing his identity with the indwelling entity (he is Maa kheru).

As this entity is the individual's share in God's essence, his established identification with it, qualifies him to pass on to the highest three spheres of the Tree of Life representing the divine faculties of omnipotence, omniscience and omnipresence which Man shares qualitatively (i.e., not in magnitude) with the Supreme Being. Had his heart weighed more than a feather, we would then have evidence that his actions were motivated by the emotional (animal) part of the spirit. In the Kamitic metaphorein of the "Weighing of the Heart," this failure is followed by the devouring of the heart by the beast Aummaum, which is part crocodile, hippopotamus and lion. It is a symbol of the destructiveness of our emotions.

Chapter 15

Levels 3 and 4

of the Meditation Process

The Last Four Stages

The successful return of the identity from the person to the indwelling intelligence, symbolized in the passing of the "Weighing of the Heart" test, enables consciousness to rise to the divine parts of the spirit. From another perspective it can be said that the ability to ignore (Men Ab) the behavioral suggestions and compulsions from the lower part of being--the person--has enabled the individual to achieve the ability to fully concentrate on a thought at the exclusion of all others, or to fully ignore all thoughts and sensory stimuli. The ability to concentrate on one thought for as long as required is the essential requirement for the work to be done in the 7th and 8th stages (spheres 3 and 2), and the ability to ignore all thoughts is the essence of the work of the last two stages of meditation.

Level 3 of the Meditation Process, Stage 7, Sphere 3

The third sphere is the seat of the creative units of spiritual power that are responsible for all of the manifestations in the mental and physical realms. These are the 50 gates of Binah through which all life forms come into and leave the world. They are the 50 matrikas (matrices) of the great Goddess Kundalini that function as the seeds (bija) or units composing the host of hekau (words of power). The ability to successfully use these hekau to affect the course of events depends, as stated above, on the ability to exclusively focus our attention on the chanting and associated graphic symbol. This ability can only be developed by the practice of Men Ab in which we must ignore the pressures of our emotions and conditioned beliefs (opinions). It is important to realize that we cannot concentrate for as long as we want, at a sit-down meditation, if we haven't broken the habit of following up the thoughts and emotions that reflex themselves into our awareness in response to the day to day challenges. The bottom line is habit. We must establish the habit of ignoring our mental activities at will. We must further realize, as you will eventually discover, that the realization of this objective is not simply based on the "will to ignore our mental

199

and emotional activities." It must be underlaid by a genuine detachment from the interests of the lower part of being-the person. In other words, we must die to, transcend the pressures and pleasures that earthly things have upon the person part of our being. This is not to say that joy or enjoyment in life will cease. We must remember, and realize that joy is no longer to be considered the engine that propels us in life. The way of life that we are to embark on at this stage, is one in which we do something because it is the truth, and let the joy for it follow from the appreciation of the good that it does. This is what was meant, but distorted, when Jesus told Satan (Set, the emotional body) to "get behind him (follow)." It is interesting to note that the Deity governing this stage, Seker, Kali, etc., rules over the dead and death.

Turning our backs on the emotionally and sensually energized way of life requires for us to discipline ourselves. But this discipline is not merely for the sake of discipline, but for the sake of coordinating our activities with the laws governing the forces (the hekau) in charge of carrying out events in our lives. As each force, for the sake of order, is assigned a place in time and space the individual must at this stage, live in harmony with the cycles governing the functions of his spirit. It is well known that the ancient Black civilizations knew about and paid strict attention to the intrinsic time for performing all activities. For example, the stomach's natural schedule to secrete digestive acids peaks at around midday, and hits rock bottom at midnight. Along with it runs the cycle for secreting the mucous that coats the stomach to protect it against this acid. When you eat a major meal past midday, especially at night, it causes the stomach to secrete acid in excess of the required amount of mucous to protect the lining of the stomach. Along with other factors, this can create or aggravate an ulcer, and definitely contribute to a host of digestive problems and malassimilation. Beyond the indigestion, all sorts of disorders will reflex themselves to distant but related parts of the body; you may suffer headaches, insomnia, emotional upsets, etc. Similarly, while the time-unconditioned voluntary (yang) part of your body will respond to your will to exercise heavily at anytime of the day, the time-conditioned involuntary portion (yin), which provides the vital support (supplies blood, clears waste, etc.), is only predisposed to handle such activities between sunrise and midday. During this period of the day, the sympathetic division of the nervous system, which is in charge of sending blood to the external organs of the body (arms, legs, etc.), is on the rise, and the body's supply of glycogen (sugar stored in the muscle and liver) is still available. Exercising during the evening, while convenient because of the economic-industrial mold controlling our lives, harms the body, not only because of the lack of internal vital support, but because it also infringes upon other functions that are naturally scheduled to take place then. It will cut into and interfere with the time allotted to the evening functions of the parasympathetic (assimilation, repair, regeneration, etc.). Then you wonder why in spite of all of your exercising, good wholesome natural diet and wondrous herbal supplements your health still breaks down, and you are still beset with spiritual and emotional problems.

A list of hundreds of facts supporting the rhythmic, and time conditioned flow of bodily functions can be given. It is enough to note a few. Independent of our activities, our temperature, pulse and breathing rates do not remain even throughout the day. They rise with the sunrise, peak at midday, drop below their mean at sunset, and bottom out at midnight. It is well known to Western scientists that all of our activities (physical labor, mental labor, left-brained thinking, right-brained thinking, eating, sleeping, etc.) have their best and worst times of the day, which times are inherently related to the forces governing the rise and fall in temperature, pulse, and the diurnal or circadian "course of the sun." Incidentally, because the people of the ancient Black civilizations synchronized the events in their lives with these cycles, ignorant Westerners accused them of worshipping the sun, the moon and the stars, which are, in reality, means of keeping track of a variety of cycles[1]. They were meditated upon, not worshipped, with the aim of understanding how to harmonize the day to day activities of our lives with the cycles they represent. Living in accordance to these cycles place limitations and disciplinary measures upon us. It is interesting to note that cycles, limitations and discipline are all saturnial keywords, and Saturn is the planetary correspondence to the third sphere.

The objective of the first meditation at this stage is to go into trance with the heka Aung Kring[2], while visualizing yourself as hawk-headed, and holding the Uas scepter, a flail and a crook (See the Seker card). The Uas scepter symbolizes the happiness and well

---

1. Of course, it is also well known that they are sources of radiations that affect organic, and inorganic processes in the world. But this is another issue.

2. The heka Kring is concealed in the land that is sacred to the deity of the third sphere, Seker. It is called Ta-Sekri.

being resulting from due attention to the flail and the crook. On one level, the flail symbolize the expansive, externalizing hot (yang) portion of the cycle of manifestation, while the crook, the internalizing cool (yin) side. Keeping them in balance leads to well being and success. In addition, the flail symbolizes the harshness with which we must deal with ourselves for violating our pledges of discipline, while the crook corresponds to the gentle meditative and ritualistic methods to the same end. Success with them qualifies us for the roles of governing and ruling others.

The second set of meditations involves the heka and symbols of the deity governing the meditation objective, as indicated by the oracle. While Nefert-Ra invoked Het-Heru during the third stage, emphasizing her enjoyment of the objective sought (she saw herself enjoying the baby she wants to have), here she will go into trance with the Het-Heru heka with the aim of becoming the deity for the sake of spiritual development. I.e., the interest here is not a personal one, as one has died to personal needs. Once one has succeeded in manifesting the deity at this level, one can generate its forces to assist others in need, or to serve as an earthly vehicle (avatar) for the will of God. I.e., the Supreme Being will use your spirit for promoting its plan in the world. With differences regarding levels of spiritual development, the procedure here is similar to the "ritual system of the afflicted" commonly practiced throughout Africa, and initiations into becoming a (living) shrine of a deity. In the ritual of the afflicted, once a person has succeeded in healing herself through the power of a particular deity, she must train to become a shrine of that deity so that she can serve as a healer to others. Hence, the invocation at this stage is to become a "power" (shekem) of the deity for the service of others, while the invocation at the 3rd stage was for the sake of one's personal needs.

Level 3 of the Meditation Process, Stage 8, Sphere 2

The Two Fundamental Actions of the Mind

Thinking vs. Thought Drift

In our "normal" waking state, on one hand, thoughts are constantly streaming into our sphere of awareness telling us what is and what is not, or suggesting what to do and what not to do. We call this "thought drift" (or unwilled thought activity). On the other hand, we are always employing our will to select and arrange these thoughts into meaningful units, or to veto or sanction the suggestions, or impulses to act according to our innate sense of logic, conditioning and acquired store of information. We call this "thinking" or willed thought activity. Although it does not concern us at this point, it is important to note that most people fail to distinguish between the uncritical acceptance of thought drifts, and the discriminating activity of willed thought activity. Only the latter is thinking proper. Both modes have their problems. It is the uncritical acceptance of thought drifts in the "normal" waking state that we label irrational and illogical behavior. Willed thought activity, on the other hand, is no better than the information that it takes as its premises. You know the old story, logical, but not necessarily true.

Ultimately, it doesn't matter how logical the reasoning is, or how pragmatic the information. All items of information are no more than labels, definitions and descriptions-that is, symbols of objective realities, and not the realities themselves. While they are 100% trustworthy for thinking about closed systems with non variable components (making or fixing machines, electronic appliances, houses, etc.), they have a delusory effect on thinking in situations in which the values of the components are subject to change as the relationship between them changes. As a result, the verbal and graphic symbols which are the foundation of our thought activities, because of their inherent finite nature, cannot cover all aspects of relational eventualities. These relational events are none other than the issues of living itself; economics, spirituality, theoretical sciences, philosophy, psychology, sociology, etc. For example, what or who is man? Is he a "rational animal?" Did he ascend from the apes, or descend from God?

If our thoughts fail to communicate to us the knowledge of reality in the higher realms of life, how then can we arrive at such knowledge? A very important clue can be found in the science of meditation which has been touted as the means to acquiring wisdom. Meditation is a process of "making the mind blank," we are told. And this is the goal that we have been seeking through the preceding 7 stages. to "make the mind blank" is to still the thought process. Thoughts that drift in must be ignored, and the habitual impulse to exert the will in directing thought activity must also be ignored. This leaves us in a state in which we are disinterested spectators to the parade of thoughts, feelings and physical percepts streaming into the sphere of awareness. Kept up long enough, we arrive at a point where the thought drift process comes to a halt. If we had been ignoring all thoughts save one, we transcend it and gain full insight into the objective reality that it represents, and if we were ignoring all thoughts, then we would arrive at a point in which all that consciousness could be conscious of, is of being conscious. The former is wisdom, and the latter is experience of Self-the indwelling source of consciousness and intelligence.

The meditation at this stage involves going into trance with the heka of Tehuti, "Aung Hung Shring," while visualizing yourself as the deity (See the Tehuti card) holding a pen to a blank sheet of paper, but not writing. Keeping the eyes open and directed toward the center of the forehead at the level of the eye brow will help to keep the attention focused on the meditation objective (this is called "tratakam"). Before meditating you will decide that your meditation objective is to come out of the state of thought free waking trance with insight into a particular subject. In the same manner that people go to sleep with a problem, and awaken with a solution without having gone through the logical sequential thought process of the "normal" waking state, we go into waking trance to still the thought processes and come out of trance with the answer. This is the process of "enlightenment," or "kensho" as it is called in Zen, or Khut as it is called in the Kamitic tradition. Sages and prophets use it to arrive at their knowledge of reality. It transcends studying, researching, thinking, reasoning and all possible forms of using the mind. It is a tapping into the omniscience of the indwelling intelligence, our true self, which is our individuated share in the life of the Supreme Being. Incidentally, all messages from such oracles as the I Ching, Ifa and the Metu Neter oracle given in this book proceed from this part of our spirit. They are the means of tapping into our indwelling omniscience, in lieu of our inability to meet the demands of this stage of meditation, which needless to say, will take a great deal of time, patience and work. Proficiency in this stage of meditation makes the person a living oracle, otherwise known as a sage or a prophet.

Level 3 of the Meditation Process, Stage 9, Sphere 1

In the preceding stage, all thoughts save one (the image of Tehuti, or the object to be known) were ignored during the meditation process. When one comes out of the trance it induces, the expectation of having a revelation is often fulfilled. The meditation at this stage involves going into trance with the heka of Ausar "Aung Ausar Hung." There are no visualizations or expectations. The attention is focused at the area about an inch beneath the navel to follow the breathing. Tratakam is also employed. Eventually, all thoughts, and awareness of the body, emotions, and environment fall away, leaving our consciousness conscious of being conscious. This is the direct experience (insperience) of our true (inner) Self,- Ausar.

The more we repeat the experience, the more we find ourselves effortlessly detached from the lower part of our being in our day to day experiences. In other words we become the mummy Ausar; decayless, immovable by emotions, etc.

Level 4 of the Meditation Process, Stage 10, "0"

This is a subtle continuation of the preceding stage. When we attain to the realization of Self, at stage 9, our consciousness of being conscious is characterized by a sense of being focused in the center of the consciousness experience. In this stage the consciousness of being conscious is decentralized, ever expansive, boundless and diffused. Thus we realize Patanjali's definition of Yoga, which "is attained from the inhibition of the mental energy/matter (citta). Then the Seer is clothed in his essential nature." We have pushed our quest of Self to its most hidden inner recess, which in the Kamitic tradition is called Amen[3] and Nu. We have thus become Neb er Tcher.

SUMMARY
THE STAGES OF INITIATION AND MEDITATION
AND SOCIAL ORGANIZATION

At this point it should already be clear, if it were not yet known, that the principles discussed from chapter 7 to the present embody the fundamental requirements that individuals must meet in order to participate harmoniously in society.

With varying degrees of spiritual understanding, the so-called puberty rites of African nations, are based on the principles of Men Ab. "Becoming of age" is not enough. To qualify for citizenship in a traditional African society, with its rights to marry, bear arms, to claim ownership of land, etc., the individual must achieve a certain degree of proficiency in the ability to ignore emotional pain, sensual temptation, physical deprivation, etc.. He

---

3. Do you know understand why Christians end all prayers with Amen?

must learn to place the needs of the many above those of the one. He must appreciate the value of accumulated experience through a show of respect for elders and wise men.

Regarding people's participation in the government of the traditional African nation, it is important to fully understand the peculiar governmental system developed in ancient Africa - the Divine Kingship. Central to the system is the concept that it is not the king who leads the people, but the Supreme Being. Even Western spiritualists who acknowledge that the true Self of man is the Supreme Being have not been able to understand this point. The man (and all others- living and deceased!) who will lead the people must be initiated into the ability to serve as a vehicle through which the Supreme Being and its agencies (the Deities) will govern the people. All leaders must, therefore, be masters of divine law, and priests of the shrines of the Deities. I will quote from *Life in Ancient Egypt*, by Adolf Erman, Dover Press, which will prove very enlightening.

> On the 14th of Paophi in the 46th year of Ramses II, we find <u>the members of the court</u> consisted of:
> "Bechenchons, the first prophet of Amon.
> Ueser-mont, the prophet of Amon.
> Ram, the prophet of Amon.
> The prophet Uennofre of the Temple of Mut.
> The prophet Amen-em-'en of the Temple of Chons.
> The (holy father?) Amen-em-opet of the Temple of Amon.
> Amenhotep, the priest and reader of Amon.
> Any, the priest and reader of Amon.
> The priest Huy of the Temple of Amon.
> The accountant Huy of the court of justice of the town."
> In this case therefore we find nine priests and but one layman, i.e., the permanent scribe of the court, who reported the lawsuit.

The author's phrase "In this case" compares this composition of the court to that of a later time (Ramses IX, 20th Dynasty) in which the court was predominantly made up of laymen. When we compare both periods we find that the latter corresponds to the beginning of the end of the Kamitic civilization. A great deal of the administration of the kingdom had fallen into the hands of foreign soldiers who had been brought in as mercenaries to staff the standing army of the country. Yet, up to the beginning of the 19th Dynasty, we find that the courts and the government of the nation are in the hands of priests-prophets. The reason for this will can be deducted from the following quotation from the same book:

"The laws which guided the king and courts in their decisions are unfortunately unknown to us. Some of them were said to be of divine origin; a deed informs us that the criminal should be condemned to the "great punishment of death, of which the gods say 'do it to him,'" and it expressly states further that this decree of the gods is written in the "writings of the divine words."" Diodorus probably says truly that he was informed that the sacred books of law had been composed by Thoth the god of wisdom.

Here we have it. A book of the "writings of divine words," i.e., the Metu Neter, which was written by Tehuti, for the use of priests-prophets, and the king in their work of administering justice. Erman also states that during the old Empire, which is the period that best represents Kamitic culture;

All the judges belonged to one of the "six great houses," that is, to one of the great law courts, in which "the secret words" were discussed . . . At the head of this court of justice stood the "Chief judge" . . . he would be one of the "high priests of the great gods," . . . the second after the king in the court of the palace." . . . At all ages of Egyptian history this was the most popular position in the kingdom. . . The popular idea was that *earthly governors and chief judges ought to vie in wisdom with their heavenly prototype* . . . He, the chief of the judges, through the words of his mouth, caused brothers to return home in peace; *the writings of Thoth were on his tongue*; and he surpassed in righteousness the little of the balance. *He knew the secrets of every one* . . . (Note: italics were inserted by me).

So what is this book of the writings of Tehuti (Thoth) which enabled the chief judge to "know the secrets of every one," that contained the "secret words" that the judges convened to discuss? I verily say to you, that it is the Metu Neter oracle that I have brought back to the world. Let those in high positions use it to govern and the world will be restored to the state of peace and prosperity known only in the days of Ausar. Let those in low positions use it, and they will inherit the staff of the lion.

Chapter 16
THE ORACLES

On the most general level, oracles are means of communicating with spiritual agencies. On the highest level, such communications take place with the wisdom faculty (sphere 2, Tehuti) of the spirit, through waking trance. This is the skill possessed by prophets and sages. On the second highest level, communications take place with the same part of the spirit through the casting of lots. These "lots" are symbolic representations of the basic categories into which the entire span of reality can be divided. Other oracles are means of communicating with the other Deities, and lower spiritual agencies through mediumistic trance or the casting of lots.

In past chapters, we looked at the process through which the world comes into being, through which order is established and maintained, the stages of initiation and meditation, and so on. Not only did we trace the sequence of unfoldment of events, but we also assigned to each shaping factor a place in time and in the hierarchy (space) of being. Thousands of years ago, Africans discovered that this system of classification and order could be represented through numerical (ordinal or binary) symbols, graphic archetypes, etc.. They further discovered that these representations, when conventionalized and arranged into a synthetical whole, could be used by the indwelling intelligence to communicate with the personality by projecting these symbols in dreams, or by drawing the attention to their physical counterparts at critical moments (omens). They further discovered that if these symbols were casted in such a manner as to allow them to fall freely, or to be gathered in a non-manipulative manner, the indwelling intelligence, acting through the life-force, would manipulate the symbols into a pattern that would communicate its message.

It should not be surprising to find that the abstract symbols used in such oracles as the Ifa of the Yorubas (Afa of the Ewes), and the Tao Te Ching, and with some modifications, the I Ching, are all based on binary mathematical principles, which are the basis of the machine language used by computers (used extensively in forecasting!). The Metu Neter oracle is composed of the combined influences of the five primary binary figures, and 14 archetypes (70 cards) of the shaping forces of all events in/as the world. These archetypes are the 14 pieces created by the dismemberment of the body of Ausar, and are related to the 14 kau of Ra. In fact, it would be correct to think of oracles as spiritual computers. They enable us to discover what shaping factors are the key effectors of a given situation.

All that reasoning, which we must use expertly, can do for us is to indicate plausibilities and probabilities. And for that it must have precedents, or some means of identifying the possible shaping factors in a situation. Oracles enable us to raise plausibilities and possibilities to the level of facts. An oracle can tell you at the moment of birth, that child "X" will grow up to be a leader or a pauper, unless he does exactly so and so. Before you even got to know him, the oracle can tell you what kinds of problems you can expect, what virtues must be cultivated, etc. if you were to get married. It is clear then that those who are against the use of oracles, do not quite understand how and why they are used. In fact, most people do not truly know what they are.

There are a few well known historical instances in the lives of Westerners regarding the oracles. Before the advent of the monarchical period in Israel, a very rudimentary oracle, the Urim and Thummim was consulted. This oracle that could only answer yes or no was the means, according to 1 Samuel 28:6, to consult the Will of Yahweh. In Ezra 2:63 a cultic problem is postponed until a priest of the oracle can be consulted. II Macc. 15, informs us that Hamman secured the deliverance of the Jews exiled in Persia, by casting the lots to choose the day for attacking the Persians. The latter were slaughtered. This event is today commemorated, although with a veil casted over it, in the Jewish feast of Purim (purim means "lots"). Another account of the Jewish use of lots is given in Acts I:26, where we are shown that Matthias was chosen through the casting of lots over Joseph Barsabbas, to take Judas' (who betrayed Jesus) place. Incidentally, it is important to remember, or note that Jesus, and his disciples never called themselves Christians. The appellation or concept did not even exist in Jesus' time. They were Jews, but that is another story. Back to the oracles. There are many more such references in the Old Testament for those who care to search for them.

Beyond indicating events and occurrences that are "around the corners" from our reasoning faculty, some oracles like Ifa and the Metu Neter are capable of indicating which word of power or

Deity is in charge of the situation at hand. Since the word of power originates, and controls the situation, word-shipping it (awakening and cultivating its power) enables us to work on the situation from the causal level. Otherwise we must work backward from effects to causes.

Chapter 17

THE DEITIES OF THE METU NETER

AMEN

Amen means "concealed." It is the Kamitic counterpart of the term "Subjective" as we have used it in this book. It corresponds to the essential nature of the Supreme Being, which is the same as the essence of Man's being. It is our unmanifested, unmanifestable unconditioned Self-That which is the ultimate source of life and consciousness. It is the unseen and unseeable that looks out into the Objective Realm of spirits, thoughts, feelings, and physical phenomena. We must return our focus of consciousness back to it by the cessation of all thought activity. Once we have established this innermost point as our place of being--i.e., living beyond emotional influences--we will attain to the state of Hetep. This is a state in which we are able to fully ignore all emotions that may rise into our awareness, and thus attain to a peace that cannot be disturbed by any challenge in life. In the Hindu tradition it is called *Parabrahm Sarvikalpa Nirvana.* This state of inner peace is the prime foundation for the functioning of the healing functions of the life-force (Ra), and is the source of all spiritual power.

AUSAR

"And God said, let us make man in our own likeness."

Now, it does not take much to realize that the likeness of God in which man is made, according to Genesis 1:26, cannot be the multitude of human frailties and sinfulness. Neither can it be the corporeal creature of earthly existence, nor the varieties of qualities that make up our personalities. For as it is said, "Make not graven images of God, thy Lord." How then are God and Man similar?

As a drop of water and the ocean are the same qualitatively, but different in magnitude, so are man and God. This fact is expressed in the Bantu's (a major group of Blacks in South Africa) categorical name for both God and Man-"Muntu" (of which Bantu is the plural). It is the same with the name that the Kamitians use for themselves-"Kam-Au." "Kam" means black, and "Au"--the root of the mantra Aung, Ausar (God/man)--was used to denote themselves.

But this Self of ours which is the likeness of the Supreme Being is, as we have so much spoken of in earlier chapters, the indwelling intelligence guiding all of the functions of our spirit, and through it the "involuntary" vital functions of the body.

We cannot leave this section without throwing some light on the Deity's name. To this date no Egyptologist can explain the meaning of, or origin of its name. The problem has its roots in the fact that the deity's name is not commonly written with alphabetic hieroglyphs, but in a "graphic metaphoric way"; an eye above or beneath a seat, which does not provide much of a clue to the true pronunciation. Although no one has ever given a good explanation, it has been commonly rendered as Asar (pronounced Euh-Sehr). The seat, which is called "ast" (pronounced Eust) is, by "punning derivation" as Budge aptly observes[1], used to represent the female aspect of the Deity. Thus they call her "Ast" (pronounced Eust). But no one can say why is a seat used as a metaphor for her, and if this is the true pronunciation of her name. Let's first deal with the meaning of the symbolism. As the ninth sphere corresponds to the first stage of the work of spiritual development, it is the foundation (Yesod) or throne or seat of spiritual evolution, meditation and initiation. All acts of the will begins with mediumistic trance. When we recall the work to be done in the first stage we will remember that it consists in going into mediumistic trance with the objective of returning our identity to the indwelling intelligence. The seat, then, is symbolic of mediumistic trance, and the eye symbolizes the indwelling intelligence. We must take a clue from the Canaanite Kabalistical tradition, in which the ninth sphere is called Yesod, which means "foundation, seat," yet, the deity of the sphere is called Shaddai El Chai. Similarly, in the Kamitic tradition, the Goddess of the ninth sphere (Isis,- the Greek name) is called a "seat" (Ast), by metaphoric punning. We understand the metaphor, but what is the pun based on? In Budge's Egyptian Hieroglyphic Dictionary, page 36a, we find the word "Aus" (Au is pronounced as the french "Eu," water!), which denotes the 3rd person, singular female. It corresponds to the Coptic "Es," which has the same grammatical role, and is also the root of "Esse," the Coptic name for the deity! On page 36a, we also find one of the few alphabetic spellings of the name: "Aus-t" (pronounced AEuset). On page 36b we find Ausars

---

1. Gods of the Egyptians, Vol. 2, page 202. Dover Press.

(AEusers). Further confirmation comes from the fact that in the Cosmological system of Annu (Heliopolis) of the Ra priesthood of the Vth Dynasty, the female counterpart of Tem or Temu (corresponding to Ausar) is called Auasasit (AEusausit). We are just not indulging here in scholarly gymnastics. The names Auset and Ausar conceal the heka "Aung," through which they are invoked. We have seen how Tehuti conceals "Hung," Seker (Sekri, Ta-Sekri) conceals the heka "Kri"; Heru (Hru) conceals the heka "Hring," and so on. When we consider the fact that these very same hekau turn up in Dravidian India in association to Goddesses that match the qualities of the Kamitic Deities-point for point, then we must realize that we have unearthed a principle that we must pay a great deal of attention to.

TEHUTI

A collection of data, however factual, is of little use until its elements are arranged according to their relationship with each other and the whole of which they are parts. For example, until Lavoisier (1743-1794), there was no science of chemistry even though there was a vast collection of chemicals in use; sulfuric acid, nitric acid, silver nitrate, chlorine, etc. and the recipes for making them. It was only when Lavoisier discovered that all atoms had a distinct weight and configuration (number of protons, electrons, etc.), and were thus subject to exact measurement, that the science of chemistry was born. *If the collection of divine laws and spiritual counsels could also be subjected to some sort of objective measurement, then the providing of guidelines for living could also be elevated to a science of living.* And such a means of measurement has already been in place in African spirituality for over 10,000 years. In other words, unlike the biblical tradition, the Kamitic spiritual tradition is not composed of a collection of spiritual guidelines; like chemistry and physics, its principles are each assigned to a specific category, which elevates it to a strict science of living. The ability to qualify life's experiences and its spiritual guidelines, through quantification and measurement, is the property of the wisdom faculty Tehuti. One of the most important rituals and spiritual practices of the Kamitic system was called the "Utchau Metut"-the "Weighing of Words."

The name Tehuti is compounded of "Tehu"[2] which means "to measure" and "ti," which means "dual." This name reveals a very

---

2. There is a great deal of controversy regarding the correct pronunciation of this Deity's name due to the fact that in most cases the Deity is represented non-phonetically. Phonetically it has been rendered as "Tchehuti," "Djehuti," and Tehuti (this "t" is a soft sort of "d"). First of all we find that the Coptic language (ancient Sahidic) which is the survival of the Ancient Egyptian language does not translate this word with either of the letters "ch" (chei), or "dj" (djandjia), or "tch" (tchima), but with "t" (tau). Dropping the final "i," a common linguistic experience, they named it "Taut," or "Tout," which is what would be expected from "Tehuti." An extensive etymological study reveals the same results. The Bohairic Coptic renders it "Thauout"; the Aramaic, "Thot"; the Babylonian, "Tihut"; and the Greek, and Phoenicians rendered it "Thout." None of them translate it with a "dj," or "tch" even though they had the means of doing so. The spelling "Djehuti" belongs to the Ptolemaic (Greek occupation of Kamit) period. It is a "punning" contraction of "Djed + Tehuti" signifying the stability (cessation) of the thought processes which lead to the manifestation of wisdom. "Tchehuti" (old and middle kingdom) is a contraction of "Tchet + Tehuti" signifying the fact that the word "tchet" (like the Hebrew "DBR") means both "word," and "physical thing" when understood from the perspective of the divine will-Tehuti-whose verbal emanations (hekau) are the causes of material things. It was also used to connect the wisdom of the deity with the serpent "tche-t" which symbolizes the aspect of Ra which is the source of the hekau (see kundalini as source of "vak," the word), as well as eternity. By punning, a prominent feature of African linguistic, they also related "tehu," meaning "to measure" with "tekh," meaning "a weight measure" through "tekhnu," a bird resembling the Ibis, which is the totem of Tehuti. The fact that "Tehu" is integrally tied in with the idea of measurement can be seen from the fact that the root of the name for Maat, which is the "sister" of Tehuti is also related to measurement. The hieroglyphic symbol for "Maa" also represents a cubit (18 inches), which is one of the main units of measurement in the Kamitic canon. We see, therefore, that on one hand, that those who call the deity "Tchehuti," or "Djehuti" do so because they have failed to understand that these terms simply relate the deity to the meditation process underlying its manifestation (Djed), and the life-force (Tchet) which is the source of the word as a vehicle of power, while, on the other hand, the use of the name "Tehuti," which is based on sound *etymological study*, fully summarizes the deity's function. The etymological principles governing the Kamitic language, and all others for that matter, prove that the Deity's name cannot be a compounding of "Tchet + Huti," or "Djed + Huti," as all meanings of "Huti" (officer, fear), or "Hu + Ti," yield fortuitous meanings. They are the types of words created via punning which is so widespread in Africa. The insight thus gained teaches that wherever knowledge, and wisdom is claimed, there must be an objective universal standard by

advance state of scientific sophistication of the Kamitic culture which cannot be doubted from the fact that they had invented the system of quadratic equations which is the foundation of the mathematical underpinning of science (the equations used in chemistry, physics, economics, etc.). That cosmology (Kabala) was related to a system of equations can be deduced from the Arabic name for algebra-"Al Jabar mu Quabalah." The dual factors by which all ideas and concepts are weighed are based on their relative place in time (temporal, cyclical) and space (hierarchic). We come across, for example, in the Chinese oracle of Wisdom, the I Ching, that "such and such" a thing is to be done or not because of its relationship to the time in the cycle (year, month, zenith, etc.). Incidentally, there might have been some cultural exportations of the Kamitic wisdom tradition to China. Let's start with noting the similarity between the root of the Deity's name, "tehu," and the Coptic derivation of the name of Tehuti, "Tout," which are very similar to the Chinese term for their wisdom tradition, the "Tao." The foundation of the Chinese oracle, the I Ching is composed of the eight Pa Kua. Similarly, Tehuti's wisdom system is also based on an ogdad representing the primal powers of the eight cardinal points. The symbol for the nome ("province") of Tehuti in Kamit was represented by four broken lines _ _ superimposed. I Ching practitioners will immediately recognize the correspondence to the yin lines, and Tao Te Ching diviners will recognize in it the 41st figure, which is the main figure of that oracular system.

The Utchau Metut

Spatial - Hierarchical Dimension

The "Utchau Metut," generally translated as the "Weighing of Words," is best translated as *the evaluation of concepts, ideas, beliefs, behavioral shaping factors, and spiritual practices.* It corresponds to the use of the Tree of Life as a device for

---

which to measure the claim. This concept found its way into the specialized meaning of the term "science," which is the Latin for "to know" (scire). When we realize that because there were no dictionaries, or encyclopedias in ancient times, the etymological relations between words were kept very tight, thus making them stores of a gold mine of information. They conceal depth meanings, and words of power which was well known to Jewish Kabalists who sought by various devices-gematria, etc. to uncover them in the scriptures.

216

categorizing and evaluating our beliefs, mental and spiritual functions, etc. By doing for the psychological shaping factors of our life (beliefs, behavioral mechanisms, etc.) what the periodical table of elements does for chemistry, the Tree of Life makes possible the creation of a science of behavior. I.e., it elevates philosophy, spiritual culture, psychology, etc. into the realm of science by providing man with a means of quantifying his ideas and beliefs regarding these subjects. For example:

The arrival at a conclusion or judgement without going through a thinking process, that is, through direct perception of the reality itself instead of manipulating the symbols representing the reality is called <u>wisdom</u>. We classify this mental process at the second sphere. The arrival at a conclusion or judgement through the manipulation of symbols embodying abstract analogies is called <u>synthesis</u>. It is related to the 4th sphere. The arrival at a conclusion or judgement through induction, deduction and inference is called <u>syllogistic logic</u>, and is related to the 8th sphere. Not only has the Tree allowed us to categorize each of these three modes of mental operations, it has also allowed us to assign a value to each. Since the Tree of Life's scale of values flows from 0-the highest, to 10-the lowest, then wisdom is the highest of the three, followed by synthesis, and in last place, syllogistic thinking. We can verify this in life. As a product of syllogistic (Cartesian) logical thinking (8th sphere), western orthodox medicine attempts to establish one to one cause and effect relationships for illnesses. Specific agent X causes specific health disorders Y, therefore, specific remedy Z must be used. Illnesses can be made to appear so specific, that the same disorder will be given different names because it manifests in different parts of the body (E.g., otitis, iritis, nephritis, colitis; lumbago, rheumatism, etc.), and in many cases, treated differently. Because remedies are similarly considered, Western physicians have fallen into the delusory belief in "side effects." Since their logical thinking is done through symbols (definitions, etc.), which can only embody a minor part of the realities they are representing, they fail to realize that the remedies, of themselves, are not limited to the effects that exist in their minds. Neither, are the disorders caused by the single agents that they have identified. This is the primary cause of many of the medical malpractices that is rampant throughout western medicine. Since many disorders can have the same underlying cause, it would make more sense to tie them together through an abstract name, than to separate them as Westerners have done. The former has been done in the Chinese medical system.

217

All disorders are given the same name, regardless of where they manifest in the body, or of their outer appearances. In harmony with this, the same remedy is given in each case. This unitary approach, which obviously, fosters order in thinking, a greater understanding and accuracy in evaluating and treating illnesses is the synthetical approach of the 4th sphere. The approach of the second sphere is even greater. Without thinking-i.e., manipulating the vast set of medical data-the second sphere is able to arrive at an understanding of the shaping factors contributing to the creation, and healing of an illness.

In addition, as the second, fourth, and eighth spheres correspond to the eighth, sixth, and second stages of initiation, respectively, it is evident that greater spiritual and mental abilities are required for the wisdom approach, and so on.

Every practice in life can be, thus, categorized and evaluated. Regarding "mental dynamics" and behavioral reshaping methods, we can arrive at the following classifications and evaluations.

Classification, and Evaluation (Utchau)
of "Ritual" Methods and Accessories

Method	Sphere(s)
Bach flower therapy	10th
Bhakti Yoga	9th
counselling	8th
Creative visualization	9th, 8th, 7th
Dianetics	9th, 8th
herbal "magic"	10th
hypnotherapy	9th, 8th
Jnana Yoga	2nd
Kamitic Initiation	10th - 0
Kula Yoga	10th - 0
mantra yoga*	3rd or 10th*
mediumism	9th
Men Ab	4th - 0
positive thinking	8th
prayer	8th
psychocybernetics	8th, 7th
sermons	8th
working with crystals	10th

*There are two forms of working with the heka (mantra yoga). Small advantages can be achieved by working with words of powers without subjecting oneself to a course of spiritual development. This is the 10th sphere level. The true and full power of hekau can only be attained at the 7th level of initiation (3rd sphere).

Classification, and Evaluation (Utchau) of Life Problems

All of life's problems can be assigned to one of three fundamental levels. The first (and lowest) level does not arise from conditionings that are opposed to our identification with Ausar and the laws of Maat, but to to our conditionings that are opposed to the contemplated objective, or from the dormancy of the spiritual power to achieve the goal. They can, thus, be overcome without transcending one's lower being. Success can be achieved by the use of such approaches that involve the use of Bach flower remedies, Bhakti yoga, counselling, creative visualization, Dianetics, herbal magic (esoteric use of herbs), animal sacrificial rituals, hypnotherapy, dianetics, mediumistic invocation of deities and ancestors, prayer, psychocybernetics, positive thinking, sermonizing, crystal working, etc. The second level of problems arises from conditionings that are opposed to our identification with Ausar and the laws of Maat. Even if we have the ability to achieve the goal, success depends on living truth at the crossroads, which is the spiritual mechanism for transcending our anti-spiritual conditionings. This type of problem can only be solved by the application of Men Ab. The third level of problems arises from the dormancy of our higher faculties (spheres 1 - 3). Can you be motivated to develop your spiritual powers for the sake of discovering and aiding God's divine plan for the world? This might require you to die to the vast amount of painfully acquired information, and to the interest accumulated from the heavy investment in your earthly social undertakings. Can you understand why Chinnamasta, the Indus Kush (Dravidian) Goddess of Wisdom, holds her severed head in her left hand, and a sword in the right? And why three streams of blood flow from her headless neck to her lips? A hint: three is Sebek's number.

From the foregoing we can see how the Tree of Life serves as a measuring rod, a slide rule if you will, for the evaluation and classification of our ideas, concepts and practices in life.

Events can also be classified and evaluated according to their relative position in time. In chapter 15 we discussed the cyclical laws governing the functions of the body and the spirit for the maintenance of order.

In many of the past chapters we discussed the spatial or hierarchical ordering of ideals, spiritual guidelines, behavioral expectations, spiritual training and virtues. It is the absence of these tools for measuring our ideas and values, why societies have become bogged down in a quagmire of opinions and ever increasing social disharmony and conflicts. Who among them is fostering the acquisition of the knowledge of reality by the stilling of the thinking mechanism? Yet, as we saw in past chapters, this is the only way of knowing truth - of arriving at the objective measurement of ideas. Of finding the "categorical imperative" that eluded the great German philosopher Immanuel Kant to the very end of his frustrated life. This categorical imperative, this yardstick of life is none other than the Tree of Life itself. Wisdom is achieved when consciousness, in considering an issue, flows through its 32 paths plus "0" to achieve a judgment.

The heka (word of power) that corresponds to this mental faculty is "Hung," which is concealed in the name Tehuti. Incidentally, the Buddhist borrowed it from the Dravidian wisdom Goddess Chinnamasta and synchretized it to their so-called "Dhyani (celestial) Buddha" Aksobhya.

It is of great importance to focus on the fact that man cannot save himself from the mere employment of his will. It must be guided by Tehuti. This is symbolized by Heru's dependence on Tehuti to defeat Set. In our day to day existence, this translates into our attainment of salvation by perfecting the meditation skill of acquiring knowledge of reality through stilling the thought processes. It is not a process of reasoning and logical manipulation of information acquired through study or observation, but one of reception of the omniscience of the intelligence dwelling within our being (our true self, Ausar) that is in charge of directing all of our physiological and spiritual functions. It is important to realize, that our physiological functions do not originate in our physical organs, but in the life-force-Ra.

It is important to realize that by stilling the thought processes (logical rationalizations, etc.) we can access a power dwelling within our being that is one with the divine entity, that the Kamitians said to have determined the revolution of the celestial bodies, the seasons, and keeps all manifestations in equilibrium. This inner intelligence also enables us to direct, protect and develop the full potential of our life-force. In this respect Tehuti is called the "mind" and "eye" (utchat) of Ra. It is Tehuti that guides us to the lifestyle and actions that enable us to maintain the equilibrium between the two metabolic (the two combatants Heru/anabolic, and Set/catabolic) processes of the life-force (Ra). Last but not least, we must note that all high oracles-Ifa, I Ching and the Metu Neter-were received by prophets and sages while meditating at the second sphere level.

SEKER

Seker (the 3rd sphere of the Tree of Life) is the divine faculty that is in charge of the life-force (Ra), which is the formative base of all things in the world. Although the source of life is infinite, each entity is allowed to share in its infinity through a series of cycles of births. Each entity is thus allotted a finite portion of this life-force at a time, for its adventure in the world[3]. This recycling principle governs the cycles of birth, growth, decay, death, rebirth and on. The life-force behaves in this manner in conformity with the divine intention of guiding man to the realization of his divinity. Would most people bother to develop themselves, and exert themselves if they were to be born with full functionality (as many reptiles and lower creatures are), eternal youth and indestructibility? We are thus spurred on to exert ourselves in our youth to provide for the days that will surely come when we will be incapable of doing so, and of course by the ultimate, which is death.

The subjection of the existence of all things to cyclical revolutions, which is governed by the "deity" (divine faculty) Khepere, divides their life term into two fundamental phases. Birth (rebirth)/growth, and decay/death (rebirth into the plane of origin!). Thus we achieve an infinitude of experiences through an infinite chain of finite existences.

The phase of birth (rebirth) is under the dominion of Khepere (Aima[4], the fertile mother in the Canaanite tradition), while the phase of decay and death is symbolized by the Hennu or

---

3. This law is taught in Chinese Taoism which states that everyone is born with a fixed amount of prenatal chi. The Taoist yoga exercises aim at preserving, and rejuvenating it, as it is not replenished by merely eating.

4. Aima is the same as Maya, the goddess who weaves the illusion that we call the world. It also conceals the heka Aing. In tantric Yoga, "Ing" is called Maya bija.

Af (dead flesh) boat in which travels the "aged Ra" (Ama, the dreaded sterile mother, and Kali).

Khepere or Aima brings all things into manifestation through the 50 sound units of power residing in the 3rd sphere. These sound units, which are the basis of all hekau, are metaphorized as the eggs of the beetle symbolizing Khepere[5], the 50 gates of Binah, the 50 skulls strung as the necklace of Kali (the Indus Kush Seker), the 50 oarsmen propelling the boat of Ausar, and they are analogous to the 500,000 or so eggs that every woman is born with. At this level, these spiritual powers do not manifest the things of which they are the germs, but the underlying structure (divine plan[6]) that provides the order governing the harmonious interaction of the forces shaping the formation of things, and their interaction. These structures appoint the places in space and time ordering all manifestations.   Incidentally, because its creative function corresponds to the female gender, which the Canaanite tradition supports (the Goddess Aima), this deity often appears (possesses) in its female form when invoked. As such, her name is Sekert.

The male side of the Deity rules over the death process. Seker was the Deity of the necropolis at Sakkara. Allied to it in this function was the "monster" Aum-mit or Aummaum, whose functions was to destroy the Ab (part of the spirit housing the conscience and will) of the deceased who failed to live in harmony with the laws of Maat (divine laws). During life, its activities are felt as the pangs of conscience, guilt, self recriminations, etc. These are warnings that we are on the path to a failed destiny.

This is to be expected as Seker governs our destiny. The Kamitic term for "destiny" is "Skher," and for "plan" is "Sekher," which are clearly etymologically related to "Seker." No two things can occupy the same place at the same time. Divine law, therefore, guarantees all things their day in the sun. Our coming into being, and the unfolding of all events in our life are controlled by the spiritual forces (Ptah) at the Seker level for the sake of maintaining

---

5. The use of the beetle to symbolize this aspect of the life-force operating at the Seker level is very rich in correspondences. The beetle, which is usually black (Seker's color) with a metallic greenlike sheen, lays a vast number of eggs in a mass of dung (another Sekerian correspondence). The hatching of the larvae by the heat of the sun is symbolical of the arousal of the force that is required in order to awaken the hekau symbolized by Khepere's eggs.

6. Note that the word for "plan" is "Sekher," which is etymologically related to Seker; Sekher Neter = Plan Divine.

order in the world. Destiny, therefore, is nothing more nor less than the expression of the structure, the plan that governs the unfolding of people's lives in order to guarantee them success. It is amazing to see how people are aware of the confusion and disorder that follow from the lack of planning and structure, yet fail to realize that the same would happen in nature and in the world, if the Supreme Being had not laid a plan to guide the lives of men and nations. As above, So below!

When we die or transcend the way of life in which earthly pleasure and personal interests are the motivating factors of our actions and undertakings, we come under the governorship of the Deity Seker. In either case, we have died to the earth-physically or spiritually. The doctrines of Seker, represent then, the *teachings that kill*. We must remember that this does not mean a joyless life. Quite the contrary, it is one, as we will later see, that leads to greater ecstasy. When we keep in mind that the spirit is essentially unconditioned, it will be realized that our spirit is ever receptive to be reprogrammed to express joy and pleasure in response to any situation or stimulus. We can therefore transcend a way of life in which our will is lead by what gives us pleasure, and change over to a way in which pleasure follows our will to live new truths.

Allied with the idea of dying to the things of the world is the host of symbols used to explain the domain of the Deity. In the *"Book of that Which is in the Underworld,"* the Fourth Hour which represents the domain of Seker is described as a region in which there are no cultivation fields to be distributed to the faithful followers of Ra. It is full of thick darkness, its floor is covered with sand, and it is lacking in water (hence, barren). This region is called Ta (land 'of') Sekri. Note that the "kri" in the name conceals the heka--Kring--of the Deity.

The truths that we must live at this sphere of the Tree of Life corresponds to the cycles governing natural phenomena. These were discussed in previous chapters. The point to note here is that the times for eating[7], exercising, having sex, performing certain types

---

7. This is not limited to the daily time of eating. In the Ayurvedic system of health from India each day is governed by a planetary energy. As foods are also conveyors of these energies, there is also a system in which the corresponding type of food is to be eaten on its planetary day. The Moon's foods (watermelon, lettuce, etc.) are to be eaten on a monday, martial foods on a tuesday, etc. Research will reveal that the name for each day is derived from the planet that governs i .

of work, meditating must not be dictated by our feelings, cravings, social or economic factors, but by the cyclical mechanisms governing nature.

The discipline of adhering to the cycles governing life that this sphere imposes upon us, is for the sake of enabling us to succeed in the use of words of power, as their manifestations are ordered by the law of cycles in order to keep them from conflicting with each other. All hekau (plural of heka) are based on 50 single sounds units which are symbolized in the Phoenician Kabalistical system as the 50 gates of Binah, or the Goddess Ama through which all things in the world come into being, and are recycled. In India she appears as Kundala or Kali, the Great Mother who wears the necklace of 50 skulls. As mistress of the words of power, and mother of all living things, she is depicted travelling in the boat of the star Sepdt (Sirius), which is propelled by 50 oarsmen. These sound units are distributed throughout the 14 chakras making up man's subtle body. As this sphere corresponds to the highest manifestation of man's spiritual power it is the dwelling place of the power aspect of his spirit. In the Kamitic tradition it is the Shekem (Sahidic Coptic "Shkum"); in the Kabalistical, the Shekinah; in the Indus tradition, the Shakti. Men who wielded this power were given the title of "Shekem." In fact this is the true title for the Kamitic king of kings[8]. The term found its way into the Arabic where we find that the great royal leaders are called Sheik. In India the kundalini yogis are called shakta, and their counterpart further up north are called shamans. It is important to note that all of these cognate terms all begin with the letter "Sh." Egyptologists commonly render the term as "Sekem," even though many words written with the hieroglyph for "S" appear as "Sh" in the Coptic, Hebraic, and Phoenician. We see the same in the Hindu rendition of many Dravidian words. For example, Shakti, and shakta are also rendered sakti, and sakta.

MAAT

Maat, pronounced "Ma aut," corresponds to the faculty within man wherein is intuited and experienced the urge to live truth

---

8. The term Pharoah was never used by the Egyptians. It was introduced by the Jews, and denotes the palace of the Kamitic king. Its use is analogous to the "White House."

(according to the laws of the indwelling self). The name and the meaning are derived from the hieroglyph that is the phonetic symbol of "Maa"-the measure of a cubit. The connection of measurement with Truth is one of the most profound achievements of the African mind. We saw that the name of Maat's complement (brother/husband), Tehuti, is also based on the idea of measurement. When something, one side of an equation, is known, it is because we have an objective standard, the other side of the equation, against which to measure it. Hence, the "double measure" or "Tehu-ti," the "utchau metut" (Weighing of Words) and the Weighing of the Heart judgement, etc.

The construction of all things and the unfolding of all events are based on universal patterns underlying the activities of all natural forces. While some of the patterns underlying physical phenomena have been discovered and codified by Western scientists (E.g., chemistry, physics), Africans and other Nonwestern people have discovered and codified the patterns governing our day to day existence and spiritual development. In other words, the quality of life, and the destiny of men and nations are ruled by forces that are as mensurable and subject to codification into immutable laws as are the factors governing physical and chemical phenomena. In the esoteric tradition, the branch of study governing these laws is Cosmology. The embodiment of these laws (moral canon), against which the actions and beliefs of Man are weighed/measured, is Maat.

By extension, the term 'maat' has several denotations in the everyday language of the Kamitic people; straight, rule, law, canon by which the lives of men is kept straight, real, unalterable ("it, the law, hath never been altered since the time of Ausar"), upright, righteous and steadfast or consistent. The last correspondence, "steadfast or consistent," is of extreme importance. In the Kamitic tradition, a person cannot claim that he is living truth if he has not been consistent in the observance of the spiritual laws at each an every crossroad situation. This is why it is said, "Today as Yesterday, Tomorrow as Today, is Truth!"

We have seen that the basis of Truth is living by a standard imposed by our essential divine nature. This leads unavoidably to the question of where does man find the strength to rise to a moral standard of which God is the standard of measure. In the Kamitic tradition the answer has been concealed in their metaphoric (so-called mythologic) mode of communicating spiritual scientific information. Maat is the daughter of Ra, we are told. But its meaning has been clouded by the popular belief that Ra represents the Sun, or the Sun God. "Ra," pronounced Rau, and not Re (hence Aur-light; Aurum-gold, oro; Aura, Aurora, RAdiation, ARdent-fiery, etc.), corresponds to the solar energy or life-force stored in physical bodies. It is the kundalini of the Hindus, the Chi of Chinese metaphysics, Aganyu of the Yorubas, Dambadah Wedo of the Fons, etc.

An abundance of life-force, which is acquired through proper diet, adequate exercise and the avoidance of sensual excesses, is required for developing the strength to live truth. The implications of this fact are that as long as people are kept ignorant of how to cultivate their life-force, and worse, kept indulging in a lifestyle characterized by wrong diet, sexual excesses, etc., they will never intuit, understand, or find the strength to live truth. Society must then be doomed to ever deepening decadence. Salvation, they teach, can supposedly be achieved by asking for God's forgiveness after a life of debauchery.

Maat is generally depicted as a woman holding the Ankh cross, symbol of the heka Aung, in one hand, and the Papyrus scepter, representing the book of the law, in the other. On her head rests the feather--her main symbol--which is the standard against which the will (the heart/ab) of the initiate is weighed. In one pan of the scale is placed the heart, and in the other, the feather, which symbolizes the lightness of truth, that is, the absence of emotional force that characterizes the action of truth. A fact little known to Egyptologists is that in her furrow (a wrinkle in her face) lays concealed the *scepter of flint* which she confers upon the initiate after he has been found to be "true of heart" (to have lived truth). That it is to be used to kindle the fire of Ra, is a hint regarding the life-force (kundalini) arousing power of living truth. This is the key of the supreme mantra caitanya (mantra awakening) secret that has eluded many yogis for millenniums[9].

HERUKHUTI

Herukhuti, also called Heru-Behutet, is the divine principle that safeguards our existence from the injustices of others. It works

---

9. Many believe that mantras can only be aroused by receiving them psychically (Shaktipat) from the Guru.

sternly through the law that states that you reap what you sow. Be consistent in being just with others, and you will be spiritually protected by this divine power.

Its aggressive power is also the foundation of the temperament of natural athletes, warriors, business executives, and so on.

In the Kamitic tradition, it is the form in which Heru fights against Set in order to regain the throne (control over one's life) that the latter usurped. The seeming contradiction that arises from considering Heru-Behutet "a form of Heru" is cleared up when we realize that ultimately there is only one Deity in the world, with different faculties. While Heru corresponds to the steady supply of noradrenalin that enables us to carry out all activities of externalization, Herukhuti (Heru-Behutet) corresponds to the extreme surges of adrenalin that support our aggressive, sexual arousal and immune responses.

HERU

There are a great deal of misunderstandings that have gained permanence in the thinking of the majority of "egyptologists." Leading these is the popular misconception that Heru is the sun god. It is damaging on two counts. For one, it is a perversion of the true meaning of the deity, and for another, it perpetuates the slur that African people worship material things (sun, rivers, lakes, animals, etc.).

In a qualified sense we can say that the sun is used as a metaphor to lead thinking to the understanding of the set of phenomena under the control of the natural force labelled "Heru." Specific to our present consideration is the division of the human metabolism into two phases; one is characterized by the rise of bodily temperature, and the other by its decrease. Each phase has its set of temperature (temperament) dependent or related physiological and psychical functions. Those that are directly related and dependent on the rise in temperature above the mean can be metaphorized as "solar" (the very extreme stages, as martial). The opposite phase is assigned to "the moon," "mercury" and "saturn." The mean between the two extremes is assigned to "venus" and "jupiter." Heru corresponds, therefore, to the "solar" phase of the psycho-physical metabolic cycle, which is mediated by noradrenalin

227

and other chemicals of the sympathetic nervous system. It enables us to become and remain awake (Pert em Heru!), to externalize our focus of consciousness, to reason, pay attention, to carry out our will, to utilize the organs and faculties of external activity (eyes, frontal part of the cerebrum, hands, legs, etc.).

Heru corresponds to our will, which is the freedom to follow or reject divine law, and our emotions. This freedom is the crux of our divinity. Without it, man would be compelled to follow the structural shaping forces of order which manifest in the 10th sphere as the "instincts" that compel all other creatures to obey the law, in which case he could not be held accountable to law, human or divine, let alone be considered the "likeness of God." Hence, spiritual growth occurs only when behavior and actions are initiated independent of emotional impulses (i.e., one ignores them). Many people are ignorant of the intrinsic freedom of their will, or are so habituated to acting out of emotional impulsion, or seeming compulsion, that they voluntarily renounce their intrinsic mastery over their spirit. This defaulting to the emotions is represented by *Heru Khenti an Maati*, or "Heru the Blind."

The other common misconception about the will is the belief that "power" is an attribute of it. The ability to achieve one's will is, therefore, spoken of as "strength of will, etc." But the very factors that make the will intrinsically free of emotional (the power part of our being) influence, also denies it of power as its attribute. A major correspondence of Heru (Shango, the "sun", etc.) is the king (and all people in authority). His function is to command the people and the army to carry out works. He does not have the power to do it himself. Similarly, when we declare our will to achieve a goal or carry out a behavior, we are commanding another part of our being which possesses the attributes of power. This is Ra, our life-force. It is of interest to note that the symbol of Ra is a serpent surmounting the solar disk, and all of its creative functions are carried out through the agency of hekau (words of power). We should not be surprised that the most primitive, hence most powerful part of our brain, the "reptilian brain" or R-complex, is responsive to sound waves and rhythm and not ideas. Perhaps some day, Western psychologists will realize that this part of the brain is the doorway to the root shaping factors of our behavior, as well as the powers of nature. The supreme way, then, of willing events is through the chanting of the heka controlling the physical manifestation. This manner of declaring our will is symbolized by *Heru-Pa-Khart*

(Harpocrates), i.e., "Heru, the child." He is depicted emerging from a lotus wearing the red and white crown, holding the flail and crook (See Appendix A) in one hand, while making the sign of silence and of chanting hekau. The lotus, which is a flower that requires a great deal of sunlight (it closes with the setting sun, opens with its rising) is a symbol of the psychic centers (chakras) wherein manifest the forces represented by the words of power. The "sign of silence and chanting hekau," which is made by pointing the index finger to the mouth, symbolizes *chanting combined with the cessation of ideation as the supreme means of expressing the will.*

Our willingness to carry out our will, as we all know so well, depends greatly on our state of vitality. Heru is assisted in his work of protecting the work of Ausar on our behalf by his four children; Hapi who represents a northern force, and protects the small viscera of the body; Tuamutef represents the eastern, and protects the heart, and the lungs; Amset represents the southern, and protects the stomach and large intestines, and Qebhsennuf represents the western, and protects the liver and gall bladder. There is more than just mere symbolism at work here. But the heart of the teaching is that by observing order, regularity, and the cycles governing the body's functions the health of the vital organs were insured, and thus the vitality. It is thus that we secure and preserve the ability to maintain the clarity of mind that is necessary for the practice of Men Ab, and the sense of vitality that supports our willingness to carry out our will. Compare this with the common belief, even among psychologists, and "mind power experts," that "will power" is developed through "mental exercises."

HET-HERU

All that strikes us as as being "beautiful"-harmoniously juxtaposed forms-in the world is the work of the Deity Het-Heru. In human life this natural intelligence manifests itself as artistic expression, social grace, charm, artistic as well as scientific invention, pleasure seeking, etc.

Het-Heru has its seat in the human body in the gonads. Its Kamitic name is an indication of this fact. Het-Heru literally means "house" (het) of Heru. Heru corresponds to those "solar" metabolic phase factors responsible for the virilization and masculinization of the adult male of the species. I.e., the metaphysical forces behind the production of androgen. In the Yoruba tradition, Heru is Shango, the patron of kings, who wears pants with exaggerated crotches to show that he "outmans" all other men. With Het-Heru, the emphasis is not on the hot gonadal expression of Heru, but on the cool, peaceful, joyous, refined, charming, sexual arousal and seductive behavior that stimulates the production of estrogen and the female reproductive system.

Concealed from the knowledge of the majority of people, is the fact that sexual arousal is an expression of the arousal of the life-force-Ra. In fact, during the earliest times in Kamitic history, Het-Heru was considered the principal female counterpart of the "deity" Ra, and therefore the mother of the deities. Her dominion over the imagination is the rationale for this association. The sensations of joy and pleasure (or negative feelings) are expressions of the arousal of the life-force, and the images that form the content of the visualization or daydreams (dhyana) are the spiritual moulds (bodies of the deities, and energized thought forms-the "elementals" of European occultism) that guide the physical forces to the realization of their goals.

In her role as the imaginative faculty she is *Nebt-Het*, the Lordess of the House. This house, of course, is the spirit. This can be easily understood from the fact that all spiritual work must be carried out through the concentration on images in a state of trance. *Images + aroused life-force (Ra) + trance (mediumistic or waking) = spiritual realization (mundane or spiritual).* Whoever remembers this formula, observes Maat, follows Tehuti, identifies with Ausar will achieve all his needs in heaven and on earth.

In her role as imagination she is also the "Eye (utchat) of Heru." That is, the eye of the will, or simply, our ability to visualize what we will to achieve. When the Kamitic texts say that the deities whose bodies where composed of light nourish themselves on the celestial light supplied to them by the Eye of Heru, they are referring to the subtle luminous matter out of which our images are formed.

SEBEK

Sebek is the name given to the planet mercury by the Egyptians during the Greco-Roman time. Earlier it was called "Sebku." In astrology, mercury is styled as "the messenger of the gods." This is because it corresponds to the language verbalizing centers--Broca, and Wernicke--that are located in the left hemisphere of the cerebrum. We must take note of the fact that all of our other faculties are only able to communicate sensations and images. Verbal thinking is a process of putting into verbal form (informing) what is felt, imaged or already known nonverbally. This will become very clear if you were to practice clipping your thought as soon as they begin to appear. You will realize that even though you suppressed the completion of the sentence or paragraph you are still able to know what the words were going to indicate. This is because the knowledge of what you clothe in thoughts precede the mental verbalization of such knowledge. Sebek translates these nonverbal messages into words. If the names, definitions, and logical activities concerning these nonverbal messages are in harmony with reality then the "way is open for the indwelling intelligence to extend its operations to the outer--career, marriage, etc.--part of our lives." Otherwise, it is closed.

It is important to note that Western psychologists have overrated the value of this faculty, obviously for the fact that it is the foundation of their technological, and commerce oriented culture. Their unqualified statement that it corresponds to language cannot be accepted. To be precise, it corresponds to the verbalizing aspects of language. It does not have the ability to process meaning (to understand) which is the function of the right side of the brain, a fact that suggests how, and why the left side of the brain is the chief source of mischief in the world. Long before Western scientists even suspected about the dualization of the brain, the Kabalistical tradition had an extensive knowledge about it. Quoting from the *Zohar* in *The Kabbalah Unveiled*, S. L. MacGregor Mathers states that:

7. When the inferior man descendeth (into this world), like unto the supernal form (in himself), there are found two spirits. (So that) man is formed from two sides--from the right and from the left.
8. With respect unto the right side he had NShMThA QDIShA, *Neschamotha Qadisha*, the holy intelligences; with respect unto the left side, NPSh ChIH, *Nephesh Chiah, the animal soul.*
9. Man sinned and was expanded on the left side; and then they who are formless were expanded also. (That is those

231

spirits of matter, who received dominion in the inferior paths of the soul of Adam, whence arouse concupiscence.).

There are few things that can rival the possession of a great deal of information without understanding.

Sebku, Sebek and Sobek are etymologically related to "Seb," from whence "Seba" and "Sebau" are derived. As "Seb" (Geb) is a name for the Earth God, Sebek or Sebku corresponds to information derived from earthly experiences (from outside of our self, as opposed to the spiritually intuited wisdom). We also have "Sba," to educate; "Sbau," school; "Sbat," pupils; and "Sbai," teacher.

Sebek is the faculty that enables us to separate and label parts of a whole, or members of a group on the basis of their external differences. Without this faculty we would look at an event, or thing and not be able to distinguish its parts or phases. Yet, because of it we segregate things, and events that belong together into air tight compartments, based on their superficial external differences, and thus create a host of problems in the world. This is the source of all the hypocritical acts, contradictions, and the failure to transfer what is learned in a situation, to analogous situations. The segregating function of Sebek is chiefly supported by the verbal functions of language; definitions, descriptions and naming. To define a thing is to explain what it is, and is not. I.e., to segregate it from other things. Few people know that verbal thinking, with its definitions, and names, is an obstruction to acquiring the knowledge of reality. When most people look at a thing, or event, they fail to see what is really there because the Sebek faculty interposes the definitions, and formulas that have been fed us via the educational process. Even where the definitions are useful and correct, there is still a process of substituting the symbols representing reality for the reality itself. Thus, to know reality, the thinking process must be stilled.

The Sebau (plural of Seba) are therefore all individuals whose lives are determined by earth-borne information, as opposed to spiritual teachings, and the intuitions from the wisdom faculty, Tehuti. This is why the Sebau were considered the enemies of Ra and of Ausar. i.e., earth-borne information closes the way to the development of our life-force and our spiritual growth.

Sobek corresponds to the side of Sebek as the guardian of the threshold. Sobek symbolized the crocodiles which closed the way to

232

Arabians attempting to smuggle themselves into Kamit. We find the same throughout Africa where cognate deities like Elegba, etc. are also the guardians at the entrance of shrines, homes, etc.

Anpu-called Anubis by the Greek-and Ap-uat (opener of the way), two aspects of the mercurial principle Sebek, shared the duty of guiding the deceased in the underworld to Maat's Hall of Justice, where the heart (will) is weighed. The deceased in this case are symbols of the person undergoing spiritual initiation, as it results in dying to certain things in the world, as well as to the personality (see Seker). This is why "reformed" Christians say that they are "born again." The "underworld" (tuat, Amenta, etc.) corresponds to the "subconscious," to which the focus of consciousness is transferred during trance.

Anpu and Ap-uat are depicted as canine headed men, because the faculty of cleverness, among others that they represent, is the dominant trait in dogs, foxes, jackals, etc. The ability of canines to learn to respond to a large number of verbal commands is also well known.

AUSET

The Goddess Auset is the embodiment of those intuitive and instinctive faculties that lay deep within our psyche, governing our ability to care for and nurture others. People in whom this faculty is strongly developed are very protective, caring and nurturing. These qualities, amongst the Kamitians and other Africans, were most desirable in mothers and wives.

In traditional African culture, social role models are based on "organic" laws that take in and integrate all aspects of man's being. It is an indisputable fact that women, as a whole, have a lower metabolic rate, and a higher parasympathetic output than men. Among many functions, the parasympathetic nervous system governs reproduction, gestation, and the trance states. These are the principles upon which women's roles in traditional African culture are defined. Activities that overstimulate the sympathetic (military, hunting, those requiring psychic aggressiveness), or diminish the capacity of the parasympathetic functions were discouraged in women. The toll to be paid is in the reduction of the quality of childbearing, social peace and harmony, and spiritual inspiration. The latter is to be understood from the intimate relationship between the parasympathetic and trance. As religion concerns itself with the inner realm of being, its main means, therefore, is the process of trance. It is a state in which an individual's externalizing faculties are "detached from the will," allowing the focus of consciousness to be internalized. Proficiency in this state of internalized consciousness gives the individual full acquaintance with the metaphysical realm. On one hand, communication becomes possible with the two classes of entities dwelling therein-the "living dead" (ancestors), and the spirits or natural intelligences (angels, deities) that administer the phenomena of the world. On the other hand, first hand knowledge of man's metaphysical vehicles (the deities of the tree of life making up his spiritual being), and his true relation with God, the divine laws, and the world is attained. Participation in African and Oriental rituals will reveal that women in general can enter into the states of trance with greater ease than men. This is why societies that utilize trance working in their religious practices have a greater appreciation and respect for women, and protect their capacity for prophetic inspiration by safeguarding them from such activities as soldiering, policing, etc.

Auset as "Mother of all living things," corresponds to the stage of conception of the will to achieve a specific goal. This conception, the uniting of the will (an image of what is to be achieved) to the life-force (Ra) is achieved through mediumistic trance. It is interesting to note that in the Kamitic language the word "Tut" means "to clothe," "Image," "to beget," etc. Out of ignorance, most of the time that people declare the will to achieve a specific goal they are in a state of externalized consciousness (non-emotional state), or verbalize it, and therefore fail to impress the idea upon the life-force. The same claim, "Mother of the Gods and the living," is made for Het-Heru, but her function deals with the gestation of the impregnated idea (daydreams in which we are enjoying the objective). In our discussion of Ausar above, we discussed the origin and meaning of Auset's name. We must add that her "special name" as Khenemet Aunkhet, also conceals the fact that she is also to be invoked through the heka "Aung" (Aunk-note that g, and k are interchangeable). In this role she shares many of the attributes of the Dravidian White Tara Goddess who combines both the qualities of Ausar, and Auset. This name Khenemet Aunkhet which denotes the "water of life and fertility" is also applied to Het-Heru. As such she corresponds to the Dravidian Green Tara. The healing and fertility giving powers of this heka "Aung

Tang" has been proven many times in the Auset and Het-Heru shrines of the Ausar Auset Society.

SEB, OR GEB, THE GOD OF THE EARTH

It has just begun to dawn, in the past decade or so, on Western scientists that the manner in which the earth maintains the equilibrium in the fluxes, and utilization of water, heat, carbon dioxide, oxygen, nitrogen, and the myriad of substances necessary to maintain life, resembles so much the picture of the homeostatic functions in living creatures, that the science of geology is best redefined as physiology, and the earth looked at as a living entity. This emerging science, which considers the earth a living being, is called Gaia. Over 6000 years ago, our African ancestors called it Geb.

Not only did they consider the earth to be alive, they noted that it played a major role in man's spiritual development. As Seb, the divine goose, the earth God broods upon the egg within which man's earthly experiences unfold. I.e., our earthly life is the embryonic stage of our spiritual development. The earthly demands, rewards (carrot on the stick!), and pressures of existence prod us toward the awakening of our spiritual talents and powers. Recall what was said about our mortality and vulnerability in the discussion of Seker. In this role as divine oxgoad, Geb is called the Erpau of the Gods. That is, it has inherited the role of the deities as the initiator of man's spiritual evolution. This is important as most people think of the earth in terms of its imprisonment of man's consciousness, without considering the fact that at the same time it provides the stimulus for escaping it. According to the *Pert em Hru (The Book Of the Dead)*, the righteous were provided with words of power that allowed them to escape the earth, while the wicked (materialists) were held fast by Seb. It must be noted that inherent in the function of the earth as the imprisoner of consciousness, and oxgoad toward spiritual development, is its role as verifier of spiritual development. A proof of spiritual development is the ability to rise above the emotional and sensual influences, which after all, are expressions of the animal (earthly) part of being; the ability to learn independently of externals, i.e., from within; the ability to control, or influence earthly events (in our bodies and environment) through the power of our life-force at the command of our will.

235

The vast majority of people who contemplate the great architectural wonders of Kamit never realize that the majority of the greatest, and most magnificent structures were built in honor of the ancestors. All traditional African societies possess the knowledge of how to communicate with the deceased. It is very important to note that although western religions believe in the existence of man's spirit, and its survival of the body after death, there are no religious or social institutions for communicating with the dead.

The most important outcome from communicating with the deceased is the realization that man's true being is not only independent of his physical body, but the fact that it precedes, and survives the existence of the body. And, finally, that it is immortal. Ultimately, a people's philosophy of life, and their cultural expression is based on their belief in the mortality or immortality of their essential being. In practice, regardless of claims, Western man lives his life as if it was the only one. Underlying western culture is the belief that life on earth is a one time experience that is to be lived for its own sake.

Spiritual philosophy begins with the understanding of the meaning of life, before and after death, which could only be empirically acquired through communications with the deceased. So great was the empirical revelation of man's immortality, that the greatest architectural wonders of Kamit were dedicated to the honor of the dead.

No less important was the fact that the ability to communicate with ancestors has enabled Africans and Orientals to unite people into kinship groups that transcended the lower and limited ties of blood. Western scientists delight in parading their erudition regarding the fact that all cells in existence today, have been in existence from the beginning of time (this is due to cellular division). Yet, for the most part, Westerners are incapable of establishing firm kinships beyond the immediate family circle of husband, wife and children. In most traditional African societies, millions of people who are, and will remain strangers to each other, are tied, through the ancestors functioning as spiritual clan heads, into a web of responsibilities that would be expected only from the immediate family. It is in this manner, out of a sense of extended

236

blood kinship, that traditional (i.e., not westernized) African societies with populations numbering in the millions, have been able to maintain law and order without police systems, ideologies, etc.

Although all ancestors have the potential to function as unifiers of the people at different levels, not all of them did so. Only such people who lived up to the standards imposed by Tehuti (Tehuti is the Great Sheps in Khemennu), earned the right, and privilege to become Sheps,-the honored living, or honored dead.

Incidentally, Africans have never worshiped ancestors. Ancestral rituals have always aimed at establishing communication with ancestors to enable them to contribute to the direction of the nation. Thus we must reject the western concept of ancestor worship.

RA

Ra (pronounced Rau, hence Aur/light, aurum (oro)/gold, aura, auraut/ureus, origin, etc.) is the active state of Nu/Nut, the undifferentiated infinite energy/matter from whence all things, living and non-living originate. It is known as Chi or Ki in the oriental tradition, Kundalini in Dravidian India, and the Aur that emanated from the union of Ain and Soph, according to the Kabalistical tradition. Although it is not correct to say that Ra is the "sun god," it is quite correct to relate its functions to the solar energy as the energy/matter basis of all manifestations in our solar system. The planets, including the earth with its life forms, owe their existence to the solar emanations. As the solar energy, then, is the material, and energy basis for the creation, and maintenance of life (physical, and metaphysical), the wisdom traditions of Africa, and the Orient devised ways of manipulating it. No! They never worshiped it. What western scholars have interpreted as sun worship are the many practices for cultivating it, replenishing it, divining its activities (as it works outside the ken of normal waking consciousness), living in harmony with the rhythmic and cyclical manifestations of its modalities ("air (wood)," "fire," "earth (metal)," and "water"). These are the subjects of pranayama (breath control), Taoist yoga, tantra yoga, so-called "fetishism" or "fakirism," hatha yoga, kundalini yoga, mantra yoga, raja yoga, tai chi, chi kung, akido, homeopathy, radiasthesia (western voodoo!), acupuncture, divination by lots, or dreams, or omens, etc.

The subjects are manifold as you can see. We must restrict ourselves to two of its most important manifestations. Our breath, which is the principal way in which we take in the life-force, is ionized into positive and negative electromagnetic polarities[10] by agents in our nostrils. These two currents of breath, which are analogous to the north and south emanations of magnets, control the two phases of our metabolism.

In his book "*Researches On the Vital Force*," translated by University Books, Baron Karl Von Reichenbach-1788-1869 (discoverer of kerosene) reports his findings from experiments on the life-force. Slow, downward passes of strong magnets (force of 10 lbs and up) close to the skin but not touching, produced in "sensitives" a sensation of agreeable coolness from one pole, and disagreeable warmth from the other pole. In some cases the energy from either pole was so strong that it caused pain, spasm, nausea, jerking of the body, faintness, etc. The warm current, which is red-orange as seen clairvoyantly, is generated by the southern or electropositive pole of the magnet. It predominates in the left side of the body, in metals, alkaline PH, moonlight, the electropositive elements, the southern node of the moon (Cauda draconis, Ketu, the dragon's tail). The cool current, which is "bluish-gray," is generated by the northern or electronegative pole, and predominates in the right side of the body, metalloids, acid PH, sunlight, light, heat, electronegative elements, the northern node of the moon (caput draconis, the dragon's head, Rahu).

It is important to note that these two currents correspond to the earth's southern, and northern magnetic poles, and hence to the electromagnetic powers flowing along the meridians of the earth. Along with the east/west currents, they play major shaping roles in the electromagnetic processes going on in all atoms, and their chemical and electrophysical activities. In the 1960's Kirlian developed a photographic process that makes it possible to photograph the radiations given off by these currents of energy. See *Psychic Discoveries Behind the Iron Curtain*, for actual photographs.

---

10. The Ida, and Pingala of Yogic science.

NEKHEBET And UATCHET

In the Kamitic tradition, the science for manipulating the two magnetic forces which form the essence of all psychic powers was subsumed in the teachings associated with the symbols of the "deities" Nekhebet, and Uatchet. These powers were considered so important that they were made the tutelary "deities" of Kamit. Nekhebet, which corresponds to the electronegative northern pole of the magnet was the chief protectress of Upper ' _thern) Kamit. She is depicted as a woman wearing the White crown of Upper Egypt, and holding a lotus scepter intertwined by a serpent, which together symbolize the electromagnetic forces (the serpent) of the psychic centers (the lotuses). Uatchet, which corresponds to the electropositive southern pole of the magnet, was the chief protectress of Lower (northern) Kamit. She is depicted as a woman wearing the Red crown of lower Kamit, and holding a papyrus scepter intertwined by a serpent. Their correspondences to the poles of the magnet are revealed in the ceremony for embalming the dead, where the priest says to the mummy, *"The goddess Uatchet comes into you in the form of the living Auaraut (uraeus), to anoint your head with their[11] flames. She (the Auraut) rises up on the left side of your head, and she shines from the right side of your temples without speech; they rise up on your head during each and every hour of the day, even as they do for their father Ra, and through them the terror which you inspire in the holy spirit is increased, and because Uatchet, and Nekhebet rise up on your head, and because your brow becomes the portion of your head where they establish themselves, even as they do upon the brow of Ra, and because they never leave you, awe of thee is stricken into the souls which are made perfect."* There are a number of very important correspondences in the above quotation.
1. The auraut (ureaus), which will be explained later, is composed of the conjunction of Uatchet and Nekhebet.
2. The statement, "and she shineth from the *right side of the temples without speech*," is exceedingly remarkable as it shows that the Kamitians possessed over 6000 years ago the knowledge that the right side of the brain is speechless. We can go further and point out that the Kamitian kings placed the head of the vulture Mut (symbol of motherhood), which corresponds to Nekhebet (the bluewish-gray cool

---

11. Their = Uatchet, and Nekhebet that together make up the Auraut (the ureaus).

239

electronegative force) on the right side of the forehead, while the head of the cobra representing Uatchet (the warm, reddish-orange electropositive force) was placed on the left side of the forehead. By this, the kings of Kamit signalled that a) psychic power was very important for the protection of the nation, and b) that the acquisitive, cool, agreeable force of Nekhebet and Mut were over the domestic policy of the nation. The southern part of Kamit, well away from the Asiatic desert homelands and nomadic routes was, for the most part, home to the chief capitals of Kamit. The northern part of Kamit was placed under the red crown, and Uatchet as a symbol of the hot offensive front protecting the motherland from the hostility of the Asiatics.

3. The statement, "they rise up on your head during each and every hour of the day, even as they do for their father Ra," is a reference to the planetary hours. A great deal of confusion has arisen from the fact that most researchers into metaphysics have failed to note that most metaphysical references to planets refer, not to the celestial bodies themselves, but to the modalities of the life-force which they symbolize. The moon corresponds to the cooling, hence moisturizing state of the life-force; the sun, to the hot, hence drying state, and so on. These "planetary" modalities dominate each hour of the day. Each day begins at sunrise with the planet that gives it its name and quality. Following the Tree of Life (the planetary spheres: 3 to 9), Saturday begins with saturn ruling the first hour from sunrise, followed for an hour each by jupiter, mars, sun, venus, mercury, the moon, and back to saturn, etc. If we followed the "planets" for 24 hours we will find that the next day, sunday, will begin with the sun governing the first hour from sunrise. It will be followed by venus, mercury, etc. The next sunrise will begin with the moon, followed by saturn, etc. For a detailed look at the subject see Llewellyn George's "*Improved Perpetual Planetary Hour Book.*"

4. The auraut or ureaus (the third eye) is none other than the ajna (brow) chakra of kundalini yoga. It is brought into manifestation through the following process: Note that in the following procedure, push your stomach out from the lower abdomen during the inbreath, and contract it during the outbreath.

The heka is as follows:

Breath
in   held   -   -   -   out

1   2   3   4 | 5   6   7, 8

Aung   Hang   Kshang | Aung   Hang   Kshang

1. Having decided the objective of your meditation, focus both eyes (open) on the center of your brow. **Breathe in during the first two counts** while mentally chanting Aung on the first count, and Hang on the second. From the third to the 6th count, hold the breath *and contract the perineum*[12]. On the third count chant Kshang and hold it through the 4th. On the 5th count chant Aung, on the 6th, Hang, and Kshang on the 7th as you breathe out, and release the perineum.

As you chant "Aung," visualize a brilliant white disk sitting on the center of your forehead. This is the undifferentiated life-force.

As you chant "Hang[13]" visualize a brilliant white cobra emerging from the left side of the disk. This is Uatchet's highest heka.

As you chant "Kshang" visualize a brilliant white cobra emerging from the right side of the white disk. This is Nekhebet's highest heka.

a) Repeatedly visualize a woman coming toward you dressed in white, holding an open white book with its pages blank. Look at the blank white page. After several repetitions of this scenario, a message will appear on the blank page. This, along with the heka given above, is a key to clairvoyance.

b) or visualize yourself as a woman (men should not worry about this) dressed in dark blue going forth, stepping out with your right foot first (THIS IS VERY IMPORTANT) to acquire a need in life. See yourself enjoying your objective. This is to be done when you get a Nekhebet reading.

---

12. The perineum is the muscle that enables us to stop our urine in midstream. Do not confuse it with the anal sphincter which is connected with defecation.

13. Hang is originally red, but in the auraut center it is white.

c) or visualize yourself as a woman dressed in red going forth, stepping out with your left foot first, to acquire your objective. This is to be done when you get a Uatchet reading.

AUNG HANG K- SHAM   AUNG HANG K- SHAM

The function of the auraut (third eye) is not limited to clairvoyance. It is the center that controls all psychic activities. Next to the crown center it is second in the hierarchy of our spiritual power. The technique given above is to be applied at the 8th stage of the meditation process. Nourishment of the auraut center through daily meditation will give you full control over the psychic influences operating in your life. Its perfection will enable you to withstand all negative psychic influences without the assistance of herbal baths, incenses, sacrifices, rituals, talismans, etc.

In future chapters we will learn about the combination of Nekhebet, and Uatchet with the seven planetary powers governing the seven days of the week. These are the powers behind the fourteen kau of Ra.

The positive, western pole of the east/west electrical current of Ra is symbolized by the Goddess Sekhet. She is depicted as a red clad, lion headed woman who delights in offerings of hard liquor, blood, and meat. She is the violent, scorching aspect of the heat of Ra, which is invoked through the heka "Rang." She works through the solar plexus (manipura) psychic center. In the form of the serpent-goddess Mehenet she emerges from the forehead of Ra pouring out her fire to destroy the enemies of Ra (one's life-force); specifically shame, spiritual ignorance, thirst, jealousy, treachery, fear, delusion, foolishness, and sadness. In the Metu Neter oracle she is represented by combinations of a negative Uatchet card with a negative Het-Heru.

The negative, eastern pole of the current of Ra is symbolized by the Goddess Bast. She is pictured as a green clad,

242

lion headed woman. She is the warm, fructifying power of the sun that is generated in the womb from sexual passion. She delights in offerings of wine, aphrodisiacs, sweets, vanilla flavored rice cream, cinnamon, honey, etc. She works through the sexual (swadhisthana) psychic center.

Chapter 18

THE METUTU

FUNDAMENTAL PRINCIPLES

**The Philosophical and Psychological Foundation of the Metu Neter
Oracle System**

The Fundamental Shaping Factors of Life
and Their Interrelation and Interdependence

Preliminary: Each card symbolizing the message from the oracle is
called a metu or metut, and their combination is called a metutu. In
the Kamitic language the plural is formed by adding a final "u."

Amen:

> The Subjective Realm, Amen, is the infinite source of the
> life-force and spiritual matter (Nut), which are the
> formative bases of the faculties and talents that enable us to
> survive, flourish, and succeed in the world. As our talents,
> and faculties originate in the universal life-force, and
> universal infinite matter (the Paut), a successful destiny can
> only be achieved by realizing that our talents are not private
> property. Amen, therefore, is the higher of the two prime
> determinants of the nature of the events in our lives. It is
> the chief stimulus of the forces urging and pushing us to
> honor the universal interests. It is seemingly directly
> opposed by the earthly influences of the 10th sphere (Geb),
> which by clothing our intrinsically indivisible being with
> physical matter creates the illusion that we are separate
> beings[1].
>
> It is of utmost importance to realize that as "the
> universal" is the source of all the individuated existences, its
> interest cannot be separated from the interests of the
> persons. This does not, directly or indirectly imply, or
> support socialistic, or communistic philosophies, as these
> systems of government, and economic distribution are the
> products of the faculties of the 7th, 8th, and 9th spheres.
> Yet, the pursuit of personal interest that is not subordinated

---

1. This is the meaning of the Amen/Geb metutu.

to the universal influences can be separated from, and can damage the welfare of the whole.

Ausar:

With its roots in Amen, Ausar is the unifying force which obliterates and overcomes all shaping factors of individuated existence. But the unity here is explicit, as there is an implicit disunity concealed in its definition and being. Unification is the coming together of parts of a whole. I.e., all things in the world are modifications of the universal energy/matter (the paut). It is the second of the chief stimuli of the forces urging and pushing us to honor the universal interests. It is directly opposed by the focal point of identification with the personality-Auset, the 9th sphere, which is the emotional instigator, and support of our personal interests. Thus we have, in the social sphere, the opposition between the universal good, and the personal good. And in the sphere of the life of the individual, we have the opposition between success in specific pursuits vs. a successful life and destiny; what is far vs. what is near, etc.

Tehuti:

With its roots in Ausar and Amen, Tehuti is the source of the intuition that shows the way to achieve the equilibrium between the interest of the whole, and of the person. It is the third of the chief stimuli of the forces urging and pushing us to honor the universal interests[2]. It is directly opposed by the influences from the 8th sphere, which is the chief provider of the arguments and rationalizations supporting the personal interests[3] and point of view.

Seker:

With its roots in Amen and Ausar, Seker guarantees the interest of the whole as well as all individuated existences by providing the structural framework that orders their coming into being, and their development[4]. It is the fourth of the

---

2. This meaning is brought out by the Amen/Tehuti, and Ausar/Tehuti metutu.

3. This meaning is brought out by the Sebek/Auset metutu.

4. This meaning is brought out by the Amen/Seker metutu.

chief stimuli of the forces urging and pushing us to honor the universal interests. It is opposed by the influences emanating from the organizing and ordering faculty of the person,-Het-Heru[5], the seventh sphere.

Maat:

Because the supreme law governing man's divinity is centered around his freedom to choose (freedom of will), the knowledge of the law is conveyed to him in such a way that allows him the freedom to follow or reject it[6]. His following it, gives him success in his individual undertakings, and it qualifies and prepares him for crossing the great abysm to partake in the divine powers of the 3rd sphere and higher. It is directly opposed by the influences from the 8th sphere, which is the chief provider of the arguments and rationalizations that support the emotionally motivated behavior of the person-centered way of life[7].

Herukhuti:

Where there is freedom of choice in an intrinsically law and order based situation, which is the fundamental nature of the world, there is bound to be transgressions. The offensive power of God, thus exists for the sake of protecting the equilibrium between the interests of the whole vs. those of the individuals. If in the exercise of our freedom to choose, we avoid obstructing others, the offensive power of God will remove all obstructions from others from our path. It is directly opposed by the seventh sphere's (Het-Heru's) receptivity to the instincts of self-preservation[8] originating in the 10th sphere.

Heru:

The possession of our will-the <u>freedom</u> to follow or reject divine law is the basis of our divinity. It is the one thing that clearly separates man from all other creatures on earth. It is the only free element in man's being. This brings us to one of the most important, if not <u>the</u> most important

---

5. This meaning is brought out by the Het-Heru/Auset metutu.

6. This meaning is brought out by the Maat/Heru metutu.

7. This meaning is brought out by the Sebek/Auset metutu.

8. This meaning is brought out by the Het-Heru/Geb metutu.

principle governing spiritual realization. While "heaven" (spheres 0-3) and "earth" (spheres 7-10) seek to coerce us to follow its mandates through structures, and impulses, respectively, living according to the principle governing the will is characterized by actions taken free of emotional coercion from below, or structural impositions from above. This is so important as most students of spirituality, so dependent on, and habituated to acting from emotional compulsion waste their opportunities for spiritual development, waiting and hoping for an impulse from above to force them to live truth. But how can we attain to freedom without effort, and how can we make the effort if there is no freedom. Yes, No freedom, No effort, and No effort, No freedom.

Het-Heru:

It is also seemingly paradoxical that sex, one of the major destroyers of spiritual careers, and quests for success, is also a major key to success in these very areas. Indulged in moderation, and with our identity transferred to our indwelling intelligence--Ausar--it is the chief means of arousing the life-force (chi, Ra, kundalini) to the level where it will enable us to achieve our goal, predominantly if not solely, through our will and spiritual faculties.

Sebek:

Perhaps the best description of the problems resulting from the use of our syllogistic logical intellectual faculty without the guidance of the synthetical faculty (4th sphere, Maat) is symbolized by the Hydra of Greek mythology. For every head that was cut off from this monster, two grew in its place. This is a very accurate characterization of the majority of proposed logical solutions. Because this faculty can only focus on a part at a time, a proposed solution to a problem creates a number of unforeseen problems in other parts. Such problems are avoided by realizing that we cannot construct wholes from the logical manipulation of species and parts (the Tower of Babel syndrome), and that the syllogistic logical function must be applied only after the whole has been perceived. The perception of concrete wholes is carried out by Het-Heru (the imagination), and the perception of abstract wholes is carried out by Maat,

247

and Tehuti. The last two faculties are the only sources of solutions to specific problems that do not create problems elsewhere (this is the function of wisdom and divine law). The second step in developing ourselves spiritually, and promoting our ability to succeed in our undertakings and in life, involves the unification of our logical intellect with the divine law.

Auset:

The upliftment of the low by the high, is the principle governing the formula for spiritual development. Auset is the beginning of this process. She is the point of bringing the highest within us-Ausar-into the vehicle of our personality (the ka) to initiate the movement toward the realization of unity within diversity, and the upward movement of our spiritual evolution.

Geb:

It is seemingly paradoxical that earthly influences which are the prime sources of our anti-spiritual behavior, should provide man with the prime impulse to his spiritual development. Without the obstructions and demands of our earthly existence, unevolved man will not stir to awaken and bring forth his spiritual powers.

In order to properly grasp the meaning of each Metut (divination symbol), and to utilize the oracle as a guide to spiritual development and mundane success, it is necessary to establish an overview showing how all the Deities--represented by the Metutu (divination symbols)--work together to bring about success on different levels. The absence of such an overview is the major cause of the failure of such oracles as the Tarot, Geomancy, Cartomancy, etc. to serve as a basis for spiritual initiation.

Shaping Factors of Success

The following principles are the embodiment of the shaping factors for success in all undertakings in life. It is important to realize that success depends on the observance of these principles in regards to content, as well as the order in which they are given. Heru is central to the means of achieving success, which according to the Kamitic philosophy is "the achievement of a mundane

248

undertaking in such a manner as to preserve, or increase our spirituality." Heru corresponds to the part of the spirit through which we express our freedom of being, and therefore assume responsibility for our destiny. It is our faculty of choosing and deciding what we will believe, do, and how we will do it. The following, then, are the steps that an enlightened will [Heru (+)] follows in order to succeed in an undertaking and in life--I.e., to achieve its mundane goals in such a manner that it will contribute to the realization of the true self.

Amen: Spiritual- An enlightened will [Heru (+)] knows that all things (life, the life-force, the potential to achieve, the materials for success, etc.) come from heaven which is infinite in its potential to give.
Mundane: Same as spiritual.

Ausar: Spiritual- An enlightened will [Heru (+)] knows that all successful undertakings (accomplishments that do not create harm--spiritual or mundane--in other ways) are performed, not by the person, but by the indwelling intelligence-the Self, Ausar.
Mundane: You must intuit the central theme underlying all parts of the undertaking or thing.

Tehuti: Spiritual: An enlightened will [Heru (+)] knows that every choice and decision affecting the course of our lives, must be guided by the wisdom of the Supreme Being. He consults high oracles, and sits humbly at the feet of the Sage.
Mundane: You must intuit how each part fits in with the whole. Its place in time (which phase) and space (its value, the priorities, its scope, etc.).

Seker: Spiritual- An enlightened will [Heru (+)] knows that before taking action on a decision, there must be the knowledge of the underlying structure (the plan) governing what must be done. As the structural framework of all events are laid down by the deities and spirits, one does not, therefore, "make up a plan." Instead, the thought processes are stilled in order to "sense" and intuit the structural framework created by the spiritual agencies. In addition, every step taken in carrying out the undertaking must follow "the plan." Incidentally, the Jewish Kabalists, not understanding that the mental process of this sphere were to be stilled, but knowing from Canaanite sources that it involved some sort of intuition, named the sphere Binah, "Understanding." As there are mental processes involving the realization of "understanding" at the 4th and 5th spheres as well, the Jewish Kabalistical correspondence must be rejected.

Mundane: You must intuit the structure that underlies, hence gives order to the unfolding of the event.

Note:

It is important to remember that the mental process operating from Amen to Seker is one of intuition, which is the ability to correctly learn from within one's own spirit. If you receive one of these Metutu in your readings and you are not able to intuit the information that is required, you must then seek counsel from capable persons represented by the respective Metut. Your meditations with the heka of the Deity will help to attract such persons. In strictly materialistic situations such persons will be, primarily, your top geniuses in science, literature, art, etc., and secondarily, your Ph.D.'s, etc. In matters regarding life, social issues, etc. such persons will be your sages.

Maat: Spiritual- An enlightened will [Heru (+)] is one that has been taught the laws that must be followed in order to receive the beneficent gifts of heaven (Amen-ta). Because of its full understanding of the law of heaven it does not chafe itself in restless rebellion against the constraints suggested by the law. It knows that the law guarantees all things its day in the sun.

Mundane: If I were a newly arrived being from another planet, and were to say to you that I observed people in New York for three months, and therefore concluded that light clothing[9] is their mode of dress, you would correct me by pointing out that although my thinking was logically correct, my conclusion was not true. Why? Obviously, I have only observed a part of the whole, while you have observed New Yorkers through all the seasons. Maat corresponds, therefore, to the ability to understand the

---

9. If the example sounds trivial, you ought to look closely around you and take note of the fact that people do not often dress functionally. Some people wear desert type clothing in temperate zones; temperate type clothing in tropical zones, etc. Of course they never know what ails them, when their health breaks down.

interdependence, and interrelationship between the parts and the whole, and with each other (synthesis), through the use of abstract analogies. It is the logical process (Cosmologics) that enables the testing of the truth of a premise. Unlike the Sebek faculty which processes connections in a sequential (serial) fashion, Maat processes them in a synchronistic, parallel mode. While we can only see how things follow each other at the Sebek level, here we can also see how they work simultaneously to carry out the central theme. Through it, we can find our way in and out of the forest, not through specific sign posts (marking certain trees, landmarks, etc.-as with Sebek), but through the ability to orient ourselves through the cardinal points (literally, or symbolically!). If you are lacking the knowledge of the cosmograms (mandalas, Tree of Life, i.e., "symbol-blueprints"), or the ability to synthesize, you must seek counsel from people who meet the criteria. Meditation with the heka of Maat will guide you to act in a manner that reflects the interdependence between all beings. You will thus widen your sphere of acquaintance, influence, and sharing (giving and receiving). As your ability to accumulate grows, your sense of interdependence between all things will prevent you from seeking more than your due.

Herukhuti: Spiritual- An enlightened will [Heru (+)] knows that the true purpose of the offensive power of the Supreme Being is not to punish the offenders of the laws of heaven, but to protect those who uphold it. It secures its objectives against the obstruction by others by treating them according to Maat.

Mundane: When parts and phases are seen from the perspective of the whole, we are able to see their complementary relationship. When they are viewed on the specific level we can only see their antagonistic relationship. For example; the watery (anabolic), and fiery (catabolic) phases of an event are cooperative when seen from the holistic perspective, and antagonistic (they check and destroy each other) when seen on their level. Herukhuti is, therefore, the ability to understand the qualities that separate parts of a whole (analysis, analogical lysis), however integral they are to the latter. It is achieved through the perception of the abstract qualities of things. It enables you to maintain your individuality (or the individuality of a set) by realizing that although all things are parts of a whole, they have been individuated for the purpose of carrying out a specific set of functions.

Heru: Spiritual- An enlightened will [Heru (+)] knows that all actions and undertakings must begin in the freedom from emotional influences. Ultimately, no sane person is ever compelled to act. He is either ignorant of his intrinsic freedom to choose to follow or reject the impulses from the animal part of the spirit (sensual cravings and emotions), or he chooses not to follow the law of heaven-Maat-which is always applied to him with the gentleness of a feather. He therefore enlightens himself regarding the true nature, and purpose of the will, and the means of effectively using it (Men Ab,-the science of using the will to secure one's goal by allowing the higher values to lead over the emotional forces).

Mundane: It is the ability to understand the abstract, and concrete unifying and separating functions of all spheres, and their coordination for the carrying out of the undertaking. If you are deficient in these abilities you must seek the assistance of one who meets the criteria. As these qualities are cultivated through supervisory and leadership positions, the people who could best assist you are those who are successful in the roles of supervisors, heads of household, bosses, kings, presidents, etc. In all cases, whether you are capable or not, your success depends on receiving counsel from someone above you. It is important, then, to cultivate respect for elders, authorities, and "masters" in particular fields, or of life matters (sages). Meditating on the heka of Heru will attract such persons to you, and assist you in establishing the mode of being receptive to higher counsel, yet, maintaining the freedom to make your own decisions (this receptivity differs from Auset's in the sense that she follows without questioning, or going through a decision process).

Note:

It is important to note that the key, mental ability functioning through spheres 4, 5, and 6 is understanding (literally, "to stand under"). It corresponds to the ability to go into waking trance

252

and perceive the abstract principles governing specifics, separating them, and unifying them. If you receive any of these Metutu in a reading and you lack the information (abstract blueprint, mandala, cosmograms, etc.), or the ability to think abstractly, you must seek counsel from one who meets the criteria.

Het-Heru: Spiritual- An enlightened will [Heru (+)] knows that there is no such thing as "will power." The realization of the will (what has been decided upon) is carried out by the life-force (Ra, chi, kundalini), which must first be receptive to what is being willed (Auset factor), and then gestated by the Het-Heru faculty. This gestation process consists of "the *enjoyment* of one's intended objective in the *imagination*." The sensations of joy and pleasure (or negative feelings) are expressions of an aroused life-force, and the images that form the content of the daydream are the spiritual moulds that guide the physical forces to the realization of the goal. As we saw in previous chapters, it is often necessary to step up the level of enjoyment through Kula yoga, "deity invocation" rituals, etc.

Mundane: It is the ability to form a concrete image of the end that you are working toward. This image has the function of organizing all of the subtle electromagnetic forces that will shape the event. On a higher level, it works through such people who have the ability to bring people together for the accomplishment of small objectives. By "small objectives" is meant those undertakings that will not stimulate conflicting conditionings within the spirit of the person(s) involved. When you receive this Metut, it means that you will most likely have to arouse your ability to be sociable, charming, etc. (invoke Het-Heru), or you may have to secure the assistance of such people.

Sebek: Spiritual- An enlightened will [Heru (+)] knows that the true purpose of cleverness (what passes for "intelligence" in the west) and education (knowledge of techniques: details of the steps, and processes of carrying out a task) are for easing the way. I.e., for the purpose of carrying out tasks with a minimum of effort and time, and maximum results.

Mundane: Same as the spiritual. In addition, it is the ability to establish the legal connection between sequential units, and between parts through their outer form. It is important to keep in mind that the reason why syllogistic or Cartesian logic cannot give insight into the truth of premises is due to the fact that it cannot establish the logical connections between parts and the whole to which they belong, as it only deals with the outer form of things. When you receive this Metut in a reading, it may mean that you may have to secure the assistance of specialists, and technicians in the field (people of "the book").

Auset: Spiritual- An enlightened will [Heru (+)] knows that there is no such thing as "will power." The realization of the will (what has been decided upon) is carried out by the life-force. The impregnation of the life-force by the will does not take place by the mere decision to achieve a goal. The life-force must first be thrown into its receptive state through mediumistic trance. Although we spontaneously and involuntarily enter into this state several times daily, it is imperative to strongly induce it at will in order to insure the conception of our will.

Mundane: it corresponds to your ability to get the support of the power that will carry out the undertaking. On the personal side, it is your life-force (Ra), and on the social side it is the assistance of followers, workers, etc. (note that while Het-Heru denotes partners, Auset denotes followers).

Geb: On one hand, Geb (+) corresponds to the mundane event that has been successfully brought about by the will that has been enlightened by its adherence to the above 10 principles. On the other hand, it corresponds to the physical resources that the life-force needs in order to carry out the undertaking. I.e., we are counselled, when we receive this Metut to adhere to the laws of the earth (health, cycles, etc.) in order to nourish, and maintain the equilibrium of Ra. Or as stated more eloquently in the Metaphoric system, "to protect Ra from the worms, and noxious serpents dwelling in Geb."

Sheps: An enlightened will [Heru (+)] knows that no man is an island. All successes in life are directly or indirectly corporate efforts. He maintains his unity with others by tracing his common ancestry with all humans through the study of history, and invocations of the ancestors.

Nekhebet and Uachet: An enlightened will [Heru (+)] knows that the life-force does not originate in the body of the person, nor can it be contained therein. Like the air, which enters us through our breathing and then leaves to be shared with others, the life-force circulates through all creatures thus putting them in touch with each other. The enlightened individual, therefore, will always observe the laws that will keep his life-force in perfect equilibrium ("psychic balance") in order to avoid the subtle negative influences of other creatures and the environment, as well as to secure their assistance toward the realization of the objective.

The Shaping Factors of Failure

Failure is just not simply, or always the inability to achieve a mundane undertaking. Whether we achieve a mundane goal or not, we fail if we have jeopardized our spirituality thereby. Central to failing is the negative state of the will, which is characterized by either the ignorance of the principles governing the will, or the unwillingness to follow them. Most people are ignorant of the fact that they are essentially free to ignore all emotional and sensual impulses, and are thus controlled by them by default. Others, pathetically, learn of their essential freedom of will, and even of the excellent means of effectively using it (Men Ab), but choose to follow these impulses just the same. The following principles which result from a negative state of the will [Heru (-)] contribute, individually or together, to failure in undertakings or in life.

Amen: An unenlightened will [Heru (-)] believes that the earthly Realm is the source of all things (life, the life-force, the potential to achieve, the material resources, etc.), and therefore, takes stock of the available material resources to calculate what it can and cannot achieve. It thus limits its potential to achieve, and out of a sense of limitation, lays the foundation for competition and conflict with others.

Ausar: An unenlightened individual [Heru (-)] believes that his natal personality is his identity. As a result he is unable to transcend its characteristics, in order to awaken his infinite potential of being to meet the infinite variety of situations confronting him. Failure comes when life demands that you manifest one of the other six personalities dormant within your spirit, and you can't because you are convinced that you are your natal personae.

Tehuti: An unenlightened individual [Heru (-)] believes that the body of information that he has acquired throughout his life, and the rationalization therefrom should be the basis of the choices and decisions affecting the course of his life.

Seker: An unenlightened individual [Heru (-)] is ignorant of, or does not believe in (lacks direct experience) the fact that deities and spirits control the course of events, for the purpose of establishing and maintaining order in the world. Thus, his plans are based on concepts for which there are no objective counterparts. He therefore runs into "delays," obstructions, denials, etc.

Maat: An unenlightened individual [Heru (-)] is ignorant of, or does not believe in divine law. His spiritually unlawful behavior brings him thus into conflict with others, and many factors opposing his will.

Herukhuti: An unenlightened individual [Heru (-)] is ignorant of the fact that by being fair to others, even at the cost of personal harm and loss, will secure divine protection. By succumbing to the fallacy that there are times when divine law can, or must be set aside (e.g., for the sake of survival), he sets in motion the pendulum of justice which must in time swing back and visit its wrath upon him.

Heru: See the opening statements to this discourse.

Het-Heru: An unenlightened individual [Heru (-)] is ignorant that all inducers of pleasure are means of arousing the life-force[10]. He thus fails to cultivate, or to moderate the indulgence of pleasure, and as a result fails due to a lack of vital force. He then speaks ignorantly of weakness of will, poor health, poor memory, and so on. His failure is compounded by his ignorance of the function of images as moulds (matrices) for physical events. He gives power of realization to unwanted or intolerable events by dwelling on them in emotionally and sensually charged visualizations. In addition, the visualization process at this level is the key for remaining motivated. The pleasure associated with the results we are aiming at serves to carry us through the various stages of the undertaking. Without it, we fail even with the assistance of schedules, day planners, etc.

---

10. This is the great key to arousing kundalini that most yogis hide from the public. All the techniques of yoga, are in reality means of intensifying the arousal, and of insuring the free flow of the force.

Sebek: An unenlightened individual [Heru (-)] believes that the purpose of his cleverness is to ease the way to his goals at the expense of others.

Auset: An unenlightened individual [Heru (-)] is ignorant of the fact that spontaneously and involuntarily, he daily goes through mild trances, which unite his will to the conceiving part of the spirit. He is therefore unaware of the fact that he is daily conceiving and reinforcing all sorts of intentions, many of which are contradictory, and in conflict with his will and destiny. He is unaware that his failure to remember what he must do to carry out his will, is an indication that he needs to reinforce the impregnation of his will upon his spirit through repeated inductions of mediumistic trance. It is important to realize that the act of remembering what we must do and the principles we must observe, is an involuntary reflex. We cannot will to remember at a specific moment. It must be automatically thrown into our awareness by the life-force.

Geb: Geb (-) corresponds to the failed mundane undertaking, resulting from the violation of the laws of health.

Dark Deceased: An unenlightened individual [Heru (-)] who perseveres in folly will throw his destiny away. His after life existence will be filled with misery and want, even if his life on earth was filled with material goods and comforts.

Nekhebet and Uachet: An unenlightened individual [Heru (-)] will be ignorant of the need to maintain psychic equilibrium, and the fact that he is spiritually in touch with all things in the world. His psychic disequilibrium will open him to the negative influences from others, and the environment.

Summary

Heru: The will is the source of Self (Ausar, unemotionally) initiated acts.

Seker: The source of the plans that must guide the steps that we take in carrying out our undertakings, and the patience to accept the limitations of the underlying structure.

Herukhuti: The source of the motive power to carry out our undertakings, and the courage to be fair (just) with others in the process.

Het-Heru: The faculty for energizing the images embodying the willed events. If the will is negative, these energized images usurp its place, and thus <u>initiate</u> events (here we are lead by the appeal that things have upon our senses).

Sebek: The faculty for <u>separating</u> the undertaking into <u>manageable steps</u>, thus easing the way. When the will is negative we delude ourselves by thinking that we can reverse the process and piece the whole out of steps, and thus arrive at an understanding of the infinite.

Maat: The <u>divine law</u> that guides the will to <u>success</u>.

The Tree of Life as a Guide to Planning

We will now look at the Tree of Life as a step by step guide to planning. You will see that the ideal way to do so, which will guarantee your success, follows the same pattern that is used by the Supreme Being in its creative activity. It stands to reason, that if Man and God are the same quality of Being, the means and methods of God must be the same for Man. This is the highest expression of the Kamitic precept *"As Above, So Below."*

Amen: "Zero out," "clear your register." Before beginning a plan, get rid of all preconceived notions, however erudite. Do not start by taking into account material resources (money, equipment, past commitments, overhead, help, time, etc.).

Ausar: Establish or discover the central theme of your undertaking. It is the god of your undertaking. It is that which will control, direct, and unify all stages of your undertaking. It is important to realize that Ra (the life-force, the subconscious) "reads" and bases its transformations (khepera) on the central theme of all that you are doing, whether you have articulated it or not, whether it is clear to you or not, whether it is right or wrong, whether it is harmful or beneficial to you. If in your mind, the central theme is "X, but in actuality it is "Y," it is the latter that will be acted upon by your life-force. You will be in for a nasty surprise. Examples: Is making money the theme of your business (or career), or is it the product or service that you are providing? Are you for democracy and the Constitution, or for "my country, right or wrong?" Is your marriage, chiefly, a vehicle for spiritual development, or did you marry for security or companionship, or out of imitation of social practices, or because you fell in love? Note that I

258

said "chiefly," for *a body can only have one head. In all undertakings there must and can only be one central theme.* All others must be subordinated. It's not up to you. It is the way the producer within you, Ra, functions. What is the theme of your life? Is it your career, or your marriage, or your spiritual development? What is the theme of your spiritual work? Is it to become a magician, realize Ausar, learn the tools to succeed in all undertakings, become versed in the teachings, and techniques of spirituality? For example, if it is becoming Ausar, then you will live truth at every crossroad, otherwise you will pick and choose when to.

Tehuti: Step #1. Consult the oracle, or the sage, or an expert to gain insight into the central theme of your undertaking, as well as the undertaking itself. The counsel will let you know whether you should be involved in the undertaking; if the theme is correct (high enough in the hierarchy to achieve your goal, in agreement with the goal, etc.); where you stand in relationship to the goal (your "chances" of success); how you should proceed, and so on. A sage, or an oracle such as the Metu Neter, or Ifa will reveal to you the heka(u) governing the situation you have undertaken. Also will be revealed to you, the spiritual meaning and value of your undertaking. You will thus find yourself involved in a deep spiritual quest through an undertaking which by mundane standards might be considered trivial. E.g., a man receives an Ausar Hetep reading on what he must do to become a salesman for a cosmetic company. While he consciously believed that his need for a job brought him to the oracle, it was the combination of the spiritual shaping forces of his life that brought him to the oracle for him to discover his spiritual condition. Instead of pointers on how to be a good salesman, or how to get the job, he received instruction in spiritual development. How he was in violation of Ausar, etc.

Step #2. Identify the means through which to carry out the central theme. Organize them in hierarchical order. The hierarchical arrangement will include the 'Two Truths' (*Maati*). That is, the means are to be classified, not only by rank, but by polarity. One will be yang (forceful, based on externals, left-brained, etc.), the other will be yin (persuasive, seductive, gentle, subliminal, based on internals, right-brained, etc.).

Seker: If you have been fortunate enough to receive training in the science of hekau, chant the heka of the Deity governing the situation to generate the underlying structure that will guide the undertaking to its completion.

Maat: At this stage you must seek out analogies to your undertaking, and its central theme. The text of the oracle reading is a good place to start. In addition, the aroused heka (Seker stage) will reveal to you the same. The best sources of analogies regarding a behavioral undertaking are the texts of the oracles, and metaphoreins (mythological stories). Similarly, the "hard" sciences have their stock of analogies that can be used. It is obvious that the conclusion that will be arrived at through this process will embody the abstract pattern, microcosmogram, blueprint, etc. of the undertaking. This is the stage of synthesis.

Herukhuti: At this stage you must arrive at the abstract distinction between the pattern of your undertaking, and those that are analogous. This is analysis (analogical-lysis).

Heru: You have now arrived at the transitional point, the crossroad. You must firmly keep in mind your readiness to run your project, and not let it run you. The work of the lower spheres must keep to the specifications of the spheres above. It is so easy, because of emotional and sensual pressures, to abandon the soundest principles, and best laid plans. Use your will. Be the king of your realm.

Het-Heru: You are now ready to visualize the various stages from the beginning to the end of your undertaking. Incidentally, it is from this stage that many people incorrectly start their planning.

Sebek: You are now ready to seek information, technical details, etc. regarding each step, phase, and means of carrying out the project. Incidentally, it is from this stage that many people incorrectly start their planning.

Auset: Once it is clear what must be done at each step, and how, you will begin work on the project. The work at this stage involves mediumistic trance meditation on each process of the undertaking. Depending on the nature of your undertaking, you may have to precede the work with the six stages of meditation.

Geb: This is the stage of physical work, and the realization of your goal.

The above formula can also be used to analyze a subject, or series of events. What is the underlying cause (central theme) of the series of international conflicts that have occured over the past 200 years? Is it ideological? Political? Economic? Religious? What is the chief method (central theme) used by modern imperialists? Is it racism? Coercing other nations into debt? Military aggression? Diplomacy, and adherence to law? Remember. A body can only have one head. Unless you find *the* main theme of an event, you will never understand it, let alone control it. All other contributing factors must be assigned their proper place in space (hierarchy).

A Place and Time For All Things

The East, Sunrise-9am, Spring (March 21-May 5), Maat:
> Your sympathetic system has just begun to put out more than your parasympathetic, just after arriving at the point of equilibrium (equinoctial point!)[11]. This is the time in the cycle (year, day) when the hot and moist energy is in activity. The body is heating up after being remoistened by the inner, and outer waters of life. It is most auspicious for the undertakings requiring jupiter's energies (the struggle for expanding one's wealth and position). Your optimism, generosity and panoramic view of things manifest themselves most strongly here. Gemmotherapeutics (drainage herbs) for the liver are in harmony with this point in your yearly cycle. At the sunrise and the equinox Nekhebet and Uachet are in equilibrium upon your brow; Aum Ham Kshang!

The South East, around 9am-Noon, May 5-June 21, Heru:
> The earth is warming up, your animal spirit is absorbing the heat, and is therefore drying out. Your moderate fire (hot/dry energy) is in activity. This is the most auspicious time to carry out such tasks that require the vitality which nourishes the ability to raise truth above our emotional and

---

11. The true meaning, and value of the equinox is that it represents the time in the year of psychic, and bodily equilibrium. It is then that the two forces of the Auarat are in equilibrium in the Ajna center.

sensual conditionings. It is the best time to impose your will upon your life-force, as the reduction of your moisture has undermined your Auset and Het-Heru faculties. Power breathing, aerobics, remedies for the cardiovascular system, etc. are in harmony with this point in your biorhythm. The bitter flavor will help your fire to rise and maintain itself. Sweets will dissipate your vitality, and give power to water (emotions).

The South, Noon-3pm, June 21-August 5, Herukhuti, Uatchet:

Your sympathetic is at its height. The earth is in its extreme point of heat absorption, and your body has lost an excessive amount of moisture. Your extreme lack of moisture (emotional factor) has brought you to your point of greatest insensitivity and fearlessness. It is most auspicious for those undertakings that require lack of fear of bodily harm, hard work and zeal. As you lack moisture, make sure that you do not engage at this time in protracted undertakings. Be careful. Do not forget to ask what is right. Do not take the exhaustion of your moisture to the limits. Illness will visit you in the North[12]. Watch your blood pressure. June 21st, the summer solstice is the most auspicious time for your Uatchet faculty; read Shakespeare's Midsummer Night's Dream, and wile away the 4 days, and 4 nights in sleep, chanting and fasting. Like "Bottoms," you will be able to play any role you chose, and "Puck" will make all of your desires come true[13]. Your parasympathetic has begun to rise, but it is still underground (putting out less than the sympathetic).

The South West, August 5-Sept. 21, 3pm-sunset, Sebek:

Your parasympathetic, although it is still underground, it has cooled down your body, with the assistance of the waning Sun. The cold and dry state of your vehicle makes this point in the cycle most auspicious for those activities that require inflexible pedantry (dry) and dispassion (cold). These are the technological subjects, trading, accounting, etc. Take your nervines, and respiratory system remedies at this point.

---

12. See the Yellow Emperor Classic of Internal Medicine.
13. Bottoms = Kundalini, Puck = Sebek.

The West, Sept 21-Nov 5, sunset-9pm, Tehuti, Sheps:

Your parasympathetic has just gotten the upper hand, just after being in equilibrium with the sympathetic (Autumnal equinox). As the sun is setting, your body is cold and dry, but your nervous system is in a state of equilibrium. It is the optimum time for querying the oracle, receiving counsel, and studying the ancient wisdom, as the basis for deciding on the course of your actions in the coming cycle. Yes, your day begins at this point, not at sunrise. When the sun rises, your plans for the day must have already been impressed upon your spirit. This is the key to success. Nekhebet and Uachet are again in balance upon your brow; Aung Hang Kshang. Before the arrival of the autumnal equinox, it is auspicious to cleanse the system by fasting with pungent herbs to purge the respiratory and mucous system. Along with reducing your salt intake from this point on to the next equinox, the fast will assist in preventing the respiratory problems (flu, etc.) that tend to break out in the winter months.

The North West, Nov 5-Dec 21, 9pm-midnite, Auset:

You have arrived at the point in your cycle where your body is cool, and has begun to remoisten itself. Your receptivity (ability to respond emotionally to ideas) is at its height. Go into mediumistic trance, renew your commitment to identifying yourself with your true Self--Ausar and meditate on realizing the objectives decided upon in the preceding period. If you have not eaten proteins in the past 3 - 4 hours, sweets will greatly enhance your ability to enter into mediumistic trance[14]. Remember that unless you impress your will on your life-force, you will suffer the host of problems that are ignorantly labelled as "lack of will power," "lack of perseverance," "lack of devotion to an objective," and so on. Now that you have impressed your will upon your life-force, it is time to go to sleep and let Khepere do the rest.

The North, Dec. 21-Feb. 5, midnite-3am, Seker, Dark deceased, Nekhebet:

Your parasympathetic has arrived at its extreme point, and your sympathetic has just been reborn! You are in non

14. Sweets release tryptophane in the system, which plays a major role in inducing sleep, and trance states.

REM sleep, or trance. The focus of your consciousness, as you sleep, has returned to the Subjective Realm, to Amen, that Ra may enter into the secret sea of marrow to be renewed in the waters of Nut. Khepera has taken the seed you sowed in the womb of Auset during the preceding period, and fashioned the egg from which it will be born into the world. In the cycle of the year, this is the winter solstice (12/21-25). This time of the year (and day) is the most auspicious time for your Nekhebet faculty (Aung Hang Kshang). During the 4 days (Dec 21-24 midnight) fast, meditate, and chant to energize the decisions made at the autumnal equinox ritual (see the West). This is definitely not the time to be caught drunk, and filled with domesticated beast in your stomach. Wonder why there has been no peace on earth? Your sympathetic has been reawakened but it is still underground. The seed has been sown, the egg has been fashioned, but the gestation has not yet occurred.

The North East, Feb 5-March 21, 3am-sunrise, Het-Heru:
You are fully remoistened by the inner, and outer waters. Your body is warming up with the gentle fructifying psychic heat of Het-Heru. These are your pleasant dreams. The most important meaning of dreams is in regards to their emotional content. Pleasant, joyful dreams presage success, and turbulent, dark, troubled, dreams are portents of difficulties. Understand that they are the signs of the gestation of the beliefs you have accepted. To control your dreams, and hence what you manifest in your life, take into mediumistic trance every night what you want to see manifesting in your life. It is important, however, to realize that your personal will must be in harmony with the will of your true self (as revealed through the oracle), otherwise you will still have bad dreams. I.e., your true self will try to warn you. To successfully interpret your dreams, review the emotions that you habitually accept throughout your life. Your dreams are their gestation, or messages from your true self, deities, and ancestors regarding the course of your life.

In order to fully benefit from the insight into the cycles provided above, it is imperative to go to bed at about 10 pm and wake up just before sunrise. You must average about 8 hours sleep, and awaken naturally (not from alarms) when the life-force (Ra) is fully regenerated. A study of the lives of the world's top executives showed that most of them observed pretty much this pattern of sleeping and awakening. You must also eat a good breakfast, after your morning meditation and aerobics. Your main meal should come at about 2 pm (mercury/Sebek = small intestine, digestion). It is important to get your full quota of calories (Maat, success = hot & moist = caloric sustenance, fuel!!). To preserve the equilibrium in your life-force, you must also avoid sleeping during the day (unless ill), exercising after sunset, avoid concentrated sweets in the morning, bitters at night. Avoid excessive fasting, excessive sexual activity, and be moderate in all things. This simple rule of living in harmony with the circadian (daily), and annual cycles of your body is the master key for success. The so called lemniscate, or infinity symbol (a horizontalized 8) above the head of the Magician card of the tarot, is in reality two superimposed sine curves which represent the flux of cycles. The four magical weapons that the magician works with in this card (and in European magic) are the four modes of the life-force. This is why in the older and better tarot decks, the magician is shown juggling these four symbols (keeping them in equilibrium). I.e., the picture states that because he observes the laws of the cycles, he is able to keep the four modes of his life-force (hot/dry=fire, cold/moist=water, etc.) in equilibrium. Therefore, he is successful at magic-the realization of what he wills, primarily through the agency of his life-force.

Chapter 19

THE METUTU

Amen

Kamitic: Amen, Nu, Nut
Canaanite: Ain, Soph, El
Kabalistical: Ain, Soph
Yoruba: Olodumare, Olokun

Underlying Principles:
+   The living of the knowledge of the essential and original unconditioned state of our spirit is a fundamental prerequisite for achieving success in all of our undertakings. The realization of this goal is the ability to maintain a state of deep inner peace that cannot be upset by externals. This condition is called Hetep. Realization of this knowledge is the final goal of life.

-        Ignorance of the knowledge of our essential state leads to the identification with our conditioned reflexes and behavioral patterns. It is the fundamental cause of all failures and evil in the world.

Keynotes: (+) Knowledge of our essence, the essence of a thing, or undertaking; (-) ignorance of the knowledge of our essence.

Spiritual Counsel

When you receive an Amen reading you are being reminded to renew your insperience of the essence of your being. You are in danger of identifying with the conditioned state of your person, thus limiting your potential to achieve. Understanding the information regarding the knowledge of Self is not enough. You must still your thoughts, and thus enable the focus of your consciousness to return to its source to drink of the Sa en Aungk (essence of Life). Your problems may have been contributed to by a lack of sleep. Most Westerners, as a result of their artificial priorities, suffer from a chronic lack of sleep, which is one of the main causes of illnesses and spiritual stagnation. Nut, which is the female counterpart of Amen is the source of Ra-the life-force. Our storehouse of Ra (prenatal chi) is replenished every night during the non-REM periods of sleep,

266

as well as through certain sophisticated yogic practices[1]. Incidentally, the fact that sleep is a process of returning the focus of consciousness way beyond the physical plane to the Subjective Realm, in order to renew our storehouse of life-force, western scientists-materialists as they are-are unable to discover, to this day, the purpose of sleeping. Get your 8 hours daily, at night!!!

Ausar

Kamitic: Ausar, Tem
Canaanite: Metatron
Kabalistical: Kether
Yoruba: Obatala
Indus Kush: Tara

Sphere	Planet	Day
1st	none	all

Color	Number	Gems
white	10	none

Time of year: Sidereal full Moon in Aquarius.

Esoteric Herbalism:
    Baths: Basil, tuberose, white roses, cotton (leaves), marjoram, sage, fennel, stephanotis (flower).
    Oils: basil, lotus, tuberose, fennel, sage, marjoram.
    Incense: myrrh, southernwood.

Hekau (mantras, words of power):
    Spiritual: Aung
    Planetary: none

Spiritual Direction: none

Personality Portfolio:
  Emotional traits: beyond the influence of emotions.
  Mental traits: the origin of all wisdom.
    Social Correspondences: God Men on earth, and in the inner planes.

---

1. See Taoist Yoga, by Lu Kuan Yu.

Careers, functions: retired from the tumult, and illusions of the world. Sages.
Places & Events: the Sekhet Aaru.

Biological correspondences:
Physiology: none
Pathology: none
Kamitic therapeutics: The healing power of hetep (an inner peace that does not depend on, or cannot be disturbed by any external influence).
Chinese Medicine: Shen strengthening herbs.

Spiritual keynotes:
Underlying Principles:
+ Perseverance in the identification with the indwelling intelligence in thought, speech and action is the substance of <u>Self-knowledge</u>, which is essential for the individual's achievement of unity in her personal and social life. Health and prosperity are achieved thereby.

Keynotes: Self-knowledge and the living of it, or the absence of it. Unity, disunion, the highest principle governing an event.

Spiritual Counsel

When you receive an Ausar reading you are being reminded to renew your experience of your true Self. You are in danger of identifying with the conditioned state of your person, thus limiting your potential to unify yourself with the world. The book knowledge regarding the knowledge of Self is not enough. You must still your thoughts, and thus achieve or renew the experience of your Self as the consciousness that is conscious of being conscious. This will shift the balance point of your being to Heru (which is biased toward the Self!), and allow you to be in the world, but not of it. This equilibrium is a major prerequisite for the manifestation of wise intuitions and spiritual power. You are also reminded that social unity is the source of the greatest power and good in mankind. This unity does not come about through the coming together of people; it results from the resolution of their differences into complementary and supplementary relationships.

Tehuti

Kamitic: Tehuti
Canaanite: Ratzi-El.
Kabalistical: Chokmah
Yoruba: Ifa, Orunmila
Indus Kush: Chinnamasta

Sphere Planet   Day
2nd   Jupiter Thursday

Color: Blue and white

Number Gems
8   Yellow sapphire, lapis lazuli

Time of year: Sidereal full Moon in Sagittarius.

Esoteric Herbalism:
    Baths: Thuja
    Oils: lotus, sweet almond.
    Incense: from the oils.

Hekau (mantras, words of power):
    Spiritual: Hung. Face Spiritual direction.
    Planetary: Aung grang gring graung.   Face mundane
    direction. Use the planetary heka for the most mundane
    undertakings.

Spiritual Direction: South East. This is the direction to face when
    you are performing your meditations and rituals for spiritual
    guidance.
Mundane Direction: West. This is the direction to face when you
    are performing your meditations and rituals for mundane
    goals.

Biological correspondences
    Physiology: See Maat.
    Pathology: See Maat.
    Kamitic therapeutics: Healing through the powers of hekau
    (mantras). See also Maat.

Chinese Medicine: See Maat.

Personality traits: See Maat

Mental functions: Stilled

Social correspondences: Sages, prophets, and through the principle
of relativity, to judges, very experienced lawyers, theoretical
scientists, theoreticians, theologians, bankers, merchants,
upper echelon priests and priestesses, fortune hunters,
officials, experts in a particular field, teachers at the highest
levels.

Spiritual keynotes:
    Underlying Principles:
    +   Guidance from the Sage, or an expert in the field
           inquired about, or oracles, or <u>intuition</u> acquired
           through Jnana Yoga (cessation of all thought
           activity) is the source of <u>good judgement</u>, and
           directions that one can place one's <u>faith</u> in.
    -      Mistaking education and information for
           knowledge will, more often than not, lead to bad
           judgements, false sense of knowledge, unfounded
           optimism.
    Keynotes: +) faith, good judgement, intuition, optimism; -)
               doubts, lack of faith, bad judgements,
               unfounded optimism.

Spiritual Counsel

When you receive a Tehuti reading, you must stop on your
forward movement to achieve your goal, and meditate on the basis
of your decision to undertake the present actions or project. The
meditation that is required at this level is based on the ability to still
the thinking process, which latter, is always based on the
manipulation of symbols standing in for the actual reality. We must
get them out of the way in order to see directly into reality. Implicit
is the fact that you are in danger of undertaking an action that will
create a problem somewhere, while solving a specific problem, or
achieving a specific goal elsewhere. As most people are unable to
still their thought processes, they are counselled to go see a master
(most likely an elder) on the subject. By a master is meant, an

individual who is able to intuit knowledge that transcends the commonly known body of information that is available on a particular subject, or the ability to intuitively apply principles to specific situations in the absence of guiding formulas. In regards to life itself, such masters are the sages. If there are no sages in your life, then you must rely on the use of oracles, until you achieve the ability to arrive at answers to problems without going through the sequential thought activity of the lower, syllogistic, Cartesian logical faculty.

On another level, the oracle might be advising you that the attainment of your goal depends primarily on the successful evocation of the powers represented by the hekau.

Seker

Kamitic: Seker, Ptah, Aummit, Khepere
Canaanite: Tzaphki-El, Ama, Aima
Kabalistical: Binah
Yoruba: Babalu Aye
Indus Kush: Kali

Sphere	Planet	Day
3rd	Saturn	Saturday

Color	Number	Gems and metals
indigo,	13	blue sapphire, onyx,
black		lead.

Time of year: Sidereal full moon in capricorn, aquarius.

Esoteric Herbalism:
>Baths: Artemisia vulgaris, jerusalem tea, bitter broom
>Oils: myrrh, cypress
>Incense: myrrh, cypress, southernwood leaves.

Hekau (mantras, words of power):
>Spiritual: Kring
>Planetary: Aung Prang Pring Praung (chant at midnight).

Spiritual Direction: East
Mundane Direction: Southwest

Personality Portfolio: Through its action on the khaibit (the animal spirit) the <u>frigid and dry energy of Saturn</u> has the following effects on the personality (sphere 9):

Emotional traits:

(+): Stable, sober, steadfast, reserved in speech, thrifty, studious, austere, steadfast in friendship, reliable, appreciative of structure, and limitations (patient, hard working).

(-): Misanthropic, taciturn, morose, depressed, covetous, jealous, mistrustful, suspicious, liar, malicious, miscontent, timorous, miserly, unappreciative of structure and limitations, acquisitive, unsympathetic, stubborn, inhibited, phobias, mistrustful, unadaptive, separative, envious, avaricious, stingy.

Mental traits:

(+): Suppression of thought processes through <u>deep concentration</u>[2] resulting from perfection in the Men Ab meditation system, leading to the ability to a) awaken and direct the units of spiritual power (neteru: deities, spirits), and b) enter in attunement with the spiritual forces that are in charge of the orderly unfoldment of events in the world; hence, good powers of <u>planning, organizing</u>, hence, <u>appreciative of structure and limitations</u>.

(-): Lack of concentration, hence, poor planning, absence of plans, unappreciative of structure, and limitations:

Social Correspondences:

Careers, functions: Elderly persons, property owners, farmers, miners, subway workers, funerary industry, Priests, and priestesses skilled in the use of words of powers.

Spiritual Portfolio: imposition of the divine law from within (by deities, and spirits), destiny, success in life, organization, structure, cycles, hierarchy, phases, limitations, delays, obstructions

---

2. The transcendence of thought forms on the Seker level is shown by the text of the fourth hour of the night of THE BOOK OF WHAT IS IN THE UNDERWORLD, "the body of Seker, who is on his sand, the hidden form which can be neither looked at nor seen."

Spiritual function: No two things can occupy the same place at the same time. Divine law and order, therefore, guarantee all things their day in the sun. The coming into being, and the unfolding of all events in life are controlled by spiritual forces for the sake of maintaining order in the world. The spiritual forces maintain order in the world by organizing all things, and their parts into a hierarchy of place and time. Regarding life events, we therefore do not make up the plans that we will follow, but seek to intuit the spiritual structure controlling the events in our lives as ordained by the spirits. Incidentally, these structures or patterns that are woven into the energy/matter substratum are analogous to the patterns that are formed when sound vibrations are deployed over the surface of water, etc. They have been reproduced in many cultures and are known as veves, yantras, etc.

People with a well developed ability to concentrate, which enables them to intuit the spiritual structures underlying events, are said to be "good planners." They also have the capacity to accept and appreciate the limitations that these structures impose on their thoughts, emotions and actions. As these structures guarantee each thing its time and place for manifesting by maintaining order, these people are successful in their lives. Those who lack the ability, or inclination to concentrate deeply enough to intuit the underlying structures of things either fail to plan, or lack the capacity to accept and appreciate structures and limitations. Thus, they run into what they interpret as obstructions, delays, etc., and lacking help from other spiritual quarters end up with a miserly existence as they live like trains trying to run without staying on the tracks.

Special Correlates:

Seker/Maat: In the process of spiritual development, we must first master the doctrine of the law as taught in the Maat stage, which precedes that of Seker. Maat is the communication of the divine law to the mind of man, while Seker is the demand to live it. Success in living the law of Maat depends on the Men Ab work at the Heru stage. See Heru.

Seker/Heru: The ability to concentrate depends on proficiency in Men Ab-the meditation discipline of the Heru stage of meditation and initiation. The taking of Men Ab to its heights involves the ability to totally ignore all instinctive, emotional and sensual impulses. Hence, we are as one who is dead. This is the basis for Seker's appellation as God of the Dead.

Seker/Het-Heru: We have seen in past chapters that the 3rd sphere, Seker is the complement of the 7th, Het-Heru. They are the complete antithesis of each other. Where Seker is fully introverted, uncaring of sensual pleasures, steady, etc., Het-Heru is extroverted, dependent on sensual pleasures, unsteady, etc. Yet, the arousal of the life-force (Chi, Ra, Kundalini) that is needed to vitalize the will to allow it to succeed in its application of Men Ab, depends on Het-Heru's indulgence in sexual and pleasurable activities. The development of the capacity to concentrate to carry out the functions of Seker is therefore strengthened by moderation in pleasure, and weakened by both the excess or suppression of sensual indulgence.

Seker/Geb: Geb's importance to Seker also revolves around the relationship between the life-force and concentration. Here attention to health in order to nourish the life-force, keeps its channels open, and its forces in harmony with each other.

Key Phrases:

Attention to cycles (E.g., stock market, and economic cycles) promotes success; "Perseverance in," steadfastness, stubbornness; patient, methodical attention to tedious details; Delays, denials, obstructions; Sobriety; Pessimism, caution, inhibition, scruples; Restraint; good organization, and planning (mental not computerized, which is Sebek); abiding by the constitution, by-laws, plan; slow at arriving at a conclusion; by being thoughtful; stop and ponder, meditate.

Biological correspondences

Physiology: the frigid and dry energy of Saturn is the basis of the crystallizing functions that govern the formation of our bony system. It is also the seat of the catabolic processes that govern aging, thus limiting the lifespan of life forms.

Pathology: Where the vitality (solar force), and immunity (martial force) are weak, the Saturnial energy generates disorders characterized by the abnormal deposition of crystallized material (stones, uric acid) in various parts of the body, thus causing gout, gall stones, rheumatoid arthritis. It is also the cause of all chronic, and deep-seated disorders; paralysis, sclerosis, blood impurities.

Kamitic therapeutics: Healing through hekau (words of power), refrigerant, hypnagogic, styptic, astringent, antipyretic.

Chinese Medicine: Spleen meridian; Cold Disease Patterns - Use warming (spleen, liver) herbs (Center Rectifying formula, Liver Warming decoction, Ephedra decoction, Wo T'ou Aconite decoction, etc.); Dryness Patterns - Nourish blood and yin; Phlegm Disease Patterns.

Spiritual Counsel

When you receive a Seker reading, you must stop your forward movement to achieve your goal, and meditate on your objective in order to intuit the structure governing your undertaking, and thus come up with a viable plan. On the level of Seker, the meditation process depends on the ability to still all thought processes ("make the mind blank") in order to "sense" the underlying structure of your undertaking. Although most people will not be able to attain this level of meditation, they should at least try to slow down the thought process in order to fully concentrate on intuiting the plan, drawing from past experiences (this is a compromise). All things considered, elders (56 and up[3]) will be most successful, as their greater experience, and lower metabolic rate (Seker's catabolic mode!) will provide them with a greater abundance of food for thought and patience. It will be advantageous for young people (under 42) who receive this reading, to seek the advice of capable elders.

On another level, the oracle may be advising you to remember that pleasure is not in the things that are enjoyed but is a manifestation of the spirit of the enjoyer. Thus, for the duration of the undertaking inquired about, you must withdraw your pleasure

---

3. The age set demarcations must be taken with flexibility. There are people who are old at 35, while others are still youthful, and vigorous in their 70's and more.

275

from earthly or personal things, and place it in universal and spiritual things. This is a requirement for manifesting the powers of Ra, which have their matrices (the eggs of Khepera, the 50 matrikas, etc.) in Sekert.

Maat

Kamitic: Maat, Seshat (Seshait, Sefkit Aubut).
Canaanite: Tzadki-El
Kabalistical: Gedulah, Chesed
Yoruba: Aje Chagullia
Indus Kush: Lakshmi

Sphere	Planet	Day
4th	Jupiter	Thursday

Color: sky blue for spiritual heka, yellow for the Planetary heka.

Number	Gems & Metal
2	yellow sapphire, lapis lazuli, Tin

Time of year: Sidereal full moon in Pisces

Esoteric Herbalism:
      Baths: thuja, anis, honeysuckle
      Oils: anise, oak moss.
      Incense: aloes, anise.

Hekau (mantras, words of power):
      Spiritual: Shring
      Planetary: Aung, grang, gring, graung

Spiritual Direction: Southeast
Mundane Direction: West

Personality Portfolio: Through its action on the khaibit (the animal spirit) the hot and moist energy of Jupiter has the following effects on the personality (sphere 9):

Emotional traits:

(+): just, equilibrated, holistic, generous, sharing, optimistic, liberal, magnanimous, moral sense, striving for advancement and wealth in a positive manner, religious, successful, "fortunate," law abiding, fair, charitable, deferring to elders, no trafficking with evil, grateful, prudent.

(-): greedy, i.e., negatively expansive (for food, sex, material things, etc.), pleasure seeking, boastful, extravagant, unlawful, materialistic, wasteful, unsocial, unsuccessful "unfortunate," hypocritical regarding religion, and the law; false religious, legal, and scientific tenets.

Mental traits: Synthesis-gaining insight into things by unifying them through the use of abstract analogies; hence well fitted for philosophical, and theoretical scientific, religious pursuits.

Social Correspondences:

Careers, functions: judges, very experienced lawyers, theoretical scientists, theoreticians, theologians, bishops, cardinals, bankers, merchants, upper echelon priests and priestesses, fortune hunters, officials, managers.

Spiritual Portfolio: doctrine of divine law & order; optimism, faith, love, abundance, success in an individual undertaking, spiritual advancement.

Spiritual function: She walks with a papyrus scepter[4]. She achieves abundance. Maat's papyrus scepter fuses divine law with the abundance that follows from living it. Its color, green, symbolizes abundance and fruitfulness, while the papyrus, which was used for writing, symbolizes the book of the law.

She realizes that even her enemies are integral parts of the whole, and thus works and shares with them. Seshat raises her consciousness to the hall of the Metu Neter and realizes the ultimate unity of all things. There are no irreconcilable opposites in the world. This is the source of an undaunted optimism, faith, and inner joy which reveal themselves in a peaceful genuine smile and relaxed (Hetep) state of being even in the midst of setbacks and the greatest of external difficulties.

---

4. See Appendix A for associated meditation.

Maat (the divine law) is the food and drink of Ra (the Life-force). She nourishes her life-force (Ra) with the divine law, and gives endlessly of her love (shares seeking nothing in return). There is no end to her worldly fortune as her giving is answered from the depths of Nut.

Perseverance in adhering to a belief system based on the Cosmological arrangement and synthesis of divine laws, such as achieved through the Tree of Life, leads to success in all undertakings, as the view of the unity that is concealed in the midst of the multiplicities that life presents to us, is never lost.

A collection of wise sayings, and divine laws, however true cannot save us, if they are not arranged into an integral system of guiding us in our day to day existence. We have seen how the abstract analogies presented in this book, especially the symbols of the Tree of Life, serve to unify specifics across general categories. Unless the elements making up our belief system (whether secular, or religious) are unified in this manner, they become enslaving agents of dogma, instead of vehicles of salvation.

Special Correlates:

Maat/Amen: Amen is the major source of the optimism, sharing, and lawfulness of Maat. The source of all things is infinite, and is held by all in common, as we all originate from, and have our being in Amen. There are no personal possessions, nothing can be lost in sharing, and what is not returned by another will come from the depths of the infinite.

Maat/Ausar: Love, which is sharing, which is giving seeking nothing in return, not asking if you deserve, but the fulfilling of a genuine need. It is the day to day expression of the unity of being represented by Ausar, and is the synthesis of all divine laws.

Maat/Tehuti: Maat is the written law that depends on the intuitions of the Sage-Tehuti.

Maat/Seker: While Maat corresponds to the communication of the divine law to man's mind, Seker is the imposition of the law from within. I.e., while we may chose to follow Maat, Seker forces us to follow the law.

Maat/Herukhuti: Without the conception of the means to enforce the law, there can be no conception of the law. See

278

Heru. Note, that while Seker forces you to follow the law, Herukhuti punishes you for breaking it.

Maat/Heru: As there is no compulsion to observe the law at the Maat stage, as is otherwise with Seker, the ability to live the law depends on the Men Ab work of the Heru stage.

Maat/Sebek: The 4th sphere, Maat, is complementary to the 8th, Sebek. While Maat corresponds to the perception of the abstract analogies that tie events and things sharing the same qualities, although they belong to separate families and species, Sebek is the perception of the concrete definitions, names, etc. that distinguish species, and parts of concrete wholes from one another. Thus, while the unifying function of Maat makes for social harmony, success and prosperity, the segregative function of Sebek is the chief source of social disharmony and difficulties.

Biological correspondences

Physiology: Like Venus, Jupiter is responsible for the conservation[5], preservation, and expansion of the life-force and spiritual power. It is the establisher of physiological equilibrium and fruitfulness, hence, it is the "fortuna major" (major fortune) and greater healing force of the body. Its action is centered in the liver where it is in charge of the production and storage of blood sugar (glycogenesis), breakdown of protein waste into urea, etc., and the creation and regulation of sex hormones (e.g., the destruction of excess estrogen, etc.). It also exerts a major influence on the arterial circulation and arterial blood itself.

Pathology: Accumulation of proteid, and other waste in the blood; liver derangements; sthenic plethora, or localized swelling; accumulation of adipose tissue; adipose sarcoma; lardaceous, and solanoid cancer of the mammary, pancreatic glands; vascular congestion leading to hemorrhages, apoplexy, epistaxis, etc.; fatty degeneration; sugar in blood (diabetes), illnesses from pleasurable excesses (diet, sex, etc.)

---

5. This conserving function is also attributed to Vishnu, who also rules the planet Jupiter (guru).

Kamitic Therapeutics: Joy, Analeptic, alterative, nurturing, spermatogenic, emollient, fattening, equilibrating, anabolic promoter (steroids, etc.).
Chinese Medicine: Liver/Gall bladder system; Damp Disease Patterns - Use herbs that clear heat, and disperse dampness (Artemisa Capillaris, Minor Bupleurum, Pulsatilla, Eight Corrections Powder, etc.).

Spiritual Counsel

When you receive a Maat reading you are being counseled to stop on your forward movement to achieve your goal, and to meditate on the abstract principles that will enable you to acquire a broad view of the subject at hand. Since the material from which you must draw upon can only be acquired through many years of study and experience, middle aged individuals (35-56) will be most successful. Although elders are most likely to possess such experiences, their metabolism, which is already on the downswing, may keep them from achieving the great success that Maat's hot and moist energy forecasts.

Herukhuti

Kamitic: Herukhuti
Canaanite: Khama-El
Kabalistical: Geburah
Yoruba: Ogun
Indus Kush: Bagalamukhi

Sphere	Planet	Day
5th	Mars	Tuesday

Color	Number	Gems
blood red, purple	11	red coral, garnet

Time of year: Sidereal full moons in aries, and scorpio.

Esoteric Herbalism:
Baths: Rompe Saraguey, Holly (Quita maldicion), Anamu, pine, Vencedor.
Oils: Pine, cedarwood.
Incense: Pine, tobacco, cedarwood.

Hekau (mantras, words of power):
    Spiritual: Hlring
    Planetary: Aung krang kring kraung

Spiritual Direction: North
Mundane Direction: Southeast

Personality Portfolio: Through its action on the khaibit (the animal spirit) the hot and dry energy of Mars has the following effects on the personality (sphere 9):
Emotional traits:
    (+): Courage manifesting as the lack of fear of bodily harm, energetic, prudent, magnanimous, forceful, enterprising, constructive, muscularly skillful, zealous, passionate; delighted, and motivated by situations involving challenges, or hard, and dangerous but relatively short work.
    (-): quarrelsome, antagonistic, pugnacious, arrogant impetuous, rash, choleric, destructive, violent, forceful, excessive, irritable. overzealous, and excessively passionate, inclined to tobacco, alcohol, murder, treason, cruelty, etc..

Mental traits: Analysis-gaining insight into things by separating them or their parts through abstract analogies.

Social Correspondences:
    Careers, functions: soldiers, fighters, warriors, executioners, butchers, slaughterers, hunters, people employed in dangerous undertakings, firemen, athletes, mechanics, surgeons, analytical theoreticians, criminal lawyers, prosecutors, policemen, shrewd and driven business executives.

Spiritual Portfolio: justice, detachment, courage, external obstructions.

Spiritual function: Let's remember that underlying all actions is the urge to succeed, which depends on following divine law (Maat). Our protection from all external obstructions is the domain of Herukhuti. But all such obstructions are the external projections of the obstructed condition of our life-force caused by our breaking of the laws of Maat in our dealings with others. By cutting (no pun intended) our identity off from our persons, and placing it firmly in our Self-the indwelling intelligence-we find the strength to be just with others in all situations. Thus, we receive protection from the Supreme Being. It also gives us the courage to sacrifice our lives for the well being of others. The failure to detach our identity from our persons compromises our sense of justice, and our ability to grow spiritually.

Special Correlates:

Herukhuti/Tehuti: The destructive side of using force is avoided by making sure that it is guided by wisdom (Tehuti).

Herukhuti/Maat: Penalties cannot be justly carried out if the law (Maat) is not clear and fair.

Herukhuti/Heru: Penalties cannot be effectively carried out, or justly applied even if the law is just, when the will is ineffective due to lack of vitality, or lack of Men Ab.

Herukhuti/Het-Heru: The 5th sphere, Herukhuti, and the 7th, Het-Heru, are complementaries. The zeal and drive to achieve of the former, combined with the creative imagination and joy of the latter, work together for the achievement of the "fortuna minore." Such successes, unfortunately, are the accomplishments that conceal future traps and problems, for we succeed at the expense of our spiritual development. We avail ourselves of this means of achievement when it is prescribed by the oracle. Beware of books that prescribe it as the chief way to success.

Herukhuti (-)/Sebek (-): This is the configuration of Set, the archminister of evil. It is the combination of the warmongering, imperialist, cruel, heartless personality traits with deception, scheming, cunning, cleverness, etc.

Key Phrases:

By setting to work; through hard, energetic effort; through zeal, drive, enterprise, initiative; through rashness, hotheadedness, arrogance, impatience, anger, violence, brutality, etc.; being guided by one's sense of power over others, or the situation; the urge to move forward, to advance; by being just, fair, courageous; by being confident, overconfident.

Biological correspondences

Physiology: It is in charge of the immune system, the voluntary musculature, elimination of toxins through the skin, focused heat production, sexual excitement.

Pathology: Acute disorders (fevers, inflammations, eruptive infectious disorders), wounds (especially from guns, knives, etc.), burns, hemorrhage, blood/skin disorders (itching, hot, eczemas, poxes, etc.), ruptures, injuries, accidents.

Kamitic therapeutics: surgery, stimulant, tonic, aphrodisiac, resolvent, caustic, rubefacient, vesicant.

Chinese Medicine: Pericardium/Triple Heater system; Heat and Fire Disease Pattern - Detoxify and drain fire, and enrichen yin (Coptis detoxifying formula, Heart-Draining formula, Great Yin supplementation pills, etc.); Summerheat Disease Pattern - (White Tiger decoction, etc.).

Spiritual Counsel

When you get a Herukhuti reading you are being warned to make sure that your zealous and courageous forward drive is being guided by wise counsel (Tehuti), a plan (Seker), knowledge of the law (Maat), and is being directed by Heru (a decision which has not been influenced by desires or emotions).

Heru

Kamitic: Heru
Canaanite: Micha-El[6]
Kabalistical: Tipareth (Rapha-El???)
Yoruba: Shango, Jakuta
Indus Kush: Bhuvaneshvari

Sphere	Planet	Day
6th	Sun	Sunday

Color	Number	Gems
red & white	6	ruby, garnet

---

6. The Jewish Kabalists give this sphere to Rapha-El. But a study of the character and metaphorein of Micha-El will show that the latter is more appropriate to the sixth sphere, and the former to the 8th.

Time of year: Sidereal full moon in Leo

Esoteric Herbalism:
Baths: poplar leaves, Paraiso, cock's comb, geranium, bay leaves, Rompe Zaraguey (Eupatorium Odorata), vencedor.
Oils: olibanum, geranium.
Incense: frankincense (olibanum)

Hekau (mantras, words of power):
Spiritual: Hrim
Planetary: Aung hrang hring, hraung

Spiritual Direction: West
Mundane Direction: Northeast

Personality Portfolio: Through its action on the khaibit (the animal spirit) the hot and dry energy of the Sun has the following effects on the personality (sphere 9):
Emotional traits:
(+): Magnanimous, desirous of power and leadership, full of vitality (hence, "strong willed"), zealous, noble, lofty, proud, ardent, authoritative, humane, reserved, above using underhanded means in the struggle against opponents
(-): arrogant, extravagant, indecisive, overbearing, dictatorial, excessive pride, devitalized (hence, "weak willed"), tyrannical, boastful yet empty, egotistical.
Mental traits: the will, circumspection, insight.
Social Correspondences:
Careers, functions: People in authoritative position (father, mother in a one parent household, king, prince, leaders, lieutenant, deputy, mayor, governor, boss, supervisor, etc.), self employment.

Spiritual Portfolio: the will, Men Ab, the determinant of character, crossroads (transitions, changes, transcending), essence of our divinity.

Spiritual function: The will is the essence of our divinity. In the same manner that we help children develop by allowing them freedom to act within a circle of limitations, the Supreme Being develops man's divinity by allowing him a certain amount of freedom within a ring passnot. The circle that man cannot pass corresponds to Seker's structural lines that keep the world and its events in place. Outside of these, man has the freedom to chose what he wills. But, as we have seen success depends on law and order. As Tehuti and Maat correspond to the communication of the divine law to our mind, and not its imposition, we have the freedom to follow or ignore it. This freedom of the will to follow, or ignore divine law is the basis of our divinity. There is no divinity where there is compulsion.

We saw in past chapters that the Men Ab system of meditation is the means of liberating and perfecting the use of the will. On our perfection of this system depends the upliftment of our character, and our spiritual growth. The only time that spiritual growth, and the transcending of our conditionings take place is when we live truth of our free will in "crossroad situations." These situations are characterized by 1) the appearance that we will lose a great deal (real, imagined, or perceived), which will be opposed to 2) the truth which must be followed and 3) the intuition of clever and seemingly convincing rationalizations for not following the truth. This latter is contributed by Set.

Special Correlates:

Heru/Ausar: There is no act of will unless we are effectively identifying ourselves with the indwelling intelligence, as opposed to our persons.

Heru/Tehuti: Tehuti, the will of God, communicates to Heru, man's will, what is to be done according to the point in the divine order, as determined by Seker. Man may ignore it and face the consequences; delays, obstructions, and failure in life. I.e., not following Tehuti leads to Sekerian repercussions, while, not following Maat leads to Herukhuhutian repercussions.

Heru/Maat: Not only does Maat guide man's will to the successful achievement of his goal, but through ordering his life, it preserves his health and therefore contributes to the full development of his life-force to enable him to succeed in his earthly and spiritual endeavors.

Heru/Het-Heru: The vitality that is needed to carry out the will, and perfect the Men Ab skill depends on a healthy attitude to the indulgence of pleasure. It is harmed by too much, as well as excessive suppression of the urge to pleasure. The process of willing an act or event must be conducted through visualization (this is the meaning of the Eye (utchat) of Heru), and not through verbal thinking. The Sesh Metut Neter--the great Kamitic system for thinking complete thoughts without verbalizing them--is a major source of success in the use of the will.

Heru/Sebek: Where there is no wisdom (Tehuti) to guide our will, we are the victims of our opinions, etc. See Sebek.

Heru/Auset: The true "strength" of the will-the ability to carry out what we will-depends on taking our goals into mediumistic trance (meditation stages 1 - 3).

Heru/Geb: The vitality that is needed to support the will depends on our adherence to the laws of health.

Summary of Heru's functions: It is the responsibility of Heru to insure that the emotions and thoughts originating from the other faculties do not interfere with the efforts of the indwelling intelligence to expand its sphere of influence to the external part of our life.

Key Phrases:

The effort, urge to rise to prominence, to be independent; urge to freedom; by cultivating expertise in Men Ab; by being "self-reliant," confident; (-) hoping to be compelled to do right, ignorance of the will's freedom from emotional compulsion, ignorance of the will's dependence on wisdom, lack of Men Ab; due to arrogance, anger, impatience; a strong (weak) life-force; through leadership, the urge to lead.

Biological correspondences

Physiology: The "Sun" corresponds to the vital energy that is the basis of our constitution (our overall ability to resist illness and heal ourselves), as well as the gauge of the spiritual force that is required for us to carry out our will. It is also the principle governing our cardiovascular system, especially the heart.

Pathology: cardiac problems, arterial circulatory problems, sthenic but not too high fevers.

Kamitic therapeutics: cardiac, alterative, constitutional homeopathic remedies regardless of organ affinity, tonics.

Chinese Medicine: Heart/Small Intestine system; Heat and Fire Disease Pattern - Detoxify and drain fire, and enrichen yin (Coptis detoxifying formula, Heart-Draining formula, Great Yin supplementation pills, etc.).

Spiritual Counsel

When you receive a Heru reading you are being reminded to perfect and utilize your Men Ab meditation skill. As Heru could only defeat Set through the wise counsel of Tehuti, and through adhering to the law of Maat, you are advised to seek counsel from someone in an authoritative, or leadership position. If you are the head person, then make sure to consult the oracle, and see a sage or master of the subject at hand.

From another perspective, you might be counselled to remember that power is not an attribute of the will. Whatever you are not in the habit of performing, or are just setting out to achieve, must be impressed upon your life-force through mediumistic trance (perhaps through hekau), and nourished through enjoyable visualizations.

Het-Heru

Kamitic: Het-Heru, Nebt-Het
Canaanite: Hana-El
Kabalistical: Netzach
Yoruba: Oshun
Indus Kush: Kamalatmika

Sphere	Planet	Day
7th	Venus	Friday

Color	Number	Gems
green, yellow	5	diamond, zircon (white, rose), white coral

Time of year: Sidereal full moons in Libra, and Taurus.

Esoteric Herbalism:
> Baths: yellow roses, honeysuckle, calendula flowers, maiden's hair, parsley, vetiver, spearmint, sandalwood
> Oils: rose, sandalwood, honeysuckle, cinnamon.
> Incense: same as oils.

Hekau (mantras, words of power):
> Spiritual: Kling
> Planetary: Aung drang dring draung

Spiritual Direction: Southwest
Mundane Direction: North

Personality Portfolio: Through its action on the khaibit (the animal spirit) the cold and moist energy of Venus has the following effects on the personality (sphere 9):
> Emotional traits:
> (+): sociable, affectionate, pleasure loving, quiet, harmonious, joyful, sweet, engaging, flexible, sympathetic, graceful, merry, cheerful
> (-): Sensually aberrated, shameless, lascivious, timorous, neglectful, lewd, idle, wasteful craving drugs, alcohol; immoral, motivated by fantasies and empty forms (hence illogical, and irrational), spendthrift, fearful, careless, narcissistic.

> Mental traits: congregative thinking: the imagination, use of metaphors, myths, metaphoreins, stories to explain.
> Social Correspondences:
> Careers, functions: Entertainers, artists, young women, the beauty, clothing, pleasure, and adornment industries.

Spiritual Portfolio: joy, pleasure, imagination, visualization.

> Spiritual function: The arousal of the life-force (Chi, Ra, Kundalini) through joy and pleasure, especially when ecstatic, provides the motive force for the accomplishment of our minor goals, and vitalization of the will. Unfortunately, most people are ignorant of this fact, and suppress their joyfulness waiting for success or overindulge

their passions, and never know why they have so much difficulty carrying out their will, concentrating, etc. Review the material given for the 3rd stage of meditation and initiation regarding the combination of creative imagery, and life-force arousal (the practice of visualizing the emotionally charged situations related to our goals, combined with special breathing techniques and asvini mudra).

A great deal of problem also arises from the ignorance of the function of the imagination. People allow themselves to indulge in the visualization of emotionally charged imagery (positive, or negative emotions and sensations) without realizing that they are thus giving power of realization to unwanted or untenable situations.

Special Correlates:

Het-Heru/Geb: As the function of the Het-Heru faculty is to organize the subtle forces of the animal spirit that are directly in control of physical phenomena, it is especially susceptible to the influence of the instincts, emotions and sensuous energies.

Key Phrases:

Love for; one is attracted to; failure to control one's attraction to; desire for; love for the external, form side of; reliance on one's beauty, grace, charm; overindulgence in; love of ease; contentment; joyfulness; following likes, and dislikes; effeminate; through creativity, and a fertile imagination; through sociableness, gentleness, cheerfulness, warmth, charm, seduction.

Biological correspondences

Physiology: the cold (warmer than the lunar energy) and moist energy of Venus induces the temperate relaxed physiological state (especially of the pneumo-gastric area; tantien) that is required by the reproductive and gestational organs (gonads, uterus, etc.). It also rules the parotid glands, kidneys, and functions in charge of generating the subtle energies behind our libido (het/house of heru/libido, vitality). It is the minor healing force (fortuna minor).

Pathology: Illnesses of the reproductive organs, mumps, gestational problems (miscarriages), varicosities (legs, scrotum), hemorrhoids, aneurysms, renal disorders, cysts, venereal illnesses, laxity of fiber, tumors, asthenic plethora, stomach disorders from dietary excesses.

Kamitic therapeutics: Joyful events, emetic, diuretic, demulcent, alterative/detoxifier.

Chinese Medicine: Kidney/Bladder system; Blood and Qi Disease Patterns.

Spiritual Counsel

Whenever you receive a Het-Heru reading you are being reminded that the purpose of indulging pleasurable (or negative) sensations is for the arousal of Ra. When they are combined with your visualizations (daydreams, meditations) of occurrences in your life (past and future), they are given the power to manifest. In the same vein, you are being warned against wasting your life-force through overindulgence, in order to avoid weakening your constitution and the ability to achieve your will.

Sebek

Kamitic: Apuat, Anpu
Canaanite: Rapha-El
Kabalistical: Hod
Yoruba: Elegba, Eshu
Indus Kush: Matangi

Sphere	Planet	Day
8th	Mercury	Wednesday

Color	Number	Gems
Saffron	3	emerald
red and black		

Time of year: Sidereal full moon in gemini, and virgo.

Esoteric Herbalism:
  Baths: Abre Camino, Arrasa con todo, Oregano, Lavender, larkspur.
  Oils: lavender, lily of the valley.
  Incense: lavender, lily of the valley.

Hekau (mantras, words of power):
        Spiritual: Aing
        Planetary: Aung Brang Bring Braung

Spiritual Direction: Northeast
Mundane Direction: South

Personality Portfolio: Through its action on the khaibit (the animal
        spirit) the cool and dry energy of Mercury makes the
        personality (sphere 9):
Emotional traits:
        (+): sharp and witty, fond of travel, critical in a positive way
        (able to separate issues based on externals), loquacious,
        diplomatic, cold and pedantic (syllogistic logical minded,
        highly dependent on information), communicative.
        Negatively critical, loquacious, busybody, opinionated,
        inconstant in belief, pretending to know yet ignorant,
        mischief   maker,   gossipper,   scheming,   cunning,
        argumentative, proud, sly, lying, selfish.

Mental traits: segregative thinking; labelling; defining; the verbal
        clothing of what is known, felt, and perceived; syllogistic
        logic; imitation.
Social Correspondences: quick-witted people, good learners from
        mere observation (even without a teacher).
Careers, functions: So called intellectuals, scholars, academicians,
        students,   teachers,   ambassadors,   astrologers,
        mathematicians,   clerks,   technicians[7],   relatively
        inexperienced lawyers, preachers, teachers, traders, young
        men, office workers, printers, schemers, schemes (financial,
        etc.), thieves, journalists, good speakers, diplomats,
        politicians, specialists.

Spiritual Portfolio:
Spiritual function: However pragmatic and necessary for the
        manipulation of physical phenomena, the mastery of
        definitions, names and descriptions-the fundamental
        elements of our education-does not constitute knowledge of

---

7. All "scientists" whose practices do not involve theoretical innovations are in reality
technicians. They merely imitate the procedures that have been taught to them.

reality. Proceeding with awareness of this limitation will bring us good fortune.

Proceeding without awareness of this limitation; Misfortune. We speak glibly of the person coming into being in the third month of gestation; of life arising out of the chance coming together of nonliving particles, in the same breath that we give better odds to a random assortment of 800,000 words and definitions on index cards being tossed in the air and falling in alphabetical order. And with pride we call ourselves scientists.

Special Correlates:

Sebek/Tehuti: To remind people that wisdom is not represented by the accumulation of information, the Kamitic men of wisdom used the dog-headed ape (Auaun), a very cunning, and imitative animal, and hence a Sebek type, to symbolize education as the aping (imitation) of wisdom. At best, the most it can do is to inspect the measuring hand of the scale of balance, record the verdicts, and chastise the pig.

Sebek/Maat: Maat is the means of giving order to thinking and provides the "truth premise" that has eluded western logicians from the days of the Greek philosophers.

Sebek/Het-Heru: This is the configuration of the "Hermaphrodite." Verbal thinking that is guided by images (description) gain coherence, unity, and a certain degree of objective reality. While we must experience something in order to describe it, we can easily delude ourselves with definitions, which essentially are "hearsay" (verbal explanations not necessarily associated with experience).

Sebek/Auset: All of the beliefs and rationalizations about life, which are carried out at the 8th sphere level are based on our identification with our persons. However lucid, they are sources of self delusion (maya) as they cannot uplift us.

Key Phrases:

Disunion due to segregative thinking; through the use of clever tactics, clever words, adroitness; by paying attention to details; pride in one's education, logical ability, verbal ability; litigations, arguments; having the facts, data, being informed;

Biological correspondences
Physiology: Mercury governs the functions of the motor, and sensory nerves.
Pathology: Neurasthenia, nervous irritability, asthma, bronchitis, stertorous breathing, neuralgia, speech impediments.
Kamitic therapeutics: nervine, emollient.
Chinese Medicine: Lung/Large Intestine system; Wind Disease Patterns.

Auset

Kamitic: Auset
Canaanite: Gabri-El
Kabalistical: Yesod
Yoruba: Yemaya
Indus Kush: Dhumavati

Sphere	Planet	Day
9th	Moon	Monday

Color	Number	Gems
sea blue	7	pearls, moonstone

Time of year: Sidereal full moon in cancer.

Esoteric Herbalism:
Baths: spearmint, lettuce, wild lettuce, purslane.
Oils: spearmint, jasmine
Incense: jasmine, spearmint

Hekau (mantras, words of power):
Spiritual: Dhum, vam
Planetary: Aung Shrang shring shraung

Spiritual Direction: East
Mundane Direction: Northwest

Personality Portfolio:

Personality traits: Through its action on the khaibit (the animal spirit) the cold and moist energy of the Moon has the following effects on the personality (sphere 9):

Emotional traits:

(+): Caring, motherliness, conservative[8], benevolent, accommodating, sweet mannered, timorous, fearful, comfort loving; wants security, and to be free of the cares and difficulties of life.

(-): Indolent, daydreaming, uncaring, vacillating, neglectful, careless, impressionable, gullible, fearful, idle, hating work, discontented, inclined to intoxicants, living beggarly, unsteadfast.

Mental traits: Mediumistic trance, imitation ("reflection").

Social Correspondences:

Careers, functions: Mother, wife, domestic life, hereditary factors, midwives, nurses, sailors, vagabonds, the masses, teachers of children, midwifes, farmers, servants, menial employment, millers, dealers and workers with liquids.

Spiritual Portfolio: devotion, humility, following, mediumistic trance, receptivity, indiscriminate imitation.

Key Phrases:

Catering to the emotions, preferences, love of ease; negligent, careless, indolent; receptivity, impressionability, gullibility; by following, by being humble; caring, nurturing; sympathetic, indulgent, compassionate; relaxed, peaceful; through mediumistic trance.

Biological correspondences

Physiology: the cold and moist energy of the Moon is the basis of the well being of the reproductive (ovaries, uterus), digestive, assimilative, autonomous nervous systems.

---

8. We cannot make the blanket statement to the effect that the Moon is changeable. As significator of women, especially mothers, it is more interested in security which is more easily attained through conservatism.

Pathology: infertility, menstrual problems, digestive problems, catarrhal conditions, chlorosis, anemia, edema, dropsy.

Kamitic therapeutics: alterative, diuretic, nutrient.

Chinese Medicine: Stomach system; Digestate Accumulation Patterns; Disease Patterns of Blood (blood vacuity, etc.); Phlegm Disease Patterns.

Spiritual keynotes: Following, humility, caring.

Underlying Principles:

+   By devoting ourselves to realizing our true Self, the indwelling intelligence, we come to realize that the true Self in all beings is none other than the Supreme Being. Thus we elevate our devotion to uplifting our character, and the caring for others to the highest levels of spirituality.

-      The ignorance of the divinity of the inner being constituting our true self, and that of others degenerates our caring for ourselves, and others into permissiveness, thus undermining our spiritual development.

Keynotes:(+) devotion to spiritual development; (-) permissiveness, loving of creature comforts, neglectful, fearful.

Spiritual Counsel

Whenever you receive an Auset reading you are being reminded that every emotional experience is a mediumistic trance induction which creates or reinforces a conditioning.

From another perspective, you may be reminded that as Auset is the point through which you express your devotion to things-emotional identification!-, it reveals to you what you truly worship. Is Ausar, the likeness of God in which you are made, what you identify with-care most for-, or is your person-the complex of conditioned thought, and emotional reactions to situations that you identify with? Do you now know which God you worship?

Geb

Kamitic: Geb (Seb)
Canaanite: Sandalphon
Kabalistical: Malkuth
Indus Kush: Bhairavi

Sphere	Planet	Day
10th	earth	all

Hekau (mantras, words of power):
    Spiritual: Aush Hrauh (Ra's heka)

Spiritual keynotes:
    Underlying Principles:
    +   Consistent adherence to the laws of health is
            absolutely necessary for spiritual development, and
            success in life.

Spiritual Counsel

When you receive a Geb reading you are reminded of the
fact that a major component of your spiritual force is sublimated
food, water, and oxygen[9]. Adherence to the laws governing health is
an essential requirement for the manifestation of spiritual power.
This is an important concept to keep in mind, as most people have
been misguided by the mistaken belief to the effect that as the
physical plane is the effect of the metaphysical forces, the earthly
laws need not be observed as all physical ills can be overcome
through spiritual work. There is a dangerous half truth at work here.
You can influence physical events through the power of your life-
force commanded by your will, only if you adhere to earthly laws.

A Geb reading may also refer to the physical resources
(money, labor, capital, energy, friends, etc.) that you have or lack for
an undertaking. It is also used by the oracle to symbolize the
"health" of an undertaking, as well as of the person inquired about.

---

9. See Chinese medicine, and cosmology where there is a full theory of the
sublimation of the gross energy, "chi (which operates the body)" into "jing (active
mental energy)," then into "shen (the peaceful state of mental energy corresponding
to the meditation state)," and finally into "wu chi" (the undifferentiated state of
energy).

Sheps & Dark Deceased

Kamitic: Sheps
Yoruba: Egungun

Esoteric Herbalism:
> Baths: Palo Espanta Muerto, Bitter broom
> Oils: Cypress, Myrrh, Olibanum
> Incense: same as oils

Spiritual keynotes:
> Underlying Principles:
> +   By cultivating a high level of spirituality one attracts positive or exalted ancestors for mutual assistance in the work of advancing the human family in its spiritual evolutionary career.
> -   Lack of consistency in the spiritual work, or trafficking with base things or people undermines the spiritual immunity and opens one to influences from dark deceased beings.

Spiritual Counsel

When you receive a Sheps reading you are reminded of your essential immortality, and your kinship with others beyond your immediate blood circle. From another perspective, the fact that there are many individuals who are in between incarnations, is a reminder that there are not enough resources for everyone to be on earth at the same time. You must therefore be grateful for the great privilege to acquire a body to come on earth to further your spiritual growth. Do not waste your short life in the pursuit of earthly things for their sake. It may also be a reminder that your present condition in life indicates your afterlife state. Earn the honor of others in life, i.e., become a Sheps now, and so will it be after life. Your name will continue to live in the memories of others, and by those who will pour libation to your Ka, to enable you to continue your role in guiding the policies of your social group, long after you have departed from the earth.

When you receive a Dark Deceased reading you are being warned that your failure to fully adhere to some spiritual law (shown by the other card) has weakened your spiritual immunity, and thus

297

opened you to the inimical forces of an earthbound spirit. It may also be a warning of what may become of your afterlife if you waste your incarnation in foolish pursuits and a dissipating way of life.

Nekhebet

Kamitic: Nekhebet, Rehu
Yoruba: Oya
Indus Kush: Rahu

Color	Gems
Dark blue	Onyx, blue sapphire

Esoteric Herbalism: See Seker

Hekau (mantras, words of power):
    Spiritual: Kshang
    Planetary: Aung hrang hring hraung

     When you receive a **Nekhebet, or Uatchet reading** you are being reminded that you are always affected, and influenced by the subtle electromagnetic forces of the earth, flowing through all things surrounding you. You must thus protect your vitality, and perfect your Men Ab to avoid being swept along by these subliminal (sublunar) forces.
     It is also calling your attention to the presence, or use of subliminal factors in a given situation. These operate on three levels. The lowest level employs embedded messages; E.g., the messages that are broadcasted below the level of normal perception (or played backward, or very fast) in department stores to discourage stealing; the so-called self improvement subliminal tapes, and other approaches. The next level employs the emotions of the practitioner synergized by the subtle radiation given off by animal, vegetable, and mineral substances. The events on this level are generally referred to as psychic phenomena, witchcraft (white & black), roots, radiasthesia, crystal healing, fetishes, etc. Its successful employment does not require spiritual power, moral upliftment, or wisdom. It is no different from mixing chemicals to achieve a mechanical effect. The third level employs all hekau, especially the heka Aung Hang Kshang as a means of uniting the will to the Ra force at the level of the Auraut (Ureus) or Ajna psychic center level.

Success in this method, which is the most powerful, comes at the 8th level of meditation. It thus requires spiritual transcendence and understanding. It is important to realize that the highest spiritual powers cannot be used by the ignorant and undisciplined. This is a divine protective mechanism.

Uatchet

Kamitic: Uachet
Yoruba: Oya
Indus Kush: Ketu

Color	Gems
Red	Cat's Eye

Esoteric Herbalism: See Herukhuti

Hekau (mantras, words of power):
      Spiritual: Hang
      Planetary: Aung shrang shring shraung
Spiritual Counsel

See above under Nekhebet.

NOTE: THE HERBS FOR WHICH SPANISH NAMES WERE GIVEN, CAN BE PURCHASED--FRESH--AT "AFRO-LATIN" RELIGIOUS STORES

Chapter 20

The Meanings of the Combined Metutu

AMEN

Amen/Amen

Amen (+)/Amen(+): Neither gain nor loss. Ultimately, there are no gains nor losses behind successes or failures. Nothing can be added to or subtracted from the substance of your being. Your spirit is essentially unconditioned.

Amen (+)/Amen(-): Striving consistently to ignore one's conditioned emotional, and sensual behavioral patterns liberates the spirit's infinite potential to achieve.

Amen (-)/Amen(+): Same as the preceding.

Amen (-)/Amen(-): Perseverance in the attachment, and receptivity to one's conditioned behavioral patterns is the fundamental cause of all failures in life.

Amen/Ausar

Amen (+)/Ausar (+):Amen and Ausar are complementaries (opposite poles of the same reality). In order to realize your infinite potential to be and to achieve, the essence of your being must be free of all conditionings (patterns of belief, emotional responses, etc.).

Amen (+)/Ausar (-): Same counsel as above.

Amen (-)/Ausar (+): Same counsel as above.

Amen (-)/Ausar (-): Failure through consistent perseverance in maintaining attachment to emotional and sensual conditionings, and the failure to transfer the self identification to the indwelling intelligence guiding all physiological and spiritual functions.

Amen/Tehuti

Amen (+)/Tehuti (+): Living the knowledge that the essential state of your being is unconditioned is the prerequisite for the manifestation of wisdom, and trustworthy intuitions.

Amen (+)/Tehuti (-): Same counsel as above.

Amen (-)/Tehuti (+): The good that can come from good counsel, correct intuitions, optimism, will be reduced by

300

attachment, and receptivity to one's conditioned behavioral patterns.

Amen (-)/Tehuti (-): Where there is attachment, and receptivity to one's conditioned behavioral patterns, there can be no receptivity to wisdom; do not trust your intuitions.

Amen/Seker

Amen (+)/Seker (+): Living the knowledge that the essential state of your being is unconditioned is the prerequisite for the manifestation of your spiritual power; Khepere rising from the waters of Nu.

Amen (+)/Seker (-): All things are the gifts of heaven. They come in their own time. One must learn to wait in cheerfulness, by cultivating appreciation for the structural spirits that maintain order in the world, although they create limitations, and "delays."

Amen (-)/Seker (+): You have good "planning" ability, but your plans are not rooted in "subjective" reality. What works in finite pragmatic situations (blueprints for machines, houses, etc.) does not work in life. We must get in tune with the spiritual entities that are the shaping forces of the structures governing events.

Amen (-)/Seker (-): attachment, and receptivity to one's conditioned behavioral patterns, combined with the incapacity to sustain deep protracted thinking, and the inability to understand the need for structure and limitations, or the lack of planning. A mean existence.

Amen/Maat

Amen (+)/Maat (+): The knowledge that the essential state of your being is unconditioned is the prerequisite for understanding the laws governing the oneness of life. Good fortune.

Amen (+)/Maat (-): The beneficent influences from heaven that are daily showered upon you will be wasted by ignorance of the law, inability to see the whole, lack of sharing, lack of compassion, etc.

Amen (-)/Maat (+): attachment, and receptivity to one's conditioned behavioral patterns will bring harm despite the possession of a view of the whole, knowledge of the law, optimism, and a sharing attitude.

Amen (-)/Maat (-): attachment, and receptivity to one's conditioned behavioral patterns combined with ignorance of the law, greed, extravagance, inability to see the whole, lack of sharing. Failure.

Amen/Herukhuti

Amen (+)/Herukhuti (+): All things arise from the same energy/matter, to ultimately serve the same purpose. They have a common divine mother and father. Fear not, for he who harms another, harms himself.

Amen (+)/Herukhuti (-): The beneficent influences from heaven that are daily showered upon you will be wasted by hastiness, arrogance, impetuousness, rashness, violence, libertinism, etc.

Amen (-)/Herukhuti (+): attachment and receptivity to one's conditioned behavioral patterns will bring harm despite hard work, zealousness, energetic action, initiative, courage, leadership, and entrepreneurship.

Amen (-)/Herukhuti (-): attachment and receptivity to one's conditioned behavioral combined with, or causing hastiness, arrogance, impetuousness, rashness, violence, libertinism.

Amen/Heru

Amen (+)/Heru (+): Take neither gain nor loss to heart. The ultimate goal of all achievements is the recapturing of the original unconditioned state of the spirit.

Amen (+)/Heru (-): The beneficent influences from heaven that are daily showered upon you will be wasted through arrogance, incorrect use of the will, strongheadedness, dictatorialness, unreceptivity to guidance.

Amen (-)/Heru (+): attachment and receptivity to one's conditioned behavioral patterns will bring harm despite good leadership quality, active will, good character, favors from people in authority, etc.

Amen (-)/Heru (-): attachment and receptivity to one's conditioned behavioral patterns combined with, or causing arrogance, incorrect use of the will, strongheadedness, dictatorialness, unreceptivity to guidance.

Amen/Het-Heru

Amen (+)/Het-Heru (+): To embrace the joy of inner peace and tranquility-unassailable by externals is happiness;

302

Amen (+)/Het-Heru(-): The beneficent gifts of heaven that are given you daily will be wasted by carelessness, negligence, illusions, addiction to pleasure.

Amen (-)/Het-Heru (+): attachment and receptivity to one's conditioned behavioral patterns will bring harm despite an outgoing joyful expression, a healthy urge to experience pleasure, favors from the many well disposed friends.

Amen (-)/Het-Heru (-): attachment and receptivity to one's conditioned behavioral patterns combined with, or causing deviations in the manner in which joy is expressed, pleasure is sought, and wrong ideas about joy (failing to make it the engine for success, and instead waiting for success to be joyful).

Amen/Sebek

Amen (+)/Sebek (+): His reasons for being, and doing are based on the knowledge of the essential state of his being. Good fortune; A good diviner of lots.

Amen (+)/Sebek (-): The beneficent influences from heaven that are daily showered upon you will be wasted by false beliefs, illogical thinking, false definitions, erroneous concepts, the desire to ease the way through schemes.

Amen (-)/Sebek (+): attachment and receptivity to one's conditioned behavioral patterns will bring harm despite a good education, good logical thinking, attention to details.

Amen (-)/Sebek (-):attachment and receptivity to one's conditioned behavioral patterns combined with, or causing false beliefs, illogical thinking, false definitions, erroneous concepts, the desire to ease the way through schemes

Amen/Auset

Amen (+)/Auset (+): Ever fruitfulness. Her receptivity goes back to the unconditioned origin of being. What can't she bring forth? When both Amen, and Auset are negative then there are deep problems as such a configuration represents indepth unreceptivity.

Amen (+)/Auset (-): The beneficent influences from heaven that are daily showered upon you will be wasted by indecisiveness, changeability, impressionability, sensitivity, emotionality, moodiness, love of ease.

Amen (-)/Auset (+): attachment and receptivity to one's conditioned behavioral patterns will bring harm despite a good memory, a fertile imagination, caring, sincerity, good trance ability, kindness, tenderness.

Amen (-)/Auset (-): attachment and receptivity to one's conditioned behavioral patterns combined with, or causing indecisiveness, changeability, impressionability, sensitivity, emotionality, moodiness.

Amen/Geb: See the section under Geb.

As stress is the mother of most illnesses, thus is Hetep, the deepest state of relaxation and inner peace, the supreme mother of healing. All emotions are conditions (conditionings) superimposed upon our essential and original unconditioned nature. In everyday life, this means that to be moved by the unmovable is the greatest manifestation of power; The infinitude of forms in the world are not individual manifestations in and for themselves. They-their infinitude-represent the infinite potential of manifestation of the Supreme Being, thus $0 = 10$.

Amen/Sheps: See the section under Sheps.

Amen(+)/Sheps(+): Success will be achieved by following the great One who rests in Amenta.

Amen/Dark Deceased: See the section under Dark Deceased.

He was shown the way of heaven, yet he did not heed. Now he rests not in peace.

Amen/Nekhebet: See the section under Nekhebet.

Amen/Uatchet: See the section under Uatchet.

AUSAR

Ausar/Amen: Amen and Ausar are complementaries. Where there is being, but no-things (the subjective realm-Amen, Tem), there is One.

Ausar (+)/Amen (+): Perseverance in living as the indwelling intelligence leads to the realization of the original, unconditioned state of the spirit. What then can be denied one?

Ausar (+)/Amen (-): The way is open for the indwelling intelligence to bring about unity, peace, and prosperity but it is obstructed by the perseverance in the attachment and receptivity to one's conditioned behavioral patterns;

Ausar (-)/Amen (+): disunion, ignorance of Self, or the failure to live according to one's true self will be transcended by consistently persevering in detaching oneself from one's emotional and sensual conditioning.

Ausar (-)/Amen (-): disunion, ignorance of Self, or the failure to live according to one's true self combined with the perseverance in the attachment and receptivity to one's conditioned behavioral patterns will keep one in bondage.

Ausar/Ausar

Ausar (+)/Ausar (+): Perseverance in the identification with the indwelling intelligence is the source of all success, health, and prosperity. It favors to go seek out one who has treaded the way back to the true Self.

Ausar (+)/Ausar (-): If today he is Ausar, and tomorrow he is his person, then he is always his person. WHO will invoke the deities on his behalf?

Ausar (-)/Ausar (+): Same as the preceding.

Ausar (-)/Ausar (-): the failure to transfer the self identification to the indwelling intelligence guiding all physiological and spiritual functions. Thus there is no unity, or purpose in his life.

Ausar/Tehuti

Ausar (+)/Tehuti (+):Living the understanding of the oneness of all life, by transcending the identification with the person, is the foundation of wisdom, wealth, and prosperity.

Ausar (+)/Tehuti (-): The way is open for the indwelling intelligence to bring about unity, peace, and prosperity but it is obstructed by incorrect intuitions, judgements, counsel, lack of faith, etc.

Ausar (-)/Tehuti (+): The failure to transfer the self identification to the indwelling intelligence guiding all physiological and spiritual functions leading to disharmony, and obstructions will be overcome by rituals to Tehuti.

Ausar (-)/Tehuti (-): obstructed by incorrect intuitions, judgements, counsel, lack of faith, etc., and the failure to transfer the self identification to the indwelling intelligence guiding all physiological and spiritual functions leading to disharmony, and obstructions; poverty, legal problems, lack of faith. Seek counsel.

Ausar/Seker

Ausar (+)/Seker (+): Living the understanding of the oneness of all life, by transcending the identification with the person, is the foundation of spiritual power.

Ausar (+)/Seker (-): The way is open for the indwelling intelligence to bring about unity, peace, and prosperity but it is obstructed by the incapacity to sustain deep protracted thinking, and the inability to understand the need for structure and limitations.

Ausar (-)/Seker (+): disunion, ignorance of Self, or the failure to live according to one's true self will subtract from the success that can be achieved through the capacity to sustain deep protracted thinking, good organizational ability, and the appreciation for structure, and limitations.

Ausar (-)/Seker (-): disunion, ignorance of Self, or the failure to live according to one's true self will exacerbate the problems arising from the incapacity to sustain deep protracted thinking, and the inability to understand the need for structure and limitations, or the lack of planning.

Ausar/Maat

Ausar (+)/Maat (+):Living the understanding of the oneness of all life, by transcending the identification with the person, is the prime requirement for understanding and living the law of God; gains through the things governed by Maat.

Ausar (+)/Maat (-): The way is open for the indwelling intelligence to bring about unity, peace, and prosperity but it

306

is obstructed by ignorance of the law, inability to see the whole, lack of sharing, faithlessness.

Ausar (-)/Maat (+): disunion, ignorance of Self, or the failure to live according to one's true self will subtract from the success that can be achieved through a view of the whole, knowledge of the law, optimism, and a sharing attitude.

Ausar (-)/Maat (-): disunion, ignorance of Self, or the failure to live according to one's true self will exacerbate the problems arising from ignorance of the law, inability to see the whole, lack of sharing.

Ausar/Herukhuti

Ausar (+)/Herukhuti (+):Living the understanding of the oneness of all life, by transcending the identification with the person, is the key for unlocking the strength to invoke the sword of justice upon one's person when one has sinned against Maat. And if you have called justice upon yourself, will not justice answer your calls for help?.

Ausar (+)/Herukhuti (-): The way is open for the indwelling intelligence to bring about unity, peace, and prosperity but it is obstructed by hastiness, arrogance, impetuousness, rashness, violence, libertinism

Ausar (-)/Herukhuti (+): disunion, ignorance of Self, or the failure to live according to one's true self will subtract from the success that can be achieved through hard work, zealousness, energetic action, initiative, courage, leadership, and entrepreneurship.

Ausar (-)/Herukhuti (-): disunion, ignorance of Self, or the failure to live according to one's true self will exacerbate the problems arising from hastiness, arrogance, impetuousness, rashness, violence, libertinism.

Ausar/Heru

Ausar (+)/Heru (+): The proper use of the will (Men Ab, following sages, oracles, and not taking the lead) leads to the realization of Self.

Ausar (+)/Heru (-): The way is open for the indwelling intelligence to bring about unity, peace, and prosperity but it is obstructed by ignorance of the law governing the will.

307

Ausar (-)/Heru (+): disunion, ignorance of Self, or the failure to live according to one's true self can be overcome through Men Ab em Aungkh em Maat.

Ausar (-)/Heru (-): disunion, ignorance of Self, or the failure to live according to one's true self will exacerbate the problems arising from arrogance, incorrect use of the will, strongheadedness, dictatorialness, unreceptivity to guidance.

Ausar/Het-Heru

Ausar (+)/Het-Heru (+): Living the understanding of the knowledge of Self, by transcending the identification with the person, is the foundation of inner joy, happiness, fellowship, peace, and harmony between men.

Ausar (+)/Het-Heru (-): The way is open for the indwelling intelligence to bring about unity, peace, and prosperity but it is obstructed by deviations in the manner in which joy is expressed, pleasure is sought, and wrong ideas about joy (failing to make it the engine for success, and instead waiting for success to be joyful).

Ausar (-)/Het-Heru (+): disunion, ignorance of Self, or the failure to live according to one's true self will subtract from the success that can be achieved through an outgoing joyful expression, a healthy urge to experience pleasure.

Ausar (-)/Het-Heru (-): disunion, ignorance of Self, or the failure to live according to one's true self will exacerbate the problems arising from deviations in the manner in which joy is expressed, pleasure is sought, and wrong ideas about joy (failing to make it the engine for success, and instead waiting for success to be joyful).

Ausar/Sebek

Ausar (+)/Sebek (+): Living the understanding of the oneness of all life, and the knowledge of Self by transcending the identification with the person, is the foundation of a proper belief system.

Ausar (+)/Sebek (-): The way is open for the indwelling intelligence to bring about unity, peace, and prosperity but it is obstructed by a false belief system, pride, selfishness, etc.

Ausar (-)/Sebek (+): disunion, ignorance of Self, or the failure to live according to one's true self will subtract from

308

the success that can be achieved through a good education, good logical thinking, attention to details.

Ausar (-)/Sebek (-): disunion, ignorance of Self, or the failure to live according to one's true self will exacerbate the problems arising from false beliefs, illogical thinking, false definitions, erroneous concepts, the desire to ease the way through schemes.

Ausar/Auset

Ausar (+)/Auset (+): The Self and the person are united in a blissful mystic marriage. Good fortune, prosperity, health, and peace.

Ausar (+)/Auset (-): The way is open for the indwelling intelligence to bring about unity, peace, and prosperity but it is obstructed by indecisiveness, changeability, impressionability, sensitivity, emotionality, moodiness. Negative mediumism.

Ausar (-)/Auset (+): disunion, ignorance of Self, or the failure to live according to one's true self will subtract from the success that can be achieved through a good memory, a fertile imagination, caring, sincerity, good trance ability, kindness, tenderness.

Ausar (-)/Auset (-): disunion, ignorance of Self, or the failure to live according to one's true self will exacerbate the problems arising from indecisiveness, changeability, impressionability, sensitivity, emotionality, moodiness. Negative mediumism.

Ausar/Geb: See the section under Geb.

Ausar (+)/Geb (+): Living the understanding of the oneness of all life, and the knowledge of Self-the indwelling intelligence - by transcending the identification with the person, is the foundation of health, and the attainment of all earthly goals.

Ausar (+)/Geb (-): The way is open for the indwelling intelligence to bring about unity, peace, and prosperity but it is obstructed by poor health, or lack of resources, etc.

Ausar/Sheps: See the section under Sheps.

Success will come from performing an Ausar ritual on behalf of your ancestor.

Ausar/Dark Deceased: See the section under Dark Deceased.

The troubled one will be uplifted by hearing the teachings of the Pert em Heru (Egyptian book of the Dead).

Ausar/Nekhebet: See the section under Nekhebet.

Ausar/Uatchet: See the section under Uatchet.

TEHUTI

Tehuti/Amen

Tehuti (+)/Amen (+): He who knows the way to the sage, and the oracles knows the way to the highest aspect of his being, and Hetep (the eternal inner peace);

Tehuti (+)/Amen (-): The way is open for success if faith, optimism in wise counsel, and correct intuitions are cultivated, but one is obstructed by the self-identification with one's conditioned being-the person.

Tehuti (-)/Amen (+): incorrect intuitions, misjudgments, bad counsel; and lack of faith will be corrected by the self-identification with one's unconditioned essential inner being.

Tehuti (-)/Amen (-): incorrect intuitions, misjudgments, bad counsel; and lack of faith coupled with ignorance of one's essence. One thus loses direction over one's life.

Tehuti/Ausar

Tehuti (+)/Ausar (+): Faith, optimism, and wise counsel complemented by Self knowledge. Good fortune. Dwelling in the inner self, instead of the person is the means of developing the wisdom faculty; trustworthy intuitions.

Tehuti (+)/Ausar (-): Faith, optimism, and wise counsel are obstructed by the lack of self knowledge, or the failure to live according to it.

Tehuti (-)/Ausar (+): Unfounded optimism, doubtfulness, bad judgement, lack of faith, obstructing the positive activities of the indwelling Self.

310

Tehuti (-)/Ausar (-): Wrong judgement, or bad counsel complicated by ignorance of Self, or the failure to live accordingly. Misfortune.

Tehuti/Tehuti

Tehuti (+)/Tehuti (+): Good counsel, or good judgement doubled. Good fortune.

Tehuti (+)/Tehuti (-): Good judgement, coupled with bad judgement. Seeking guidance in too many places, or failing to give one's head up when seeking counsel will only lead to confusion.

Tehuti (-)/Tehuti (+): Same as the preceding.

Tehuti (-)/Tehuti (-): Doubts, unfounded optimism, bad judgements, lack of faith; untrustworthy intuitions. You must go to counsel.

Tehuti/Seker

Tehuti (+)/Seker (+): Wise counsel, and good judgement coupled with discipline, organizational ability, and the appreciation for structure (limitations) are the skills that lead to success in large, time-consuming, and complex undertakings; Without wisdom there is no spiritual power, nor trustworthy plans.

Tehuti (+)/Seker (-): Although there can be good fortune arising from optimism, wise counsel, and good judgement, the lack of discipline, structure will create delays, or failure. Beware of poverty.

Tehuti (-)/Seker (+): incorrect intuitions, misjudgments, bad counsel, and lack of faith will be corrected by deep meditation, and strict adherence to structural guidelines.

Tehuti (-)/Seker (-):Bad judgement, delays, obstructions. Beware of legal troubles, separations.

Tehuti/Maat

Tehuti (+)/Maat (+): The way is open for a joyful period, contentment, well being, expansion, success.

Tehuti (+)/Maat (-): There is good judgement but a view of the whole is lacking; beware of extravagance, greed, false sense of security from the belief that you know.

Tehuti (-)/Maat (+): the inability to identify the applicable principle in a given situation even though there is a view of the whole, knowledge of the law. Danger from dogmatism, unjust laws.

Tehuti (-)/Maat (-): Bad judgement coupled with ignorance of the law, of cosmologics, etc. Misfortune.

Tehuti/Herukhuti

Tehuti (+)/Herukhuti (+): Wisdom coupled with force. Wise counsel carried out with zealousness. Success. Successful business executives, negotiators.

Tehuti (+)/Herukhuti (-): Hotheadedness, opposition to wise counsel, extravagance, opposition to the law.

Tehuti (-)/Herukhuti (+): incorrect intuitions, misjudgments, bad counsel; and lack of faith serving as the foundation of hard work, zealousness, energetic action.

Tehuti (-)/Herukhuti (-): hastiness, exaggeration, intemperance, disputes, extravagance, anarchy, lack of enterprise.

Tehuti/Heru

Tehuti (+)/Heru (+): The will is successful through maintaining faith, and optimism in wise counsel; He lets the oracle, and the sage guide his decisions. Good fortune.

Tehuti (+)/Heru (-) Arrogance, and unreceptivity to wise counsel. Misfortune. Trouble with officials, the law.

Tehuti (-)/Heru (+): incorrect intuitions, judgements, counsel; lack of faith, etc. guiding the will, decisions, the policy of people in authoritative positions, the head of household, father, etc.

Tehuti (-)/Heru (-): obstructed by arrogance, incorrect use of the will, strongheadedness, incorrect intuitions, judgements, counsel, lack of faith, etc. A very dangerous reading as there is a severe lack of receptivity; beware of extravagance, extremes, greed, overconfidence, overexpansiveness.

Tehuti/Het-Heru

Tehuti (+)/Het-Heru (+): maintaining faith, and optimism in wise counsel coupled with a joyful expression, and healthy sexual attitude leads to success, charming and pleasurable life experiences; a happy marriage, wealth, and health; the successful arousal of Ra. Good health, power, and good fortune.

Tehuti (+)/Het-Heru (-): The way is open for success if faith, optimism in wise counsel, and correct intuitions are cultivated, but one is obstructed by deviations in the manner in which joy is expressed, pleasure is sought, and wrong ideas about joy (failing to make it the engine for success, and instead waiting for success to be joyful).

Tehuti (-)/Het-Heru (+): incorrect intuitions, judgements, counsel, etc. acting in combination with a joyful expression, and healthy urge for pleasure. Enjoyment and happiness will give way to disappointment, and disillusionment. Hung String Aung heka.

Tehuti (-)/Het-Heru (-): incorrect intuitions, misjudgments, bad counsel; and lack of faith coupled with deviations in the manner in which joy is expressed, pleasure is sought, and wrong ideas about joy (failing to make it the engine for success, and instead waiting for success to be joyful).

Tehuti/Sebek

Tehuti (+)/Sebek (+): When education, beliefs, and rationalizations are in harmony with the oracles, and the counsel from the sage, the way to success is open.

Tehuti (+)/Sebek (-): the success that can be achieved through maintaining faith, and optimism in wise counsel is jeopardized by false beliefs, illogical thinking, false definitions, erroneous concepts, the desire to ease the way through schemes.

Tehuti (-)/Sebek (+):incorrect intuitions, misjudgments, bad counsel; and lack of faith serving as the premise for reasoning. Grave errors will result.

Tehuti (-)/Sebek (-): incorrect intuitions, misjudgments, bad counsel; and lack of faith coupled with wrong education, faulty logic, pride, selfishness, a trickster mentality; foolhardiness, craziness, insanity. Rituals to Sebek, and Tehuti. Palm oil oleation therapy (see Ayurvedic medicine), nervines, etc. Seek counsel, but be honest, and sincere. You can only trick yourself.

Tehuti/Auset

Tehuti (+)/Auset (+): maintaining faith, and optimism in wise counsel from oracles, and sages, and correct intuitions

313

coupled with an unswerving devotion to uplifting your character (identifying with Ausar), and the care of others is the foundation for building strong humanistic institutions (family, nation, fraternal organizations, etc.).

Tehuti (+)/Auset (-): The way is open for success if faith, optimism in wise counsel, and correct intuitions are cultivated, but one is obstructed by a lack of receptivity, and self-identification with one's person.

Tehuti (-)/Auset (+): incorrect intuitions, misjudgments, bad counsel, and lack of faith acting as the thought components of well meaning feelings. Problems in spite of sincerity.

Tehuti (-)/Auset (-): incorrect intuitions, misjudgments, bad counsel; and lack of faith coupled with a careless, negligent, "emotionally sensitive," unreceptive attitude. Be humble, allow yourself to be guided.

Tehuti/Geb: See the section under Geb.

Tehuti (+)/Geb (+): A way of life in which faith, and optimism in wise counsel are maintained are keys to maintaining good health, and the successful attainments of earthly needs.

Tehuti (+)/Geb (-): Measures to improve health, and secure the earthly needs will be helped by maintaining faith, and optimism in wise counsel.

Tehuti (-)/Geb (+): incorrect intuitions, misjudgments, bad counsel; and lack of faith will be reversed by improving your health, and conditioning.

Tehuti (-)/Geb (-): incorrect intuitions, misjudgments, bad counsel; and lack of faith influenced by poor health; see the Tehuti physiological data.

Tehuti/Sheps: See the section under Sheps.
Tehuti/Dark Deceased: See the section under Dark Deceased.
Tehuti/Nekhebet: See the section under Nekhebet.
Tehuti/Uatchet: See the section under Uatchet.

SEKER

Seker/Amen

Seker(+)/Amen (+): Great spiritual power (shekhem ur) is achieved through the consistent perseverance in the detachment from one's emotional and sensual conditioning; By living in harmony with the cycles one comes to understand that all things ultimately come from heaven, and in their own time. Patience, and submission to the will of heaven is the way to a successful destiny.

Seker(+)/Amen (-): the success that can be achieved through the capacity to sustain deep protracted thinking, good organizational ability, and the appreciation for structure, and limitations is jeopardized by the perseverance in the attachment and receptivity to one's conditioned behavioral patterns.

Seker(-)/Amen (+): lack of spiritual power, lack of success in working with hekau (words of power), lack of concentration will be corrected by consistently persevering in detaching oneself from one's emotional and sensual conditioning.

Seker(-)/Amen (-): lack of spiritual power, lack of success in working with hekau (words of power), lack of concentration is caused by, or is exacerbated by the perseverance in the attachment and receptivity to one's conditioned behavioral patterns.

Seker/Ausar

Seker(+)/Ausar (+): the capacity to sustain deep protracted thinking, good organizational ability, and the appreciation for structure, and limitations is instrumental in achieving the realization of the true self.

Seker(+)/Ausar (-): the success that can be achieved through the capacity to sustain deep protracted thinking, good organizational ability, and the appreciation for structure, and limitations is jeopardized by disunion, ignorance of Self, or the failure to live according to one's true self.

Seker(-)/Ausar (+): lack of spiritual power, lack of success in working with hekau (words of power), lack of concentration will subtract from the success that can be achieved in spite of self knowledge. The essence of spiritual

315

development is practice, not mere sermonizing, and studying.

Seker(-)/Ausar (-): lack of spiritual power, lack of success in working with hekau (words of power), lack of concentration will exacerbate the problems arising from disunion, ignorance of Self, or the failure to live according to one's true self.

Seker/Tehuti

Seker(+)/Tehuti (+): He stills the thought processes and intuits the knowledge of the underlying tracts leading to Khemennu. His infinite patience, and wisdom makes him an indefatigable teacher. You must go see him; Success in large, and time consuming undertakings.

Seker(+)/Tehuti (-): Despite the ability to provide a good structure, and good organization, delays, or failures will result from incorrect intuitions, misjudgments, bad counsel; and lack of faith.

Seker(-)/Tehuti (+): lack of planning, or the incapacity to sustain deep protracted thinking, and the inability to understand the need for structure and limitations will subtract from the success that can be achieved through maintaining faith, and optimism in wise counsel.

Seker(-)/Tehuti (-): incapacity to sustain deep protracted thinking, and the inability to understand the need for structure and limitations coupled with incorrect intuitions, misjudgments, bad counsel; and lack of faith will lead to failures, delay, poverty, legal problems, temptation to ease the way through antisocial behavior, misanthropy.

Seker/Seker

Seker(+)/Seker(+): the capacity to sustain deep protracted thinking, good organizational ability, and the appreciation for structure, and limitations.

Seker(+)/Seker(-): The success that is promised by good planning is in danger because of pessimism, doubts, worries, etc.

Seker(-)/Seker(+): Same as in the preceding.

Seker(-)/Seker(-): the incapacity to sustain deep protracted thinking, and the inability to understand the need for structure and limitations, or the lack of planning combined with, or causing pessimism, worries, depression, etc.

316

Seker/Maat

Seker(+)/Maat (+): the capacity to sustain deep protracted thinking, good organizational ability, and the appreciation for structure, and limitations coupled with a view of the whole, or knowledge of the law is the foundation for long lasting success in business, religious, and theoretical sciences; wealth, prosperity, good health.

Seker(+)/Maat (-): the way is open for success through the capacity to sustain deep protracted thinking, good organizational ability, and the appreciation for structure, and limitations, but there is obstruction caused by ignorance of the law, inability to see the whole, lack of sharing. Business failures, financial losses.

Seker (-)/Maat (+): lack of planning, or the incapacity to sustain deep protracted thinking, and the inability to understand the need for structure and limitations will subtract from the success that can be achieved through a view of the whole, knowledge of the law, optimism, and a sharing attitude

Seker(-)/Maat (-): incapacity to sustain deep protracted thinking, and the inability to understand the need for structure and limitations coupled with ignorance of the law, inability to see the whole, lack of sharing, and faithlessness. Deep financial losses, unhappiness, separations, law suits.

Seker/Herukhuti

Seker (+)/Herukhuti (+): the capacity to sustain deep protracted thinking, good organizational ability, and the appreciation for structure, and limitations working combined with zealous, and energetic action. One can overcome great obstructions encountered in large, difficult, complex and even dangerous projects.

Seker (+)/Herukhuti (-): the success that would otherwise come from good organization, structure, and limitations is jeopardized by the lack of enterprise, or hastiness, arrogance, impetuousness, rashness, violence, libertinism disguised as the love for freedom; Reticence, and reserve in speech, and actions will avoid conflict.

Seker (-)/Herukhuti (+): incapacity to sustain deep protracted thinking, and the inability to understand the need for structure and limitations will subtract from the success

317

that can be achieved through hard, and indefatigable work. Small success after much delay. Wasted effort due to lack of, or the inability to plan. Seek the assistance of elders, or the experienced. One has given too much thought to an issue, act!

Seker(-)/Herukhuti (-): Strong inner conflict caused by the opposition between inhibitions, and sensual impulses; between the desire to overcome an opposition and too much thinking about it. Difficulties from rogues; attempts to overcome obstructions, and denials through violence.

Seker/Heru

Seker (+)/Heru (+): the capacity to sustain deep protracted thinking, good organizational ability, and the appreciation for structure, and limitations in associations with an enlightened will, and magnanimity is the foundation of good government, and administration. It will lead to power, honors, appreciation from people in authority, success in litigation. Success in undertakings demanding steadfastness, reliability, slow and steady growth.

Seker (+)/Heru (-): the administrative success that would otherwise be achieved through the capacity to sustain deep protracted thinking, good organizational ability, and the appreciation for structure, and limitations is thrown away through arrogance, dictatorialness, extravagance, lack of vitality.

Seker (-)/Heru (+): the absence of a plan, or the incapacity to sustain deep protracted thinking, will undermine a strong and enlightened will. There will be a lack of staying power and steadfastness.

Seker (-)/Heru (-): severe restrictions, limitations, delays, and obstructions which will not be adequately met due to a lack of vitality, or an ignorant will; officials may be demoted due to gross mismanagement.

Seker/Het-Heru

Seker (+)/Het-Heru (+): A serious attitude towards love, art, and social protocols; a sense of duty in love relations, the taking of life seriously yet joyfully, fully enjoying pleasures yet limiting them, relations with older people, a deep and powerful imagination, clairvoyance.

318

Seker (+)/Het-Heru (-): the success that can be achieved through the capacity to sustain deep protracted thinking, good organizational ability, and the appreciation for structure, and limitations is jeopardized by carelessness, playfulness, negligence, extravagance.

Seker (-)/Het-Heru (+) inner tension, and conflict caused by inhibitions, or unnatural scruples in opposition to the urge to experience joy, and pleasure.

Seker (-)/Het-Heru (-): jealousy, sexual inhibitions, coldheartedness; separations, aberrant urges.

Seker/Sebek

Seker (+)/Sebek (+): the capacity to sustain deep protracted thinking, good organizational ability, and the appreciation for structure, and limitations coupled with good attention to definitions, descriptions, phases of operation, logics, and details. Success in scholarly, philosophical, and scientific endeavors.

Seker (+)/Sebek (-): the success that can be achieved through a good plan, organization and structure is jeopardized by false beliefs, illogical thinking, false definitions, erroneous concepts, the desire to ease the way through schemes. A reputation built through many years of hard work is jeopardized by slanderers, mischief workers, gossipers. The young and inexperienced should let the elder, and experienced lead.

Seker (-)/Sebek (+): incapacity to sustain deep protracted thinking, and the inability to understand the need for structure and limitations will be compensated by a good education in the subject inquired about.

Seker (-)/Sebek (-): One is afflicted by the incapacity to sustain deep protracted thinking, and the inability to understand the need for structure and limitations coupled with false beliefs, illogical thinking, false definitions, erroneous concepts, the desire to ease the way through schemes. Lack of planning coupled with wrong ideas, and illogical thinking. There will be delays, failure, false theories. Beware of misrepresentations; mistrustfulness. Nervines, and rest might prove helpful.

Seker/Auset:

Seker (+)/Auset (+): The capacity for deep concentration combined with trance ability; a successful medium. Steadfast in caring for others, sense of duty, a strong home life, a strong nation; a stern mother.

Seker (+)/Auset (-): The capacity for deep concentration combined with negative, careless, or untrained mediumism, daydreaming; a good plan fails due to carelessness.

Seker (-)/Auset (+): Overthinking (causing brain fag, and confusion), or the incapacity to think deeply will be overcome through rituals to Auset, trance work.

Seker (-)/Auset (-): Overthinking (causing brain fag, and confusion), or the incapacity to think deeply combined with impressionability, daydreaming leading to fearfulness, depression, lack of self-confidence, inhibitions, vacillation, moodiness. Bad effects of excessive sedentary habits; the constant dwelling on morbid thoughts.

Seker/Geb: See the section under Geb.

Seker/Sheps: See the section under Sheps.
Seker/Dark Deceased
Seker/Nekhebet: See the section under Nekhebet.
Seker/Uatchet: See the section under Uatchet.

MAAT

Maat/Amen

Maat (+)/Amen (+): Your wealth ultimately comes from heaven where it is owned in common with all others.

Maat (+)/Amen (-): the success that can come from having a view of the whole, knowledge of the law, optimism, and a sharing attitude will be jeopardized by attachment and receptivity to conditioned behavioral patterns; Material success, but spiritual failure.

Maat (-)/Amen (+): Establish yourself in Hetep, and your "luck" will change for the better.

Maat (-)/Amen (-): A man seeks to accumulate wealth to satisfy his inner emptiness. There will be disappointment, and unhappiness in the midst of plenty.

Maat/Ausar

Maat (+)/Ausar (+): Observing the divine law in our daily lives is the substance of our identification with the divine part of our being; Your greatest wealth is your oneness with others.

Maat (+)/Ausar (-): It matters not how well you know the divine law. If you do not identify with your true self-the indwelling intelligence, there will be evil.

Maat (-)/Ausar (+): ignorance of the law, inability to see the whole, lack of sharing and optimism will be reversed through rituals to Ausar.

Maat (-)/Ausar (-): ignorance of the law, inability to see the whole, lack of sharing, faithlessness combined with ignorance of Self, or the failure to live according to one's true self. There will be much evil, and problems in life.

Maat/Tehuti

Maat (+)/Tehuti (+): The way is open for a joyful period, contentment, well being, expansion, success.

Maat (+)/Tehuti (-): Although there may be a view of the whole, the inability to identify the applicable part will lead to wrong judgements. Problems with the judiciary system.

Maat (-)/Tehuti (+): ignorance of the law, inability to see the whole, lack of sharing, faithlessness. See the sage, expert, teacher, use the oracles consistently.

Maat (-)/Tehuti (-): ignorance of the law, inability to see the whole, lack of sharing combined with incorrect intuitions, misjudgments, bad counsel; and lack of faith. Failure, poverty, misfortune, trouble with the law.

Maat/Seker

Maat (+)/Seker (+): the capacity to sustain deep protracted thinking, good organizational ability, and the appreciation for structure, and limitations coupled with a view of the whole, or knowledge of the law is the foundation for long lasting success in business, religious, and theoretical sciences; wealth, prosperity, good health.

Maat (+)/Seker (-): The success that is readily available through a view of the whole, knowledge of the law, a sharing heart, optimism is jeopardized by incapacity to sustain deep protracted thinking, and the inability to understand the need

321

for structure and limitations; from lack of or bad planning. Unfounded optimism.

Maat (-)/Seker (+): the capacity to sustain deep protracted thinking, good organizational ability, and the appreciation for structure, and limitations, or good planning will compensate for ignorance of the law, inability to see the whole, lack of sharing, faithlessness. Small success will come from long, hard work, and thoughtful planning. There will be some losses.

Maat (-)/Seker (-): greed, overexpansiveness, false beliefs, ignorance of the law combined with a disregard for structure, and plans; depression, worries, separations, mean behavior, erroneous theories and philosophies; Poverty.

Maat/Maat

Maat (+)/Maat (+): One succeeds, accumulates wealth, friends, position, fame by abiding in the law, and a loving, compassionate, and sharing attitude.

Maat (+)/Maat (-): Only a fool attempts to maintain a book of accounts on the living of truth. It is only truth when it is lived daily. Today as yesterday. Tomorrow as today. Truth!

Maat (-)/Maat (+): Same as in the preceding.

Maat (-)/Maat (-): ignorance of the law, inability to see the whole, lack of sharing, extravagance, greed

Maat/Herukhuti

Maat (+)/Herukhuti (+): The law (spiritual, or mundane) is backed by force. The young spirit will not embrace truth for the love of it. Until maturity is attained, the law must be backed by force. A strong faith in the law wedded to a strong enterprising spirit. Major success.

Maat (+)/Herukhuti (-): the success that can be achieved through a view of the whole, knowledge of the law, sharing is in jeopardy by hastiness, arrogance, impetuousness, rashness, violence, libertinism. Beware of extravagance, overconfidence.

Maat (-)/Herukhuti (+): Fearlessness, zealousness, the capacity for hard work will compensate for the ignorance of the law, inability to see the whole, lack of sharing. Perseverance in this unfortunate way will yield little net returns. One will work hard with little cooperation from others, without joy. What is made will be lost as quickly as earned.

Maat (-)/Herukhuti (-): extravagance, greed, rashness, extreme sensuality, libertinism, opposition to rules and order. Trouble, and failures. Injustice.

Maat/Heru

Maat (+)/Heru (+):an enlightened will is guided by the view of the whole, knowledge of the law, optimism. Success; good character; a religious individual.

Maat (+)/Heru (-): success can be achieved through a view of the whole, knowledge of the law, optimism, and a sharing attitude, but it is jeopardized by arrogance, incorrect use of the will, strongheadedness; unmerited wealth.

Maat (-)/Heru (+): ignorance of the law, inability to see the whole, lack of sharing, and faithlessness will subtract from the success that can be achieved through a good character, good leadership, and the proper use of the will. Nourish yourself with the teachings of Maat.

Maat (-)/Heru (-): ignorance of the law, inability to see the whole, lack of sharing, greed, faithlessness combined with arrogance, incorrect use of the will, strongheadedness; problems with people in position of authority, the law.

Maat/Het-Heru

Maat (+)/Het-Heru (+): a view of the whole, knowledge of the law, optimism, and a sharing attitude combined with an outgoing joyful expression, a healthy urge to experience pleasure; a happy marriage, success in business, a harmonious partnership, good health; Maat is the food and drink of Ra. An abundant life-force is aroused by living the law in combination with a healthy expression of joy. Great success.

Maat (+)/Het-Heru (-): Wealth and success will be jeopardized by sensual excesses.

Maat (-)/Het-Heru (+): Very much like the following but with better chances of redemption; redemption through rituals to Maat, and study of the law.

Maat (-)/Het-Heru (-): excessive love, and greed for sensual gratification; great dissipation; extreme carelessness, love of ease, craving for "nice things"; spends millions on artwork, jewelry; profligate.

Maat/Sebek

Maat (+)/Sebek (+): a view of the whole, knowledge of the law, optimism, and a sharing attitude coupled with a correct belief system, and good logical thinking. The ability to relate specifics to their parental general principle. Success.

Maat (+)/Sebek (-): the matter is known generally, but one is unable to identify the related specific examples. For example, a person may know that it is unlawful to poison others even though death, or severe illness does not ensue, but they fail to realize that forcing others to inhale their cigarette smoke is a species of the same general principle. Improperly applied laws, bad rulings.

Maat (-)/Sebek (+): ignorance of the law, inability to see the whole, inability to share are the foundation of the premises upon which the reasonings of the subject are based.

Maat (-)/Sebek (-): ignorance of the law, inability to see the whole, lack of sharing combined with false beliefs, illogical thinking, false definitions, erroneous concepts, the desire to ease the way through schemes. Very irrational behavior.

Maat/Auset

Maat (+)/Auset (+): One has achieved one's goal through the power of mediumistic trance (the full moon!). There will be good fortune as long as one does not fall into the belief that this is the way, as it does not, by itself, lead to spiritual development.

Maat (+)/Auset (-): the wealth that you have accumulated, or can accumulate through observance of the law, optimism, etc. is jeopardized by indecisiveness, changeability, impressionability, sensitivity, emotionality, moodiness, carelessness.

Maat (-)/Auset (+): the negative side of Maat can be overcome through mediumistic trance.

Maat (-)/Auset (-): ignorance of the law, inability to see the whole, lack of sharing, greed, extravagance combined with indecisiveness, changeability, impressionability, sensitivity, emotionality, moodiness, carelessness.

Maat/Geb: See the section under Geb.

Maat/Sheps: See the section under Sheps.
Maat/Dark Deceased: See the section under Dark Deceased.
Maat/Nekhebet: See the section under Nekhebet.
Maat/Uatchet: See the section under Uatchet.

HERUKHUTI

Herukhuti/Amen

Herukhuti (+)/Amen (+): true justice is achieved when law enforcers are consistently persevering in detaching themselves from their emotional and sensual conditioning.

Herukhuti (+)/Amen (-): although law enforcers mean well, their attachment to their emotional, and sensual conditioning will lead to injustice (revenge, etc.).

Herukhuti (-)/Amen (+): hastiness, arrogance, impetuousness, rashness, violence, libertinism will be overcome by consistently persevering in detaching oneself from one's emotional and sensual conditionings; Working without seeking credit will avoid conflict.

Herukhuti (-)/Amen (-): hastiness, arrogance, impetuousness, rashness, violence, libertinism will be exacerbated by attachment and receptivity to one's conditioned behavioral patterns.

Herukhuti/Ausar

Herukhuti (+)/Ausar (+): He cuts himself from his person to identify with his Self; the source of true courage.

Herukhuti (+)/Ausar (-): hard work, zealousness, energetic action will be jeopardized by disunion, lack of self knowledge.

Herukhuti (-)/Ausar (+): hastiness, arrogance, impetuousness, rashness, violence, libertinism will subtract from the success that can be achieved by the harmonizing influences of the indwelling intelligence.

Herukhuti (-)/Ausar (-): hastiness, arrogance, impetuousness, rashness, violence, libertinism. The failure to transfer the self identification to the indwelling

325

intelligence; great danger. Accidents, wars, violent confrontations, brutality, or lack of ambition and enterprise.

Herukhuti/Tehuti

Herukhuti (+)/Tehuti (+): Force must be complemented and guided by wisdom. Good fortune.
Herukhuti (+)/Tehuti (-): Zealous, and energetic action will meet with failure due to bad judgement, or unwise counsel.
Herukhuti (-)/Tehuti (+): hastiness, arrogance, impetuousness, rashness, violence, libertinism will subtract from the success that can be achieved through good counsel, correct intuitions, optimism; The conflict will be resolved by the source of truth that is beyond all question of bias. What other than the oracle is there?
Herukhuti (-)/Tehuti (-): hastiness, arrogance, impetuousness, rashness, violence, libertinism will be exacerbated by incorrect intuitions, misjudgments, bad counsel; and lack of faith.

Herukhuti/Seker

Herukhuti (+)/Seker (+): analytical ability combined with good powers of concentration, and organizing; scientific researchers. Capacity for hard and long sustained work; The army is lead by elders. Good fortune; One goes forward with a plan, organization, and discipline. Good fortune.
Herukhuti (+)/Seker (-): the success that can be achieved through hard work, zealousness, energetic action, initiative, courage, leadership, and entrepreneurship is jeopardized by lack of planning, steadfastness.
Herukhuti (-)/Seker (+): hastiness, arrogance, impetuousness, rashness, violence, libertinism will subtract from the success that can be achieved through the capacity to sustain deep protracted thinking, good organizational ability, and the appreciation for structure, and limitations; One is checked in one's forward movement by the inner forces of order. Submit in humility.
Herukhuti (-)/Seker (-): hastiness, arrogance, impetuousness, rashness, violence, libertinism be exacerbated by the lack of spiritual power, lack of success in

working with hekau (words of power), lack of concentration; Starting, or going forward without a plan will lead you into complications, and obstructions.

Herukhuti/Maat:

Herukhuti (+)/Maat (+): They are supplementaries. Herukhuti receives from Maat the foundation for its execution of justice. Without Herukhuti how many will listen to Maat? Their working together is the preservation of order, and harmony in society; The carrying out of penalties, wars, and the use of force to right or prevent wrongs must be based on divine law.

Herukhuti (+)/Maat (-): the success that can come from hard work, zealousness, energetic action is jeopardized by ignorance of the law, inability to see the whole, lack of sharing.

Herukhuti (-)/Maat (+): hastiness, arrogance, impetuousness, rashness, violence, libertinism will subtract from the success that can be achieved through a view of the whole, knowledge of the law, optimism, and a sharing attitude; Sticks and stones are stronger than words, thus you proceed on the offensive. But as right is not on your side, humiliation. Thus the gentle feather of Maat restrains the strong.

Herukhuti (-)/Maat (-): hastiness, arrogance, impetuousness, rashness, violence, libertinism combined with ignorance of the law, inability to see the whole, lack of sharing; greed, problems with the law and officials.

Herukhuti/Herukhuti

Herukhuti (+)/Herukhuti (+): success through hard work, zealousness, energetic action, initiative, courage, leadership, and entrepreneurship. Maintain awareness of the principles of just treatment of others. It is the source of the divine assistance for the overcoming of the obstructions in your way.

Herukhuti (+)/Herukhuti (-): the success that can be achieved through hard work, zealousness, initiative, courage is in jeopardy by accidents, arrogance, rashness, etc.; beware of fire, weapons, sharp instruments, etc.

327

Herukhuti (-)/Herukhuti (+): Your opponent's strength is superior to yours. Retreat; curb your rashness, overconfidence.

Herukhuti (-)/Herukhuti (-): hastiness, arrogance, impetuousness, rashness, violence, libertinism; danger from fire, weapons, accidents, mean people, alcoholic indulgence, drugs, tobacco.

Herukhuti/Heru

Herukhuti (+)/Heru (+): the capacity for hard work, zealousness, energetic action, enterprise, initiative, fair play combined with an enlightened will, and magnanimity are qualities that make for powerful leadership, and great accomplishments. Beware of overstrain; The confidence of the warriors will be bolstered if the leader fights with them.

Herukhuti (+)/Heru (-): the success that can be achieved through hard work, zealousness, energetic action, initiative, courage, leadership, and entrepreneurship can be jeopardized by arrogance, incorrect use of the will, strongheadedness, dictatorialness.

Herukhuti (-)/Heru (+): hastiness, arrogance, impetuousness, rashness, violence, libertinism will subtract from the success that can be achieved through good administrative abilities; The conflict, and contention can be resolved by a person who possesses the authority, and impartiality (independence of the will); There are times when a man has no choice but to proceed with a dangerous enterprise. Men Ab is the key for successfully treading on the tail of a tiger, as it is the foundation of caution, and circumspection.

Herukhuti (-)/Heru (-): hastiness, arrogance, impetuousness, rashness, violence, libertinism combined with an ignorant self-willedness; An army without leadership. Mob violence.

Herukhuti/Het-Heru

Herukhuti (+)/Het-Heru (+): inflamed passions, sexual desire; zealousness, energetic action combined with a fertile imagination, the ability to coordinate; small successes.

Herukhuti (+)/Het-Heru (-): the success that can be achieved through hard work, zealousness, energetic action, initiative, courage, leadership, and entrepreneurship is

328

jeopardized by carelessness, negligence, illusions, addiction to pleasure; surgery of the female organs.

Herukhuti (-)/Het-Heru (+): over exaggerated sensualism and passion, too amorous, hard to satisfy

Herukhuti (-)/Het-Heru (-): immorality, wayward impulses, wanderlust, excessive passion, tactlessness; excessive menstrual flow.

Herukhuti/Sebek

Herukhuti (+)/Sebek (+): analytical ability combined with attention to details are essential for discriminating, and separating issues in a complex situation. Success in litigations, scientific inquiries, difficult negotiations. Championing a cause through the media.

Herukhuti (+)/Sebek (-): Differences are understood generally, and in principle, but there is an inability to identify the specific manifestations associated with them. One is up to the struggle but fails to clearly communicate one's position.

Herukhuti (-)/Sebek (+): Despite the correctness of one's logic, and rationalizations, one is not motivated by truth but by anger, revenge, rash impulses, zealousness, etc.

Herukhuti (-)/Sebek (-): hastiness, arrogance, impetuousness, rashness, violence, libertinism combined with false beliefs, illogical thinking, false definitions, erroneous concepts, the desire to ease the way through schemes.

Herukhuti/Auset

Herukhuti (+)/ Auset (+): the courage to sacrifice for others.

Herukhuti (+)/Auset (-): the success that can be achieved through hard work, zealousness, energetic action, initiative, courage, leadership, and entrepreneurship is jeopardized by indecisiveness, changeability, impressionability, sensitivity, emotionality, moodiness.

Herukhuti (-)/Auset (+): excitable behavior, excessive emotionalism, very impulsive.

Herukhuti (-)/Auset (-): very impulsive behavior, exaggerated emotionalism.

Herukhuti/Geb: See the section under Geb.

Herukhuti/Sheps: See the section under Sheps.

Herukhuti/Dark Deceased: See the section under Dark Deceased.

Herukhuti/Nekhebet: See the section under Nekhebet.

Herukhuti/Uatchet: See the section under Uatchet.

HERU

Heru/Amen

Heru (+)/Amen (+): Perseverance in the practice of the Men Ab meditation system will lead to realization of the essence of one's being; striving consistently to ignore one's conditioned emotional, and sensual behavioral patterns will liberate the will from the domination of the animal spirit.

Heru (+)/Amen (-): the success that can be achieved through a "strong will," good administrative skill, and magnanimity is jeopardized by attachment and receptivity to one's conditioned behavioral patterns.

Heru (-)/Amen (+): arrogance, incorrect use of the will, strongheadedness, dictatorialness, unreceptivity to guidance can be overcome through consistent perseverance in maintaining detachment from one's emotional and sensual conditionings.

Heru (-)/Amen (-): arrogance, incorrect use of the will, strongheadedness, dictatorialness, unreceptivity to guidance is exacerbated by attachment and receptivity to one's conditioned behavioral patterns; He gives up because of the difficulties encountered in getting an enterprise started. One must not persevere in such behavior.

Heru/Ausar

Heru (+)/Ausar (+): perseverance in the self-identification with the indwelling intelligence, maintaining a sense of unity with all will liberate the will from the domination of the animal spirit.

Heru (+)/Ausar (-): the success that can come from a strong will is jeopardized by the failure to transfer the self identification to the indwelling intelligence guiding all physiological and spiritual functions leading to disharmony, and obstructions.

Heru (-)/Ausar (+): arrogance, incorrect use of the will, strongheadedness, dictatorialness, unreceptivity to guidance will be corrected through rituals to Ausar.

330

Heru (-)/Ausar (-): arrogance, incorrect use of the will, strongheadedness, dictatorialness, unreceptivity to guidance combined disunion, ignorance of Self, or the failure to live according to one's true self.

Heru/Tehuti

Heru (+)/Tehuti (+): success results from allowing the will to be guided by wise counsel, optimism. A sharing, magnanimous, joyful attitude; The wise king has made the oracle the first, and final arbiter of all conflicts, and the indicator of all policies in the realm. His nation survives even after all of its citizens have been dispossessed from their homeland and scattered around the globe.

Heru (+)/Tehuti (-): the success that can be achieved through a strong will, and good administrative ability is jeopardized by incorrect intuitions, misjudgments, bad counsel, and lack of faith. In spite of your strong powers of observation, and great intelligence, you will not make it through a strange forest without a guide.

Heru (-)/Tehuti (+): arrogance, incorrect use of the will, strongheadedness, dictatorialness, unreceptivity to guidance will lead to failure unless the individual allows himself to be guided by wise counsel. Beware of extravagance.

Heru (-)/Tehuti (-): arrogance, incorrect use of the will, strongheadedness, dictatorialness, unreceptivity to guidance combined with incorrect intuitions, misjudgments, bad counsel; and lack of faith.

Heru/Seker

Heru (+)/Seker (+): An enlightened individual knows that before taking action on a decision there must be the knowledge of the underlying structure (the plan) governing what must be done. As the structural framework of all events are laid down by the deities, and spirits one, therefore, does not "make up a plan." Instead, the thought processes are stilled in order to "sense," and intuit the structural framework created by the spiritual agencies. In addition, every step taken in carrying out the undertaking must follow "the plan"; The capacity to lead long term, large, and difficult projects; before acting, he pauses and keeps his heart still (Men Ab). Thus he is able to see that all things are achieved in six stages, which he patiently goes through.

Heru (+)/Seker (-): the success that can be achieved by an enlightened will, and magnanimity is jeopardized by the incapacity to intuit the underlying structure of things; the lack of planning. You must persevere in your Men Ab.

Heru (-)/Seker (+): An unenlightened individual is ignorant of, or does not believe in (lacks direct experience) the fact that deities and spirits control the course of events for the purpose of establishing and maintaining order in the world. Thus, his plans are based on considerations that lack objective reality. He therefore runs into "delays," obstructions, denials, etc.

Heru (-)/Seker (-): arrogance, incorrect use of the will, strongheadedness, dictatorialness, unreceptivity to guidance combined with the incapacity to sustain deep protracted thinking, and the inability to understand the need for structure and limitations, or the lack of planning.

Heru/Maat

Heru (+)/Maat (+): the successful cultivation of the will is essential for developing the capacity to live truth; An effective will combined with optimism, and knowledge of the law. Great fortune. As your will is free, you may chose to continue on the road of amassing wealth, and fame, or you may cross the great abysm and continue on the path to the realization of your true self. Has not your heart been made as light as a feather to facilitate your flight across the great abyss?

Heru (+)/Maat (-): the success that can be achieved through a strong will, and administrative ability is jeopardized by ignorance of the law, inability to see the whole, lack of sharing.

Heru (-)/Maat (+): arrogance, incorrect use of the will, strongheadedness, dictatorialness, unreceptivity to guidance will lead to failure unless a view of the whole, knowledge of the law, optimism, and a sharing attitude are cultivated.

Heru (-)/Maat (-): arrogance, incorrect use of the will, strongheadedness, dictatorialness, unreceptivity to guidance combined with ignorance of the law, inability to see the whole, lack of sharing.

Heru/Herukhuti

Heru (+)/Herukhuti (+): the capacity for hard work, zealousness, energetic action, enterprise, initiative, fair play combined with an enlightened will, and magnanimity are qualities that make for powerful leadership, and great accomplishments. Beware of overstrain.

Heru (+)/Herukhuti (-): hastiness, arrogance, impetuousness, rashness, violence, libertinism will subtract from the success that can be achieved through good administrative abilities.

Heru (-)/Herukhuti (+): the success that can be achieved through hard work, zealousness, energetic action, initiative, courage, leadership, and entrepreneurship can be jeopardized by arrogance, incorrect use of the will, strongheadedness, dictatorialness.

Heru (-)/Herukhuti (-): hastiness, arrogance, impetuousness, rashness, violence, libertinism combined with an ignorant self-willedness.

Heru/Heru

Heru (+)/Heru (+): A man of worth and upright character has set himself up as the leader of his life, or of others by his own judgement. There will be some success, but in the long run there will be failure.

Heru (+)/Heru (-): Stop vacillating, persevere in Men Ab.

Heru (-)/Heru (+): failure will result if arrogance, incorrect use of the will, strongheadedness, dictatorialness, unreceptivity to guidance is persevered in. Fortunately, the subject of this metut (symbol) can change and allow himself to be guided.

Heru (-)/Heru (-): Believing that strength resides in the will itself, and that the freedom of the will is absolute, he does not follow sages, wise teachings, or believe in destiny. He will be crushed by his titanic aspirations.

Heru/Het-Heru

Heru (+)/Het-Heru (+): An enlightened will knows that there is no such thing as "will power." The realization of the will (what has been decided upon) is carried out by the life-force (Ra, chi, kundalini), which must first be receptive to what is being willed (Auset factor), and then gestated by the Het-Heru faculty. This gestation process consists in "the

333

enjoyment of one's intended objective in the imagination."
The sensations of joy, and pleasure (or negative feelings)
are expressions of the arousal of the life-force, and the
images that form the content of the daydream are the
spiritual molds that guide the physical forces to the
realization of the goal. As we saw in previous chapters, it is
often necessary to step up the level of enjoyment through
Kula yoga, "deity invocation" rituals, etc.

Heru (+)/Het-Heru (-): the success that can be achieved
through the proper exertion of the will is jeopardized by
carelessness, negligence, illusions, addiction to pleasure, etc.

Heru (-)/Het-Heru (+): An unenlightened individual [Heru
(-)] is ignorant that all inducers of pleasure are means of
arousing the life-force1. He thus either fails to cultivate, or
to moderate the induction of pleasure, thus failing due to a
lack of vital force. He then speaks ignorantly of weakness
of will, poor health, poor memory, and so on. His failure is
compounded by his ignorance of the function of images as
molds (matrices) for physical events. He gives power of
realization to unwanted or intolerable events by dwelling on
them in emotionally, and sensually charged visualizations.

Heru (-)/Het-Heru (-): arrogance, incorrect use of the will,
strongheadedness, dictatorialness, unreceptivity to guidance
combined with carelessness, negligence, illusions, addiction
to pleasure. Addiction to drugs, alcohol, fears.

Heru/Sebek

Heru (+)/Sebek (+): An enlightened individual knows that
the true purpose of cleverness (what passes for
"intelligence" in the west), and education (knowledge of
techniques: details of the steps, and processes of carrying
out a task) are for the easing of the way. I.e., for the
purpose of carrying out of tasks with the less effort, and
time, and maximum results; an enlightened will, and
magnanimity combined with attention to details, and good
logical ability. Successful middle management. Supervisors;
decisive actions further.

---

1. This is the great key to arousing kundalini that most yogis hide from the public.
All the techniques of yoga, are in reality means of intensifying the arousal, and the
insuring the free flow of the force.

Heru (+)/Sebek (-): the success that can be achieved through the exertion of the will, good administrative ability is jeopardized by false beliefs, illogical thinking, false definitions, erroneous concepts, the desire to ease the way through schemes; vacillation, and indecision due to confused thinking, or erroneous facts; Interference with the center of command. Dissension, insubordination..

Heru (-)/Sebek (+): arrogance, incorrect use of the will, strongheadedness, dictatorialness, unreceptivity to guidance will subtract from the success that can be achieved through a good education, good logical thinking.

Heru (-)/Sebek (-): arrogance, incorrect use of the will, strongheadedness, dictatorialness, unreceptivity to guidance combined with false beliefs, illogical thinking, false definitions, erroneous concepts, the desire to ease the way through schemes; indecision; being led astray by irrelevant issues; biased and prejudiced leadership; Rising to fame, and honor through questionable means.

Heru/Auset

Heru (+)/Auset (+): an enlightened will, and magnanimity, upright character combined with a positive receptivity, caring, patience, kindness, trance ability; A good family life, domestic policy, the foundation of society; Good relations between husband and wife; A calm and sympathetic leader; The will has been conceived, but it is not yet time to act. Continue to nourish the will to achieve your goal and your identity with Ausar through mediumistic trance.

Heru (+)/Auset (-): The exertion of the will achieves nothing if there is no harmony between it and the executive part of the spirit.

Heru (-)/Auset (+): the dominance of the will by the emotional side of life; A calm and sympathetic leader, or person in position of authority, yet unreceptive to opposition; Perfection in mediumistic trance will lead nowhere if we do not cultivate our will.

Heru (-)/Auset (-): an unstable will, inner contradictions, conflicts between what is known, and what is felt; ignorance of the proper use of the will, and of the function of mediumistic trance. Unproductiveness, stagnation; easily led to anger when opposed.

Heru/Geb: See the section under Geb.

Heru/Sheps: See the section under Sheps.

Heru/Dark Deceased: See the section under Dark Deceased.

Heru/Nekhebet: See the section under Nekhebet.

Heru/Uatchet: See the section under Uatchet.

HET HERU

Het-Heru/Amen

> Het-Heru (+)/Amen (+): the true source of joy is within. Can you recreate the smell of a rose in your imagination? Of course you can. Then why not persevere in recreating a feeling of peace by merely willing it? Why hold such an important thing as peace (Hetep) ransom to externals over which you have no control?
>
> Het-Heru (+)/Amen (-): the success that can be achieved through an outgoing joyful expression, a healthy urge to experience pleasure is jeopardized by attachment and receptivity to one's conditioned behavioral patterns.
>
> Het-Heru (-)/Amen (+): deviations in the manner in which joy is expressed, pleasure is sought, and wrong ideas about joy (failing to make it the engine for success, and instead waiting for success to be joyful) can be overcome through consistent perseverance in maintaining detachment from one's emotional and sensual conditionings.
>
> Het-Heru (-)/Amen (-): carelessness, negligence, illusions, addiction to pleasure is exacerbated by attachment, and receptivity to one's conditioned behavioral patterns; A man seeks pleasure in order to escape the boredom which has been caused by his inner emptiness. He will never find satisfaction. He may blame it on others, or the environment, or the situations in his life, and lose his most precious friend.

Het-Heru/Ausar

> Het-Heru (+)/Ausar (+): the love for unity, and peace. But little will be achieved as there is the inability to penetrate into the underlying shaping forces of unity; desire for unity, as opposed to the understanding of the factors that bring about true unity; they dedicate their love relationship to their mutual spiritual upliftment. Good fortune, but they must be guided by the sage.

336

Het-Heru (+)/Ausar (-): the success that can be achieved through an outgoing joyful expression, a healthy urge to experience pleasure is jeopardized by disunion, ignorance of Self, or the failure to live according to one's true self.

Het-Heru (-)/Ausar (+): deviations in the manner in which joy is expressed, pleasure is sought, and wrong ideas about joy (failing to make it the engine for success, and instead waiting for success to be joyful) can be overcome through perseverance in the self-identification with the indwelling intelligence, maintaining a sense of unity with all.

Het-Heru (-)/Ausar (-): carelessness, negligence, illusions, addiction to pleasure is exacerbated by disunion, ignorance of Self, or the failure to live according to one's true self.

Het-Heru/Tehuti

Het-Heru (+)/ Tehuti (+): an outgoing joyful expression, a healthy urge to experience pleasure combined with faith and optimism in wise counsel. good fortune.

Het-Heru (+)/Tehuti (-): a joyful expression, and healthy sexual attitude is obstructed by incorrect intuitions, judgements, counsel; lack of faith, etc. Errors in choosing a partner.

Het-Heru (-)/Tehuti (+): deviations in the manner in which joy is expressed, pleasure is sought, and wrong ideas about joy (failing to make it the engine for success, and instead waiting for success to be joyful) can subtract from the success that can be achieved through maintaining faith, and optimism in wise counsel.

Het-Heru (-)/Tehuti (-): carelessness, negligence, illusions, addiction to pleasure, combined with incorrect intuitions, misjudgments, bad counsel; and lack of faith. Errors in choosing a partner.

Het-Heru/Seker

Het-Heru (+)/Seker (+): a powerful, and positive imagination combined with good powers of concentration.

Het-Heru (+)/Seker (-): inner tension, and conflict caused by inhibitions, or unnatural scruples in opposition to the urge to experience joy, and pleasure.

Het-Heru (-)/Seker (+): carelessness, playfulness, negligence, extravagance will subtract from the success that can be achieved through the capacity to sustain deep protracted thinking, good organizational ability, and the appreciation for structure, and limitations; He does not take life seriously. If discipline is not applied, he will throw his life away.

Het-Heru (-)/Seker (-): jealousy, sexual inhibitions, coldheartedness; separations, aberrant urges, phobias; Worn out, and prematurely aged from sensual excesses.

Het-Heru/Maat

Het-Heru (+)/Maat (+): a view of the whole, knowledge of the law, optimism, and a sharing attitude combined with an outgoing joyful expression, a healthy urge to experience pleasure; a happy marriage, success in business, a harmonious partnership, good health.

Het-Heru (+)/Maat (-): the success that can come from an outgoing joyful expression, a healthy urge to experience pleasure is jeopardized by ignorance of the law, inability to see the whole, lack of sharing.

Het-Heru (-)/Maat (+): carelessness, negligence, illusions, addiction to pleasure will subtract from the success that can be achieved through a view of the whole, knowledge of the law, optimism, and a sharing attitude.

Het-Heru (-)/Maat (-): extravagance, sensual greed, bad judgement; losses.

Het-Heru/Herukhuti

Het-Heru (+)/Herukhuti (+): an energized healthy attraction to pleasure, and imagination. Significant success can be achieved, if one remains aware of the ever lurking danger of overindulgence. Men Ab!; a strong manifestation of the Ra force.

Het-Heru (+)/Herukhuti (-): As above, with the difference that there is greater danger of being carried away.

Het-Heru (-)/Herukhuti (+): As below, but with less drive to indulge.

Het-Heru (-)/Herukhuti (-): immorality, wayward impulses, wanderlust, excessive passion, tactlessness; excessive menstrual flow.

338

Het-Heru/Heru

Het-Heru (+)/Heru (+): an enlightened will in combination with a vivid imagination. Success will come from vision, inventiveness, flexibility.

Het-Heru (+)/Heru (-): there is danger of excesses, and waywardness in the expression of emotion, romance, the pursuit of pleasure because of "weakness of the will"; extravagance, intemperance.

Het-Heru (-)/Heru (+): the success that can be achieved through an enlightened and "strong" will is jeopardized by carelessness, negligence, illusions, addiction to pleasure.

Het-Heru (-)/Heru (-): arrogance, incorrect use of the will, strongheadedness, dictatorialness, unreceptivity to guidance combined with carelessness, negligence, illusions, addiction to pleasure. Addiction to drugs, alcohol, fears.

Het-Heru/Het-Heru

Het-Heru (+)/Het-Heru (+): an outgoing joyful expression, a healthy urge to experience pleasure will nourish your vitality (Ra) and bring about success in relatively small undertakings.

Het-Heru (+)/Het-Heru (-): Unstable in the expression of affection, joy, and the capacity to enjoy. The source of an unstable will.

Het-Heru (-)/Het-Heru (+): In love with love. Many people are more interested in being in a relationship than the person with whom they are involved. He collects art more for the gratification of the senses, than for a true appreciation of the intrinsic values.

Het-Heru (-)/Het-Heru (-): A fool who will not heed, must be left to learn from his own foolhardiness.

Het-Heru/Sebek (hermaphrodite)

Het-Heru (+)/Sebek (+): a strong and positive imagination combined with attention to details, and good logical thinking; creative writing, charismatic speaker, poetry, inventiveness (scientific, and artistic).

Het-Heru (+)/Sebek (-): illusions: a powerful, and fertile imagination combined with false beliefs, illogical thinking, false definitions, erroneous concepts, the desire to ease the way through schemes

Het-Heru (-)/Sebek (+): carelessness, negligence, illusions, addiction to pleasure will subtract from the success that can be achieved through a good education, good logical ability.

Het-Heru (-)/Sebek (-): carelessness, negligence, illusions, addiction to pleasure combined with false beliefs, illogical thinking, false definitions, erroneous concepts, the desire to ease the way through schemes.

Het-Heru/Auset

Het-Heru (+)/Auset (+): Contentment with a peaceful, comfortable situation. Good relations with women. A joyful, pleasurable situation.

Het-Heru (+)/Auset (-): unstable, changeable, unpredictable relationship, social situation.

Het-Heru (-)/Auset (+): Same as in the preceding.

Het-Heru (-)/Auset (-): excessive craving for creature comforts; insecurity, indecisiveness, impressionability, emotionality, delusions.

Het-Heru/Geb: See the section under Geb.

Het-Heru/Sheps: See the section under Sheps.

Het-Heru/Dark Deceased: See the section under Dark Deceased.

Het-Heru/Nekhebet: See the section under Nekhebet.

Het-Heru/Uatchet: See the section under Uatchet.

SEBEK

Sebek/Amen

Sebek (+)/Amen (+): the way is open to Self realization, and great spiritual power by persevering in making our essential unconditioned being the premise for all the reasons we give ourselves for what we do. See the second stage of initiation, and meditation.

Sebek (+)/Amen (-): the success that can be achieved through a good education, good logical thinking, attention to details is jeopardized by attachment, and receptivity to one's conditioned behavioral patterns

Sebek (-)/Amen (+): false beliefs, illogical thinking, false definitions, erroneous concepts, the desire to ease the way through schemes can be overcome by consistent perseverance in maintaining detachment from one's emotional and sensual conditionings.

Sebek (-)/Amen (-): false beliefs, illogical thinking, false definitions, erroneous concepts, the desire to ease the way through schemes is exacerbated by attachment, and receptivity to one's conditioned behavioral patterns.

Sebek/Ausar

Sebek (+)/Ausar (+): a good education, good logical thinking, attention to details combined with perseverance in the self-identification with the indwelling intelligence, maintaining a sense of unity with all.

Sebek (+)/Ausar (-): the success that can be achieved through a good education, good logical thinking, attention to details is jeopardized by disunion, ignorance of Self, or the failure to live according to one's true self

Sebek (-)/Ausar (+): false beliefs, illogical thinking, false definitions, erroneous concepts, the desire to ease the way through schemes, segregative behavior can be overcome through perseverance in the self-identification with the indwelling intelligence, maintaining a sense of unity with all.

Sebek (-)/Ausar (-): false beliefs, illogical thinking, false definitions, erroneous concepts, the desire to ease the way through schemes is exacerbated by the failure to transfer the self identification to the indwelling intelligence guiding all physiological and spiritual functions leading to disharmony, and obstructions; beware of trickery, selfishness, con artists.

Sebek/Tehuti

Sebek (+)/Tehuti (+): When education, beliefs, and rationalizations are in harmony with the oracles, and the counsel from the sage, the way to success is open; Despite his good education, he gives his head to the sage. Good fortune.

Sebek (+)/Tehuti (-): in spite of a good education, good logical thinking, attention to details, success is jeopardized by incorrect intuitions, misjudgments, bad counsel; and lack of faith.

Sebek (-)/Tehuti (+): He fails to offer his head to the teacher. Misfortune. The way is open for success if faith, optimism in wise counsel, and correct intuitions are

341

cultivated, but one is obstructed by the failure to recognize that the possession of an education-knowledge of definitions, and descriptions, and the ability to derive logical permutations from them, does not in itself constitute knowledge of reality; pride; shallow and linear thinking; desire to ease the way through schemes; To repeatedly question the oracle, or the teacher on the same subject because of doubt, mistrust, or argumentativeness will bring humiliation.

Sebek (-)/Tehuti (-): incorrect intuitions, misjudgments, bad counsel; and lack of faith coupled with wrong education, faulty logic, pride, selfishness, a trickster mentality; foolhardiness, craziness, insanity. Rituals to Sebek, and Tehuti. Palm oil oleation therapy (see Ayurvedic medicine), nervines, etc. Seek counsel, but be honest, and sincere. You can only trick yourself.

Sebek/Seker

Sebek (+)/Seker (+): the capacity to sustain deep protracted thinking, good organizational ability, and the appreciation for structure, and limitations coupled with good attention to definitions, descriptions, phases of operation, logics, and details. Success in scholarly, philosophical, and scientific endeavors.

Sebek (+)/Seker (-): the success that can be achieved through a good education, good logical thinking, attention to details is jeopardized by the incapacity to sustain deep protracted thinking, and the inability to understand the need for structure and limitations, or the lack of planning, overthinking.

Sebek (-)/Seker (+): the success that can be achieved through a good plan, organization and structure is jeopardized by false beliefs, illogical thinking, false definitions, erroneous concepts, the desire to ease the way through schemes. A reputation built through many years of hard work is jeopardized by slanderers, mischief workers, gossipers. The young and inexperienced should let the elder, and experienced lead.

Sebek (-)/Seker (-): One is afflicted by the incapacity to sustain deep protracted thinking, and the inability to understand the need for structure and limitations coupled with false beliefs, illogical thinking, false definitions, erroneous concepts, the desire to ease the way through schemes. Lack of planning coupled with wrong ideas, and illogical thinking. There will be delays, failure, false theories. Beware of misrepresentations; mistrustfulness. Nervines, and rest might prove helpful.

Sebek/Maat

Sebek (+)/Maat (+): a view of the whole, knowledge of the law, optimism, and a sharing attitude coupled with a correct belief system, and good logical thinking. The ability to relate specifics to their parental general principle. Success.

Sebek (+)/Maat (-): the success that can be achieved through a good education, good logical thinking, attention to details is jeopardized by ignorance of the law, inability to see the whole, lack of sharing.

Sebek (-)/Maat (+): false beliefs, illogical thinking, false definitions, erroneous concepts, the desire to ease the way through schemes can be overcome through a view of the whole, knowledge of the law, optimism, and a sharing attitude.

Sebek (-)/Maat (-): false beliefs, illogical thinking, false definitions, erroneous concepts, the desire to ease the way through schemes is exacerbated by ignorance of the law, inability to see the whole, lack of sharing; Inability to unify ideas due to the inability to perceive the whole.

Sebek/Herukhuti

Sebek (+)/Herukhuti (+): a good education, good logical thinking, attention to details combined with hard work, zealousness, energetic action, initiative, courage, leadership, and entrepreneurship; success in litigations, conducting the fight through the media.

Sebek (+)/Herukhuti (-): the success that can be achieved through a good education, good logical thinking, attention to details is jeopardized through hastiness, arrogance, impetuousness, rashness, violence, libertinism; negotiations, and arguments that degenerate into violence.

Sebek (-)/Herukhuti (+): false beliefs, illogical thinking, false definitions, erroneous concepts, the desire to ease the way through schemes will subtract from the success that can be achieved through hard work, zealousness, energetic action, initiative, courage, leadership, and entrepreneurship.

343

Sebek (-)/Herukhuti (-): nagging, nervousness, argumentative, a libertine, a busy body, verbal abuse.

Sebek/Heru

Sebek (+)/Heru (+): a good education, good logical thinking, attention to details combined and controlled by an enlightened will, and good administrative skills.

Sebek (+)/Heru (-): the success that can be achieved through a good education, good logical thinking, attention to details is jeopardized by arrogance, incorrect use of the will, strongheadedness, dictatorialness, unreceptivity to guidance.

Sebek (-)/Heru (+): false beliefs, illogical thinking, false definitions, erroneous concepts, the desire to ease the way through schemes can be overcome by Men Ab; Success through cultivation of sincerity. It is found not in clever words, but in the uprightness of one's character (Men Ab).

Sebek (-)/Heru (-): Argumentative, proud, and disrespectful of people in authoritative positions. As a result unity with others cannot be achieved.

Sebek/Het-Heru

Sebek (+)/Het-Heru (+): a strong and positive imagination combined with attention to details, and good logical thinking; creative writing, charismatic speaker, poetry, inventiveness (scientific, and artistic).

Sebek (+)/Het-Heru (-): the success that can be achieved through a good education, good logical thinking, attention to details is jeopardized by carelessness, negligence, illusions, addiction to pleasure.

Sebek (-)/Het-Heru (+): illusions: a powerful, and fertile imagination combined with false beliefs, illogical thinking, false definitions, erroneous concepts, the desire to ease the way through schemes.

Sebek (-)/Het-Heru (-): carelessness, negligence, illusions, addiction to pleasure combined with false beliefs, illogical thinking, false definitions, erroneous concepts, the desire to ease the way through schemes.

Sebek/Sebek

Sebek (+)/Sebek (+): Very good logical ability. Success in finite situations (technological undertakings).

344

Sebek (+)/Sebek (-): Your intentions are sincere, but everything you say is distorted by others out of mischief; Some people are incapable of discerning the logical from the illogical. They believe that all perspectives are valid, and must be given a chance to play a role in decision making. Misfortune.

Sebek (-)/Sebek (+): Wrong ideas, wrong facts can be corrected by educating oneself on the situation. Check your logic. Remember the chief rule of logic,- "logical but not necessarily true."

Sebek (-)/Sebek (-): In the end, you can only fool yourself.

Sebek/Auset

Sebek (+)/Auset (+): a good memory, a fertile imagination, caring, sincerity, good trance ability, kindness, tenderness combined with a good education, good logical thinking, attention to details; creative writing.

Sebek (+)/Auset (-): the success that can be achieved through a good education, good logical thinking, attention to details is jeopardized by indecisiveness, changeability, impressionability, sensitivity, emotionality, moodiness.

Sebek (-)/Auset (+): false beliefs, illogical thinking, false definitions, erroneous concepts, the desire to ease the way through schemes will subtract from the success that can be achieved through a good memory, a fertile imagination, caring, sincerity, good trance ability, kindness, tenderness.

Sebek (-)/Auset (-): indecisiveness, changeability, impressionability, sensitivity, emotionality, moodiness combined with false beliefs, illogical thinking, false definitions, erroneous concepts, the desire to ease the way through schemes;

Sebek/Geb: See the section under Geb.
Sebek/Sheps: See the section under Sheps.
Sebek/Dark Deceased: See the section under Dark Deceased.
Sebek/Nekhebet: See the section under Nekhebet.
Sebek/Uatchet: See the section under Uatchet.

AUSET

Auset/Amen

Auset (+)/Amen (+): devotion to realizing Self; consistent perseverance in maintaining detachment from one's emotional and sensual conditionings.

Auset (+)/Amen (-): successful trance work will be wasted due to attachment, and receptivity to one's conditioned behavioral patterns.

Auset (-)/Amen (+): indecisiveness, changeability, impressionability, sensitivity, emotionality, moodiness will be corrected by consistent perseverance in maintaining detachment from one's emotional and sensual conditionings.

Auset (-)/Amen (-): indecisiveness, changeability, impressionability, sensitivity, emotionality, moodiness is exacerbated by attachment, and receptivity to one's conditioned behavioral patterns; negative mediumism.

Auset/Ausar

Auset (+)/Ausar (+): perseverance in the self-identification with the indwelling intelligence, maintaining a sense of unity with all is the foundation of religion, and spiritual development. In every person there is an urge to follow someone, or something. While upright people are the proper role models for us to follow in our youth, we must come to realize eventually that Ausar is our true Self, and the deities are the true models (archetypes) of the personality masks that we must assume in order to meet the various situations in life.

Auset (+)/Ausar (-): the success that can be achieved through a good memory, a fertile imagination, caring, sincerity, good trance ability, kindness, tenderness is jeopardized by disunion, ignorance of Self, or the failure to live according to one's true self.

Auset (-)/Ausar (+): indecisiveness, changeability, impressionability, sensitivity, emotionality, moodiness can be corrected by perseverance in the self-identification with the indwelling intelligence, maintaining a sense of unity with all.

Auset (-)/Ausar (-): indecisiveness, changeability, impressionability, sensitivity, emotionality, moodiness is

exacerbated by disunion, ignorance of Self, or the failure to
live according to one's true self

Auset/Tehuti

Auset (+)/Tehuti (+): a good memory, a fertile
imagination, caring, sincerity, good trance ability, kindness,
tenderness combined with good counsel, correct intuitions,
optimism.

Auset (+)/Tehuti (-): a good memory, a fertile imagination,
caring, sincerity, good trance ability, kindness, tenderness
combined with incorrect intuitions, misjudgments, bad
counsel; and lack of faith.

Auset (-)/Tehuti (+): indecisiveness, changeability,
impressionability, sensitivity, emotionality, moodiness will
subtract from the success that can be achieved through good
counsel, correct intuitions, optimism.

Auset (-)/Tehuti (-): incorrect intuitions, misjudgments,
bad counsel; and lack of faith combined with indecisiveness,
changeability, impressionability, sensitivity, emotionality,
moodiness

Auset/Seker

Auset (+)/Seker (+): a good memory, a fertile
imagination, caring, sincerity, good trance ability, kindness,
tenderness combined with the capacity to sustain deep
protracted thinking, good organizational ability, and the
appreciation for structure, and limitations; deep
mediumistic trance; the power to successfully manifest the
powers of the hekau;

Auset (+)/Seker (-): the success that can be achieved
through good counsel, correct intuitions, optimism is
jeopardized by the incapacity to sustain deep protracted
thinking, and the inability to understand the need for
structure and limitations, or the lack of planning.

Auset (-)/Seker (+): indecisiveness, changeability,
impressionability, sensitivity, emotionality, moodiness will
subtract from the success that can be achieved through good
planning, assistance from elders.

Auset (-)/Seker (-): indecisiveness, changeability,
impressionability, sensitivity, emotionality, moodiness
combined with the incapacity to sustain deep protracted
thinking, and the inability to understand the need for

structure and limitations, or the lack of planning; are not your excessive love of ease, and receptivity to your creature comforts omens that the winter of your life is just around the corner?; "Street people," vagrants, the homeless, rolling stones.

Auset/Maat

Auset (+)/Maat (+): a good memory, a fertile imagination, caring, sincerity, good trance ability, kindness, tenderness combined with a view of the whole, knowledge of the law, optimism, and a sharing attitude; success through popularity, a joyful caring, patient attitude in dealing with others; a humble follower of the law, but lacking in the understanding of its intricacies. Great success, nevertheless.
Auset (+)/Maat (-): the success that can be achieved through a good memory, a fertile imagination, caring, sincerity, good trance ability, kindness, tenderness is jeopardized by ignorance of the law, inability to see the whole, greed; Sincere, and humble, but following a wrong belief system, ignorant laws.
Auset (-)/Maat (+): indecisiveness, changeability, impressionability, sensitivity, emotionality, moodiness will subtract from the success that can be achieved through a view of the whole, knowledge of the law, optimism; unreceptivity to the law due to fears, irrationality, etc.
Auset (-)/Maat (-): indecisiveness, changeability, impressionability, sensitivity, emotionality, moodiness combined with ignorance of the law, inability to see the whole, lack of sharing. Needs outside help.

Auset/Herukhuti

Auset (+)/Herukhuti (+): the "courage" to sacrifice for others due to love, and devotion.
Auset (+)/Herukhuti (-): impulsive behavior, exaggerated emotionalism, tendency to violent emotions.
Auset (-)/Herukhuti (+): indecisiveness, changeability, impressionability, sensitivity, emotionality, moodiness will subtract from the success that can be achieved through hard work, zealousness, energetic action, initiative, courage, leadership; unstable in enterprise.

348

Auset (-)/Herukhuti (-): very impulsive behavior, exaggerated emotionalism, violent emotions. inner conflict between anger and fear.

Auset/Heru

Auset (+)/Heru (+): a good memory, a fertile imagination, caring, sincerity, good trance ability, kindness, tenderness in combination with an enlightened will, and magnanimity; He takes an upright man as his role model. Although there will be success, in the long run it must be transcended. See Auset/Ausar.

Auset (+)/Heru (-): the success that can be achieved through a good memory, a fertile imagination, good trance ability, is jeopardized by arrogance, incorrect use of the will, strongheadedness, dictatorialness, unreceptivity to guidance.

Auset (-)/Heru (+): Indiscriminate imitation of others, however upright they may be, will only serve to compound the difficulties involved in the quest for Self realization.

Auset (-)/Heru (-): Indiscriminate imitation of the unworthy. This is a common feature in today's society. It is customary to make role models out of people for their talent without regard to their character.

Auset/Het-Heru

Auset (+)/Het-Heru (+): A good memory, and receptivity combined with a joyful disposition, and a fertile imagination. Good potential for psychic, mediumistic, creative, artistic works; a sweet, loving, kind, charming person, or situation. Success in small things; psychic achievements which by themselves will not increase the level of spiritual development.

Auset (+)/Het-Heru (-):the success that can be achieved through a good memory, a fertile imagination, caring, sincerity, good trance ability, kindness, tenderness is jeopardized by carelessness, negligence, illusions, addiction to pleasure.

Auset (-)/Het-Heru (+): indecisiveness, changeability, impressionability, sensitivity, emotionality, moodiness will subtract from the success that can be achieved through an outgoing joyful expression, a healthy urge to experience pleasure.

Auset (-)/Het-Heru (-): indecisiveness, changeability, impressionability, sensitivity, emotionality, moodiness compounded by carelessness, negligence, illusions, addiction to pleasure, and the bad effects of wasted vitality.

Auset/Sebek

Auset (+)/Sebek (+): a good memory, a fertile imagination, caring, sincerity, good trance ability, kindness, tenderness combined with a good education, good logical thinking, attention to details; creative writing.

Auset (+)/Sebek (-): the success that can be achieved through a good memory, a fertile imagination, caring, sincerity, good trance ability, kindness, tenderness is jeopardized by false beliefs, illogical thinking, false definitions, erroneous concepts, the desire to ease the way through schemes.

Auset (-)/Sebek (+): indecisiveness, changeability, impressionability, sensitivity, emotionality, moodiness will subtract from the success that can be achieved through a good education, good logical thinking, attention to details; interrupted education, an unreliable clerk.

Auset (-)/Sebek (-): indecisiveness, changeability, impressionability, sensitivity, emotionality, moodiness combined with false beliefs, illogical thinking, false definitions, erroneous concepts, the desire to ease the way through schemes;

Auset/Auset

Auset (+)/Auset (+): success through a good memory, a fertile imagination, caring, sincerity, good trance ability, kindness, tenderness, messages received through dreams.

Auset (+)/Auset (-): Overdependence on the success achieved through spiritual receptivity, or mediumistic (hypnotic) trance ability. Aware that many of their hunches, dreams, come true (they conveniently ignore those that don't--ok), many people believe that they do not have to exert themselves further in spiritual training, and development. The same is true for many trance mediums who mistake their ability for wisdom, and spiritual power. They are unaware that they have not even taken the 1st of the 10 steps towards the realization of their true self. Emotional instability.

350

Auset (-)/Auset (+): Same as in the preceding.

Auset (θ)/Auset (θ): failure through an overlaxed st e of being manifesting indecisiveness, changea ility, impressionability, sensitivity, emotionality, moodiness. Correct it through exercise.

Auset/Geb: See the section under Geb.
Auset/Sheps: See the section under Sheps.
Auset/Dark Deceased: See the section under Dark Deceased.
Auset/Nekhebet: See the section under Nekhebet.
Auset/Uatchet: See the section under Uatchet.

GEB

All of the readings of Geb indicate the interactions between the physical body and the mental/emotional faculties.

Geb as the first card symbolizes the effect that the deity (second card), especially the emotions, and lifestyle has upon the health.
Geb as the second card symbolizes the effect that the physical health has upon the emotions, and thus the mental activities symbolized by the deity.

It is very important to note that often times, the oracle will utilize Geb metutu as metaphors for the state of "health" of an undertaking. Meditate clearly on all readings.

SHEPS

All Sheps readings indicate that a beneficent ancestor will assist in the undertaking under the guidance of the deity indicated in the other half of the reading. Where the deity card is negative, then corrective measures regarding the faculty represented should be taken.

DARK DECEASED

All dark deceased readings indicate that a disturbed ancestor will interfere in the undertaking under the guidance of the deity indicated in the other half of the reading. Uplift the deceased

351

by invoking the deity represented in the other half of the reading, and meditating on the virtues of the deity.

Dark deceased/Sheps: Invoke Tehuti on behalf of the deceased.

Dark deceased/Dark Deceased: An intractable deceased. Strong methods must be used. See a competent traditional African priest, or priestess.

NEKHEBET

In all of the metutu that follow Nekhebet (+) symbolizes the attainment, protection, etc. through psychic influences, regarding the affairs under the dominion of the respective deity. Nekhebet (-) symbolizes obstructions, and dangers from receptivity to, or generation of negative psychic energies. Review Chapters 18, and 19.

The following formula is to be followed in understanding the various combinations:

Nekhebet/Deity
    Nekhebet (+)/Deity (+): Success through psychic forces, in the affairs governed by the deity (E.g.: Heru- promotion, favor from people in authority, etc.; Sebek,- litigation, business, studies, writings, etc.)
    Nekhebet (+)/Deity (-): The assistance of psychic influences are nullified by deficits, and negativities represented by the deity.
    Nekhebet (-)/Deity (+): Negative psychic influences will interfere with success in spite of the good qualities.
    Nekhebet (-)/Deity (-): Negative psychic influences combined with deficiencies in your being.

Nekhebet/Amen
    (+): striving consistently to ignore one's conditioned emotional, and sensual behavioral patterns (cultivating Hetep) is the chief means of safely, and effectively developing one's psychic powers, and protecting oneself from negative psychic influences; The power derived from

352

an offering of Hetep (unassailable inner peace) is superior to the ashe of blood, plants, stones, etc..

(-): the reversal of the above.

Nekhebet/Ausar

(+): perseverance in the self-identification with the indwelling intelligence, maintaining a sense of unity with all is the chief means of safely, and effectively developing one's psychic abilities.

(-): perseverance in the self-identification with the indwelling intelligence, maintaining a sense of unity with all is the chief means of protecting one's person from negative psychic influences (exorcism, hex breaking, etc.).

Nekhebet/Tehuti

(+): Thursday during the two hours of the jupiter, wear white, and blue, face west, chant Ung (oong), and visualize your objective. Offer, and eat rice mixed with cow's or soya milk, and the articles of Tehuti. Better results in the waxing moon.

(-): Beware during the period of 1:30 p.m. - 3:00 p.m.

Nekhebet/Seker

(+): Saturday during the two hours of Saturn, wear indigo, face South, chant Ong, and visualize your objective. Offer the articles of Seker. Better results in the waxing moon.

(-): Beware during the period of 9 a.m. - 10:30 a.m.

Nekhebet/Maat

(+): Thursday during the two hours of the jupiter, wear yellow, face west, chant Ung (oong), and visualize your objective. Offer, and eat rice mixed with cow's or soya milk, and the articles of Maat. Better results in the waxing moon.

(-): Beware during the period of 1:30 p.m. - 3:00 p.m.

Nekhebet/Herukhuti

(+): Tuesday during the two hours of Mars, only if you have been just, wear red, face east, chant Ang, and visualize your objective. Offer red objects (red candle, cloth, etc.), and the articles of Herukhuti. Better results in waxing moon.

(-): Beware of period from 3-4:30 pm, tuesdays.

353

Nekhebet/Heru

(+): Sunday during the two hours of the Sun, face north, wear red, and white, chant Ang, visualize your objective. Offer the articles of Heru. Better results in the waxing moon.

(-): Beware during the period of 4:30 p.m. - 6:00 p.m.

Nekhebet/Het-Heru

(+): Friday during the two hours of venus, face north, wear yellow and green, chant eng, and visualize your objective. Offer the articles of Het-Heru. Better results in the waxing moon.

(-): Beware during the period of 10:30 a.m. - 12 noon.

Nekhebet/Sebek

(+): Wednesday during the two hours of mercury, face west, wear white, chant iing, and visualize your objective. Offer Sebek's articles. Better results in the waxing moon.

(-): Beware during the period of 12 noon - 1:30 p.m.

Nekhebet/Auset

(+): Monday during the two hours of the moon, face south, wear white, chant eng, and visualize your objective. Offer rice mixed with cow's or soya milk, and Auset's articles. Better results in the waxing moon.

(-): Beware during the period of 7:30 a.m. - 9:00 a.m.

Nekhebet/Geb

(+): Improve your psychic vitality through kundalini yoga breathing practices. Dhumo (Gtummo), Surya Bedhana, Chandra Bhedana, Nadi shuddi, Bhastrika, etc.

(-): Psychic imbalance due to violations of health laws. Clogged psychic channels. Acupuncture, and/or moxa will help.

Nekhebet/Sheps

Beneficent psychic influences acting in concert with a helpful ancestor.

Nekhebet/Dark Deceased

Negative psychic influences acting in concert with a dark deceased. See a competently trained traditional African priest, or priestess.

Nekhebet/Nekhebet

(+): Positive psychic influences are surrounding you. To the degree that you can maintain your aura pure, and your vitality strong (avoid sex, and dissipating pleasures) you will attain successes in material undertakings, especially from favors of others. Chant Aung Hrang Hring Hraung, offer Heru's articles, and visualize your objective.

(-): Negative psychic influences are surrounding you. Pay attention to all of the things that will reestablish your vitality. Chant Aung Hrang Hring Hraung, offer Heru's articles, and visualize your objective.

Nekhebet/Uatchet

(+): Psychic forces responsible for assistance from others, psychic affairs, meetings with spiritualists, etc.; Psychic protection.

(-): Negative psychic forces inspiring meetings with low minded people, and all sorts of malefic experiences; Psychic disequilibrium. Are you performing psychic, yogic, and Chi practices without proper guidance?

UATCHET

Uatchet/Uatchet

(+): Psychic influences can aid you in business, and negotiations, contest, etc. making you more shrewd. Be mindful of staying within the boundaries of what is right; Assistance from grandparents, trade with foreign countries, religious pilgrimages, psychic affairs; Psychic protection. Chant Aung shrang shring shraung, offer Auset's articles, and visualize your objective.

(-): intrigues, hidden enemies, illegal activities, suicide, murder, contagious diseases, etc. inspired through subtle forces. Chant Aung Shrang shring shraung, offer Auset's articles, and visualize your objective. Improve your vitality through aerobics, deep diaphragmatic breathing, etc. You are too lax. Pay attention to what you are receptive to, who, and what you follow.

For all other combinations of Uatchet, read Nekhebet's material.

355

Chapter 21

CONSULTING THE ORACLE

Your Very First Reading

Please read this entire chapter before your first reading.

Because high oracles are means of communicating with the divine part of your spirit (the second sphere), it is very important to establish and maintain a proper relationship with the oracle. Before performing your very first reading you must bathe just before the reading, and put on clean clothes. Spread a new cloth (about 24" X 24"), white, and or blue, on a clean spot, and say the following prayer. It is part of the material inscribed on the back of the cards.

As Tehuti, semaaukheru Ausar er Kefta-f
Hail Tehuti, making victorious Ausar over his enemies.
Kerh pui en auba
On the night that of battle
au en arit saut Sebau
and of making the fettering of the Sebau.
Heru pu en hetem-tu kefta nu Nebertcher.
day that of destroying the enemies of Nebertcher.
Kerh pui en seauha Djed em Djeddjedtu.
Night that of making to stand the Djed in Djeddjedtu.

this is to be followed by the following which does not appear on the cards.

Anetch Hrauten Atef-Mut Neter
Salutation of Power Father-Mother Supreme Being
Ita em Tehuti
Who comes as Tehuti
Tua en Metu Neter
Thanks for the Words Divine
Pai-a Ab ani Tu.
My Heart (will/head) belongs to You.
Ab ani Tu.

From time to time (daily if you want to master divination) you should meditate on the meaning of the prayer. The Sebau correspond to your earth-born stock of information, as opposed to spiritual intuitions. Nebertcher means "Lord of the World." the "djed" is the symbol of the stability of heart achieved through mastery of Men Ab meditation. Ausar is your true self.

This prayer must also be said before your first reading of the day.

A most important observance that **women must** uphold is to **refrain from performing readings, or handling their cards when on their menses,** as menstrual blood-which is the ejection of an unfertilized egg-is a very powerful attractor of sublunar forces. She can however, receive readings.

The State of Mind, and Motives For Readings

We must keep uppermost in mind that the purpose of the oracle is to provide such counsel that will lead the querent to spiritual perfection by showing the spiritual meaning of mundane undertakings. You must therefore observe the following rules, and remain aware of the following principles in querying the oracle, otherwise you may get answers that may not be clearly intelligible, or might turn out to have been apparently the wrong counsel.

1. Avoid questions that are purely materialistic.
2. If your question involves a problem with someone, you must keep in mind that the oracle will exhaust all possibilities in favor of restoring peace. You must therefore refrain from going to the oracles to seek an advantage over others out of anger, hurt, sheer competitiveness, selfishness, revenge, and so on. Many people fail to benefit from oracles because they query them seeking confirmation that they are right in an altercation or conflict, instead of seeking a solution to the problem.
3. Meditate on the answer that you receive. Do not repeat your question, especially through rephrasing.
4. Above all refrain from "testing" the oracle. You are communicating with that portion of God that is at the core of your being-your true Self. It will take no more than a few readings for you to realize the accuracy, and high spiritual counsel of the oracle,

especially if you carefully meditate on the answers and are diligent in carrying out the instructions.

5. Do not ask questions that are aimed at finding out if you can get away with an immoral or unlawful act. You might get a rhetorical answer from the oracle and not realize it. By this is meant, an answer which seems to be saying that it is allright to do the act, when in reality, you are being instructed by being shown the example of the correct thing to do in the situation. If you think that such answers are trick answers, you are right. But they are justified by the fact that such questions are asked with the knowledge that what is being contemplated is wrong.

Suggested Questions

1. What is the most important thing that you must learn and master in order to open the way to the realization of the reason for your incarnation (destiny)?

2. What are the principles governing your name? The name (Ren, in the Kamitic tradition) is an integral component of the Sahu part of the spirit. Because they do not know that as an integral part of the spirit, the name plays a shaping role in the life of the person, Westerners treat it as a mere label for the purpose of identification. Our name should summarize, and where possible, carry the energies of the virtues that we must cultivate for the realization of our destiny. If your present name does not reflect these virtues, you should seriously consider changing it,-legally if possible. Unlike Westerners, the names of people in many other cultures reflect the person's relationship with the deities, etc.

3. Questions #1 and #2 are the essential requirements for the performance of a naming ceremony for an infant.

4. Questions seeking to discover, not necessarily if you should marry, or marry a certain person, take a job, undertake a career, etc., but how would you fare in the situation, what forces (deities, and the virtues represented by them) will guide you to success, what are the odds against you (according to your state of conditioning). If you get a Herukhuti (-)/Het-Heru (-) reading for a marriage, you are being warned that you might experience many fights, or that the basis of the marriage is sensual. You may marry just the same, and either fail, which is most likely, or you may rise to the heights of spiritual challenge and transcend the problems. The value of the oracle in that situation is in its ability to enable you to enter into the situation with the foreknowledge of what kind of problems you will encounter,

why, and how to confront them. What words of power to use, what gems, herbs, etc. to employ to psychically influence a favorable outcome of the event, as well as to turn the mundane undertaking into a mini spiritual initiation. Or, of course, to decline involving yourself.

5. Understand that the Metu Neter oracle, unlike Tarot, etc., is a spiritual tool; a means of personalizing your spiritual curriculum. Do not treat it as a fortune telling device.

6. Consult the oracle with a mind to finding out "what to do spiritually in order to succeed." Most Westerners are so entrenched in the misconception that all that is required for success in life, is to be properly informed. Information does not do much to alter behavior. How many times have you done the wrong thing, in spite of knowing what to do? Incidentally, this is one of the reasons why in spite of the great teachings that we find in the major western religions, there is so much decadence amongst the children of very religious and God fearing, church going parents. Sermons don't cook the food. Remember, that unless you take in what you will into mediumistic trance, it will not be impressed upon the life-force, which is in charge of carrying out your beliefs. *The Truth AND Spiritual Power will Set You Free.*

How to Consult

Step 1: On a 24" x 24" blue and or white cloth, fan the cards face down so that their faces cannot be seen, after shuffling them (avoid such sophisticated procedures that will unnecessarily reduce the life of your cards, or mark them, etc.). Pick a card and make a note of it (it is best to write it down). If the card picked is of the Hetep suit (see below), your reading is complete. I.e., this one card will make up your reading. Otherwise, proceed to step 2.

Step 2: **Return the card to the deck**, reshuffle the cards, and pick another card (note that it is possible to choose the first card again). Study the reading according to the rules explained in chapter 22.

Remember, that if the first card picked belongs to the Hetep suit (See below), you do not pick another card. This card, by itself, will make up your reading. Any other suit, will require you to draw again. In this case, your reading will be composed of two cards. As you returned the first card to the pack, and shuffled it, your reading could be composed of the doubling of the same card. E.g., Sebek tu maat/Sebek tu maat.

Note, that in consulting for another, do not let them touch or handle the cards. Let them point to, or touch the cards with an object that you have selected to serve as a pointer. Something like a chop stick, a fancy one of course, will do. In this way, the cards will not pick up inimical vibrations. For the same reason, it is advised that cards should not be shared, and care must be taken regarding where readings are done, and where the cards are kept when not in use. Keep them wrapped in the cloth described above.

Recording the Cards

The names of each of the 14 cards were given in chapter 17 on. The names of each of the five suits modifying each of the cards are as follow: Note that the first three suits are positive (Tu =yes), while the last two are negative (tem = no).

(+)	(+)	(+)	(−)	(−)
Hetep	Tu Maat	Tu Tchaas	Tem Maat	Tem Tchaas
O	O	O	●	O
O	O	O	●	●
●	O	O	●	●
●	O	●	●	●

Your recordings of the readings will be as follows: Het-Heru Tu Maat and Maat Tem Maat (i.e., Het-Heru (+)/Maat (−)); Others are Sebek Hetep; Auset Tem Maat/Tehuti Tu Tchaas, and so on.

Chapter 22

INTERPRETING THE ORACLE

Before Your first Attempt at Interpretation

Before attempting your first interpretation, it is imperative that you have a working knowledge of the material from chapter 4 on, especially the stages of initiation, meditation, and the material from chapters 16 - 19. Not only will this aid you in understanding the readings, but more importantly, to frame your question properly. It is with the proper phrasing of questions that the successful comprehension of the reading is secured. If you understand the material taught in the past chapters you will not ask questions that, for example, implicitly or explicitly reflect identification with your person as the essence of your being. E.g., "Given my fear of X, should I do so and so?" As the oracle is a means of communicating with your true Self, you may not comprehend, or be prepared for the answer. From the preceding chapters it is evident that there is a great deal of information to be coordinated i. order to arrive at the proper understanding of the reading.

The Preliminary Keynotes of the Reading

Step #1: Read the meanings (+ and -) denoted by the Deity of each card in chapter 19. Be sure you have a clear comprehension of the mental, emotional, physiological, social, and spiritual correspondences of the Deity or Deities denoting the reading. Details of this step are given below.

Step #2: If you received two cards (i.e., your first card was not a Hetep suit), read the combined meaning (+ and -) of the cards in chapter 20.

Step #3: Read the material for the Deities under "shaping factors of success and failure" in chapter 18.

Step #4: Take note of how the role that the Deity or Deities governing your reading contributes to success or failure (chapter 18).

If you have carefully noted and studied the above material, you are now in possession of **the basic keynotes of the reading.** I.e., what the Oracle is saying about the situation. It is important to understand that you do not yet have a clear means of extracting from the list of correspondences, the information that would indicate the actual occurrence. This is accomplished by identifying the significators of the event, and the key person or persons that will aid in the undertaking. There is an extensive list of correspondences at the end of this chapter to assist you in this process. Examining it will show that Auset is the significator of the conception and gestation of pregnancy, duties of the wife and mother, etc.; Het-Heru, to the gestation of pregnancy, the sensual expression in marriage, etc.; Herukhuti, to martial activities (the army, police, etc.), athletics, and so on.

Step #5

The Significators of the Event and Its Uses

Let's say that a person consults about taking a job as a guard, and receives a Sebek Tu Tchaas/Auset Hetep reading [Sebek (+)/Auset(+)]. According to the list of significators, Herukhuti is the significator of this occupation. By implication, the oracle is stating that this person will not bring the specifically required traits to the job. It then identifies what resources the person has that can be readily adapted to the situation. Thus we have that this person, in order to succeed in this position will have to be creative in his/her thinking, and persuasive and clever, in order to make up for the lack of fieriness which is the ideal requirement for the job. When confronted with danger he will be more successful, on a whole, by talking his way out of the situation than by fighting. However, given the anomaly of the situation, in spite of the positive denotations of the Tu Tchaas (+) of Sebek, and the Hetep (+) of Auset, this person will best utilize his skills in more suitable occupations. If he is forced by circumstances to carry out the task, then it should be temporary, or with help, and with clear awareness of the shortcomings.

Implicit Data and Counsel

From the preceding, we have seen that there are implicit data and counsel in a reading that are derived from the lack of agreement between the significators of the event, and the reading received. The oracle will inform you as much by what it tells you, and by what it doesn't.

Adaptation of Resources

        We also saw that when the person lacks the capacity, or ought not to transform his/her being to manifest the powers of the significator of the event, the oracle shows what spiritual resources the person will use to formulate a strategy for handling the situation. This is a widespread practice in life. Many lawyers adapt a Het-Heru strategy in their profession which is governed by Sebek; many creative writers and musicians adapt a dry technological Sebek approach to their profession which is governed by Het-Heru; many athletes (long distance runners, especially) push themselves out of sheer Seker doggedness, to compensate for the lack of Herukhuti, and so on. It goes without saying, that it is best when the reading matches the significator.

The Significator of the Subject of the Reading

        This step is full of potential problems, and although useful, it must be used either with a grain of salt, or only when you are absolutely sure. When properly used, it can be a tremendous help. It may be skipped in most cases.

        It involves classifying the subject into a specific category. This is easy and relatively safe when the subject(s) in the situation has a well defined social position, provided that the latter is relevant to the reading. If the question relates to a promotion, or family, or corporation, then Heru signifies the boss, the father (or mother if she is single), president, or boss, and so on. In previous chapters we saw that certain undertakings were more natural to certain age groups and sex gender because of the energies involved. Thus we can establish a young woman as signified by either Auset, or Het-Heru, a young man by Sebek, or Heru, and so on. But this latter procedure is precisely where we can go wrong because it involves guessing at the internal makeup, and transcendental abilities of the individual. If you use it, treat it as a "what if scenario." You might want to establish other "what if" models. Suppose, let's say that the person who inquired about the guard job was a 60 year old man, or a 25 year old woman, who do you think, is most likely to better carry out the Sebek/Auset strategy? Do you think that the 60 year old man, given the strong Seker energies (scruples, experience, ponderous thoughtfulness, etc.) working through him, might be somewhat more inhibited in his creativity and cleverness than the young woman?

Step 6

The Suits

The suits are a guide to your likelihood of succeeding or failing through the strategy and faculties you are using in the given situation.

Hetep represents the greatest likelihood of success. You could still fail, however, as it does not predict success without effort. It is like being shackled with a light chain that can be easily slipped off, but you must make the effort. This is why you must always read both the (+) and the (-) correspondences of a metu. Hetep does not mean the absence of negativity. It means that it is relatively easy to transcend it. Whether you are aware of it or not, it means that **the way is open** for "heaven"- the indwelling intelligence -to assist you through the faculties represented by the deity of the reading. I cannot overemphasize the need to take note of the fact that the step of considering the suit comes **after** the study of the correspondences of the cards, and its comparison with the significator of the situation. In the above example we can see the possible catastrophic results that would occur if prior to step 5 the person concluded that because the Auset card was Hetep, the reading presaged success in the undertaking. Placed in the proper perspective, it indicates that the individual is likely to succeed as a guard by adapting a Sebek/Auset strategy to the situation. We would be more comfortable, however, for the safety of the guard, and the property guarded, if the guard had received a Herukhuti Hetep, or Herukhuti tu Maat, etc.

Tu Maat means that **the way is opening** for the influence of the indwelling intelligence to assist you in your undertaking. You must focus on living (just not knowing) the truths and virtues associated with the deity of the reading. Your meditations and rituals must focus on what must be done in order to carry out the counsel of the oracle.

Tu Tchaas means that **the way is opening** for the influence of the indwelling intelligence to assist you in your undertaking. You must focus on increasing your stock of information regarding the situation, through study and meditation. You must also meditate on impressing these ideas upon your spirit (first level of the meditation process).

Tem Tchaas means that **the way is closing** to the indwelling intelligence to assist you in your undertaking, due to your vulnerability to the wrong beliefs denoted by the card.

Tem Maat means that **the way is closed** to the indwelling intelligence to assist you in your undertaking, due to your vulnerability to the wrong beliefs and emotions denoted by the card.

It is obvious that the lowest suits indicate that there is more work to be done, more obstructions to be overcome, and a greater chance of failing. In most cases, it is advisable to avoid undertakings when the two latter suits are drawn. If they must be done, a great deal of care, meditation, and study must be observed.

Positive Readings

By now it should be clear that positive readings-Hetep, Tu Maat, and Tu Tchaas- simply mean that the way is open or opening. You must still apply yourself to studying, meditating and living truth to succeed. *A positive reading does not necessarily state that the subject is free of negative traits, but that the way is open to transcend them.* It is important then, to study the negative side of the card as well. As it is virtually impossible to measure effort, it would be foolhardy to adapt an attitude of taking it easier than you would, had you received a negative reading. The ultimate purpose of labelling readings as negative is to serve as a means of directing the subject away from certain undertakings. When we must do something, regardless of the reading, we must give it our best.

Negative Readings

If we must engage in an undertaking, the factors that are indicated by the negative readings must be converted into positives. Thus, when a negative reading is received, you must also study the positive correspondences of the card. Obviously you must meditate study, and be consistent in living truth.

Details of Step # 1

Using the Correspondences of Chapter 19

Chapter 19 presents us with an array of correspondences which can singularly, or in combination indicate the outcome of the reading. In some cases, it will be easy to see which apply, but in others, there will be a great deal of work required. In a Seker reading, for example, the key to the meaning of the reading could be the mental trait (good, or poor planning), or the emotional trait (patience, lack of appreciation for limitations, etc.), or the social correspondences (assistance from elders, priests, supreme court judges, etc.), or health problems (depression, arthritis, etc.), or by cultivating the spiritual skills and virtues of the deity.

For example, in a recent case, a couple placed a $30,000 deposit on a house, and later asked to be reimbursed because the owner failed to tell them that the house was haunted. The judge sided with the seller, and refused the buyers their desire to back out of the deal. The reading that was done to see what was the Metu Neter's commentary on the judge's actions was Maat Tem Maat/Sebek Tem Tchaas [i.e., Maat (-)/Sebek (-)]. Had this reading been done for the couple before they purchased the house, they would have been made aware that they would face problems due to incorrect application of, or ideas concerning the law (Maat -), wrong ideas, lack of facts, deception (Sebek -), contractual problems, and so on. In this reading, the health, personal spirituality, emotional traits of the couples were not the factors, the social correspondences were. Incidentally, as neither Maat nor Sebek is a significator for purchasing a house, but are significators of lawyers, judges, contracts, legal matters, etc., the pointers to the meaning of the reading in this case are easy to figure out.

So far we have only considered the correspondences from chapters 18, 19 and 20. Although the oracle must not be used for trivial matters, there are some situations that are not very critical or so important. The material from these chapters will suffice. Questions regarding very important matters (What must be cultivated in order for this marriage to be successful? What career should I pursue? Etc.) require a deeper understanding of the reading. It is important to fully study the correspondences to your card(s) in chapters 4 - 17. Suppose you receive for a marriage reading, Heru tem tchaas/Tehuti Hetep. Your experience will not just simply be limited to the Men Ab meditations of Heru, and following a sage, or a marital counsellor, etc. You will find that many of your marital experiences are your personal living examples of the metaphorein (so called myth) of Ausar vs. Set, of sections in the *Pert em Heru (Egyptian Book of the Dead)*, and so on. By making correspondences to the Yoruba religion, you will find that many of the patakis (metaphoreins) of the Yoruba wisdom system concerning Shango (Heru), and Ifa (Tehuti) are archetypes of the personality qualities that you must cultivate in order to succeed in your marriage. You will see that your bringing of projects into manifestation are microcosmic versions of the creation of the world as shown in chapters 4 - 6. You will find rich material in the spiritual literature to guide your steps. You will experience the reality that true religious stories are not accounts of "historical events," or have their values as such, but are universal archetypes serving as guides to the gamut of life experiences. More importantly, you will grow in your appreciation for the Tree of life because of its ability to serve as a means of cataloguing each archetype, and relating them to the host of human traits and experiences.

The Utchau Metut and Interpretation

The Utchau Metut, which was discussed in chapter 17, is one of the most important elements in the interpretation of readings. High oracles, like the I Ching, Metu Neter and Ifa, do not merely prognosticate. The counsel that they give is based, fundamentally, on the weighing of the shaping factors of an event. All attempts must be made to determine the place in time and space (hierarchy) of the various factors of the reading and the situation, as revealed by the metutu.

Modes and Levels of Interpretation

There are several levels, and modes of interpreting the Metu Neter oracle, according to levels of ability and temperament. The 1st level and mode, which all beginners must go through, is the Sebek mode. It is the process outlined so far. It entails reading, studying, and logical reasoning about the correspondences and suits. Because of the large number of correspondences owned by each deity (mental, emotional, social, etc.), you will never know from this method, exactly how the situation will unfold, although you will know the basic path that it will take. Nevertheless, you will be prepared for the various events as they unfold. A person running for a political post receives Uatchet (-) on the outlook on his election. It is easy to logically rule in favor of sabotage by spies from the other camp, or treason from members of his campaign, or damage through slander, than to consider the other correspondences; suicide, murder, assassinations, witchcraft, etc. (he did not get the cat's eye talisman, nor did he work with the heka, thus he lost the election, as predicted). The second level and mode involves taking the reading into mediumistic trance, through the heka or hekau of the deity or deities governing the reading. Depending on the skill and psychic equilibrium of the medium, it will be possible to ferret out very out of the way facts. A person gets Uatchet Hetep for the likelihood of getting a bank loan. There is no way that the Sebek approach would have arrived at the realization that the person will witness a hold-up of a bank (a Uatchet correspondence is robbers!), and in assisting the bank officer, secures the latter's good will, and thus gets the loan. And at the time, he had merely gone to the bank to make a routine deposit (the success came from chanting the heka of Uachet over a cat's eye talisman [jewelry]). A good medium, focusing on the question, and guided by the heka of Uatchet can predict such events, days and years in advance, down to the color of the underwear worn by the bank officer, and the caliber of the pistol used by the robber. The danger of the mediumistic approach is that the psychic equilibrium needed for consistent and high accuracy is hard to achieve, and maintain. In addition, many revelations are received in parables, symbols, or fragments. In touching up and interpreting them, the message is often perverted. A medium receives a fragmentary message that there is a conflict between the subject of the reading and another person. Failing to realize that the subject may have been, or will be the wrong doer, warns him that he has "an enemy" that will get him in trouble. If you have this ability well developed, you should use it, but combine it with the Sebek approach as a check. The third mode and level is the Maat approach. Here an attempt is made to take the abstract principles behind the correspondences into waking trance. By seeking to discover analogies to the picture emerging out of the reading, and the abstract principles governing the mental and emotional traits (hot/dry, cold/moist, etc.) you will find other situations in your experiences that were produced by the same forces. Since they have the same underlying structure, the set of events making up the prior occurrence will serve as a basis for "predicting" what will occur in the situation at hand. This is no different from the practice of economists who, for example, were able to predict the coming recession of the 1990's because it represents the recessionary point in the 60 year economic cycle. The last major recession began at the end of 1929, and hung in for the first half of the 30's. This Maat (synthesizing) mode to interpretation is an excellent and very accurate approach, when used in a state of waking trance. While most people will be more dazzled by the feats of the mediumistic approach, the synthesizing method is superior by its ability to give insight into what will take place, its spiritual meaning, and how to solve the problem. The fourth mode is the <u>Tehuti approach</u>. It entails meditating on the card, or a representative metut (see Appendix A), and the heka of the deity. All thinking about the correspondences of the cards, shaping factors of the situation, etc. must be suppressed to allow the indwelling intelligence to reveal the specific application of the reading to the situation.

Why Should Oracles be Used?

Incidentally, some of the examples of readings given above-the haunted house, and the bank loan-are good supports for the argument in favor of using oracles. Some people argue that the use of oracles detracts from the exercising of one's rational ability[1]. But there is no way that reason would have warned the couples of the outcome of their purchase. Neither could one have arrived through reasoning at the manner in which the young man secured his loan. To cap it all, we should note that the greatest Western minds have been employed in putting the Europe 1992 project together. Had they consulted an oracle, they would have spared themselves the humiliation that is waiting for them. Seker Tem Maat/Ausar Tem Maat. The Metu Neter is saying, on the Seker (-) side, that there will be delays due to the lack of planning ability, problems due to the lack of appreciation for structure and limitations, and so on. On the Ausar side, it is saying that, true unity will not be achieved, because there is no spiritual tradition of the essential divinity of man's Self in Western Europe. Imprisoned in their personal and national idiosyncrasies, they will not be able to effectively, and significantly escape the chains of tribalism and parochialism. American business men should take heed, for they are caught up in the greener grass syndrome, and are thus on the verge of throwing away billions of dollars . . . at the expense of the welfare of the have-nots, and have

---

1. If they were really sincere they will stop drinking alcohol, smoking, and eating junk food. These are the real killers of people's brains.

369

little of America. It seems that nothing has been learned from the Babel tower metaphorein. A similar reading was received for South Africa for the year 1990. Seker tem maat/Heru tem maat. While the Seker tem maat is to be understood as explained above, the Heru part of the reading shows that there will be problems on the governmental level; dictatorialness, administrative failures, weakness, etc. Black Africa, for the decade, received Het-Heru tu maat/Geb tu maat, which predicts relatively minor prosperity (Het-Heru tu maat) through the exploitation of natural resources (Geb tu maat). The minor success indicated by Het-Heru, if we apply the Utchau Metut, will be caused by the failure to transcend certain fundamental errors in cultural, and political identity. If they were to study this reading and make the necessary corrections, major succcess can be achieved. The way is implied in the correlates of Het-Heru (Seker), and of Geb (Amen). Seker/Amen will entail a return to their original spiritual science based cultural, and political systems of organization.

Direct and Indirect Responses

The responses from the oracle fit into two categories. The first, which is the direct mode is as the term says of itself. In the example readings that we have looked at so far, the responses identified what was wrong, or what resources were available, and so on. Sometimes, for its own reasons, the oracle responds indirectly. It usually does this when the answer is, or should have been obvious to the querent. If you ask the oracle a question such as "would it be okay for me to use the company's paper to make unauthorized reproductions for personal or community purposes?" you may get an answer such as Maat Hetep. Since Maat denotes strict adherence to divine law, the oracle is not telling you to go ahead and misappropriate the company's property. The reading is reminding you of the law, and the good consequences of upholding it. Or you could have received a Sebek Hetep reading, because you have been very clever in the way you have been going about using the company's property, or because of the persuasive rationalizations you have been employing to assuage your conscience. Thus, the Sebek Hetep is reminding you of the proper use of this faculty. As people do, the Metu Neter oracle will sometimes counsel you by focusing on the negative side, or the positive side of an issue.

An interesting indirect response was received from the oracle to the question as to what were its thoughts in regards to

370

being introduced to the world. It gave Maat tem maat/Geb tem maat! I immediately went into trance, whereby Maat and Geb informed me that the world at present is not dominated by divine law, and as a result widespread disasters (illness and poverty) will be suffered by rich and poor, high and low through ecological imbalance. None will escape. It has come to establish the throne of Maat upon the earth, and redeem it through the powers of the 750,000 waiting at the threshold of the shrine of Khemenu. This time it shall not be the 42, but the 750,000 that shall deliver the Ab of the Sebau to the jaws of Aum-mit. It is important to note that in answering with Maat tem maat/Geb tem maat, the oracle painted a picture of the present condition of the world. It singled out the greed, waste and extravagance [Maat (-)] of those in control, who are disequilibrating the earth. What can you do? Saturate the earth's electromagnetic field with Maat's heka (Aung Shring), learn-teach the divine law, love one another, and respect the earth and your body. Reject not the cornerstone of the temple not built with hands.

Implications and Greater value of Readings

You do a reading regarding health, or a very mundane quest (buying a house) and receive Maat Tem Tchaas as part of your reading, showing that you lack the knowledge of cosmograms, divine law, or the ability to perceive the whole governing the situation. It could very well be a reflection of how you are living your life in general, or some other area of your life. In addition to receiving insight into your health, or getting a house, you will gain insight into your spirituality, and other areas in your life, as the skills and occult powers that are developed for a specific situation can be utilized in all other areas of life.

Significators

accidents	Nekhebet
accountants	Sebek
adventure	Nekhebet, Herukhuti
advertising	Sebek, Maat
airplanes	Sebek

371

ambassadors	Sebek, Maat
artists	Het-Heru
ascetics	Uatchet
assassinations	Uatchet, Herukhuti
astrology	Sebek, Maat
auctions	Sebek, Maat
aviation	Sebek, Herukhuti
beasts of prey	Herukhuti
bedroom	Het-Heru, Auset
bilious temperament	Heru
blood	Auset, Geb
bloodshed	Herukhuti
bondage	Seker
bones	Seker
books	Sebek, Maat
book dealers	Sebek
brother	Herukhuti
builders	Herukhuti, Seker
burns	Herukhuti
business success	Maat, Het-Heru
caring	Auset
cars	Herukhuti
Cartesian logic	Sebek
cemeteries	Seker, Nekhebet
charity	Maat
chemists	Heru, Sebek
children	Auset
circumspection	Heru
clothes	Auset
colors, variegated	Het-Heru
con artists	Sebek

confinement	Seker
conflicts	Herukhuti
constitution, the	Seker
contractors	Sebek
cooperation	Het-Heru
copper	Het-Heru
corals, pink	Het-Heru
coronation	Heru
corpulence	Maat
Cosmogony	Maat
courage	Heru
cracks	Nekhebet
criminals	Herukhuti
cultivation of land	Auset
cunning	Sebek
deception	Uatchet
decorations	Het-Heru
defense	Herukhuti
dentists	Herukhuti
deserts	Herukhuti
dexterity	Sebek
diplomacy	Maat
draftsmen	Sebek
druggists	Heru
duplicity	Nekhebet
earthquakes	Herukhuti
education	Sebek, Auset
education, higher	Herukhuti, Maat
education, spiritual	Maat, Tehuti
elders	Seker
elders, respect for	Maat
electricity	Herukhuti
endurance	Herukhuti
entertainment	Het-Heru
epidemics	Nekhebet
exile	Nekhebet
explosions	Herukhuti
faith	Maat
father	Heru

fire	Heru
fire, firemen	Herukhuti
gems	Auset, Het-Heru
ghosts	Nekhebet
gold, goldsmiths	Heru
guards	Herukhuti
guns	Herukhuti
heart	Heru
honors, honorable	Maat
hot & pungent	Heru, Herukhuti
impediments	Seker
indolence	Auset, Het-Heru
infamous men	Nekhebet
insurance	Sebek, Seker
intoxicants	Het-Heru
intoxicants	Seker
intrigues	Uatchet
inventors	Nekhebet
iron	Herukhuti
journalists	Sebek
journeys	Sebek
judges	Maat, Tehuti
kings	Heru
knives	Herukhuti
kulayoga	Het-Heru
lawyers, young	Sebek
lead	Seker
leaders	Heru
lecturers	Nekhebet, Sebek
legal matters	Maat
litigation	Herukhuti, Sebek
litigation	Nekhebet
low lifes	Seker
low lifes	Uatchet, Nekhebet

marriage	Het-Heru
masses, the	Auset
mathematics	Sebek
mediums	Auset
men, appx 28-56	Heru
men, young	Sebek
merchants	Sebek
military	Herukhuti
milk	Auset
mines	Seker
morality	Maat
mother	Auset
motors	Herukhuti
nervines	Sebek
nurse, nursing	Auset
optimism	Maat
ornaments	Het-Heru
oracle	Tehuti
pearls	Auset
philosophers	Maat
plans	Seker
plots	Nekhebet
poets	Sebek/Het-Heru
poisons	Nekhebet
poisons	Uatchet
policemen	Herukhuti
political power	Heru
politicians	Sebek
pregnancy	Auset, Het-Heru
presidents	Heru
prostitutes	Het-Heru
psychism	Nekhebet, Uatchet
psychosomatic power	Auset, Het-Heru
psychosomatic power	Nekhebet, Uatchet
rain	Het-Heru
red	Herukhuti
red & white articles	Heru

religious institutions	Maat
religious science	Maat
religious resignation	Uatchet
road	Sebek
romance	Auset, Het-Heru
rotten things	Sebek
sailors	Auset
salesmen	Sebek
salt	Auset
scars	Herukhuti
scars	Nekhebet
scientific theory	Maat
scriptures	Sebek
secrecy	Uatchet
self-reliance	Heru
serpents	Nekhebet
serpents	Uatchet
servitude	Seker
sexual pleasure	Het-Heru
sharing	Maat
shrines	Nekhebet
social events	Het-Heru
soldiers	Herukhuti
sorrows	Seker
speakers	Sebek
speculation	Maat
spies	Nekhebet, Uatchet
spiritual power	Seker
steel	Herukhuti
stones	Nekhebet
strength, physical	Herukhuti
stubbornness	Seker
subliminal seduction	Uatchet, Nekhebet
subway	Seker
sudden, unexpected events	Nekhebet
suicide	Uatchet
surgery	Herukhuti
synthesis	Maat
talismans	Uatchet

thieves	Seker
trade, foreign	Sebek, Tehuti, Maat
trading	Sebek
trains	Herukhuti
travellers	Nekhebet
travelling agents	Auset, Sebek
truth	Maat
vegetation	Auset
vegetation	Het-Heru
venereal disease	Het-Heru
visions	Auset
warriors	Herukhuti
water, rivers, sea	Auset
wealth, wealthy people	Maat
weapons	Herukhuti
white articles	Auset
widows	Nekhebet
wife	Het-Heru
will	Heru
wit	Sebek
women, young-49	Auset
wounds	Herukhuti
writers	Sebek

The Western Legal System vs. the Kamitic

The Kamitic System

	Significators
Judges	Tehuti, Maat

The Western System

	Significators
Supreme Court judges	Tehuti
Judges	Maat
Lawyers	Sebek

District Attorneys	Sebek/Herukhuti
Jury	Auset

It is important to note that in the Kamitic system, only Tehuti and Maat--significators of judges--play a role in the judgement of court cases. As we saw in chapter 15, such individuals qualified for these positions through spiritual initiation. As fulfillment of the initiation and meditation requirements of the 6th and 8th stages of spiritual development places the initiate beyond the sway of emotionalism, bias, and narrow mindedness, such initiates were selected for adjudicating court cases. The plaintiff submitted his charges in writing (to avoid biasing the case through oratory rhetoric), and these were read to the defendant. He in turn, submitted his rebuttal in writing, which were then read to the plaintiff. And the cycle was repeated until enough insight was produced. The judges then used their full knowledge of the law of God, and of the land, and their meditation and prophetic skills to render judgement. Why call judges "judges," if they don't render judge-ment? Were they not trained in the science and art of arriving at correct judgement? Why then, in Western society, is the passing of judgement in the most important court cases in the hands of people (Signified by Auset) who are 1) not trained in the science of judgement? 2) Are most likely to be swayed by the clever oratory of Sebek (lawyers)? It is no secret that lawyers decide the outcome of court cases more so than judges. Does this not make the Western legal system a contest of cleverness, as opposed to the administration of justice? Is it that they do not trust their judges? Why are law enforcers so frustrated? Why are most people so afraid to go out of their houses, or even, stay in them? You must keep these points in mind when consulting on legal matters, as the oracle may often slant its counsel toward the truth, while cleverness is the main factor at work in many legal cases. If you receive a reading showing that success is outside of the established law, you may have to prepare yourself for an intense, and protracted set of rituals if you hope to invoke divine assistance to influence the changing of the law. Such procedures are justified, when we have rulings, for example, that allow drug dealers to escape their deserved punishment, people with AIDS to transmit their disease with impunity, because a particular state does not have a specific law on the subject on its books, and so on.

Rituals and the Readings

The most important aspect of the Metu Neter oracle is the fact that even if you are not able to identify how the reading will specifically manifest itself, you can still help yourself, and succeed by meditating and performing rituals based on the words of power. Barring great psychic abilities which very few people will ever possess, hardly anyone would have been able to predict, in the above example regarding the house purchase, that the problem would center around the house being haunted. Successful chanting of the hekau of the Deities governing the reading--Aing and Shring, in this case (Sebek/Maat reading)-would have either forced the truth out in the open in a timely manner, or would have blocked the sale from going through, or would have influenced the judge to rule in favor of the buyers. In another situation, a man who needed a bank loan received Uachet Hetep. He bought himself a Cat's Eye ring, and chanted the planetary heka Aung shring shrang shraung. One day while making a routine deposit at the bank, he found himself in the middle of a Uatchet situation; a bank robbery (Uatchet (-) governs all kinds of low-lifes, robbers, criminals, sorcerers, con artists, etc.). As a result of his cooperation-as a witness-with the bank officials, he received the loan, after other banks had previously turned him down because of "inadequate credit." Uachet! Don't leave home without it.

It is important to also note that you are not restricted to the ritual material given in this book. If you are a Yoruba, you may do the rituals of your tradition by making the correspondences of the Yoruba Orishas to the Kamitic Neteru (Deities). The same goes for other traditions (American Indians, Akans, Ewes, etc.).

Rituals and the Significators

One of the most important aspects of spiritual phenomena is the Deities' use of their significators (the things of the world that are under their dominion) as means of communication with people. Once you begin to perform the rituals as they are explained in this manual, you will discover that so many aspects of the unfoldment of the undertaking are significators of the deity that there is no room for attributing them to coincidences. A person involved in a Sebek ritual, for example, finds that the key events happen on a Wednesday, or any day at 3:00 o' clock, on the 3rd, or 13th, or 30th of the month, or in 3 days (Sebek's "mystic" number is 3); involved will be people wearing red and black, or yellow clothing, or red and black things; critical events will happen at corners, intersections (crossroads), at doorways (Sebek is the opener of the way, and guardian of portals, etc.). Iron clad meeting will be set for 10:00 am to take place on the 8th floor, but "unforeseen" events will force the meeting to begin at 3:00 pm, and be held on the 13th floor, and so on. Person's involved with an Auset ritual will find that the key person involved might be a woman of childbearing age, wearing a blue dress; events will happen mostly on a Monday, or the 7th of the month, or at 7:00 o'clock; water, lettuce, etc. will be involved; your car might be involved in an accident with a blue vehicle, and so on.

This is the manner in which the Deities let you know that you have successfully invoked them, and that they are on the case. That they are in control, and fully in charge of the situation. Such revelations are very important as they help you to keep the faith, and, of greater importance, they serve as one of the best evidence of the existence of the spiritual entities, and the science for dealing with them. When you pray or meditate without awareness of the specific Deity in control of the event, and all events are controlled by some aspect of God, you miss the wealth of "signs" (omens and portents) that the Deity uses to inform you of its presence and the progress of the situation. You have no way of getting feedback of how things are progressing, or what you must do to help the situation along. In preparation for a group healing ritual for women, I dreamed that a beautiful young woman visited my house, and when I asked her what could I offer her, she asked for Pulsatilla soda. As Pulsatilla is one of the major feminine homeopathic remedies, I realized that the woman was Auset. The next day, I happened to pass by a flower shop, and for the first time, after several years of visiting the store, it just "came" to me to inquire about the name of a particular flower that "caught" my eye. It was Pulsatilla. When I placed an order for these flowers for all of the women who were participating in the ritual it came up to $70.00. 7 is Auset's mystic number. They placed the flowers in pouches and wore them around their womb area, as they went into trance and invoked Auset through the heka Aung Vang Dhung. The next day most of them had their menses, way off schedule, and as the time progressed, many problems, including infertility, painful menses, etc. cleared up without the administration of medicines, or other changes in lifestyle, except the observance of the laws (spiritual counsel material) of the Deity.

When we speak of initiation, we must distinguish between the formal vs. the informal approaches. In the formal approach, the initiate goes through a step by step, stage by stage process of spiritual practices. The observances of each stage are applied to all aspects of life. In the informal approach, a spiritual observance of any of the 10 stages is prescribed by the oracle in relation to the undertaking inquired about. Obviously, the latter approach is the subject of this book. A young woman receives a Maat reading in a situation regarding the guidance of her wayward teenage son. Although she must go through the first 6 meditation stages, and should go through the higher ones, the focus of the experience is the 6th stage of initiation. She has to become the embodiment of Maat in order to succeed. Nefert-Ra, the fictitious character that we discussed in the meditation chapters must become the embodiment of Het-Heru in order to heal her female organs and get pregnant. These "initiations" differ from the formal ones, in that they are "mini-initiations," i.e., the observances of the stages of meditation are somewhat limited to the subject inquired about. This distinction, however, cannot be applied too narrowly. According to the nature of the situation, it is possible to often find that the observances must extend to all areas of life. The ideal of course is to use both approaches simultaneously.

Finally, it is of utmost importance to note that only an abbreviated set of meanings of the oracular combinations has been given. The 3934 ($56 \times 70 + 14$) base combinations have been reduced to about 400, as the full presentation would have added several hundred more pages to this volume. I have reserved a future volume for the full treatment of the combinations, which amount to 55076 (3934×14) combinations when the 14 sets of significators are considered.

Chapter 23

Underlying Principles of the Practice

of

Meditations and Rituals

Meditation is the science of manipulating our <u>focus of consciousness (the will)</u>. Through meditation we are able to internalize it or externalize it at will, and focus it and unfocus (relax) it at will. **Ritual** deals with the science of <u>manipulating Ra (the life-force)</u>, i.e., <u>our so called subconscious, id</u>, etc.

Meditation

We must begin by removing certain major popular misperceptions and misconceptions regarding the states of consciousness before we can fully understand the mechanism of meditation. The greatest impediment to the understanding of meditation and spiritual practices has been the popular division of consciousness into "waking consciousness," and "sleeping consciousness" to identify what we normally call "being awake," and "being asleep," respectively. The observation is as correct as the "self evident truth" that heavier bodies fall at a faster rate than lighter ones. If you keep in mind the following substitutions, you will establish a sound foundation for understanding meditation and ritualistic procedures. The state that we normally call "being awake," in which we are aware of the external environment, is a "<u>modality of the extroverted state of consciousness</u>." And what we normally call "being asleep" is a "<u>modality of the introverted state of consciousness</u>." The gist of the problem resides in the popular miscomprehension of the objective reality behind the words "waking" and "sleeping," although most people will swear that their understanding of the realities behind them is accurate.

Our consciousness has 2 fundamental modes, with 3 sets each, yielding 6 modalities.

A **Introverted**		**B** **extroverted**
1a focused/awake active	1b	focused/awake active
2a focused/awake relaxed	2b	focused/awake relaxed
3a unfocused/ asleep	3b	unfocused/ asleep

What is "normally" called "**sleeping**" is 3a-the <u>unfocused introverted state</u>. The introversion of consciousness is the cause of the detachment from the environment, and the unfocusing is the cause of the undirected stream of imagery we call dreaming, and the "unconsciousness" experienced during the non-REM period of sleep. Being "**awake**" is 1b-the <u>focused, and active extroverted state, with minor periods of 2b (daydreaming)</u>. This adds up to about 18% of our mental states. When we add to it the 3a state we see that most people are using about 35% of the potential of their states of consciousness. The remaining 65% corresponds to the states of trance, which is the means of accessing the unused portion of the brain (the 80% or so that most people do not use).

State of Trance

Waking Trance States

1a: We can introvert our focus of attention, so that we detach our consciousness from the environment and the body, and yet, remain awake and mentally active. The will in this state is still active, sanctioning, and directing thought associations.

2a: We can introvert our focus of attention, so that we detach our consciousness from the environment and the body, yet remain awake (the will is focused), but mentally passive (the will is relaxed). In this state, the life-force is free to throw up all associated thoughts, and spiritual agencies-deities, ancestors, etc.--are able to enlighten the meditator. We are here <u>dreaming, yet awake</u>. And unlike "sleep dreaming," and the height of mediumistic trance (3b), we are able to clearly remember everything that transpired during trance.

383

The introversion of consciousness in both of the above states, reduces the receptivity to the distractions from the environment, and the left side of the brain. Thus we can concentrate and avoid the resistance to changing our behavior patterns that stream in from the lower faculties of the left side of the brain.

Mediumistic Trance

When we are extroverted, thus communicating with the environment and the body, but with our will in a passive state, we fall into mediumistic trance. The "person" walks around, dances, talks, etc., but all activities are being guided either by Ra-the life-force (subconscious)-or by the will of another entity (spirit, deity, hypnotist, initiatior, etc.). This state is popularly known as one of possession or obsession according to the directing agency. In possession, the direction is coming from a deity or ancestor, and in obsession, the direction is coming from a highly charged passion.

BREATHING THE KEY TO MEDITATION

When you want your car to turn left, you do not exit the car, and turn the wheels to the left, just because they are directly involved in the turning of the car? You know that the wheels are indirectly controlled from the steering wheel. It is the same with the control of mental activities and emotions. The main "switch" is not located in the "mind" but in the body. We must understand the scope of activity allocated to the will. It is like the banks of a river. While it can direct the flow of the water, it cannot stop its flowing.

Most people are under the misconception that thoughts can be controlled through mental effort. If you tried, you will discover that thoughts come and go independent of your will. Even when you attempt to focus your attention on one object or line of thought, it isn't long before you notice that your awareness of your self, and what you were concentrating upon is returning to you. You realize that without realizing when it was happening, your attention drifted off unto something else, which you may or may not be able to recall. You rededicate yourself to the task, only to find the same thing happening all over again. And again, and again. If you were attempting this exercise because you received instructions from one of the hundreds of books on meditation, which direct you to "chose

384

"X" object or subject and to concentrate upon it, you would be told that "If your attention wanders bring it back, keep it fixed, etc.." It wouldn't be long before you gave up and declared yourself a failure at meditation, and a "weak-willed" person who is incapable of concentrating etc.

The first thing about your Self, and meditation that you must know is that thought control is not under the dominion of the will. It's function is to direct how thoughts come together for making meaningful units in conformity to logical principles, facts, and Truth. The misconception that the will is in charge of controlling the coming and going of thoughts is so easy to form given the fact that it is directly involved with them. This is like believing that the wheels of a car must be turned directly. But the fact, which has been known, and verified for thousands of years is that the manifestation of thoughts, as well as sensations (emotions, etc.) are to be controlled through the manipulation of the diaphragmatic muscles. This is the set of muscles located in the lower abdoMen About an inch below the navel. This location is called the Tan Tien in the Chinese tradition, the Tanden in Japanese Zen tradition, the Hara in Japanese martial arts, and is the "guts " from where we derive our physical and moral strength.

We have already experienced, but may not have noticed the thought and emotion restraining power of this center. At the moments when we are bracing ourselves to withstand a blow, or intense cold, or some painful event we may tighten this area. We instinctively summon strength in this manner. What most people fail to notice is that at such moments thought activity stops completely. You can prove it to yourself. Put the book down right now and take a deep breath, push out the lower abdomen and tighten it, while holding the breath and ignoring all thoughts that may tend to rise. Hold your breath for as long as you can and just stare straight ahead. The instruction to "ignore all thoughts that may tend to rise" is for the initial period of the exercise before the force fully sets in. Afterward it will wipe out all thoughts on its own. The holding of the breath and counting to ten to negate emotions is based on the same principle, just that people fail to tighten the lower abdomen, or might draw in the upper chest and hold the breath with catastrophic effects- they are vanquished by the emotion. You may have heard people speak of their courageous acts in critical moments. Underlying all such accounts is the fact that they acted without time

385

to think. Whenever we act positively and successfully in a critical situation, you can be sure that strength was instinctively thrown in the lower abdomen. Had we stopped to think, not only would we have come up with the wrong plan for action, but we would not have found the strength to succeed, as summoning strength is incompatible with thinking. The two activities operate in opposed psycho-physical settings. This is a crucial point to remember.

Tension Diaphragmatic Breathing

Tension diaphragmatic breathing is the key to concentrating the attention and summoning strength; spiritual, mental or physical. The essence of this form of breathing is in the handling of the outbreath. Just before we breathe out, the lower abdomen must be in a state of expansion (a mild pot belly). As we breathe out, we pull in the abdomen, without releasing the tension. The result is a restrained exhalation in which the lower abdomen is contracted. This is the essence of pranayama.

The restraint of the exhalation in this fashion slows the breath down to the point of stopping it from time to time. The stoppage that occurs when the exhalation is being restrained in this manner is called Kumbhaka in the yogic tradition. In Lesson II, verse 77 of the *Hathapradipika* is stated, **"Consciousness should be emptied of objects through kumbhaka."** The perfect Raja Yoga state is attained by practicing in this manner. When meditation is conducted with this mode of breathing, eventually the restraining of the breath changes over from willed to automatic activity as the meditator enters into the state of trance. In fact it is in the state of trance that the held breath is truly effective. In the *Hathapradipika*, Lesson II, verse 73: "When siddhi (perfection through/in trance) in Kumbhaka is attained (which is then called Kevale) nothing in the three worlds can be said to be unattainable by the Yogi." The understanding behind this statement is that in Yoga philosophy, the Yogi seeks to carry out all activities in, or through trance as it is the vehicle of perfection. All difficult Asanas (postures) become easy, or are entered into automatically, and spontaneously when the practitioner attains to the trance state. And breath retention is no different. The breath is manipulated in such a manner as to induce the state of trance, in which the cultivated procedure of breathing will continue without direction of the will once the trance is established. Then its power comes into being. The same holds true for the working with words of power. Uttered in the everyday

386

externalized state of consciousness nothing happens. In trance, their powers come into manifestation. The experience of hypnosis is the same. Mere suggestions, which have no effect on the individual, have the power in trance, to remove pain to the extent that open heart surgery can be conducted without anesthesia, etc.

To summarize, we must fully understand that by the proper restraining of the breath during exhalation, trance, the objective of meditation is attained. And when that form of breath restraint is continued automatically- now directed by the spirit and not the will!- which is called Kevale Kumbhaka, the power of the spirit to achieve is fully awakened.

The Physiological Basis of Kumbhaka

Applying tension to the lower abdomen presses against the pneumo-gastric nerve which is the main nerve of the parasympathetic division of the nervous system, stimulating it, thus, to higher activity. As its activity inhibits that of the sympathetic division of the nervous system which is in charge of externalizing consciousness, and preparing us for external action, consciousness is thus withdrawn into the inner plane. In addition, the stimulation of the pneumo-gastric sends nervous impulses to the wakefulness center in the posterior hypothalamic region of the brain, which in turn, excites the cerebral cortexes, contributing thus to the increased activity of these higher brain centers. It is important to realize that all involuntary/autonomous functions of the body have a reflex center from which they can be influenced. Chinese acupuncture is based on this fact. A point on the finger can be stimulated to cause increased activity of the heart, for example. The same is true of the mechanism of thought control. The switch is located, not with the mental faculties, but in the "gut."

BREATHING AND THE INTERNALIZATION OF CONSCIOUSNESS

It is obvious from the preceding material, that if we are restraining the outbreath, the overall rate of breathing will slow down. And it is the rate at which we breathe that controls whether our consciousness is externalized or internalized. When we are concentrating on a thought we automatically hold our breath. This is

387

an instinctive act to withdraw the consciousness from the external plane to focus it in the mental plane. In addition it helps to slow down thought activity. Marksmen, golf players, basketball players, pitchers instinctively hold their breath as they concentrate on focusing in on the mark. When we find it difficult to stay awake we get fresh air, or walk about to get the lungs working more.

Normally, the adult breathes an average of 18 breaths per minute, when subjected to very light activity or seated at rest. When we are concentrating heavily on a subject our rate of breathing automatically drops to about 9 breaths/min. Now, we may have noticed that usually protracted concentration work readily runs into a state of sleepiness. This is due to the diminished intake of air. Now, to induce trance, the meditator lowers the rate of breathing to 7.5 breaths/min, or 6, or 4.5, or 3. Each rate tunes us into a different level of consciousness. It is important to note that all books on meditation that instruct to breathe slower, betray that the author lacks mastery of the subject.

THE HARMONICS OF BREATHING

All things vibrate, including the human spirit and body. And each thing vibrates to its specific "Key." The vibrating mechanism of the human body is the breathing system. When we are seated at rest, the spirit vibrates (we breathe) at 18 waves per minute. Comparing the cyclical values of our respiratory and circulatory systems with that of the Solar system yields some very revealing facts.

Let's begin with the fact that there is a 1:4 ratio between our breathing and pulse rates (18 breaths to 72 pulses), and the rate of the Earth's rotation and the time it takes to rotate (1 degree every 4 minutes). A good meditation objective would be to see if the 1:4 relationship between our breathing and pulsation rate was determined by the clocking mechanism that controls the Earth's rotation around its axis.

The average rate of 18 breaths per minute equals 25920 breaths a day. This figure, 25920, corresponds to the number of years that it takes the north pole to trace a complete circle in the heavens in its precessional movement. The significance of this relationship has been known for thousands of years, although its true meaning has been lost to all authors since the destruction of the Temple (library) of Luxor.

The knowledge of the harmonics of breathing survives veiled in the Hindu allegory of the Yugas, and Chaldean sacred cycles of the Saros and Naros. According to the Hindu allegory, Man has not always behaved as he currently does. There was a time when all Men were honest and truthful. This was during the first of four ages in which the history of mankind is divided. This age was called the Golden Age or Krita Yuga[1] or Satya Yuga (Satya: truth, honesty), and lasted for 1,728,000 years. It was followed by other ages in which Man's goodness and power degenerated by degrees. Following the Golden Age was the Silver Age, known as Treta Yuga[2]. It lasted 1,296,000. This was followed by the Copper Age, called Dvapara Yuga, and lasted 864,000 years. The last Age, in which we are now living (supposedly started in 3150 B.C. with the death of Lord Krishna) is the Iron Age, which is known as Kali Yuga, and will last for 432,000 years. Together they add up to a great period, or Maha Yuga of 4,320,000 years.

Most books on Hindu culture simply mention this allegory, or unprovable "scientific fact," and leave it at that. Now, if we compare these cycles to those of the solar system we discover some startling correspondences. It was said earlier that the North pole describes a complete circle backward through the zodiac in a period of 25,920 years[3]. It moves at a rate of 1 degree each 72 years (the number of our pulses/minute, by the way). As there are 30 degrees in a zodiacal sign (or Age) it takes 2160 (72X30) years to span a sign (or an Age). As there are 12 signs in the zodiac, it takes 25,920 years (2160 X 12, or 72 X 360 degrees) to span the 12 signs of the zodiac (or Ages). The key figures here are the period of 25,920 years and the 12 signs of the zodiac. The division of the Period of 25,920 years by the 12 zodiacal signs, and its factors.

---

1. Krita conceals the heka Krim (Sekr, Ta-Sekri), the power of the third sphere of the Tree.

2. As treta means three, how can it be the second age? Clearly there is a blind here. It only makes sense when we understand that it corresponds to the third in a series. We must therefore count from the bottom. But count what, if we are not dealing with the sequence of ages? It is the third level that is reached in the process of the internalization of consciousness as the rate of breathing is reduced. The same holds for the so called third age, "dvapara." Dvapara means two. It is the second level. The first level of internalization is the Japa point which corresponds to the alpha brain wave state.

3. This is due to a wobbling motion of the earth.

We get the following:

```
25,920 DIVIDED          Length of Ages
BY
12 =   2160
6  =   4320             432,000   Kali   Yuga
                        4,320,000 Maha Yuga
4  =   6480
3  =   8640             864,000   Dvapara Yuga
2  =  12960             1,296,000 Treta Yuga
1  =  25920
```

The missing Age, Krita is 4 X 4320 X 100 = 1,728,000.

The figures resulting from the Division of 25,920 by 12 and its factors follow the overtone, or harmonics of musical tones. When we strike a tone, although we only hear one tone, it is a synthesis of itself and a series of overtones that it generates. We can chart this as follows:

Let's say that we strike a note that vibrates at the rate of 2160 waves per second. And let's say that the note is "C." Then we get the following:

Note	Vibration Rate	Division
C	2160	1/1
C	4320	1/2
G	6480	1/3
C	8640	1/4
E*	10800*	1/5*
G	12960	1/6
G	25920	1/12

*Note: The 1/5th interval--the third of the triad--introduces the emotional factor in musical harmonics.

In other words, when we strike "C" at 2160 vibrations/second, what we actually hear is a fusion of this C with the C eight notes above (4320), the G above the preceding C, the following C, the following E, the following G, and the G an octave above. There are other overtones that are generated between the 1/6th and the 1/12th divisions, but the principle discussed here is limited to the tones that define the tone (the unison, third, fifth, and octave).

The third column labeled "division" refers to the subdivisions that every vibrating medium goes through in producing a tone and its overtone. For example: the C at 2160 is produced by the vibration of the full length of the string. Simultaneously, the string is vibrating at 1/2 half its length, twice as fast to produce the C an octave above. It also subdivides itself by thirds to produce the G at 6480 (3 times the rate of the base tone C/2160). Another point to note that the division of the string produces the series of notes */1, */2. */3, */4, */5, */6, and */12 (SEVEN IN ALL!). Applying the harmonics to the breath we get the following:

Note	Vibration Rate	Division	Breaths/ minute	Yugas
C	2160	1/1	1	Maha
C	4320	1/2	3	Satya
G	6480	1/3	4.5	Treta
C	8640	1/4	6	Dwapara
E*	10800*	1/5*	7.5	Japa point
G	12960	1/6	9	Bala Rama point
G	25920	1/12	18	Kali Yuga

18 breaths--6+6+6--(666) the Beast!,
Kali Yuga

Above I have given the proper allocation of the yugas to the rates of breathing.

From all the above facts we can begin to understand that the periods measuring the yugas are really key ratios in the human breathing cycle. An average of 18 breaths per minute yields 25,920 breaths / day; 9/min. = 12,960; 7.5 = 10800, and so on. Students of spiritual science will recognize all of these numbers as the so called "sacred numbers" spoken of in many texts but never has any practical elucidation about them been given. The data regarding the so-called qualities of men that lived in each Yuga are allegories for the effect that each rate of breathing, sustained through meditation has upon the person. If we average 1 breath /min. (breathing according to the techniques of meditation, pranayama and kumbhaka) we will make contact with our divine nature. At such a slow rate we would succumb to the grand slumber that Vishnu is said to enjoy in Maha Yuga. At 3 breaths per minute all thought processes stop, and we attain to Satya. That is, the ability to intuit all knowledge. Constant meditation at this pace will heal the body, and prolong life. In addition we will also activate the Kriya power that will enable us to attain whatever we desire in the world. 4.5 breaths per minute will place us in the Treta Yuga state. Although intuition does not function perfectly at this pace, as thoughts can still intrude, understanding of spiritual truths is very high when we are in waking trance at this rate of breathing. This is the characteristic of the men of the silver age. 6 breaths /min. will place us in the Dwapara yuga stage which is excellent for learning material facts. 7.5 breaths per minute is the rate for performing japa (protracted repetition of mantras). In this practice a rosary of 108 beads is used to keep track of the count which is invariably placed at 108, 1080, 10800, etc. This practice is caused by the unfortunate failure to understand the connection of the number 10800 (108, 1080, etc.) with japa. It is the key to the rate of breathing at which japa is effective. Once you are in trance, it matters not if you repeated the mantra once, or 10,000 times. Once trance is achieved, the power of the mantra is awakened. 9 breaths /min. corresponds to the rate at which we must breathe when performing Hatha Yoga asanas. It is excellent for strengthening the body, and correcting certain infirmities. Bala Rama, to which this rate corresponds, is the Hindu Hercules. 18 breaths /min. is the rate at which we are very externalized, and fully subject to the domination of thoughts and emotions. It is therefore the number (rate) at which the *Beast* (animal soul) within us lives, and does its thing. 18 = 666 (6+6+6). To control it, and transcend it, all that we have to do is to deny it of its breath. It is as simple as that. Some scholar may, no doubt, take exception to this interpretation of the yugas, but they should ponder the fact that there is nothing in the word "yugas" that means an "age," the true name for which is a "Kalpa." "Yugas" is a variant of "yoga," and clearly has to do with the meditation process. And as far as I know, this is the only valuable information that has ever been given on the Yugas. The author received this insight into the Yugas from one of his ancestors. Otherwise, it has always been introduced as an odd curiosity.   Here we find that it is the key to a most, hitherto unknown, important factor in meditation.   We just don't simply breathe slower.   Slowing down the breath over an extended period should not be taken lightly, as the respiratory mechanism is at the center of the body's and the spirit's rhythmical equilibrium.   We must breathe at a rate at which stability can be maintained.   Guided by the harmonic progression we find that breathing will best stabilize itself at the 1/2, 1/4, 1/6, and 1/12 divisions.   These are the tonic, and dominant tones in the harmonic series.   We must note that the third (the 1/5th division) does not arise when we apply the division by 12 and its factors.   The exclusion of the third in this matter will be clearly understood by music theoreticians.

BREATHING AND WAKEFULNESS

We have seen that reducing the rate of breathing brings on sleepiness.   We may wonder how then is it that meditation leads to a greater degree of wakefulness.   The compensation for the reduced rate of breathing is in the increase in the amount of breath taken in (We must remember that the tension in the lower abdomen is another contributing factor).

BREATHING CAPACITY

ml	Total	"Normal"	Meditation	Limits Upper	Lower
5700					
2800					
2300					
1200					
0					

From this chart we can see that although the total capacity of the lungs is 5700 ml, we normally take in and expel 500 ml, between 2300 and 2800.   We don't take in all the oxygen that we can, and neither do we expel all the carbon dioxide in the lungs.   Of course, as we can see, it is impossible to breathe in to the full capacity as there is an upper limit at about 2900 ml.   Neither can we expel all of the carbon dioxide as there is a lower limit at 1200 ml. But we can certainly take in more than the 500 ml that we normally

393

do. This shallow everyday breathing is the cause of our health problems, failure to perform to our mental optimum, and to develop spiritually. When we meditate or exercise vigorously we normally take in up to 1700 ml. between 1200, and 2900 ml. The difference between exercising, and meditating is of course the rate of breathing, and the fact that in meditation, the vast amount of oxygen taken in, goes to energize the spirit, while in exercising it is expended in muscular activity. Meditation is to the spirit, what exercising is to the body. Do you exercise your spirit daily? Do you realize the consequences of not keeping the body in shape? The spirit in shape?

The 1200 ml. of air taken in and expelled above the normal 500 (1700 ml. in all), during meditation has the effect of fully waking us up. And this is one of the most important distinguishing factors of meditation. With meditation proficiency, we will come to realize that our "normal state of being awake" is not one of full wakefulness. In this state, there is a blend of thought direction (willed activity), and the perception and passive following of thought drifts (dreaming). Clear perception will reveal that we dream while we are awake, and while we are asleep. It is this thought drift (dreaming) activity that leads consciousness astray in its attempt to follow a trend of thought to its logical end, or to substitute symbols to stand in for the realities that the Self is trying to gain knowledge of. The combination of the tension exerted at the lower abdomen, with the increased intake, and expulsion of air, fully awakens us, thus putting a stop to the parade of thoughts (dream activity). In other words, the sphere of awareness ("mind") is emptied of thoughts. In this state we can then 1) look directly into the nature of things and reality or 2) think (string thoughts with each other) logically and analogically (synthetical thinking), without loosing our concentration or 3) concentrate our attention on words of power and their vessels (images) or 4) insperience the reality of our Self, and the formless, unmanifested reality.

Rituals

While meditation deals with the manipulation of the focus of consciousness so as to effectively put the will in communication with the life-force, ritual deals with the means of effectively directing the life-force to the intended objective, once it has been united to the will. Incidentally, this union of the will with the life-force is the other side of the coin of the definition of yoga. The other side is the unification of our identity (person) with our true self. Ritual is thus a process of programming (conditioning), or deprogramming the spirit to manifest desirable effects in our lives. *The assumption of responsibility for the conditioned state of our spirit-what we like; what we can do; how we feel; how we spontaneously react to situations, etc.- -is the foundation of spiritual work.* Ultimately, if you do not know this, you have no knowledge of spirituality. And if you don't know how to control the conditioned states of your spirit, you are not living spiritually. In spite of your wealth of spiritual information, you would not be in control of your behavior, and the course of your life.

The principles of ritual are based on the reality that Ra, the life-force, does not respond to the meaning of words[4]. It is an energy system, and thus, responds to force and forms. In place of ideas, it is directed through words of power, colors, odors, images, electromagnetic forces, etc. In fact, the specific effect of each color, sound, odor, etc. upon the life-force has been identified, catalogued, and cross-referenced by Black scientists, in very much the same manner as has been done with the chemical elements. For example, the heka "gang," one of the 50 matrices of Khepera, belongs to the heart psychic center, is orange, and excites the life-force to remove obstructions; "tang" belongs to the heart center, is a brilliant yellow, and awakens the healing modality of the life-force; "B-hang" belongs to the navel center, is orange, and awakens Ra's power to destroy evil spirits, and so on. The effects of the electromagnetic radiations of plants, gems, colors, odors, etc. have been similarly catalogued.

In past chapters, the correspondences of the deities to gems, colors, oils, baths, etc. were given. These are to be used in association with the meditations. In carrying out a Het-Heru ritual you should wear green, or green and yellow, use sandalwood incense and oil, or rose, etc. Before the meditation, a bath composed of the infusion of spearmint, yellow roses, culantro, sandalwood oil, and so on will help to change your aura (the electromagnetic radiation from your body) to that of the deity. As the first, eight, and fifteenth hours of Friday (during the waxing moon) are the times of the week when her vibrations are strongest, it is auspicious to do her rituals then. The energy generated during the ritual can be "captured" in a

4. The practice of hypnosis and autosuggestion would seem to contradict this. But it is the key for understanding the so called differences in hypnotic susceptibility between people. The "most susceptible" individuals are better able to translate verbal information into images, and sensations.

gem (ring, bracelet, necklace, etc.) appropriate to the deity (white coral for Het-Heru, Ruby for Heru, etc.), or leaves of associated plants (see Chapter 19) which can be carried somewhere on your person. In this manner, the effect of the meditation is made to last much longer, or is rendered portable.

In relationship to these ritual aids a special comment must be made about oils. If their use is fully restricted to ritual purposes, you will discover in them very potent forces. For example, I restrict the use of honeysuckle oil to a Het-Heru meditation for improving my finances, and to achieve success in my goal. When I find myself in a similar situation in the future, It would not be necessary for me to repeat the entire process. By just putting on the oil, or imagining its scent (and mentally chanting the heka), the forces that were cultivated through the meditation will be aroused even though I am not in trance at the moment. This cannot be done, if you are using the oils non ritualistically. I.e., to "smell good," etc.

Chapter 24

HOW TO MEDITATE AND PERFORM A RITUAL

The key to meditation is in the management of the breath. And the key to the management of the breath is in the management of the posture. Proper posture has two aims. It automatically promotes correct breathing, and it prevents the body from distracting and calling the attention outward to the body and the external environment.

POSTURE IN MEDITATION

There are 3 sets of observances to achieve the correct posture:

1.   The <u>focal point</u> of the posture in meditation is in the <u>small of the back</u>. It must be slightly tucked in at the waist level (the third lumbar vertebra) so that the back depicts a slight "S" in shape. You will find that this automatically forces you to breathe correctly from the lower abdomen. If, instead, we experimented with the posture in which the abdomen is caved in, and the back depicts a "C" shape, we will see that breathing is automatically focused in the upper chest, and made shallow. This is the wrong way to breathe. It cultivates illness, proneness to emotionality, tension, irrational, and foggy thinking, weakness (physical, mental, moral, and spiritual), etc. Incidentally, the correct posture is to be cultivated, not only in meditation, but at all times. It is incorrect posture that unbalances our breathing, and makes us vulnerable to being controlled by our emotions, reducing our clarity of perception, and activity of the will during the course of the day.

2.   Care must be taken to insure that <u>the only tension point</u> in the body is <u>at the lower abdomen</u>, an inch below the navel, where breathing is concentrated. Every other part of the body must be relaxed. Especially the shoulders, which most beginners tend to pull up at the suggestion to keep the back straight. Straightening of the back takes place by pulling in the small of the back at the waist level.

3.   When meditation is done in a seated position, the feet must be flat on the ground, hands must be resting palms down (it is preferable to the palms up that is usually recommended) on the lap, the head is to be slightly tilted downward. Meditation can also be conducted lying down, flat on the back, no pillows, and hands resting palms up (Corpse Asana), or lying on the right side, head resting on the right hand, right leg drawn up perpendicular to the body, and bent at the knee. Beginners are recommended to stick with the seated position until proficient, because, in lying they will either fall asleep, or fail to fully awaken themselves. There is this life long association of this position with sleeping, or relaxation of the will, and diffusion of consciousness. For the very proficient, meditation can also be conducted while walking very slowly.

THE PROCEDURE

First of all, note that given the nature of the breathing, this meditation should be done either before eating, or at least 3 to 4 hours after a meal.

PRELIMINARIES

1.   Begin by assuming the proper posture. Make sure that the seat is not too high, or low. The deep diaphragmatic breathing must proceed naturally without any difficulties. Most beginners may become fatigued quickly from this posture as they are now using muscles that they have neglected for so long. They will find it helpful to tuck a small pillow or rolled towel between the small of the back and the chair's back rest.

2.   Close your eyes. Some books recommend that the eyes should be kept open. Although this is best for advanced work, it is not recommended for beginners, as it leads to distraction.

3.   Place the tongue on the gum at the line where it meets the teeth. This unites the negative (Jen Mo), and positive (Tummo) currents of energy in the body. Unfortunately I cannot go into details. Consult books on Chinese Yoga, and Acupuncture for details. Besides, it keeps the tongue from

wandering in the mouth, which produces an excess of saliva, which in turn interferes with keeping the attention inward. Keep the tongue relaxed.

BREATHING (Always though the nostril, and smoothly)

4.   Breathe in slowly, pushing out the lower abdomen.
5.   Tense the lower abdomen slightly.
6.   While maintaining the tension, breathe out very slowly, contracting the lower abdomen. Note that the contraction is being opposed by the tension that is being held.   This restrained contraction is the essence of pranayama (prana = breath, yama = restraint).
7.   From this point on, the in breath is done in two stages
a)   At the end of the outbreath, the lower abdomen is fully contracted and mildly tense. Therefore, the first stage of the inhalation is conducted by simply letting go of the abdomen, that it may fall outward by itself. Breathe in at the same time.
b)   Pause slightly, then deliberately push the stomach out, while taking in more air. This form of in breathing is called "pot belly" breathing by the Tibetan Yogis.
8.   Repeat from 5 to 7b for the duration of the meditation.

These steps are to be memorized with 100% accuracy. Any sloppiness might lead to failure or illness.

FUNCTIONING IN THE MEDITATION STAGE

As you begin to meditate, your brain is still generating 50 microvolts in the beta frequency of 13 - 28 Hz., therefore consciousness is still oscillating between the lower half of the 6th, and the lower spheres. It is useless at this point to try to concentrate on something, or to expend efforts to achieve clear, vivid images. This is not the state in which these mental effects manifest naturally. In meditating we must know what mental activities naturally express themselves in what states of consciousness. Attempt to manifest a clear vivid image in the beta state, and all you will get is a fuzzy, grey or impermanent image. In the alpha, and theta stages you will see that the image will be vivid, and will remain in consciousness without effort.

In the course of the meditation you will (must!) begin to feel some of the signs of coming trance. Your eyelids may feel heavy, flutter, become glued to your eyes; your body may feel heavy, like lead, or feel light. You might feel like you are floating away. Or, you may feel detached, a stranger to your body, etc. These off-bodily sensations are the result of the partial withdrawal of consciousness from the 10th sphere; The body might feel as if it would rock from side to side (allow it if you want to achieve mediumistic trance, otherwise ignore the feeling); You may also feel currents of energy travelling through the body, heat, flashes of light, hear sounds, see colors, etc. These are all natural to the state of trance. You will not experience all of them. Neither will you always experience the same ones each time that you meditate. This has no meaning.

The key experience to look for are the points 1) at which your body feels very heavy, or very light and floating. 2) At which you find that there are no thoughts drifting into your awareness. Your "mind" is a blank screen. It is at these points, especially the latter, that you can shift your attention from the lower abdomen to your creative visualization work.

Accompanying these experiences is the feeling that your breathing no longer wants to proceed at the direction of the will. It has been taken over by the life-force. Let the breathing proceed on its own. You will find that it becomes very smooth and fine, slows down, comes to a stand still, and resumes by itself. This is the moment of Kevala Kumbhaka. You have achieved an effective state of trance.

Managing the Sphere of Awareness During Meditation

Throughout the chanting it is important to keep the attention focused on the image that has been chosen for the meditation objective. While chanting the heka of Ausar for the purpose of healing a friend, I visualize myself wearing the white crown (see the Ausar card), passing the Uas staff (symbol of well being, and happiness--see Appendix A). This image and the mantra are the entire contents of the sphere of awareness. There must be no verbalized thoughts about reasons, stages, process of healing, etc. Critical for success in meditation is the unification of the two hemispheres of the brain. This is achieved by giving the left side of the brain a right-brained task. Rhythm, melody, and repetition are intrinsic to the functions of the right side of the brain. When the left side of the brain is deprived of its "straight line" sequential mental processing, and given right brained processing-circular (repetitive) and rhythmic tasks-it unites itself to the latter. In addition, the circular activity of chanting concentrates the attention to one spot.

Meditating on your Readings

The format to be followed is the same one detailed in chapter 13. Regardless of your reading you must go through the 4 meditations of stage 1, and the meditation of stage 2. In stage 3 you will work on the heka of the deity, or deities of your reading, using the appropriate image (see Appendix A) for your objective. Then continue with the Men Ab practices of stage 4 (Chapter 14), and the meditations of stages 5 and 6. As for the last four stages, you should make a good go at it.

HEKAU OF THE DEITIES

Coordinating the Breathing with the Chanting

Note that the inbreath occurs during the 1st, and 2nd counts. It is held from the 3rd to the 6th, and the outbreath occurs during the 7th, and 8th. The perineum is contracted at the 3rd count and held until the 6th.

The Rate of Breathing

Mediumistic trance induction takes place at 7.5 breaths per minute (each count lasts about a second). The depth of breathing is slightly greater than normal, but not too deep.

Waking trance induction takes place at 4.5 and 3 breaths per minute. At 4.5 breaths per minute each count will last slightly under 2 seconds. At 3 breaths per minute, each breath count will last about 2.5 seconds. The depth of breathing must reach the full capacity.

The following chants are to be done at the three prescribed rates. The 3 breaths per minute should not be attempted until the 4.5 rate can be handled with ease for over an hour.

Following are the instructions for coordinating the breathing with the chant. The chanting must be done mentally. The music score for the hekau has been placed at the end of the book. Cassette recordings of them are available, as well. They can be ordered from the publisher. See the address on the front page of the book.

Ausar

	Aung	Ausar	Hung		Aung	Ausar	Hung
count 1	2	3	4		5	6	7 8
Breath:							
	in	held					out

Tehuti

Aung	Hung			Shring	Aung	
count 1	2	3	4	5	6	7 8
Breath:						
	in	held				out

Seker

Aung	Kring		Aung	Kring	Aung	
count 1	2	3	4	5	6	7 8
Breath:						
	in	held					out

Maat

	Aung	Shring	Aung	Shring		
count 1	2	3	4	5	6	7 8
Breath:						
	in	held				out

Herukhuti

	Hlring			Hrah		
count 1	2	3	4	5	6	7 8
Breath:						
	in	held					out

Heru

			Heru	Ausar	Hrah		
Aung							
count 1	2	3	4	5	6	7	8
Breath:							
	in	held				out	

Het-Heru

			Kling	Sauh			
Vang							
count 1	2	3	4	5	6	7	8
Breath:							
	in	held				out	

Sebek

			Aing		Aung		Aing
Aung							
count 1	2	3	4	5	6	7 8	
Breath:							
	in	held				out	

Auset

			Vang	Duhung		
Aung						
count 1	2	3	4	5	6	7 8
Breath:						
	in	held			out	

Planetary
They all use the same melody

Aung	Shrang	Shring	Shraung	Aung		
count 1	2	3	4	5	6	7 8
Breath:						
	in	held			out	

SESH METUT NETER

The Sesh Metut Neter-the Book (of the) Word (of) God-is the work of the Goddess of wisdom, Seshat. This sister of Maat, hence belonging to the 4th sphere, corresponds to a faculty in the right side of the brain which processes the abstract meanings of images, and aids in the internalization of the focus of consciousness. The term "metut" is a very interesting example of the Kamitic linguistic process. It is a punning derivative of "metu" (word, speech), and "tut" (image, beget, clothe, collect, resemblance, statue). While "metu" primarily, though not exclusively denotes the phonetic, definitive (masculine) side of words, "metut" denotes, in most cases, the graphic, descriptive (feminine) side. As a derivative pun it combines the sound "tu" common to both words, with the related communication and creative functions of phonetic symbols-"metu," and graphic symbols-"tut." The denotations of "tut" can be easily related. "To beget" corresponds to the creative functions of "imagery." We thus find "tut" in such phrases as "Tut Meshes Neteru," meaning "the image producer of the deities." "To collect" is to be understood in two ways. On one hand it refers to the concentration, or the ingathering of the faculties by focusing it on something. We find the following phrases in the literature, "tut ma" (to concentrate the vision, to gaze intensely on something), "tut ab" (to concentrate the will, to keep the will focused on something. I.e., keeping the attention focused on an image is one of the major keys to keeping the attention focused on the object of meditation). On the other hand, it refers to the synthesizing, and condensing power of images. As it is said, "a picture is worth a thousand words." The last meaning, as seen earlier, is the function of the 4th sphere.

From these we can understand why the Kamitians gave such importance to the hieroglyphic script, and the graphic arts (paintings, and statues). To this day, egyptologists are unable to give an intelligent reason for the fact that the Kamitians never gave up their hieroglyphic script with all its difficulties and cumbersomeness (hundreds of symbols), in spite of having produced the phonetic scripts (demotic, and hieratic) of about 27 symbols which form the basis of the very same script in which this book is written, and which most European, and Semitic people use. The key is to be found in the fact that the hieroglyphic (metut) script was used for most religious, literary, and wisdom texts, while the phonetic (metu) script, once created, was used for accounting and legal documents. Once today's psychologists and scholars understand that descriptive language (showing), and graphic symbols are superior to phonetic language (telling) for the realization of understanding, then they will understand the Kamitic attitude to hieroglyphs.

The Sesh Metut Neter is a set of symbols tightly woven into the Kamitic cosmology which enables us to think complete and interrelated ideas on all subjects without verbalizing our thoughts. The fundamental principle behind this system resides in the fact that verbal thinking is the property of the left side of the brain which externalizes consciousness and is thus an obstructor of meditation. It is also the seat of our conditioned and earth born beliefs (the Sebau-enemies of Ra and Ausar), and thus the obstructor of our efforts to transcend our lower self. This is the substance of the saying, "Never let your left hand (should be, left side of the brain) know what the right hand is doing." Hypnotherapists may find this very useful, as one of their greatest problems is the depotentiating of resistances in the subject.

Meditation, therefore, relies heavily on the use of concrete and symbolic images. In the Kamitic tradition this was accomplished through the so-called "determinatives" of the hieroglyphic script, and the paintings, and statues of the deities that were so abundantly displayed in Kamitian society. Given the high degree of spiritual, and psychological sophistication behind the use of imagery, we must, from one point of view, forgive the Semitic and European people for their inability to do anything more than invent the concept that Africans were worshipers of idols. How could they understand that they were using a device for minimizing or excluding the involvement of the left side of the brain in their mental processes that were aimed at extracting meaning, or shutting out the verbal thought processes in order to bring to the fore the higher mental faculties?

If Westerners truly understood religion, and the processess of the brain, they would surround themselves with synthesizing images of divine themes, as Africans do, in place of all the "synthesizing images of materialism and hedonism" with which they surround themselves; billboards for tobacco, junk food, sex, alcoholic drinks, gambling, etc.

Following are a few basic symbols that can be used to non-verbally express your intention while meditating. Note that although they are

405

each associated to one of the stages of the meditiation process, they can be used in any stage.

Note: The illustrations for these metutu are given at the end of this book.

1. The Ab: associate with it all information relating to the will, Heru (Shango, Shemesh, etc.), self reliance, confidence, courage to submit to truth, and wise counsel from a sage, etc.. Use it in place of such suggestions as "I follow my will," "my will is strong, and effective," "I have confidence in my Self," "I am self-reliant." To say that you are righteous, or that you follow divine law, see your heart balancing a feather on the scales (see the Maat card). Stage 1 - 4 of meditation.

2. The Aungkh: It is the hieroglyphic represetation of the heka "Aung." Use it to symbolize giving, or receiving the life-force. As it corresponds to the undifferentiated life-force, you will have to combine it with other metut (symbols). With the Uas staff for health and happiness; with the Menat for joy; with Khepera for spiritual, or intellectual, or physical fertility, etc. 1st stage of meditation. In stage 1, and 3 of the meditation see a brilliant white aungkh entering your body, or of someone else, as a symbol of healing.

3. Apep: Associate with it all negative emotional, and sensual behavior patterns. In constrast to Westerners, who glorify or categorize these behaviors as human traits, the Kamitians classified them as animal traits. The serpent will remind you of the ambushing, and venemous nature of emotions, and sensuality. As the "serpents" and "worms" were the chief enemies of Ra, using them as symbols of your emotions, will help to keep uppermost in mind that the uncontrolled indulgence of emotions will rob you of your vitality, upon which depends your ability to invoke the deities (i.e., manifest the powers of the hekau), and through them to control the events in your life. See yourself cutting off the heads of the serpents, and stabbing them. 4th stage of meditation.

4. Auset: Associate all ideas of making the realization of your divinity the top priority in your life. First four stages of meditation.

5. The Ba: This is the part of the spirit in which dwells the Ausar faculty. Having realized some of the values of Ausar in your

daily life, chant Aung Hang Kshang, see yourself as the Ba bird wearing the White Crown of Ausar, and astral project to wherever you need to go.

6. The sistrum: Sistrums sound like tambourines without resonance. In Kamit they were used along with Het-Heru chants to drive away the depressive emotions (evil spirits) which drain away the life-force. As you meditate on the Het-Heru chant visualize yourself dancing, and shaking the sistrum. Hear the sound. Use this meditation when depressed in place of dwelling on the thought content of your depression. 3rd stage of meditation.

7. The Bennu: This is the so-called phoenix which rises out of the ashes. It is the symbol of succeeding in holding on to the values of Ausar when strongly tempted to function according to the lower self. The ashes are symbolic of having been burned by the heat of Ra (tapas) that is generated in all difficult situations in which we are challenged to live Truth. Rather than verbalizing your thoughts, see yourself as the Bennu bird flying away from the situation. Associate all Ausar information with it. 1st - 4th stages of meditation.

8. Bes: Symbol of merriment, and joy. Bes is a "celestial" musician that is in charge of inducing merriment, which is a healing source, especially for the female reproductive system.

9. The Shepherds' Crook: This is a sign of dominion, and leadership through inner force. It is gentleness without, and force within. Use to meditate on a situation that requires working with inner force, as opposed to the outer display of power. This is especially important when you get a Heru/Auset reading, as well as Heru readings dealing with domestic, and family matters. Stages 1 - 3.

10. The Djed: It symbolizes the backbone of Ausar. Associate all ideas about stability, the stilling of thoughts, and so on, with it.

11. The Ausar glyph: Associate all Ausar material with it. Use it to remind yourself of the importance of stage one-the foundation-of the meditation process. Stages 1 - 4.

12. The Flail: This is the sign of dominion, and leadership through the outer show of force. But this is the force of Heru who declares his authority by being an exemplar of strength of character, and the rule of truth, as opposed to Herukhuti's outer display of force through threats of harm. Stages 1 - 4.

13. Heru-Pa-Khart: See Chapter 17 under Heru. Use it to remind yourself (stage 1 - 3) of the role of hekau in the use of your will.

14. The 4 supports of heaven: Associate with it all ideas of the role of order and cycles in your life. The 4 supports of heaven are the cardinal points which as symbols of the 4 basic phases of cycles, and the 4 sources of the electromagnetism influencing all events on earth are used to symbolize the divine order that controls life. Stages 1 - 8.

15. The Heh glyph: It is a symbol of eternity ("the millions of years"). See yourself holding these two branches as a means of indicating that your life, or the life of your enterprise (a business, marriage, etc.) will last a long time. Stages 1 - 3.

16. Arrows of Neith: Visualize it as the insignia of a shield or banner, to symbolize a means of protecting the person (Ka).

17: Khepera: It is a symbol of spiritual and physical fertility. Kamitian women used to eat them-especially the green variety-on the belief that they increased fertility. Stages 1 - 3.

18. Khenemu: This is the symbol of the elemental spirits that carry out the work of the hekau on the level of the animal spirit.

19. The Lotus: The fact that lotuses have their roots in water, and open and close their flowers in relationship to the amount of sunlight they receive, make them apt symbols of the chakras (psychic centers). They too have their roots in the waters (Nut), and require the arousal of Ra in order to become fully active. Use it to remind yourself of the processess that you must use in order to achieve your goals in a spiritual fashion.

20. The Papyrus Scepter: Papyrus was the plant used by the Kamitians to make paper, hence the source of the word itself. The scepter then, is a symbol of the dominant role, or importance of written records in our life, especially, the recordings of divine law,- the scriptures, cosmologies, scientific principles, and data, etc. Use it to meditate on your need to be more informed of laws, scientific principles, and data. Stages 2, and 4 of the meditation process.

21. The Menat: Associate all ideas of joy to it.

22. Min: This Deity represents the attainment of success, through discipline (symbolized by the flail raised overhead), and the cultivation of a high libido, yet moderated sexual indulgence (symbolized by the erect phallus). Min was chiefly depicted

in this form, standing at the top of stairs, where he received the offerings of the first fruits.

23a. Left Utchat: Aabit, the left, lunar eye of Ra. It corresponds to the right side of the brain. Associate all ideas regarding the use of visualizations that are aimed at gaining insight, especially when the breath is flowing predominantly through the left nostril. You can tell by placing a mirror under the nostrils to see which one makes a greater fog. This power is also greater during the waxing half of the month, the second half of the day, the second half of the year, etc.

23b. Right Utchat: Aakhut, the right, solar eye of Ra. It corresponds to the left side of the brain. Associate all ideas regarding the use of visualizations that are used aggressively or defensively. This eye is more powerful when the breath is flowing predominantly through the right nostril.

24. The Uas Scepter: This is the symbol of well being, happiness, and good health.

25. The Sa: It corresponds to the mode of energy/matter that the spirit uses to form our sense images (imaging of tastes, smells, etc.).

26. The Shekem staff: Use it to represent all ideas regarding the manifestation of power on the third sphere level of being.

27. The head of Set: This symbol is used to represent the use of clever rationalizations and force to oppress and control others.

28. Tem's Crown: The crown of two plumes is used to identify yourself with Tem, the representative of Ausar in the Ra system.

29. The Tet: This symbol, popularly known as "Auset's buckle," in reality, depicts the union of the organs of generation. It is the Kamitic counterpart of the linga-yoni of Dravidian India. Use it to denote the idea of becoming pregnant, or the idea of uniting the will to the spirit, through mediumistic trance.

30. Sma Taui: This symbol represents the unity of all dualities. The papyrus plant represents the left side of the brain and all yang correspondences. The lotus plant represents the right side of the brain and all ying correspondences.

31. Hetep: Use it to denote the idea of the state of peace that cannot be upset by any externals. As this is the source of power, it can also be extended to denote the idea of the ability to

409

generate the power to achieve a goal by maintaining an unshakeable inner peace.

These are but a few of the symbols composing the Sesh Metut Neter. If you work consistently with all of them you will establish a sophisticated means of communicating with your life-force. Once programmed into the spirit, the divine intelligences (Deities), and ancestors will use these symbols to communicate with you during dreams, and meditations.

Select Bibliography

Avalon, Arthur. *The Serpent Power*. New York: Dover Publications, Inc.1974.

Baron Von Reichenbach, Karl. *Researches on the Vital Force*. Secaucus, New Jersey: University Books, 1974.

Budge, E. A. Wallis. *The Book of the Dead: The Papyrus of Ani*. New York: Dover Publications Inc., 1967.

Budge, E. A. Wallis. *The Gods of the Egyptians: Or Studies In Egyptian Mythology. Vol. I*. New York: Dover Publications Inc., 1969.

Budge, E. A. Wallis. *An Egyptian Hieroglyphic Dictionary*. . New York: Dover Publications Inc., 1978.

Butt-Thompson, F.W. *West African Secret Societies: Their Organisations, Officials and Teaching*. Argosy-Antiquarian LTD., 1969.

Cabrera, Lydia. *El Monte (Igbo-Finda; Ewe Orisha. Vititi Nfinda)*. Miami, Florida, 1983.

Cameron, Barbara. *Turning The Tables*. American Federation of Astrologers, Inc., 1984.

Chattopadhyaya, Sudhakar. *Reflections on the Tantras*. Delhi: Motilal Banarsidas, 1978.

Cheng-Yu, Li, and Paul Zmiewski (eds.). *Fundamentals of Chinese Medicine*. trans. Nigel Wiseman, and Andrew Ellis Brookline, Massachusetts: Paradigm Publications, 1985.

Digambarji, Swami, and Pt. Raghunathashastri Kokaje (eds.). *Hathapradipika of Svatmarama*. Lonavla, Dist. Poona: Kaivalyadhama, S.M.Y.M. Samiti, 1970.

Erman, Adolf. *Life In Ancient Egypt*. New York: Dover Publications, Inc., 1971.

Evans-Wentz, W.Y. *Tibetan Yoga and Secret Doctrines*. Oxford University Press, 1958.

George, Llewellyn. *Improved Perpetual Planetary Hour Book*. 11th ed. rev. St. Paul Minnesota: Llewelly Publications, 1975.

Graves, Robert, and Raphael Patai. *Hebrew Myths: The Book of Genesis*. New York: McGraw Hill Book Company, 1964.

Harris, J.R.(ed.). *The Legacy of Egypt*, 2d ed. Oxford: Clarendon Press, 1971.

Hawkes, Jacquetta. *The First Great Civilizations*. New York: Alfred A. Knopf, 1973.

Hawkes, Jacquetta, and Sir Leonard Woolley. *History of Mankind vol I. The Beginnings of Civilization.* New York and Evanston: Harper & Row, 1963.

Jahn, Janheinz. *Muntu: The New African Culture.* Grove Press, 1961.

Kunte, M.M. *The Vicissitudes of Aryan Civilization In India.* Delhi: Heritage Publishers, 1974.

Mackenzie, Donald A. *Indian Myth and Legend.* New Delhi: Sona Publications, 1971.

McKenzie, John L. *Dictionary oof The Bible.* New York, London: Macmillan Publishing Company, 1965.

Rawson, Philip. *The Art of Tantra.* New York and Toronto: Oxford University Press, 1978.

Simmonite, W.J. *The Arcana of Astrology.* Hollywood, Calif.: Newcastle Publishing Company, Inc., 1974

Tripathi, R.S. Deli: *History of Ancient India.* Varanasi: Patna Motilal Banarsidass, 1942.

Walters, Derek. *The T'ai Hsuan Ching The Hidden Classic.* Wellingborough, Northamptonshire: The Aquarian Press, 1983.

Wilhelm, Richard, and Baynes, Cary F. *The I Ching.* Princeton University Press, 1967.

Worthington, Vivian. *A History of Yoga.* Routledge & Kegan Paul, 1982.

Yu, Lu K'uan. *Taoist Yoga: Alchemy and Immortality.* New York: Samuel Weiser Inc., 1973.

0 sphere 85, 96, 97, 99, 136
10th sphere 63, 95, 96, 97, 98, 99,
         104, 133, 138, 244
12 Hours of the Night 88
14 chakras 224
14 kau of Ra 210
1st division of the spirit 59
1st sphere 59, 69, 85, 96, 99, 101,
         160, 167
    See Ausar 59
2nd sphere 60, 69, 71, 79, 86, 96, 101,
         102, 103, 121, 153, 159, 160,
         167, 199
33 degrees of Masonry 131
3rd sphere 60, 70, 73, 80, 84, 86, 96,
         102, 158, 167, 199, 246
4th division of the spirit 59
4th sphere 57, 61, 70, 71, 73, 75, 88,
         92, 95, 96, 103, 104, 112, 134,
         157, 158, 167, 170, 217, 218
50 Gates of Binah 57
50 matrikas 57
50 Oarsmen of the boat of Ausar
         57
50 creative forces 87
50 sound units of power 158, 222
50 units of power 57
5th division of the spirit 59
5th sphere 57, 61, 71, 75, 81, 89, 96,
         104, 156, 157, 167
6th division of the spirit 59
6th sphere 36, 57, 62, 71, 80, 90, 91,
         92, 96, 104, 156, 167, 168,
         186, 196
7th division of the spirit 59
7th sphere 57, 62, 71, 75, 80, 83, 92,
         93, 96, 102, 109, 127, 135,
         145, 152, 167, 180, 246
8th spere 63

8th sphere 72, 76, 79, 83, 93, 96, 102,
         103, 108, 126, 127, 128, 129,
         130, 133, 134, 135, 142, 145,
         152, 166, 178, 245, 246
9th sphere 36, 58, 63, 72, 79, 93, 95,
         96, 99, 101, 102, 104, 127,
         133, 139, 152, 162, 166, 174,
         213, 245
Ab 57, 88, 107, 122, 123, 222
Ab division of the Spirit 152, 156,
         157
Ab Man 105, 110
Abortion 128
Absolute Being 77
Abstract ideals 183
Abstract relational category 119
Abstract thinking 84
Abstractions 89
Abundance 277
Acacia tree 141
Acid PH 238
Acupuncture 238
Administrative organs of Being 59
Adversities 160
Af 222
Africa, for the decade 370
Africa, traditional 11
Aganyu 226
Age regression meditation 178
Agriculture
    13000 B.C. 34
Aima 221
Ain 77, 160
Aisha 98
Ajna 240
Akan 51, 55
Akans 57
Akhenaten 51
Aksobhya 44, 220
Al Jabar mu Quabalah 216

413

Alchemy 74
Algebra 216
Alkaline PH 238
Alpha state 399
Ama 222
Amandhla 58
Amen 53, 77, 160, 167, 205, 212, 244
     See Subjective Realm 69
Amenta 233
Amorites 30
Amset 229
Analogies 260
Analysis 10, 18
Analysis, defined 89
Anandamaya Kosha 55
Ancestor communication rituals 128
Ancestor worship 128, 237
Ancestors 14, 20, 234, 236
Ancestry 254
Angels 15, 36, 64
     are deities 37
Anger 145
Animal division of Man's spirit 98
Animal sacrificial rituals 219
Animal spirit 98, 127, 129, 133, 152,
     181
Animal-headed people 192
Animals 98
Animism 18
Ankh cross 226
Annu 214
Anpu 145, 178, 192, 233
Anthropomorphism 117
Anubis 145, 233
Anuk, and aunk 144
Ap-Uat 143, 233
Apep 98
Aphrodisiacs 148
Aquarius 267
Archangels 36, 64

Archetypes 184, 209
Armenians 30
Arphaxad 31
Artistic faculty 92
Aryan 43, 148
Aryans 34
As above, So below 223, 258
Asamprajnata Sarvikalpa Nirvana
     53
Asamprajnata Samadhi 165
Asanas 147, 386
Asar 213
Asceticism 150
Ashiah 58
Association, law of 190
Astral body 58
Astral Light 58
Asvini mudra 149, 185
At-onement 165
Atheism 140
Atziluth 55
Auaraut 239
Auasasit 214
Aum 38, 43
Aum Ham Kshang 261
Aum-mit 222
Aummaum 198, 222
Aung 213, 214, 226, 234
Aung Aing 179
Aung Ausar Hung 204
Aung Hang Kshang 263
Aung Hlring 195
Aung Hring 195
Aung Hung Shring 204
Aung Kring 201
Aung Shring 196
Aung Tang 234
Aung Tang sutcha-a Het-Hert 185
Aung Vang Duhung 176
Aunk 234

414

Aunk cross 60
Aupep 145
Aur 50, 237
Aura 395
Auraut 240
Aus 213
Aus-t 213
Ausar 54, 55, 79, 82, 106, 118, 126,
        127, 128, 130, 140, 143, 152,
        153, 156, 160, 166, 172, 174,
        175, 178, 180, 183, 212, 219,
        245, 248
    African kingship 21
    See indwelling intelligence 142
    See the 1st sphere 59
Ausarian metaphorein 162, 188
Ausars 82, 213
Auset 21, 72, 79, 127, 129, 152, 162,
        184, 214, 233, 248
Auset's devotion 141
Austerities 138
Avatar 202
Awakened, becoming 152
Ayurvedas 139
B-hang 395
Ba 55, 56, 122
Ba Division of the Spirit 160
Ba Man 112
Babalu Aye 56, 271
Baboons 177
Bach flower remedies 219
Bala Rama 392
Bandhas 147
Bantu 17, 51, 55, 212
Bantus of South Africa 10
Bast 242
Belief system 100
Belief system, reshaping 142
Belief systemss 172
Believing acquired information 133

Beni Alohim 57
Beta state 399
Bhakti yoga 219
Bhuddism 43
Binah 56
Boddhidharma 44
Boddhisattvas 54
Book of Knowing the Manifestations
        of Ra 51, 82
Book of that Which is in the
        Underworld 223
Born again 233
Brahmins 42
Brain 176
    comprehension 9
    left hemisphere 9
    right hemisphere 9
Briah 56, 57
Broca 231
Buddhism 43, 44
Cabala
    See Kabala 35
Canaan 24, 28, 29, 30
Canon 71
Caput draconis 238
Caring 295
Cartesian logic 10
Casting of lots 209
Categorical imperative 220
Cauda draconis 238
Causal level 211
Causative mechanism, the 63
Celestial government 70, 110
Chakras 229
Challenges in life 155
Chanting 87
Chi 138
Chi kung 238
Chiah 56
Chinese medical system 217

Chinnamasta 44, 56, 219, 220
Chokmah 56
Christ 184
Christian tradition 184
Christianity 141, 158
Citizenship 205
Civilization 8, 68, 126, 130, 168
    racial contact 24
    why created by Blacks 18
Civilization, founders
    racial identity 22
Civilization, origins
    hieroglyphic system 25
Clairvoyance 241
Clan heads, into a web of
        responsibilities that would
        be expected only from the
        immediate family. 236
Clarity of mind 229
Classification set of species 57
Cleverness 134, 233
Closed systems 203
Cold and moist 95
Colors 162
Communicating with the dead 236
Communications media 132
Concentrate 273
Concentration 164, 199, 386
Conditioned reflex 85
Conflicts in society 90
Congregative thinking 92
Conscience 222
Conscious effort 43
Consciousness
    Subjective 69
Consciousness, described 163
Consciousness grasps consciousness
        165
Consciousness of being conscious
        164, 205

Consciousness raising 139
Consciousness, states of 164
Contradictions, exposing 142
Copper Age 389
Coptic language 27, 33
Cosmo-logical method 112
Cosmo-logical thinking 88
Cosmogonies
    are systems theories 66
Cosmogony 65, 68
    function of 52
Cosmology 49, 65, 68, 225
    definition of 47
Counselling 219
Creation
    goal of 71
    reasons for 53, 61
Creative 'imaging 102
Creative organs of Being 59
Creative vehicles of Neter 61
Creative visualization 129, 219
Criminal acts 125
Crook 202
Crossroad 155, 195, 225, 260
Crossroad, the 187
Crossroads 158, 188, 219
Crystal healing 298
Crystal working 219
Cultural expressions 20
Culture
    biological factors 19
Cycles 200, 216, 229, 274
Cycles of the body 166
Cyclical alternation of phases 139
Dambadah Wedo 226
Darwinism 23, 28
Dasas 34
Dasyus 34
Deceased 233
Definitions 111, 156, 232

Deities 64, 67, 83, 100, 167, 171, 181, 183
Deities are hekau 87
Deity 153
Deity invocation 182
Deity invocations 253
Descriptions 232, 292
Desire 187
Desires 97, 152, 153
Destiny 153, 188, 222, 245, 358
Detachment 195, 205
Details, how coordinated 92
Devil 129, 135
Devotion 129, 136
Dhumo 154
Dhung 142
Dhyani-Buddhas 43
Dianetics 219
Diaspora, the 131
Diet, and spiritual culture 138
Discipline 155
Divination by lots 238
Divine historical plan 159
Divine Kingship 206
Divine law 222, 248
Divine plan 116, 219
Divine power 97
Divine powers 116, 173
Djed 357
Dog-headed ape (Auaun) 292
Dogons 19
Doomsday 125
Dravidian India 214
Dravidians 34, 39, 139
Dream activity 166
Dreaming 383
Dreaming state 164
Dreams 209, 264
Drugs 149
Duality 99

Duality of our nature 194
Duality principle 96
Duality, principle of 77
Dualization 5, 18
Dvapara Yuga 389
E-motive force 185
Earth 247
Earthborn ideas 179
Earthly life, reason for 167
Eber 31
Economics 122, 123, 203
Ecstasy 159
Ecstatic trance 129, 145, 151
Education 94, 124, 291
Effects to causes 211
Egotism 18
Egyptian Book of the Dead 155, 179
Egyptian language 12
Egyptian way of thinking 12, 17
Ejaculation 147
El 36, 73
Elders 252
Electromagnetic currents 162
Electromagnetic energies 98
Electromagnetic forces of the earth 298
Electromagnetic motive force 59
Electropositive elements 238
Elegba 36, 233
Elohim 73
Embalming 178, 179
Emotion, defined 192
Emotion, etymology of term 146
Emotional expressions 176
Emotional suppression 139
Emotions 97, 112, 144, 150, 179, 185, 189, 190, 192
Emotions, cravings, and desires can never be guides to living. 99

417

Empire 126
Endocrine organs 150
Enlightenment 204
Equilibirium
    Law of 62
Equilibrium 245, 246, 265
    and the spheres 54
Equilibrium, doctrine of 78, 90, 91
Equinox 263
Eros 145
Erpau of the Gods 235
Esse 213
Essential state of the Supreme Being
    82
Etheric double 58
Ethiopia 33
Europe 1992 369
Evil 134, 266, 282
Evil, foundation of 134
Evil spirits 395
Evolution 84, 157
    Stage 1 107
    Stage 2 110
    Stage 3 112
Evolution, spiritual 157
Evolutionary ladder 100
Evolutionism 17, 183
Exploitation 134
Eye of Heru 230
Failure 255
Failure, causes 86, 87
Failures 266
Fakirism 238
Fall of Man 98
Fasting 139, 263
Fear 156
Feather 226, 252
Fertility 234
Festivities 146
Fetishes 298

Fetishism 238
Field theory 66
Fiery 95
Fiery person 182
Fire 92
First 28 years of our life 83
Flail 202
Following 94
Forces of nature 100
Forgetting 141
Four elements 74, 139
Four-fold organization 57
Fourteen kau of Ra 242
Fourteen pieces 128, 131
Fractional abstraction 184
Full moon 142
Gaia 235
Gang 395
Garden of Eden 98
Geb 58, 133, 235, 248
Gematria, 144
Genesis 1
    26 197
Genesis I
    27 73
Geology 235
Geomancy 248
Gestalt theory 66
Gestation of the impregnated idea
    234
God 119
    definition 258
God-head 49
Goddess 147
Goddess of wisdom 170
Golden Age 389
Golden mean 90
Gonads 150, 229
Good vs. evil
    foundations of 18

Government 89, 126, 202, 206
Gtummo 154
Guide of the Dead 145
Habit 129
Ham 25, 26, 28, 29, 119
Hang 241
Hapi 229
Happiness 98, 99, 162
Happiness, misdefined 97
Happiness, quest for 96
Harappa 39
Harpocrates 229
Hatha yoga 238
Hatha Yoga asanas 392
Hawk 177
Hawk of gold 183
Healing 212, 234
Health 8, 162, 201
Hearsay 111
Heaven 55, 247
Hebrew language 25
Heka 36
    and creation 62
    See mantras 80
    See sound waves 80
Hekau 112, 199, 219, 228, 260
Hemispheres of the brain 9, 19, 20,
        28
    and culture, sexes, races 10
    and history, anthropology as
            science 10
    and religion 13
Hennu 221
Hercules 392
Hermaphrodite 292
Herodotus 26
Heru 111, 127, 129, 130, 131, 152,
        155, 162, 163, 184, 192, 227,
        229, 246, 248
Heru against Set 136

Heru defeats Set 132
Heru Khenti an Maati 228
Heru over Set 136
Heru the Blind 228
Heru, the child 229
Heru's initial failure to defeat Set
        188
Heru-Behutet 226
Heru-Pa-Khart 228
Herukhuti 152, 226, 246
    See 5th sphere 75
Het-Heru 129, 135, 150, 151, 152,
        185, 229, 242, 247, 370
    See 7th sphere 76
Het-Heru, meaning of name 150
Hetep 97, 160, 212, 266
    See peace, happiness 98
Hierarchical administration 119
Hieroglyphic script 169
Hieroglyphic system 28
Hieroglyphs 25, 111, 169, 192
Hinayana 43
Hinduism 39, 78, 150
Historical events
    biological factors 19
Hittites 30
Hod 57
Holistic thinking 10
Homeopathy 238
Homosexuality 104
Honhom 55
Hot and dry 95
Hring 100
Hu, God of the senses 144
Hum 44
Human classes 95
Hung 220
Hydra 247
Hydra serpent of Greek mythology
        101

Hydration (water) factor 74
Hyksos 24
Hypnosis 175, 387
Hypnotherapists 180
Hypnotherapy 219
Hypnotic autosuggestions 156
Hypnotic trance
    See mediumistic trance 144
Hypnotist 164
I Ching 209, 216
Identification of our Selves with
        Ausar 140
Idols 169
Ifa 56, 209
Illness 139
Illusion of being separate 95
Image 253
Images 80, 181, 230
    ordering function 72
Imagination 80, 92, 102, 135, 148,
        150, 181, 230, 247, 289
Imitation 94, 176
Immaculate conception 129
Immorality 84, 88
Immortality 15
Immune responses 227
Immunity 156
Imperialism 130
Incarnation of a Deity 100
Individual, defined 99
Indivisible duality 77
Indus Kush 55, 87, 219
Indus Valley 24, 39, 53, 54
Indwelling intelligence 140, 142, 162,
        166, 220
Infidelity 151
Information 134
Initiation 133, 137, 138, 381
    a goal 153
    candidates 139

dead, the 159
goal of 161
level 1 136
level 2 136
level 3 136
level 4 136
stage 1 139, 142
stage 10 160
stage 2 142, 145, 160
stage 3 145, 152, 153
stage 4 152, 156
stage 5 156, 157
stage 6 157, 158
stage 7 158, 159
stage 8 159
stage 9 160
Initiator 164
Intellect, lower 129
Intellectualism 43
Interdependence 157
Intuitive cosmologically ordered
        thinking 88
Invention 109
Involuntary functions 141, 153
Involuntary" vital functions 213
Iron Age 389
Irrational 125
Irrationality 94, 203
Isis
    See Auset 21
Isitunsi 58
Israel 31
Israel, origins
    Hittite, Amorite 29
Iye 58
Jackal 177
Janheinz Jahn 11
Japa 117, 392
Japheth 25
Jewish kabalism 156

Jewish polytheism 36
Jivan Atma 72
Jnana Yoga 270
Joshua 32
Joy 145, 196, 200, 223, 230
Judiciary system 207
Jupiter 152, 158
Jusitice, basis of 90
Justice 104, 156, 195, 227
Ka 58, 72, 181, 248, 297
Kabala 35, 37
Kabalistical method 112
Kali 56, 200, 222
Kali Yuga 389
Kalunga 56
Kam 25, 212
Kam-Au 212
Kamakhhyatantra 149
Kamau 26
Kant 220
Kaos 48
Kematef 127, 129
Kensho 204
Kether 55, 69, 156
Ketu 238
Kevala Kumbhaka 400
Kevale Kumbhaka 387
Khab by the Kamitians, and .i.Guph
     58
Khaibit 58, 107, 109, 133, 135
Khemenu 371
Khenemet Aunkhet 234
Khepera 51, 82
Khepere 183, 221, 263
Khu 56, 107, 112, 121
Khu Division of the Spirit 159
Khut 204
Ki 138
King 124
Kingdom of God is within 141

Kingship 16, 184
Kingship, divine 128
Kinship groups 236
Kling 100
Knowing 12, 133
Knowing vs. believing 134
Knowledge 107
Knowledge of God 134
Knowledge of scripture 134
Knowledge of Self 5, 46, 61
Knowledge of words 134
Kri 60
Krita Yuga 389
Kronos 29
Kshang 241
Kula Yoga 149, 253
Kula Yoga Ritual 147
Kumbhaka 386
Kundala 224
Kundalini 57, 58, 87, 127, 129, 138,
     145
Kundalini, dangers of arousal 149
Kundalini Tantric Yoga 87
Kundalini Yoga 88, 156, 238
Lakshmi 89
Language 93, 231
Language, and initiation 143
Lavoisier 214
Law and order 88, 237
Law, Divine 88
Law enforcement 124
Laws 207
Laws, divine
     purpose 59
Laws, Kamitic 207
Leaders 206
Learning 94, 109
Learning, accelerated 168
Left hemisphere 19, 20, 66, 67, 108,
     179, 194, 201, 231, 240, 384

and meditation 168, 174
deactivating 169
Legal 13
Liberation, the Great 86
Libido 145, 150
Life after death 15
Life, purpose for manifesting 99
Life-force 138, 180
Linga Sarira 58
Living truth 225
Logic 13
Lotus 229
Lotus scepter 239
Love 89, 134, 196, 278
Love, falling in 151
Lower (northern) Kamit 239
Lower Yetzirah 57
Maa 111
Maa kheru 197
Maat 61, 89, 111, 143, 152, 172, 173,
185, 219, 222, 224, 246, 247,
273
feather 196
Maau 51
scale 196
See 4th sphere 75
See order 71
See synthesis 75
Maati 19
Macrocosm 48
Magic 80
Magnets 238
Maha Yuga 389
Mahamudra 115
Mahamudra Yoga 114
Mahayana 43
Man
purpose of 82
Man, "the likeness of God," 197
Man-Godhood 65

Mandalas 71
Manipura 242
Mantra
See heka 36
Mantra caitanya 226
Mantras 44, 80, 87, 100
See heka 80
Mars 152
Masculinization 229
Masses 105
Masses, the 131
Matrices 161
Matrikas 87
Maya 292
Meaning 231
Measurement 214
Meditation 140, 141, 158, 168
level 1 171
level 2 172
level 3 173
level 4 173
stage 1 166, 167
first meditation 174
fourth meditation 178
second meditation 175
third meditation 176
stage 10 167, 205
stage 2 166
first meditation 178
stage 3 166, 180
stage 4 167, 187, 195
stage 5 167, 195
stage 6 167, 195
stage 7 167, 199
stage 8 167, 203, 242
stage 9 167, 205
Meditation, essence of 163
Meditation, highest aim 163
Meditation process 115
Medium 368

Mediumistic trance 129, 141, 144,
    151, 164, 166, 181, 187, 193,
    209, 254, 257, 263, 264, 368,
    383, 400
Mediums 85, 153
Mehenet 242
Memory 94, 141
Men
    three types 7
Men Ab 205, 219, 229
Men Ab em Aungk Em Maat 189
Men Ab em Aungkh em Maat 155
Mercury 152, 230
Merimden culture 34
Messenger of the gods 230
Metalloids 238
Metaphorein 126
Metaphoreins 260
Metaphoric punning 213
Metaphoric stories 133
Metatron 267
Microcosm 48
Mindfulness 141, 194
Miracles 120
Mohenjo Daro 15, 39
Monotheism 67, 176
    thingish thinking 67
    unitary living 67
Monotheism versus Polytheism 65
Moon 142, 152, 240
Moonlight 238
Moral behavior 88
Moral developmen 83
Moral faculties 84
Morality 88, 104, 127
Moses 51
Mother of all Living things 63, 162
Mothers 233
Motivation 256
Motivation, secret of 148

Movement, origin of 96
Mudras 147
Mula bandha 185
Multiplicity of approaches 12
Mummification 178
Mummy 205
Muntu 143
Music 146
Mut 239
Myths 126, 134, 151
    origins 22
Nachash 98
Nada 60, 63
Nadhi Shuddi Pranayama 139
Nak 98
Naming ceremony 358
Nana Esse 72
Neb er Tcher 49, 205
Nebertcher 51, 357
Nebt-Het 127, 129, 230
Nekhebet 239
Nephesh 58
Nervous system 147
Neshamah 56
Neter 128, 174
Neter, defined 49
Neteru 64
Neurosis, a cause 150
Nkra 57
Noah 25
Non-REM 165
Non-REM period of sleep 383
Non-REM periods of sleep 266
Northern node of the moon 238
Notaricon 144
Noumenal plane
    definition 55
Ntu 51
Nu 50, 51, 55, 78, 160, 205
Nubians 24

423

Nummo serpents 19
Nut 55, 237
Nyakonpon 55
Nyame 51
Obatala 38, 55
Objective Realm 49
Obsession 149, 165, 384
Occult powers 117
Odomankoma 56
Odors 162
Offensive power of God 246
Offerings 155
Ogdad 216
Ojiji 58
Okra 57
Oladumare 51
Old Testament 30
Olodumare 266
Olokun 266
Omens 209
Omnipotence 60, 102
    defined 52
Omnipresence 60
    definition 52
Omniscience 60, 113, 144, 159, 173,
        204
    definition 52
One solution, one problem 176
Oneness, experience of 84
Oneness in action 91
Oneness of being 103
Open the Way 166
Opening of the Way 142, 180, 231
Opinions 199, 220
Optimism 167
Oracle 155, 202
Oracles 132, 153, 158, 159, 204, 209
Oracular readings 154
Order 71
    based on oneness 73

Order, explained 71
Order, program of 8
Orgasm 145
Orishas 64
Osiris
    See Ausar 21
Overtones 390
Pa Kua 216
Pachad 156
Padma Sambhava 44
Paganism 134
Paganism, true 148
Papyrus scepter 226, 239, 277
Parabrahm Sarvikalpa Nirvana 212
Parasympathetic nervous system 233
Patakis 367
Patanjali 165, 205
Path Without Form 114
Paut 183
Paut Neteru 63, 83
Pavlov 190
Peace 86, 97
Perineum 149, 241
Periodical table of elements 68
Periodical table of elements 217
Persians 30
Person 100, 116, 135, 140, 171, 178,
        182, 197
    See external part of being 8
Person, defined 100, 116
Personal good 245
Personalities 85, 100
Personality 165
Personality archetype (a deity) 164
Personality complex 85
Personality fragment 164
Persons 137
Persuasion 151
Pert em Heru 155, 166, 179, 194, 228
Pert em Hru 183

Phenomenal plane
    definition 55
Phenomenal plane, the 58
Phoenicia 24, 31
Photographic memory 141
Places in space and time 222
Placid Temples 10
Plan 153
Planetary hours 240
Planning 258
Pleasurable experiences 148
Pneumogastric nerve 193
Police systems 237
Policing system 127
Polytheism 36, 119, 126
    segregative living 67
Positive thinking 101, 178, 219
Possession 36, 148, 164, 384
Pot shaped breathing 114
Pranayama 147, 238, 386, 399
Pranayama Kosha 58
Prayer 219
Predestination 153
Prenatal chi 266
Primeval matter 82
Problems in the world 88
Problems, master causes 101
Prophets in government 206
Prosperity 86, 93
Prostitution 148
Psychic centers 229
Psychic healing 148
Psychic phenomena 145, 298
Psychic power 150, 158, 240
Psychic powers 139, 239
Psychics 85
Psychocybernetics 219
Ptah 222
Puberty rites 205
Punning derivation 213

Punt 25
Purim 210
Qadan culture 33
Qebhsennuf 229
Quadratic equations 216
Queen Mothers 16
Ra 50, 58, 87, 138, 145, 155, 166, 220,
    225, 228, 230, 237, 242, 258,
    259, 278, 395
Ra ritual system 156
Ra theology 88
Racism 157, 169
Radiasthesia 238, 298
Rahu 238
Rang 242
RaphaEl 36
Ras Shamra 31
Rationalizations 179
Rationalizations, basis of 134
Reality, defined 103
Reap what you sow 156
Reason
    not opposed to religion 13
Red crown 239
Relational eventualities 203
Relational thinking 67
Relaxation 99
Religion 104, 119, 234
    Ab Man 119
    and brain hemispheres 13
    definition 13
    law 13
    Sahu Man 119
    true 19
Religion and government 123
Religion, false definition 120
Religion, true 8
Religion,defined 118
Religions
    world's major 21

Religious consciousness 125
Religious stories 367
Religious systems 125, 131
Remembering 257
Ren 358
Reptilian brain 228
Resistance to change 151
Resolutions 141
Revelations 142
Revenge 104
Revolutionaries 131
Revolutions 131
Right hemisphere 19, 20, 24, 28, 48,
        67, 108, 201, 239
    and meditation 168, 174
    and systems thinking 66
Right side of the brain
    See right hemisphere 48
Ring passnot 285
Rishis 42
Ritual 141, 395
Ritual, essence of 163
Ritual system of the afflicted 202
Rituals 155, 158
River 129
Roots 298
Rosary 392
Rudrayamala 147
Sacred numbers 391
Sage 130, 159
Sages 85, 98
Sahu 58, 106, 109, 110, 112, 122, 123,
        125, 133, 135
Sahu division of the Spirit 139
Sahu is the 5th division of the spirit.
        .i.spirit
    5th division 105
Sahu Man 105, 107, 109, 114, 118,
        119, 122, 142, 179
Sahu men 127

Salvation 125
Samadhi 56, 165
Samadhi Sarvikalpa Nirvana 97
Samprajnata Samadhi 165
Sargon I of Akkad 130
Satan, origin of 135
Satipatthana 189
Satori 97
Saturn 201
Scepter of flint 226
Science 216
Science of chemistry 214
Scientists 292
Scriptures 121
Seb 232, 235
Sebau 126, 179, 232
Sebek 126, 128, 129, 133, 135, 219,
        230, 247
    See 8th sphere 76
    See brain
        left hemisphere 9
Sebek
            faculty of rationalization
        189
Sebku 230
Secret languages 143
Secret words 207
Sefkhit Aubut 170
Segregation 109
Segregation, racial, etc. 93
Segregative thinking 93, 102
Seker 56, 159, 221, 245, 285
Sekert 222
Sekhet 242
Sekhet Aaru 268
Sekmet 178
Self 99, 100, 140, 152, 156, 160, 163,
        182, 197
    Knowledge of vs. Belief 114
Self knowledge 115, 165

Self-identity 85
Self-image 116
Semites 25, 130
Semitic languages 31
Senses, stilling them 144
Sensory body 95
Sermon on the Mount 117
Sermons 144, 359
Sesh Metut Neter 169, 176, 184, 286
Seshat (also Seshait) 170
Set 124, 126, 127, 129, 130, 131, 135,
         143, 145, 151, 163, 174, 177,
         178, 192, 282
Set's penalty 132
Sex 138, 147, 150, 247
Sexual arousal 230
Sexual excitement 145
Sexual intercourse 148
Sexual passion 243
Sexual perversions 150
Sexual power 155
Shaddai 36
Shaddai El Chai 213
Shakti 39, 224
Shamanism 145
Shango 184, 230
Shapes 162
Sharing 158, 196
Shekem 56, 202, 224
Shekem Division of the Spirit 158
Shekinah 56, 145, 224
Shem 25, 31
Shemsu Heru 23
Sheps 237
Shinear 25
Shiva 39, 55, 117
Shri Deva 89
Shrine 202
Shrines 128, 129, 131
Shu 51, 74, 82

Sign of silence 229
Significators 362
Silver Age 389
Sky god 55
Sleep 154, 266
Sleeping 382
Smoking 84
Sobek 232
Social conflicts 132
Social role models 233
Solar force 149
Solar plexus 242
Soph 50, 78
Sound waves 80
South Africa 212, 370
Southern node of the moon 238
Space 216   ,
Sphere of Being 63
Sphere of awareness 394
Sphere of Living 63
Spirit
      5th division 107
      Khaibit 107
      Sahu 105, 107
Spirit, not Self 115
Spirit, programming 164
Spirit's program 164
Spiritual curriculum 154
Spiritual development 138, 143, 235
Spiritual development, measuring
         154
Spiritual exercises 158
Spiritual force 296
Spiritual growth 152, 155, 188
Spiritual immunity 297
Spiritual infancy 94
Spiritual liberation 150
Spiritual power 72, 126, 138, 155,
         298

Spiritual power intensification rituals 153
Spiritual protection 195, 227
Spiritual stagnation 266
Sramanas 42
St John 116
Sub-conscious 180
Sub-conscious mind 140
Subconscious 153, 233, 258
Subconscious mind 161
Subjective Being 61
Subjective Realm 49
Subjective state 69
Subliminal factors 298
Subliminal seduction 148
Subtle physics 173
Success 101, 158, 162, 248
Sufism 44
Sumer 24, 33
    source of Semitic culture 35
Sumerians 23
Sumsum 58
Sun 152, 240
Sun worship 237
Sunlight 238
Sunyatta 160
Super learning 18
Suppressed thoughts 94
Suppression 191
Supreme Being 83, 140
Supreme Being as the core of our being 140
Swadhisthana 243
Sweets 263, 265
Syllogistic logic 88, 217
Symbols 217
Sympathetic division of the nervous system 200
Sympathetic nervous system 228
Synchretism 44

Syntheism 35
Synthesis 10, 18, 75, 89, 92, 111, 169, 217, 369
Synthetical power of pictorial symbols 169
System 65
    defined 65
Systems theory 66
Systheism 120
Ta Neter 25
Ta-ui 19
Table of Nations 25
Tai chi 238
Talents 80
Tan Tien 385
Tang 395
Tantra 146
    bhuddhist 43
Tantra yoga 238
Tantric Buddhists of Tibet 114
Tantric Yoga System 147
Tao 216
Tao Te Ching 209, 216
Taoist yoga 238
Tar Lam Yoga 114
Tara 38, 44, 55, 234
Tarot 248, 265, 359
Te 183
Tefnut 51, 74, 82
Tehu 215
Tehuti 56, 127, 130, 132, 144, 145, 153, 159, 170, 188, 204, 209, 245, 248
Tem or Temu 214
Tem, Temu 53
Temperamental classes 95
Temperaments 100
Tension 97, 99, 166
Tension diaphragmatic breathing 386

Theme 140
    function of 258
Thermal (heat) factor 74
Theta state 399
Thingish thinking 67
Thingish thinking 48
Thinking 113, 115, 203, 217, 231
    abstract 106
Thinking, relational 108
Thinking, stilling 159
Thinking, unification of 170
Thinking, verbal 232
Third eye 240
Third eye, awakening 240
Thought drift 166, 202
Thoughts 181
Thoughts, stilling 386
Time, definition 96
Tower of Babel 247
Trance 8, 14, 20, 114, 121, 129, 141,
        142, 153, 168, 233
    and women 15
Tratakam 204
Tree of Life 61, 64
    a cosmogram 71
Treta Yuga 389
Trinity, the 56
True of heart 226
Truth 197, 225
Truth of a premise 251
Truth of premises 254
Tuamutef 229
Tuat 233
Turn the other cheek 158
Tut 234
Two Truths 19
Uas scepter 201
Uas staff 169
Uatchet 239, 262
Unconsciousness 383

Understanding, failure 94
Underworld 233
Unevolved Man 104
Unification of experiences 141
Unifying force 245
United Nations 132
Unity 101
Unity vs. diversity 91
Unity within diversity 248
Upanishads 43
Upper (southern) Kamit 239
Upper Ruach 57
Upper Yetzirah 57
Uraeus 239
Uranous 29
Ureaus 240
Urim and Thummim 210
Utchat of Heru 230
Utchat of Ra 221
Utchau Metut 214, 216, 370
Utiwemuntu 57
Utiwetongo 55
Vairocana 44
Vedanta 44
Vedas 43
Venus 151, 152
Verbal thoughts 111
Veves 273
Virtue 165
Virtues 158
Vishnu 392
Vitality 229
Voodoo 238
Waking center of the brain 193
Waking consciousness 382
Waking state 154, 164
Waking trance 154, 165, 167, 193,
        194, 209, 368
Wars 90
Waters of Life 63

Watery person 182
Way, the 143
Wealth 97
Wealth, source of 8
Wealth, spiritual definition 89
Weighing of the Heart 198, 199
Weighing of Words 214
Wernicke 231
Western 'logical' mind 17
White crown 239
Will, and emotions 193
Will, deactivated 165
Will of Yahweh 210
Will, personal 153
Will power 253
Will, the 69, 86, 87, 101, 110, 129,
        130, 136, 146, 150, 152, 153,
        162, 164, 222, 228, 230, 234,
        246, 252, 286, 383
    man's will 6
Will, the + 187, 195
Will's function of grasping 166
Willed thought activity 203
Wisdom 79, 86, 112, 125, 144, 159,
        204, 217, 220, 248
Witchcraft 298
Woman 43
Women 22, 233
    in Black cultures 20
Word of power 82, 117
Word-shipping 211
Words of power 84, 102, 116, 129,
        149, 168, 173, 229, 379, 386
    See heka 36
World Soul 55
Worms 179
Worship 120, 227
Yang 51, 200, 202
Yantras 273
Yardstick of life 220

Yechidah 55
Yemaya 72, 184
Yesod 213
Yetzirah 57
Yin 51, 152, 200, 202
Yin and Yang 19
Yoga 118, 147, 394
    origins 39
Yoga, definition 165
Yoga of the Simultaneously-born
        Great Symbol 114
Yogic teachings 147
Yogis 91

ILLUSTRATIONS

THE SESH METUT NETER

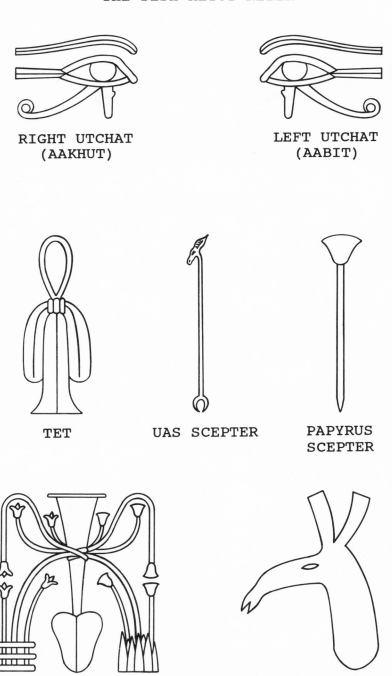

RIGHT UTCHAT
(AAKHUT)

LEFT UTCHAT
(AABIT)

TET

UAS SCEPTER

PAPYRUS
SCEPTER

SMA TAUI

ŚET

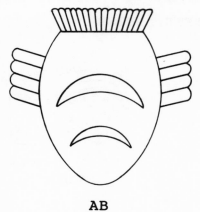

AB

AUNGKH CROSS

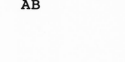

APEP

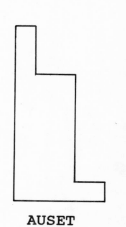

AUSET

BA

SISTRUM

BENNU

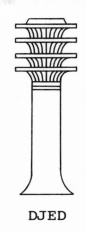

DJED

BES

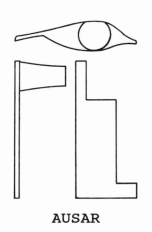

AUSAR

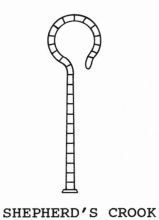

SHEPHERD'S CROOK

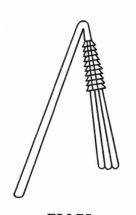

FLAIL

HERU-PA-KHART

ARROWS OF NEITH

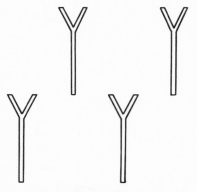

FOUR SUPPORTS
OF HEAVEN

KHEPERA

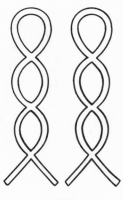

HEH

KHENEMU

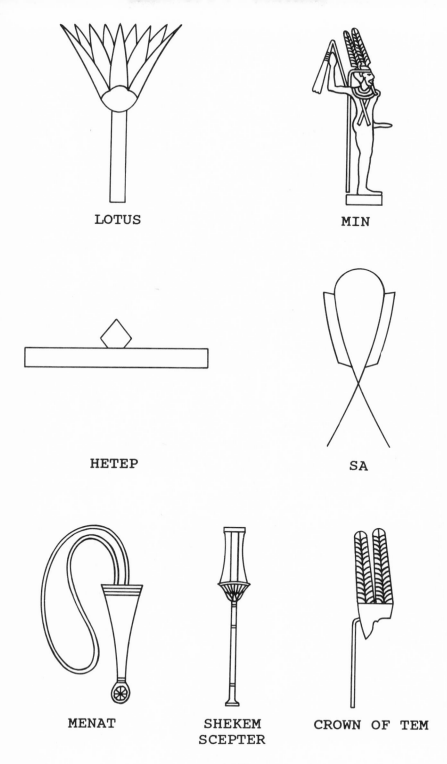

LOTUS

MIN

HETEP

SA

MENAT

SHEKEM
SCEPTER

CROWN OF TEM

THE METU NETER

AUSAR

HERU

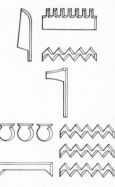

AMEN

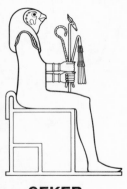

SEKER

TEHUTI

MAAT

HET-HERU

HERUKHUTI

438

AUSET

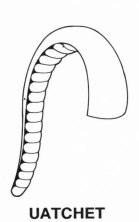

SHEPS

**DARK
DECEASED**

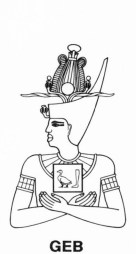

SEBEK

UATCHET

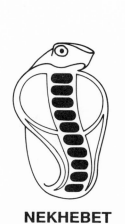

NEKHEBET

GEB

439

OTHER BOOKS BY RA UN NEFER AMEN I

THE REALIZATION OF NETER NU, A Kabalistical Guide to the Realization of Self, 1975

MEDITATION TECHNIQUES OF THE KABALISTS, VEDANTINS, AND TAOISTS, 1976

THE ORACLE OF THOTH, A Kabalistical Guide to the Tarot, 1977

ORACLE OF MERCY, (A Play), 1977

BLACK WOMAN, BLACK MAN IN A QUANDARY, 1977

HEALTH TEACHINGS OF THE AGELESS WISDOM, VOL I, 1980

BLACK WOMAN'S BLACK MAN'S GUIDE TO A SPIRITUAL UNION, 1981

FEMALE HEALTH DISORDERS, 1982

HEALTH TEACHINGS OF THE AGELESS WISDOM, VOL II, 1983

A NUTRITIONAL, HERBAL, AND HOMEOPATHIC GUIDE TO HEALING, 1988

AUSAR AUSET NUTRITION HANDBOOK, 1988

OPTIMIZING HEALTH THROUGH NUTRITION, 1988

THE RITUAL SYSTEMS OF ANCIENT BLACK CIVILIZATIONS, VOL. I: INTRODUCTION TO MEDIATION

THE RITUAL SYSTEMS OF ANCIENT BLACK CIVILIZATIONS, VOL. III: OPENING OF THE WAY, 1988

For on-going information by the Author - on health, history and African spiritual culture, please subscribe to the METU NETER Magazine, (1 year subscription is $15.00, money order or check payable to Khamit Corp.) Khamit Corporation, P.O. Box 281, Bronx, N.Y. 10462. This magazine is published by RA UN NEFER AMEN I.